SAINT VENERATION AMONG THE JEWS IN MOROCCO

SAINT VENERATION AMONG THE JEWS IN MOROCCO

ISSACHAR BEN-AMI

WAYNE STATE UNIVERSITY PRESS • DETROIT

01 00 99 98 5 4 3 2 1

Library of Congress Cataloging-in-Publication Data

Ben-Ami, Issachar.
[Haʿaratsat ha-ḳedoshim be-ḳerev Yehude Maroḳo. English]
Saint veneration among the Jews in Morocco / Issachar Ben-Ami.
p. cm. — (Raphael Patai series in Jewish folklore and anthropology)
Includes bibliographical references and index.
ISBN 0-8143-2198-4 (alk. paper)
1. Zaddikim—Morocco. 2. Judaism—Morocco. I. Title. II. Series.
BM440.M8B44 1998
296.6′1′0964—dc21 97-15878
CIP
r97

Designer:

Cover art:

Grateful acknowledgment is made to Mr. Nissim Krispil for the photographs that appear in this volume.

To my wife Paulina, without whose collaboration and faithful and dedicated support this work would not have been possible.

CONTENTS

ILLUSTRATIONS

Following p. 197:

PART ONE

1

INTRODUCTION

VENERATION OF SAINTS IS A UNIVERSAL PHENOMENON. ALL MONOTHEISTIC and polytheistic creeds contain something of its religious dimension as well as certain historical, sociological, folkloristic, economic, cultural and political manifestations of its presence. Researchers have recently focused on the significance of one or more of these manifestations, but relevant studies do not provide a comprehensive, inclusive understanding of the phenomenon.[1]

Among Moroccan Jews saint worship is a highly important cultural characteristic, pervasively present in all strata of the population. Nevertheless, from many standpoints exceptional features characterize this Jewry's collective perception of saints. It would therefore seem to be fertile ground for an in-depth study that is significant in and of itself, and also of much wider application.

The present study of saint worship among Moroccan Jews is based primarily on fieldwork conducted over a period of almost ten years.[2] It includes an exhaustive list of 656 saints,[3] twenty-five of them women. It illuminates the intricate network that connects the saint and his faithful followers, while revealing the ideological fundamentals that sustain the interrelationship and ensure ritual continuity. Much attention is devoted to a description of the cult and the many miracles associated with it. This implies depicting the values and concepts pertaining to veneration of saints and the influence those values and concepts exert on the communal and social order — an influence that has undoubtedly been reciprocal.

This is not a historical study, nor does it deal with the saints' histories or presume to treat sociological, socio-psychological or scientific-religious fields, although elements of these and other disciplines are certainly present. Rather, the study is both folkloristic and descriptive, an attempt to present the important manifestation of saint worship as it still exists today among Moroccan Jews. Veneration of saints by these Jews evolved in Morocco, but it did not cease upon their immigration to Israel,[4] where it continues to follow traditional lines and simultaneously finds new channels of expression.

The manifold aspects of the phenomenon can only be understood in direct reference to the saints who elicit it; such understanding also presupposes thorough consideration of all testimony dealing with saint worship. Hence, for a comprehensive grasp of the subject, it is vitally important to present the material as narrated by the informants, even at the occasional risk of repetition. There is little written material on the subject,[5] and thus any available information, reference or story is endowed with the utmost importance. Such testimony is important not only for its intrinsic value, but also as a link in a remarkable chain that is unwound here for the first time.

Throughout the period devoted to this study I worked with a sense of urgency and national obligation, a feeling that time is of the essence, because the material is rapidly disappearing. Virtually all Moroccan Jews have left their country of origin, and for the first time a real possibility has arisen that Muslim traditions in relation to saints will supersede Jewish traditions. In effect, the memory of many of the Jewish saints may be lost forever as they are taken over by Muslims. In this connection it is of interest to note that as early as the eighteenth century, visitors to Morocco were surprised to find — despite the generally disparaging attitude of the Muslims toward the Jews — the practice of joint Muslim-Jewish veneration of a Jewish saint.[6] This manifestation prompted the French scholar Voinot[7] to try to determine, primarily from a statistical survey, the dimensions of such shared veneration.

The present study reflects ideas and concepts, historical and legendary types of saints, customs and beliefs that have grown up around them, and practices and ceremonies that take place during and outside of the *hillulah*. It also reflects the economic situation, the organizations and institutions responsible for maintaining the saints' sanctuaries and burial sites. Further, it includes popular creative works such as legends, stories and songs extolling the greatness and miraculous deeds of the saints. The material included herein has been selected from more than 1,200 statements accumulated in the course of my research. It can be divided into five major categories:

1. Folk tales, particularly legends about saints transmitted from generation to generation.
2. Descriptions of miracles—some of which are known to many Moroccan Jews and therefore can be considered folk material, and some of which are personal miracles experienced by the informants.
3. Dreams, most often individual, personal ones, although some of them are familiar and widespread among Moroccan Jews in general.
4. Descriptions of experiences primarily associated with the *ziyara* and *hillulah* in homage to saints, but also related to various aspects of daily life that express affinity with the revered figure.
5. A few historical traditions.

At least two genres are apparent in this hagiographic material:[8] the saint's legend and the sacred legend. The first genre encompasses all the legends recounting the lives and remarkable deeds of the saints themselves; the second genre contains legends focusing on miracles and ceremonies connected with the saint. A more thorough study of this material, together with hagiographic literature originating in other areas, would probably lead to the identification of additional genres characteristic of Jewish saints' legends. All religious tales contain an admixture of realistic and supernatural elements.

The saints are listed in Part Two in alphabetical order by their first names, and the burial site appears in parentheses alongside the name. I have included factual details about the life of each saint, insofar as they are known. The environs of the grave and its proximity to that of other saints are described, together with any family connection by which one saint may be related to another. I have also transmitted further details—gleaned either in the course of my research or from relevant literature—about additional names by which the saint is known, the day of his *hillulah,* whether the Muslims also venerate him, and so forth. This information provides either important testimony about a particular saint or examples of miracles and unique experiences associated with veneration of saints in Morocco as a whole.

Following folkloristic practice, the entire testimony of each informant was recorded in his or her own words in native Judeo-Arabic speech. From the standpoint of style and form, the very fact that testimony was not transmitted in writing but was tape-recorded led to difficulties of literal rendition, first in Hebrew and subsequently in English, and occasionally made comprehension difficult. Yet it must be emphasized that this method facilitated, for the first time, a close scrutiny of the narrative tradition of Moroccan Jews. With vivid imagery, formulaic mode of expression and fluent eloquence, their storytelling includes all the traditional earmarks of folk literature—for example, the laws of three, of repetition and of contrast. It also includes direct speech, rhetorical questions, a tendency to play on words,[9] and so on.

The material itself functions as a primary source for studying the culture of Moroccan Jewry, and it may also serve as a basis for further research. Thus particular attention was given to the collection, selection and presentation of this material. In the following expository chapters I have tried to designate the essential themes that inform the material, but I am nonetheless aware that there is a potential for more comprehensive analysis than is provided here. While I have offered as many descriptions, analyses and hitherto unknown sources as possible, I have not passed judgment or arrived at final assessments, for I believe that due to the broad scope of the study it is still too early to draw definitive conclusions. For much the same reason I have chosen not to engage in an extensive discussion of the problems relevant to this subject in Judaism as a whole,[10] but have touched on them only as essential points of reference and comparison.

Because of its novel approach, this work has been accompanied by much soul-searching and inner debate. From the outset it has been clear that a single study could not exhaust all facets involved in veneration of saints and there is need for further research in the field. As stated above, the fieldwork was accompanied by a feeling of urgency, a sense that time is running out, as can be seen by the cultural transformations Moroccan Jews have undergone in the present generation. As this study brings to light various aspects of their tradition, it contributes to a better understanding of the cultural contribution made by Jews of Morocco to their immediate surroundings, as well as to Jewry as a whole.

Notes

1. See: R. P. Werbner (1977); *Les Pèlerinages* (1960); F. Raphael (1973); R. Oursel (1978).
2. During this period about five hundred Jewish informants originating from all regions of Morocco were interviewed. The fieldwork was performed by a group of researchers of the Folklore Research Center of the Hebrew University of Jerusalem, with the aid of the Memorial Foundation for Jewish Culture, New York.
3. This is undoubtedly not an exhaustive list. I strongly believe that names of additional saints will be added to this list in future studies. In former works, I have cited lower cyphers. See I. Ben-Ami (1981a, p. 283, note 2).
4. See I. Ben-Ami (1977) and (1980c).
5. The sources of this material can be classified in different groups:

   a. Works about one or more saints in Hebrew or in Judeo-Arabic: see I. Ben-Ami (1973a); (1975b); (1975c); and (1980a); A. Mograbi (1968); M. Mazal-Tarim (1939); Moshe Wazana (1936. *Book of Miracles of the Saints from Buhlo.* Casablanca) (Judeo-Arabic); Haim Suissa (1945. *The Saint's Joy.* Casablanca) (Judeo-Arabic); Albert Suissa (*The Beloved Saints.* Casablanca, n. d.) (Judeo-Arabic); J. Lasri (1978); Y. Benaim (1931); D. Hassin (1931); Y. Bilu (1993);

   b. Literature in French: see L. Voinot (1948); E. Doutté (1914); J. Bénech (1940); J. Goulven (1927); and F. Legey (1926);

   c. Printed leaves, including *qasidot,* that were distributed in the area around saints' graves;

   d. Letters, reports and other documentation written by officers in charge of the holy places in the name of the Jewish community;

   e. Manuscripts; and

   f. Oral information, on which this study is mainly based.
6. See L. de Chénier (1787); L. Godard (1859); E. Mauchamp (n.d); E. Doutté (1905).
7. L. Voinot (1948, pp. 1–20).

8. This is among the most complete hagiographical material as yet published in the Hebrew literature. Regarding Jewish saints in other geographic areas, see also: "Hagiography" in *Encyclopaedia Judaica* (1971, vol. 7, pp. 1116–20); D. Ben-Amos and J. Mintz (1970); Y. Avida (1958); and G. Nigal (1982). For traditional hagiographic material of Morocco, see D. F. Eickelman and B. Bouzekri (1973).
9. A. Dundes (1965, "Forms in Folklore"); A. Olrik (1965); R. Dorson (1972, pp. 53–159); S. Thompson (1967); L. Röhrich (1973); A. Dundes (1975); D. Ben-Amos (1976).
10. The pilgrimage to saints' tombs is a very ancient custom among the Jews. According to the *Aggadah,* when Caleb was sent to Canaan as a spy by Moses (*Num.* 13), he paid a special visit to the grave of the Patriarchs in Hebron to pray for their help against the evil intentions of the other spies (*Sot.* 34b). The scholar Rashi (*Yebamot* 122:2) is of the opinion that in Talmudic times the Jews were already accustomed to going in pilgrimage to the tombs of saints, particularly on the anniversary of their deaths. See also A. Ben-Jacob (1973, pp. 11–34) and M. Hakohen (1971).

2

TERMS USED TO DESIGNATE SAINTS

VARIOUS TERMS ARE USED TO DESIGNATE THE JEWISH SAINTS OF Morocco.[1] Some are titles added to the personal name; others are expressions applicable to given saints. Some terms are used by all Moroccan Jews, while others are typical of certain areas.

The most widespread term for a saint among Moroccan Jews is *saddiq* or *tsaddiq* (righteous or saintly one), especially in the plural form, *saddiqim,* often followed by *el-ʿzaz,* "the dear (or beloved) saints." When pronouncing these names, Jews raise one hand and kiss it. Five saints are known with names that include the term *tsaddiq.* Their identity is unknown, the name being derived solely from the site of their tomb: Tsaddiq ʿAyn Nzar, Tsaddiq Azru, Tsaddiqe ʿAyn Diab, Tsaddiqe ʿAyn Um-Krima and Tsaddiq Kelaat Al-Mguna. The appellations *Rav* and *Rabbi* (my teacher, master) are also very common among Moroccan Jews, particularly preceding the saint's name.[2]

Another very widespread general term is *ḥakham* (sage). Moroccan Jews say they are "going to the sage" when they set off to visit the tomb of a saint.

Mul, meaning "master, lord, ruler" in Arabic, is a common element in the names of many saints, as is its plural *mwalin.* The title *mul* is usually given to a saint who is foremost among many saints interred in a given place, or, if he is named after a certain area, *mul* means Lord of that area. Many saints bear the title *mul.* It is interesting to note that the vast majority of these names are connected with elements of the natural world, as in the case of Mul Taurirt (Master of the Hill), Mul Jebel El-Kebir (Master of the Great Mountain), Mul Shejra (Master of the Tree), Mul El-Karma (Master of the Fig), and so on. Other names relate to objects traditionally connected with a saint, such as Mul Tefillin (Master of the Phylacteries), and Mul Sandoq El-Khdar (Master of the Green Box). Other saints are known by their personal name and a second name preceded by the title Mul, such as R. Shelomoh Bar-Beriro (Mul Absar), R. Mussa Ben-Yishay (Mul Tsor), R. Abraham Azulay (Mul Imitk), R. Yitsḥaq Yisra'el Ha-Levi (Mul El-Barj), R. Makhluf Ben-Yosef (Mul El-Qantra), R. Yaᶜaqob Ashkenazi (Mul Anmay or Mul Almay) and R. Yehudah Halaḥmi (Mul Tasqast). R. Eliyahu of Casablanca is said to be Mul El-Blad, that is, Master of the City.[3] The plural form *mwalin* is an element in the name of two groups of saints, Mwalin Bu-Ḥlu and Mwalin El-Gomra; it is also part of an additional name of two saints, Mwalin Dad (R. Abraham Awriwer) and Mwalin Tassabrant (R. Yehudah Ben-Yisra'el Ha-Levi).

The title *mulay*[4] is less common among Moroccan Jews, but is familiar to many because one of the most widely revered Jewish saints is called Mulay Ighi. There are six saints whose names begin with the title *mulay:* Mulay Ighi, Mulay Inguird, Mulay Sedra, Mulay Tabia, Mulay Tamran and Mulay Yaᶜqub, as well as R. Abraham Cohen, who is also known as Mulay Matil, R. Ḥabib Ha-Mizraḥi, also called Mulay Tadot, and R. Moshe Ben-Zohra, known also as Mulay Twabit. In these instances, too, the saints' names are associated with places (Ighi and Tabia) or with a tree (Sedra).

The Arabic title *sayyid,* meaning "master," is not commonly used by Jews to designate their saints. At least two saints bear that title: Sayyid El-Merhirha and R. Aharon Ha-Cohen (from Demnate), also called Sayyid Aharon Cohen or Sayyid Aharon by the Jews. The saint Qayid El-Ghaba is called Sayyid El-Yahud by the Muslims. The Jews use the title *sayyid* more frequently when they refer to a certain saint as "a great *sayyid.*" They also use the forms *sidna* (our master) and *syadna* (our masters). Far more common is the term *sidi*[5] (my master) as an element in the names of many saints who are venerated by both Jews and Muslims, and in the names of other saints who are explicitly said to have been adopted by the Arabs from the Jews. These phenomena explain the use of the term *sidi* as well as the fact that some Jewish saints have Arabic names, such as Sidi Ḥmad El-Kamel and Sidi Moḥammed U-Belqassem, or Arabic nicknames such as Sidi Brahim and Sidi Mussa. The most renowned saint in this group is Sidi Bu-ʿAissa U-Sliman.

The Hebrew term *ḥazzan* is widely used by Muslims when referring to a Jewish saint, but Jews rarely use it. The names of three saints are preceded by this title: Ḥazzan Izzo, Ḥazzan El-Ḥili and Ḥazzan of Tirhermine, the latter two being venerated by Muslims as well as Jews. The Jews call R. Aharon Cohen Ḥazzan Haron or Ḥazzan Haron Cohen.

Another widespread term among the Jews is *baba,* meaning "father." This would seem to be an affectionate name usually given to saints during their lifetime. It is used particularly with reference to the descendants of R. Yaʿaqob Abiḥatsira[6] and R. David Ben-Barukh.

For female saints the term *saddiqah* or *tsaddiqah,* the feminine form of the title *tsaddiq,* is sometimes used. It appears as part of the name of the most renowned female saint, Sol Ḥatshuel, also known as Sol Ha-Tsaddiqah or Solica Ha-Tsaddiqah. The most widespread term for a female saint in Morocco is *lalla,*[7] meaning "lady" in Berber. In one case, the two titles are combined in the name Lalla Tsaddiqah, the saint buried in Imi n'Timouga. In two other instances both titles are prefixed to the name of the saint, Lalla Sol Ha-Tsaddiqah and Lalla Miryam Ha-Tsaddiqah. The name of one female saint bears the term *imma* ("mother," in Hebrew), Imma Esther, and the name of another the term *setti* ("lady," in Arabic) combined with the title *lalla:* Lalla Setti Ben-Sasso.

The Jews frequently add titles such as *ʿzizi,* "my beloved," and *ḥbibi,* "my dear," to the names of saints. Jews of southern Morocco use the term *el-ʿnaya,* meaning Providence.[8] Jews of Draa in the vicinity of Mḥamid use the term *el-ghassi* (community, crowd, congregation).

Occasionally other titles are added to the names of saints. Thus some are called *sbaʿ*[9] (lion) or *sbaʿ el-kebir* (the great lion) or *sbaʿ el-ʿziz* (the beloved lion). Only a few saints from the south are addressed thus; examples are R. David U-Moshe, R. Ḥananiah Ha-Cohen, R. Makhluf Ben-Yosef Abiḥatsira, R. Moshe Ben-Ḥammu and R. Yosef Dayyan. Another title for a renowned saint is *azzogh,* a Berber word meaning "great." Thus we have R. David Ben-Barukh Cohen Azzogh, R. David U-Moshe Azzogh and R. Pinḥas Ha-Cohen Azzogh.

Notes

1. In Hebrew, the words *qadosh* (saint) and *tsaddiq* sometimes have the same meaning. See Z. Werblowski (1977, pp. 146–47 and 164–65); E. Urbach (1969); R. Mach (1957); I. Tishbi (1957). In North Africa, *qadosh* is usually connected with miracle workers. For terms used by the Muslims in North Africa with regard to their saints, see E. Doutté (1900, pp. 34–43); E. Westermarck (1926, vol. 1, pp. 35–36).
2. In the alphabetical list arranged according to the saints' given names, the term Rabbi (R.) was not taken into consideration. All the other terms are presented as an integral part of the name.
3. R. Eliyahu is the most important saint of Casablanca, and as Lord of the City he is responsible for and protects Casablanca. Patron saints are also known in other cultures: A. van Gennep (1951, tome 1, vol. 5, p. 2451); P. Brown (1981, p. 41).
4. The term *mulay* is very common among the Muslims in North Africa. It is written *moulay* by E. Dermenghem (1954), *mouley* by L. Voinot (1948) and *muläi* by E. Westermarck (1926). E. Doutté (1900, pp. 36–37) writes *moulaye* and ascribes its origin to the term *ouali* or *wali,* used when referring to saints. The term *mulai* or *moulaye,* employed originally to honor the shereef in Morocco, is now used to designate all Muslim saints in Morocco, even those that are not shereefs.
5. Many of the Jewish saints bearing the term *sidi* are known only by their first names. This is the most usual term for designating the Muslim saints, although it is used also in respect to any person one wishes to honor. See E. Westermarck (1926, vol. 1, p. 36); L. Brunot (1952, vol. 2, pp. 391–92).
6. R. Yisra'el Abiḥatsira, the Baba Sale, who lived and died in Netivot, Israel, is the most famous descendant of R. Yaʿaqob. R. Yisra'el's brother, R. Yitsḥaq, who was the chief rabbi of Ramleh, Israel, was known as Baba Ḥaki.
7. This is also the term generally used by the Muslims in Morocco to designate their female saints: E. Doutté (1900, p. 40); E. Westermarck (1926, vol. 1, p. 36); L. Brunot (1952, vol. 2, pp. 741–42).
8. N. A. Stillman (1982, p. 493) translates the term as "divine solicitude."
9. Some Muslim saints also bear this title. E. Westermarck (1926, vol. 1, p. 36): "The epithet *sbaʿ* (plur. *sboʿa*), which properly means 'lion,' is especially given to saints who are much feared in oath-taking or otherwise."

3

GENESIS OF A SAINT

THE QUESTION OF HOW SAINTS IN GENERAL COME INTO BEING IS A MOST intriguing one, but it is even more interesting in the specific context of the cult in Morocco, where so many saints are venerated by Jews. Sometimes the objects of veneration seem to have lain dormant through the ages—until one day they rise up in the form of saints. It is difficult to comprehend the process by which a saint is born, what it is in one's lifetime or after one's death that turns an individual into a saint. How does a real historic figure or an imaginary entity become an object of veneration?

It should be noted at the outset that most saints venerated by Moroccan Jews were recognized as such only after their death. Exemplary behavior or exceptional erudition exhibited by certain individuals during their lifetimes prepared the ground for the bestowal of sainthood after death. Few achieved the distinction while still alive.[1] Another group of saints—many of them fictitious or legendary figures[2]—were revealed in a dream or through the medium of some natural phenomenon. To generalize, then, a saint manifests himself or herself primarily through the performance of miracles or by exemplary personal behavior; this revelation may be through a dream or by the occurrence of some extraordinary event at the time of death or burial.

1. Performing miracles

One of the clearest hallmarks of a saint is the manifestation of supernatural powers through performance of miracles. Famous rabbis and sages became saints only when their names were associated with some miracle they brought about. Although magical deeds are usually attributed to the saints after their death, during their lifetimes holy people will sometimes display supernatural power such as magically curing the sick, saving an entire community, or, like R. Yaʿaqob Abiḥatsira, walking on water. It is told that with his stick, R. Eliʿezer Davila stopped the sea from inundating its shores. R. Ḥayyim Toledano retrieved a crate a Jewish merchant had lost at sea. R. Ḥayyim Pinto the Younger, R. Pinḥas Ha-Cohen, R. Raphael Anqawa, and R. Re'uben Azini made predictions that always came true. During their lifetimes R. Moshe Ḥaliwa and R. Raphael Anqawa cured the sick. R. Pinḥas Ha-Cohen brought about many miracles in his lifetime and saved the pasha of Marrakech several times, as did R. David Bussidan from Meknes.

2. Exemplary Behavior

Exemplary behavior and an ascetic life-style—particularly devout prayers, zealous studying under unusual circumstances (above all studying with Elijah the Prophet), prolonged fasts, frequent and constant charitable activities—can turn one into a saintly figure revered by the people.[3] Obviously most saints who actually existed lived in exemplary fashion; witnesses can always be found to extol the deeds they performed in the course of their lives. The very same deeds, however, have been attributed retrospectively to legendary saints.

Protracted fasting or abstemiousness characterize certain saints: R. Eleʿazar Ha-Cohen would break his fast only twice a year, on the Jethro *Sabbath* and the New Year. Lalla Solica Waʿqnin fasted constantly (once doing so sixty times consecutively, each time for six days in a row), breaking her fast only at night. R. Abner Ha-Tsarfati would eat meat only on the *Sabbath.* All his life R. Shelomoh Suissa ate no eggs but those laid by a chicken he raised in his own house. And R. Raḥamim Mizraḥi ate nothing but dry bread dipped in water throughout his lifetime. Morning and evening, R. David Bussidan ate nothing but a piece of carob.

A distinguishing mark of a saint is intensive study of the *Torah*, above all with Elijah the Prophet. Many of the saints are said to have been granted such an exceptional gesture. It is interesting to note that attainment of this degree of excellence is also attributed to saints after they have died, and many traditions tell of saints studying after their death, at or near their tombs. Among those who studied with Elijah are R. Abraham Ben-Ibgui, R. David Bel-Ḥazzan, R. David Perets (Telouet), R. Ḥayyim Pinto (Mogador), R. Ḥayyim Toledano, R. Mordekhay Dayyan, R. Shalom Bar-Ḥani, R. Shelomoh Tangi and R. Yaᶜaqob Abiḥatsira. Studying usually took place at night. R. David Bel-Ḥazzan always studied after midnight, and R. Mordekhay Dayyan from eight in the evening until noon the following day. R. Shelomoh Tangi and R. David Perets would study with Elijah the Prophet every Saturday night. Once every two weeks R. David Perets would disappear, and the story would go around that he was in heaven with the Prophet.

To see Elijah the Prophet or hear his voice was considered a very special sign of grace. The wife of R. David Bel-Ḥazzan would bring her husband a cup of tea and, although she heard two voices, would find him studying alone. The wife of R. Shelomoh Tangi once peeked in and saw the rabbi studying with Elijah, the entire room glowing with light. R. Ḥayyim Pinto's servant, R. Aharon Ibn-Ḥayyim, once heard two voices coming from the rabbi's room and brought him two cups of coffee; when the rabbi asked why and learned that his servant had heard two voices, he blessed the man for having been granted the privilege of hearing the voice of Elijah the Prophet. R. Yaᶜaqob Abiḥatsira's female servant once saw three visitors in the holy man's room and sent the male servant in with four cups of coffee. When he entered the room, the man found the rabbi alone. The saint immediately understood the great privilege that had been bestowed upon his female servant.

Such a privilege is not without risk. One who sees Elijah the Prophet or hears his voice must keep it a secret. A neighbor of R. Yaᶜaqob Abiḥatsira who once saw a great light coming from the rabbi's room and did not heed the warning not to look in there again was stricken blind; only after much pleading did R. Yaᶜaqob agree to restore his sight. When the daughter of R. Ḥayyim Pinto entered his room suddenly and saw two people there, her father told her that she had seen Elijah the Prophet, something she was not worthy of; when she married, he said, she would either die or go blind — a fate that was later cancelled by virtue of her good behavior. R. Ḥayyim Pinto asked his servant, who heard the voice of Elijah the Prophet, not to reveal the secret until after the rabbi had died, and so it was.

Charitable deeds redound to one's favor and can endow a person with sainthood. Many saints are known for the particular charitable deeds they performed: R. David of Ait Yaᶜish and the elder R. Ḥayyim Pinto are among those. Every Monday and Thursday the latter would sit in his doorway and collect alms for the needy. R. Ḥayyim Pinto the Younger took care of the poor and treated the sick, while the wise R. Mordekhay Turjman always helped his students. Among the female saints whose charitable deeds became famous were the El-Khwatat sisters, one of whom dispensed oil and the other fat to any poor person who came to their house. Lalla Solica Waᶜqnin gave alms to the needy every holiday eve and looked after the *yeshibah* students; and Lalla Saᶜada always gave generous contributions to charity.

A strict moral code and extreme modesty are criteria by which a saint can be identified.[4] R. Eleᶜazar Ha-Cohen conscientiously avoided looking at women; going from his home to the synagogue and back he would wrap himself from head to foot in his prayer shawl to keep from seeing them. When he sat outside, both Jewish and Muslim women were careful not to walk down the street past his house. Women were forbidden to kiss R. David Naḥmias's hand. R. Yisra'el Cohen and R. Shelomoh Ben-Tameshut were killed by Muslims for refusing to lie with Muslim women. According to one tradition, Sol Ha-Tsaddiqah, the female saint, was killed by a Muslim because she refused to give herself to him.

A single exemplary act can sometimes bestow the title of saint on an individual, as in the case cited above of Sol Ha-Tsaddiqah who, rather than marry a Muslim, chose martyrdom and death as an undefiled Jewess. Bent El-Ḥmus let herself be killed by Muslims in order to save a group of rabbis and wise men from the Holy Land who were lodging in her house and were accused by officials of selling wine to Muslims. Lalla Luna Bat-Khalifa dedicated herself to the care of the saint R. Yehudah Gadol Gilᶜad during his lifetime, and after his death she devotedly tended his grave. By virtue of this devotion she herself became a saint.

A number of saints endowed with this title while still alive belonged to Jewish families whose sainthood was transmitted from generation to generation. Belonging to such a family does not automatically bestow the prestigious honor,[5] but when accompanied by exemplary behavior, it does give one a certain advantage. Baba Du—R. David Abiḥatsira—went to his death in place of other Jews whose lives were threatened by Muslims; R. Ḥayyim Pinto the Younger became known for his charitable deeds; and R. Meir ʿArama from Ait ʿArama was known for his asceticism: he subsisted on donations.

3. Revelation through a Dream

Dreams play a decisive role in the creation of saints among Jews of Morocco.[6] The historical existence of the saints revealed in dreams is not questioned by these Jews. Most saints who revealed themselves in a dream belong to the group of legendary figures, and therefore no historic or factual details are known about them. It is also interesting to note that these saints are generally thought to have originated in antiquity, often in the Holy Land. Perceived as the medium through which a saint or some other entity is conveyed, the dream has an absolute intrinsic value of its own, and any message transmitted thereby must be heeded. From the standpoint of the believer, and this should be stressed, there is no doubt that the saint who reveals himself in a dream was once a real live person.

In the dream the saint usually tells something about himself or herself and asks people to come and prostrate themselves on his or her grave or erect some sort of memorial to him or her. Sometimes he or she gives his or her name and details about where he or she is buried, as did R. Abraham Darʿi, R. Yitsḥaq Ha-Levi and R. Masʿud Mani—all three of them buried on the mountain Imi n'Tanoute. Others who identified themselves in dreams include R. Abraham Ben-Salem, R. Abraham Cohen (Mulay Matil), R. Abraham Makhluf Ben-Yaḥya, R. Abraham Mul Annes,[7] R. Mimun Elghrabli, Mul Timḥdart, R. Nwasser, R. Shem-Tov Ha-Mizraḥi, Sidi Moshe, R. Yaʿaqob Bardiʿi and R. Yehudah U-Re'uben. Sometimes the saint gives only his or her name and orders the dreamer to find his or her tomb. Thus, after an arduous search, a Jew from Casablanca who dreamed of R. Eleʿazar Ben-ʿArakh found his grave under a heap of stones in Iguenisaine.

There are times when the saint does not identify himself, in which case he is given a name that refers to his place of burial. One example of this is Mul Jebel El-Kebir, who appeared to a Jew of Sefrou in a dream and told him he was buried on the mountain of that name. The saint may reveal himself in a dream to a Jew who is visiting the tomb of another saint nearby. Thus R. Abraham Bu-Dwaya and Mul Sedra at Ksar Es-Souk were revealed to people who had come to prostrate themselves on the graves of saints buried there.

A saint may even bring about a miracle in the course of the dream in which he reveals himself. R. Eliyahu of Casablanca, for example, cured a blind woman. R. Aharon Assulin, appearing in a dream to a Jew from Tinejdad, informed him that the river was about to overflow its banks but the Jews need not worry because he would protect their village. One Friday, R. Yehudah Halaḥmi appeared in a dream to a ritual slaughterer sleeping under a tree and told him where to find the knife he needed for the slaughter. The rabbi even stopped the sun so that all slaughtering could be finished before the *Sabbath.*

The saint may also reveal himself in a dream to a Muslim. Rabbi David Alshqar (also known as Mulay Ighi) appeared in a dream to the Muslim who guarded the Jewish cemetery in Casablanca and showed him where he was buried. The *dayyanim* therefore built a monument to the saint at the site. R. Yitsḥaq El-Qansi revealed himself to the people of Debdou in a dream, after having appeared to a Muslim woman who lived near the Jewish cemetery. An interesting case is that of a saint who revealed himself to a Muslim woman who lived near the sanctuary of R. Makhluf Ben-Yosef Abiḥatsira; she set aside a place for him in her house and would beg Jews who visited R. Makhluf to come and light candles in her house, too.

A few saints whom some traditions hold revealed themselves in dreams have been reputed by other traditions as disclosing their existence in other ways. R. David U-Moshe is said to have told one of the villagers in a dream that he was buried under a certain stone, but the more accepted tradition is that he died in a field in exchange for the lives of the people of Timzerit. Alongside the tradition that Mul Timḥdart manifested himself in a dream, he is also said to have been revealed during an epileptic attack. Some traditions, alongside those telling how R. Eliyahu of Casablanca made himself known in a dream, explain why he was buried at the city gate rather than in the cemetery. Traditions telling of the death of Mulay Ighi in Ighi exist alongside those that claim he revealed himself as R. David Alshqar to a Muslim guard who was dreaming in the Casablanca graveyard.

4. Revelation through an Extraordinary Phenomenon at Time of Death

One sign of sainthood is the occurrence of an extraordinary phenomenon while the deceased is being bathed, during his burial or immediately thereafter. Such an event may or may not be related to the man's activities while he was alive. Dying on the *Sabbath* Eve, the time most saints are said to have died, is also a mark of great merit.

The revelation can assume the form of a strong light that appears at the moment of death or while the body is being tended. It is said that when R. Yosef Elmaleḥ died, light beams flashed on him. When the pious Mul Sandoq El-Khdar died, a shaft of light covered his body. A witness who had been standing near the body of R. Raphael Anqawa related that the ineffable light of the *shekhinah* had illuminated the saint. Because of his lameness, R. Raḥamim Mizraḥi was held up to ridicule by children, and yet, on the day of his death, with people of the Burial Society standing around his body, the entire room was suddenly suffused with powerful light: the *shekhinah* had descended upon the rabbi, and he was buried as a saint.

Saintliness can also be revealed by the body of the deceased rising up. R. Meir Bar-Sheshat was from Mogador but died in Marrakech. His body rose twice. Understanding that the dead man was thus revealing saintliness, the men of the Marrakech Burial Society decided to inter him in their city, despite protests on the part of the members of the Mogador Burial Society. When R. Yosef Knafo died, he rose from his litter and his face turned red. It is also a sign of saintliness if the body, while being washed, stands upright on the board. R. Yosef Dayyan stood up on the washing board and would not permit his body to be bathed until, after two futile attempts, the people of the Burial Society had purified themselves thoroughly and conjured him in the name of the saints.

Difficulty in lifting the litter of the deceased indicates both saintliness and an unfulfilled wish of the deceased. Of R. Aharon Monsonego they say that it was impossible to carry his litter because of its great weight until the rabbi received certain passages from the book of *Torah* which he had ordered be buried with him. Attempts to lift the pallet of R. Yosef Bajayo were unsuccessful because the rabbi wanted to be buried at Ntifa, not at Tabia where he had died. R. Yosef Turjman's pallet could not be lifted until the market through which the funeral procession was to pass had been thoroughly cleaned.

The day of a saint's death is sometimes accompanied by drastic—usually inauspicious—changes in weather; this is generally interpreted as an indication that nature is mourning the death of the saint. There was total darkness on the day R. David Abiḥatsira died. When Mul El-Ḥazra El-Menzura was buried, large hailstones fell and covered the grave. When R. Yosef Bajayo died, the heavens opened: lightning flashed and fierce rain beat down. The day R. Shelomoh Cohen died, a sandstorm raged and walls collapsed. R. Pinḥas Ha-Cohen died in the very rainy month of *Tebet,* but as the funeral took place the sun came out.

A holy man's body never rots, and this, too, is a sign of saintliness.[8] R. Masʿud Naḥmias died and was buried in a village far away from his home; in a dream he ordered his wife to transfer his body to Marrakech, and when the grave was opened one month after the burial, the body appeared exactly the same as it had on the day of death. It is also told that some time after the death of the saint R. Iza Cohen, his body looked as it had when it was buried. The saint's shroud, too, may remain white after many years in the grave. When R. Raphael Berdugo's mortal remains were being moved from one place to another, they found the cloth enshrouding his body still pure white.

Some traditions tell that chains descended to lift certain saints heavenward at the time of their burial, as happened to R. Yaḥya Laḥlu and R. Mordekhay Dayyan. It is also told that angels have come down to take a saint to heaven: R. Mordekhay Turjman and the rabbi of the village where ʿAsarah Be-Kever are buried were granted this privilege. It is said that angels gave R. Yosef Turjman, who was very old and wanted to die, the exact date of his death: on the night of the second *Seder.* There is also a belief that saints can lift body and soul into the skies. And so it is told that a Muslim woman saw R. Yosef Bajayo rise into the sky; that Mul Tefillin raised body and soul upward, leaving only his *tefillin* behind; and R. ʿEli Ben-Yitsḥaq, too, rose toward the heavens.

5. Revelation through a Pillar of Fire or Light over the Grave

Another sign of a saint is the presence of a pillar of fire. A flaming column above a grave is a sign that a saint is buried there[9] and must be visited. Thus it was with R. Eliyahu Dahan of Ait Yaish: the flame chased away Muslims who wanted to extinguish the fire and dig up the grave. According to one tradition, Mul Terya, Master of Light, is a tree on which flames descend from the heavens all night; according to another tradition, the fire descends every *Sabbath* Eve and burns throughout the *Sabbath*. Jews and Muslims would see fire descend on R. Moshe Ben-Yaʿaqob Ḥayon's grave every Friday, on the first of every month and the eve of every holiday. It is told of R. Ḥayyim Cohen that the night after his burial, a *Torah* student and his family who lived near the cemetery saw a strong light shaped like a bowl on the rabbi's tomb. When R. Yosef Dahan died and was buried, a *qadi* who lived close to the cemetery saw two pillars of light, one green and the other like a large candle flame, coming down from the sky. The *qadi,* the only one in his entire entourage who saw this, was frightened and went away. When those preparing the body of R. Yosef Dayyan for burial finally succeeded, after three attempts, in washing it, they saw a light descend and cover the grave; it was even seen by Muslims in the vicinity.

6. Other Manifestations that Reveal Sainthood

Sometimes a saint reveals himself by means of an epileptic fit. Thus, while having a seizure, a woman from Tabia pronounced Mul Timḥdart's name. A well-known case is that of R. Daniel Hashomer Ashkenazi, who revealed himself to a demented Arab youth. When the boy ran outside, the saint was revealed to him in the fields, told him his name and where he was buried. He also cured him. A few days later the boy, returning home healthy, told everyone about the saint.

The present study led to only one case of sainthood associated with a person suffering from a psychological disturbance.[10] This was the case of R. Re'uben Azini, who sometimes seemed mad to the people around him. Nevertheless, things he predicted would actually happen. After his death, therefore, visitors came to worship at his tomb.

There is also a single instance of one saint being revealed by another. When R. Moshe Mimun struck a rock during a fierce drought and a spring bubbled up at the spot, he informed the Jews that a saint by the name of Qayid El-Ghaba was buried there and wanted to be visited.

Certain animals, particularly doves,[11] are a sign of sainthood. Two doves always rested on the branches of a certain palm tree, and people understood that a saint must be buried at its roots. One day, when Jews were reading Psalms in the shadow of the tree, R. David Ha-Levi Draʿ appeared, identified himself, asked them to tell about him, and announced that he would save them from Muslim thieves.

Sometimes Muslims are responsible for the revelation of a Jewish saint. R. Moshe (buried near Mulay Ighi) was revealed when Muslims who were plowing nearby found a tombstone inscribed with the date of his death. Another Muslim saw R. Raphael Ha-Cohen (Achbarou) enter his grave, which closed over him. The Muslim told a passing Jew that this was the site of the master of the Jews. The passerby began to dig and found a tombstone with a date. When he informed the Jews of the nearby village, they came out of their houses and announced that a rabbi by the name of R. Raphael Ha-Cohen had been revealed as a saint, and they began to worship at the site.

The relationship of saints, usually legendary ones, with natural objects—stones, rocks, springs, mountains, trees, and so on—is interesting. It may come about in one of the several ways described above, although most often the connection is made in a dream. Cases in point are R. Abraham Darʿi, R. Abraham Makhluf Ben-Yaḥya, R. Eleʿazar Ben-ʿArakh, R. Masʿud Mani, R. Mimun Elghrabli, Mul Jebel El-Kebir, Mul Sedra, R. Yehudah U-Re'uben, R. Yitsḥaq El-Qansi and R. Yitsḥaq Ha-Levi. There is also the appearance of illumination on a tree, as in the case of Mul Terya, or, as in the case of Qayid El-Ghaba, there may be a connection with nature as one saint is being revealed by another.

Notes

1. The process of sanctification among Jews is different from that among their Muslim neighbors. See E. Dermenghem (1954, pp. 26–33); C. Langlois (1955, pp. 5–118).

2. See N. Slouschz (1927, p. 438): "Cemeteries are filled with saints, real or imaginary."
3. The same criteria are current among the Muslims in North Africa. See E. Dermenghem (1954, pp. 26–27, 31–32); E. Westermarck (1926, vol. 1, p. 44): "A person may, furthermore, become a saint by extraordinary piety and devotion—by incessant praying, diligent fasting in the day time, giving an abundance of food to the scribes and alms to the poor, and abstaining from every forbidden act."
4. In this aspect the Moroccan Jews differ from their Muslim neighbors. See E. Westermarck (1926, vol. 1, p. 198): "Sexual intercourse with a saintly person is considered beneficial"; E. Doutté (1900, pp. 97–98); E. Doutté (1914, p. 187); E. Dermenghem (1954, pp. 242–43).
5. Among the Muslims in Morocco, see E. Westermarck (1926, vol. 1, pp. 36–40): "No man has possessed more *baraka* than the prophet Muḥammad. His *baraka* was transmitted to the shereefs, that is, the descendants in the male line of his daughter Fatimah. But although every shereef is thus born with more or less *baraka* . . . there are only comparatively few who have so much of it that they are actually regarded as saints."
6. The very great number of dreams, including saints' revelation dreams, collected in the framework of this study is an indication of their importance among the Moroccan Jews. No similar phenomenon is found among the Muslims in Morocco.
7. The historian D. Corcos (1976, p. 211) heard the evidence directly from the person to whom the saint was revealed in a dream.
8. See Z. Vilnay (1985, p. 28); E. Westermarck (1926, vol. 1, p. 159, note 2).
9. The same belief is found among the Muslims. See E. Westermarck (1926, vol. 1, p. 161): "Strange phenomena of light are often connected with dead saints. In Dukkala, *ignis fatuus* in a desert place is taken for the sign of an unknown saint having died there."
10. The belief in a link between mental disorder and sainthood is very common among the Muslims. See E. Dermenghem (1954, pp. 29–31); E. Westermarck (1926, vol. 1, pp. 47–48); E. Doutté (1900, p. 73).
11. See E. Westermarck (1926, vol. 1, p. 105): "Pigeons are sometimes supposed to be dead saints in disguise."

4

FAMILIES OF SAINTS AND THEIR DESCENDANTS

SAINT VENERATION AMONG THE MUSLIMS OF MOROCCO IS ORGANIZED around religious orders dominated by saintly dynasties. Although the overwhelming majority of saints venerated by the Jews of Morocco are individuals, references may be found to familial ties among various saints revered by Jews. The list of saints in the appendix includes several brothers, fathers and sons, grandfathers and grandsons, and even four married couples, all of whom are saints. There is also a small number of families in which two or more generations of saints and their descendants continue to enjoy the family fame.

A number of saints are mentioned as brothers of other saints. The kinship usually exists only in tradition, which explains the occasional multiple traditions connected with the same saint as well as the variety of siblings attributed to him. It is interesting to note that the number of brothers usually mentioned is two, three[1] or seven.

The most famous and widely venerated brothers are the seven Ulad Zemmur in Safi. In Todgha, seven brothers called Esqlila are buried side by side. R. Abraham Awriwer is said to be buried with six of his brothers.

Three illustrious brothers are Sidi Bu-ʿAissa U-Sliman, R. Yitsḥaq Ben-Sliman and Sidi Ftaḥ Ben-Sliman, who are all thought to be sons of King Solomon. The renowned R. David Ha-Levi Draʿ is believed to have two sainted brothers, R. Yehudah Ben-Yisra'el Ha-Levi and R. Yitsḥaq Yisra'el Ha-Levi. The saintly brothers Sidi Abraham, Sidi Yaʿqub and Sidi Mussa are buried in the Sous region. One tradition tells that R. Ḥananiah Ha-Cohen, R. Moshe Cohen and R. Raphael Ha-Cohen (buried in Achbarou) are brothers; another tradition maintains that R. Ḥananiah Ha-Cohen and R. Raphael Ha-Cohen are the brothers of R. David Alshqar. A local tradition in Tazzarine tells that R. Ḥayyim Lashqar, who is buried there, is the brother of R. David Alshqar and R. Shelomoh Ben-Lḥans.

Pairs of sainted brothers include R. Yisra'el Ben-Moḥa and R. Masʿud Ben-Moḥa in Marrakech; R. Yisra'el Danino and R. Ḥayyim Danino in Ait Boulli; and R. Mussa U-Re'uben and R. Yehudah U-Re'uben in Tadrhia. Various traditions mention that R. Yaḥya El-Khdar and R. Eliyahu (of Casablanca) are brothers, as are Mulay Ighi and Sidi Rghit, as well as R. David Ha-Levi Draʿ and R. ʿObadiah Ha-Levi.

R. ʿAmram Ben-Diwan (of Ouezzane) and R. Ḥayyim Ben-Diwan (of Anrhaz) are mentioned as father and son, as are R. Abner Azini and R. Re'uben Azini, who are buried in Sefrou, R. Yehudah Elmaleḥ and R. Abraham Elmaleḥ, who are buried in Amizmiz; R. Yehudah Ben-Shabbat and R. Mordekhay Ben-Shabbat, who are buried in Tillin; R. Yaʿaqob Bibas and R. Yosef Bibas, who are buried in Salé; R. Shelomoh Bar-Beriro and R. Yitsḥaq Bar-Beriro, who are buried side by side in Bechar; R. Masʿud ʿArama and R. David ʿArama, who are buried in Skoura; R. Yosef Ha-Cohen and R. Yaʿaqob Ha-Cohen, who are buried in Tazenakht; R. Yaʿaqob Ben-Walid and R. Moshe Ben-Walid, who are buried in Rabat; R. Shalom Dahan and R. Eliyahu Dahan, who are buried in Ait Yaish; R. ʿAmram Abiḥatsira and R. Yosef Abiḥatsira, who are buried in Telouet; R. Makhluf Ben-Yosef Abiḥatsira and R. Eliyahu Abiḥatsira, who are buried in Tarkellil; and R. David Bel-Ḥazzan and his son called "the Prophet," who are buried in Mogador—all of these are reputedly father and son. There are also traditions about a parent and son who are buried side by side, though only one of them is designated a saint, as in the case of R. Yehudah Ben-Baba (of Tagounit) and R. Yitsḥaq Davila (of Sidi Rahal), both of whom are buried next to sons whose names are unknown. There is a tradition that R. Daniel Hashomer Ashkenazi's mother is buried next to him, and that seven of the female saint Lalla Rḥima Ha-Cohanit's sons are buried at her side in Iguidi.

In Demnate we find the saints R. Yosef Ḥayyim Boḥbot and his grandson, R. Ḥayyim Boḥbot. In Sefrou R. Abba Elbaz and his cousin R. Raphael Moshe Elbaz are buried near each other. There is a tradition that R. David Alshqar and Mulay Ighi are cousins.[2]

According to various traditions, Lalla Saᶜada was the wife of R. Eliyahu, and they are buried side by side in Casablanca. Lalla Mima was the wife of R. Yisra'el Cohen and is buried by his side in Tabia. Other sainted couples are R. David Ben-Yamin of Beni Mellal and his wife, Lalla Kherwiᶜa, who is buried alongside him; and R. Ḥayyim Cohen and his wife, Lalla Cohen, who are buried in Fez.

Several families in Morocco have produced a number of saints who are renowned throughout the country and even beyond its borders. Other families are known only in their immediate vicinity. Some saints bear their family name, such as Abiḥatsira, Pinto and Ben-Barukh Ha-Cohen. Others are designated by a general term, such as *Ulad,* meaning "sons of,' or *Ait,* meaning "family of," "tribe" or "clan"—the designation encompassing the entire family. There are also groups of *Cohanim* who are buried together, although the link between them is unknown and indeed there may be none at all.

Three large families in Morocco have produced several saints and illustrious rabbis: Abiḥatsira, Pinto and Ben-Barukh Ha-Cohen. To this day they are considered holy, and their descendants share the family's distinguished reputation.

The Abiḥatsira family originally came from Tafilalet. Its founder was R. Yaᶜaqob Abiḥatsira,[3] who was born in Rissani in 1807 and died in 1880 in Damenhour, Egypt, on his way to the Holy Land. The *hillulah* in his honor is still celebrated by masses of his followers on the 20th of *Tebet* in numerous places in Israel and all over the world.[4] R. Yaᶜaqob had four sons and one daughter: R. Masᶜud, the eldest; R. Aharon; R. Abraham; R. Yitsḥaq; and Esther, who married R. Dahan. All four sons were sainted, but R. Yitsḥaq, who is buried in Toulal, is particularly venerated. His grandsons who are considered saints include the three sons of R. Masᶜud: R. David, who is buried in Rissani; R. Yitsḥaq, who was known as Baba Ḥaki and is buried in Ramleh, Israel; and R. Yisra'el, who was known as Baba Sale and is buried in Netivot, Israel, where he lived until his death in 1984. The two sons of R. Aharon also deserve mention: R. Yisra'el, also called

Baba Sale, who is buried in Bechar, and R. Eliyahu, buried in Erfoud, as well as R. Yitsḥaq's son, R. Abba (buried in Boudenib). His great-grandson, R. Meir (buried in Israel), acquired a reputation as a miracle worker.

The Pinto family originally came from Mogador. The dynasty was founded by R. Ḥayyim Pinto,[5] who was born in Agadir but at age ten moved to Mogador, where he died on the 26th of *Elul* 1845. His son, R. Yehudah Pinto, also buried in Mogador, was highly revered as a saint. R. Yehudah's son, R. Ḥayyim—called R. Ḥayyim Pinto Ha-Qatan (the Younger), in order to distinguish him from his grandfather, who was called R. Ḥayyim Pinto Ha-Gadol (the Elder)—became very famous as a saint active in Casablanca, where he died in 1937.

The Ben-Barukh Ha-Cohen family originated in Taroudant. The founder of the dynasty was R. David Ben-Barukh, also known as R. David Ben-Barukh Ha-Cohen *Azzogh* or "the High Priest." His grandsons, the brothers R. Yamin Ha-Cohen and R. Barukh Ha-Cohen, and his great-grandsons, R. Pinḥas Ha-Cohen (son of R. Yamin) and R. David Ben-Barukh (son of R. Barukh)—dubbed Baba Dudu or R. David Ben-Barukh Ha-Qatan (the Younger, to distinguish him from his illustrious great-grandfather)—enjoyed great fame as saints. Even today many large *hillulot* are celebrated in their honor in Israel and elsewhere.

Other families have produced saints, although the relationship among the various descendants is not always known or clear. Here it is possible to cite the Ulad Dayyan, buried in the Draa Valley, who include, among others, the saints R. Mordekhay Dayyan and R. Yosef Dayyan; Ulad Zemmur in Safi; Ait Ben-ʿAmram or Ait Yaʿaqob Ben-ʿAmram in the village of Iguitimisa, named for one of the most prominent saints in the family; Ait Naḥmias, buried in Tazda, the most prominent of whom are R. David, R. Yosef and R. Yaʿaqob Naḥmias; Ait ʿArama in Skoura, whose members include R. David, R. Meir, R. Makhluf and R. Masʿud ʿArama; Ait Lʿasri in Ksar Es-Souk, represented by R. Yaʿaqob Lʿasri; Ulad Siggar in Tagounit; Ulad Bu-Ḥlu near Demnate, which includes the saints R. Mussa Ben-Yishay and R. Yannay Mul Lmekhfiya; Ait Azilal in Tamnougalt, of which R. Yosef Dahan is a member; Ait Idbud Fassin in Assaka, and Ait Ḥaqon in the Sidi Rahal region, of which only R. Yaʿaqob Ḥaqon is known; the Abikhzer family in Marrakech, to which the saints R. Abraham, R. Yaʿaqob and R. Yisra'el Abikhzer belong; the Davila family in Rabat, to which the saints R. Ḥayyim and R. Eliᶜezer Davila belong; the Wazana family, one of whose members is R. David Wazana; the Ait Oḥayon, whose members, according to tradition, are buried in Meᶜarat Oufran (the Cave of Oufran); the Tangi family in Ait Abbas, whose sainted members are R. Abraham, R. Yosef and R. Shelomoh Tangi; the Turjman family in Beni Sbih, to which R. Abraham Turjman belongs; the Ben-Safet family in Marrakech, including R. David Ben-Safet and one of his descendants, R. Yitsḥaq Ben-Safet; and the Dahan family in the Mzab region, which includes R. Aharon, R. Yosef and R. Moshe Dahan.

Groups of *Cohanim* buried together in various places visited by pilgrims should also be noted: Ait El-Cohen in Imini and several other places (Amzerkou, Imerhane, Talate, Tamnougalt, Tarkellil and Tazenakht); Ait Bu-Aharon in Aghmat; the Cohanim of Beni Hmad, Marrakech, Mogador and Oulad Mansour; and the Cohanim and Leviim near the *mellaḥ* of Tadmout of Ait Otman. The members of these groups of *Cohanim* seem to belong to different families.

Another interesting phenomenon is the connection between the burial places of saints who were great rabbis and the graves of their students. Various traditions tell that a hundred-and-fifty disciples—also known as Ulad Lyeshibah, or "Students of the *Yeshibah*"—are buried near R. Abraham Awriwer. R. Aharon Ha-Cohen from Demnate continues to study with his students, who are buried near him and called Mwalin El-Gomra, meaning "Masters of the *Gemara*" (the Talmudic commentaries they study). R. Nwasser is buried in Oulad Yahia with some twenty-four of his students, who apparently died along with him. And in the *mellaḥ* of Tillin, according to tradition, Mul El-Ḥazra El-Menzura and ten of his students are buried.

Notes

1. Seven and three are formulaic numbers. See A. Dundes (1968, pp. 401–24); E. Tavenner (1916); E. Lease (1919); O. Schnitzler (1970).
2. The most current tradition says that both names designate the same saint.
3. According to tradition, R. Yaᶜaqob is a descendant of R. Shemuel Elbaz, whose name was changed to Abiḥatsira, meaning 'Master of the Mat,' after he miraculously sailed the seas on a mat. Another tradition tells that the miracle on the sea involved R. Yaᶜaqob

himself. The genealogical tree of the Abiḥatsira family is depicted in D. Manor (1982, p. 238). See also A. Mograbi (1968) and Y. Benaim (1931, p. 66).

4. The great *hillulah* takes place in Ramleh, Israel, with the participation of members of the Abiḥatsira family and hosts of followers. Since 1980, worshippers from Israel and all over the world go on yearly pilgrimage to his grave in Damenhour, Egypt, and celebrate the *hillulah* in honor of the saint.
5. See I. Ben-Ami (1974a, pp. 45–47), (1975b); M. Mazal-Tarim (1939).

5

THE SAINTS AND *ERETS YISRA'EL*

EVER SINCE ANCIENT TIMES, NORTH AFRICAN JEWRY HAS CHERISHED all things associated with the Land of Israel—*Erets Yisra'el.*[1] The cult of sainthood is a conspicuous manifestation of this close bond. According to tradition, many of the saints venerated by Moroccan Jews were born in the Land of Israel.[2] The research described here has netted a list of eighty-four such saints.[3] In addition to these, one must add the *Torah* Scrolls—the Sepher Tislit[4] and Sepher Ait Yitsḥaq—which are reputed to have come from the Holy Land. There are also Meʿarat Oufran—the Cave of Oufran—and the Imin wa-Mumen cemetery,[5] in which saints from *Erets Yisra'el* are buried.

Throughout history rabbis have come from Israel to Morocco. A number of saints are said to have come during the days of the Second Temple, among them Mulay Inguird, Mulay Tamran and Mul El-Bit. R. Yaḥya Laḥlu is said to have arrived in Morocco during the period of the First Temple. The Sepher Tislit is a *Torah* Scroll from the Temple of Jerusalem, and the Sepher Ait Yitsḥaq has been preserved from the time the First Temple was destroyed. It is said that rabbis who came to Morocco from the Holy Land during the First and Second Temple periods are buried in the cemeteries of the Cave of Oufran, Imin wa-Mumen, Ksar Es-Souk, and near Gourama.[6]

Records of the present study show that almost twenty percent of all the male saints were born in *Erets Yisra'el.* They are important not only because of their numbers, but above all because of their intrinsic merit and the great veneration they elicited. Among the twelve saints who attract huge crowds at their *hillulot,* ten originated in *Erets Yisra'el;* these include R. ʿAmram Ben-Diwan, R. David Ha-Levi Draʿ,[7] R. David U-Moshe and Mulay Ighi.

An examination of the ramified connections between Morocco and Israel within the framework of the saints originating in both lands reveals a number of fascinating aspects. The connection is not limited to technical issues of the arrival of the emissary in Morocco, his death there and eventual transformation into a saint. These individuals came to Morocco from Israel for specific purposes, about which there are many and varied traditions.

One legend states outright that in ancient times at least one group of seven rabbis came to convert the Berbers.[8] Viewing this tradition from a historical perspective, it seems likely that it originated during the first centuries of the Christian Era, when the fathers of the church in North Africa attempted to counteract the influence of the Jews[9] by encouraging conversion to Christianity.

Another story, originating in Beni Mellal, tells of a famous rabbi who taught in the Temple. He had many students, ten of whom he particularly favored. One day they decided to test him and deliberately omitted a passage of the text they were reading. The rabbi noticed it and dismissed them, telling them they would be dispersed and would die in foreign lands, bearing non-Jewish names.[10] A related tradition tells that Elijah the Prophet wanted to test ten pupils. He ordered them not to laugh if they saw someone with parched, cracked lips holding a psalter. If they failed the test, the punishment would be exile. One pupil burst out laughing when he saw King David with a psalter, his upper lip seeming cracked. At that very moment the pupils were dispersed, each flying in a different direction. That is how R. Raphael Ha-Cohen and R. Ḥananiah Ha-Cohen came to the city of Marrakech and Mulay Ighi came to the mountains. These oral traditions usually refer to seven[11]—sometimes ten—rabbis. One of the stories tells of seven, while at least eight others were about ten rabbis,[12] the most noteworthy one being that of the Jews of Tidili.[13]

A Muslim tradition relates that R. David Ha-Levi Draʿ was a rabbi in Jerusalem at the time of Jesus: when he saw that the Jews were torturing Jesus and distorting the words of the covenant, he sentenced himself to exile and went to Morocco.

Morocco not only assimilated sages from Jerusalem who were sent there as special emissaries or came as a result of historical dispersion. It also served as a refuge for saints who were persecuted in Israel. A story tells that when R. ʿAmram Ben-Diwan and his son, R. Ḥayyim Ben-Diwan, were being pursued by Muslims in the Cave of Makhpelah in Hebron, they left through a side gate with the help of the Patriarchs Abraham, Isaac and Jacob, and found themselves in Azjen, Morocco.

Moroccan Jews have interesting traditions about Biblical[14] and Talmudic figures who came to Morocco and were buried there. Noah's Ark, for example, is said to have landed in Morocco. The prophet Daniel[15] is buried in that country, as are the prophet Jonah,[16] Yoab Ben-Tseruyah,[17] and the three sons of King Solomon—R. Yitsḥaq Ben-Sliman, Sidi Bu-ʿAissa U-Sliman[18] and Sidi Ftaḥ Ben-Sliman. R. Eleʿazar Ben-ʿArakh, R. Hillel Ha-Galili,[19] R. Yosef Ha-Galili, R. Shimʿon Bar-Yoḥay[20] and R. Meir Baʿal Ha-Nes[21] are also buried in Morocco. Even the Baʿal Shem-Tov[22] has a connection with the country: one tradition maintains that he wrote the Sepher Tislit, and therefore he is revered by Jews of Morocco.

The connection between Moroccan Jewry and *Erets Yisra'el* focuses on the concept of redemption. An interesting tradition tells that many saints of unknown identity are buried in the Jewish cemetery at Ksar Es-Souk. The day they are identified, the Messiah will come, bringing redemption for all the people of Israel. The Cave of Oufran also has a story relating to the redemption. When a Jewish shoemaker entered the cave to bring out the sword of the governor's son, he found the saints sitting there. They informed him that had he greeted them, salvation would have come to the world that very day. Another tale tells[23] that there was a hidden trail by which it was possible to reach Jerusalem from Oufran in only a few hours. Every morning a certain cow from Oufran went to graze in Jerusalem, and every evening she returned to Morocco. Wise men of Jerusalem noticed the cow and fed her a slip of paper on which they wrote that she came to Jerusalem every day. One day the cow touched a child, and the child's father demanded that the animal be slaughtered. After she was slaughtered, they found the note and great was the sorrow of the people of Oufran when they realized that the hour of redemption had been postponed again.

The same legend that tells of the dispersion of the ten students who failed to pass Elijah the Prophet's test also records that Elijah promised early salvation if the students would follow his orders. God struck Elijah for wanting to bring redemption before its time.[24]

On the one hand, these legends offer an explanation of why so many saints from Israel are found in Morocco. On the other hand, they clearly indicate the functional connection between the Jews of Morocco and the people of Israel. Indeed, rabbis were banished because they did not pass a test, but their covert as well as overt presence represents an important, if not prime, link in the messianic process. Saints from *Erets Yisra'el* buried in Morocco wait to be revealed. Sometimes they reveal themselves, and here, too, there is a clear etiological element in the ritualistic system and arrangements surrounding Morocco's saints. But it is impossible to know the extent to which their full revelation depends upon the saints themselves and to what extent it depends upon the Jews of Morocco. Moroccan Jewry's devoted veneration of saints, and the consequent privilege granted them of revealing those saints, is an important aspect of the ramified ties binding them. It is not a great step from this to a general awareness of Moroccan Jewry's active role in the coming of the redemption and the Messiah. In the process of redemption, Moroccan Jews believe they have a crucial function to perform within Jewry as a whole. This makes perpetuation of their physical existence absolutely essential: to enable these Jews to fulfill their designated task, the saints protect and fight for them when annihilation threatens.

The bond with the Land of Israel in all that involves Moroccan Jewry's cult of sainthood acquired a new dimension when these Jews began to emigrate to modern Israel. This represents an interesting development: the saints are returning from Morocco to Israel, either through revelation in a dream, as with R. David U-Moshe, or through a miracle whereby the body of a wealthy Jerusalemite who has died is exchanged for that of R. Shelomoh Ben-ʿAttar.

It should be noted that while Moroccan sages paid due respect to rabbis and emissaries from the Land of Israel, Moroccan wise men remained fully aware of their own worth. In many cases they came to the assistance of their colleagues from the Holy Land—and the scales were often tipped in favor of the Moroccans. There are traditions telling of emissaries sent to Morocco by the wise men of *Erets Yisra'el* to seek the advice of R. David Ben-Barukh the Elder and R. Yehudah U-Re'uben, in connection with matters the sages of *Erets Yisra'el* had difficulty interpreting. The two rabbis knew in advance that an envoy was on the way; they not only resolved the issue at once, but sent him home with a loaf of fresh bread in his hand. The envoy concluded that the sages of Morocco were wiser than their counterparts in *Erets Yisra'el.* With a wave of his hand, R. David Ben-Barukh transported a Jerusalem envoy who longed for his family. Telling the rabbi that he was indeed wise, the envoy declared that he would be his slave.

The Moroccan sages would not forgive an insult on the part of emissaries from the Land of Israel. It is told that one of these envoys, R. Raḥamim Meyuḥas, attended a circumcision in Mogador at which R. Ḥayyim Pinto was also present. Without asking permission, R. Raḥamim blessed the wine; when R. Ḥayyim Pinto spoke of this to him, he retorted that sages from *Erets Yisra'el* did not need permission. They argued and cursed one another. A few days later R. Raḥamim Meyuḥas died.

Notes

1. See H. Z. Hirschberg (1965, vol. 1, pp. 226 *sq.*); J. Toledano (1972, p. 305).
2. Moroccan Jews said "Jerusalem" meaning *Erets Yisra'el*—the Land of Israel.
3. The list includes the following saints: R. Abraham Awriwer, R. Abraham Azulay (Iguenisaine), R. Abraham Bu-Dwaya, R. Abraham Cohen, R. Abraham Cohen Bu-Dwaya, R. Abraham Yafe, R. Aharon Cohen, Ait El-Cohen (Imini), Ait El-Cohen (Talate), R. ʿAmram Abiḥatsira, R. ʿAmram Ben-Diwan, R. Ben-Zḥila, R. Daniel Hashomer Ashkenazi, R. Daud, R. David Alshqar, R. David Cohen (Azjen), R. David Ha-Levi Draʿ, R. David Tsabbaḥ, R. David U-Moshe, R. Didokh, Irhir Izid, R. Eleʿazar Ben-ʿArakh, R. Eleʿazar Ha-Cohen (Aiounil), R. Eliʿezer Ashkenazi, R. Eliʿezer Turei-Zahav, R. Eliyahu (Casablanca), R. Ḥabib Ha-Mizraḥi, R. Ḥananiah Ha-Cohen, R. Ḥananiah Ḥaliwa, R. Ḥayyim Ben-Diwan, R. Ḥayyim Ha-Mizraḥi, R. Ḥayyim Lashqar, R. Ḥayyim, R. Ḥayyim Waʿqnin, R. Hillel Ha-Cohen, R. Hillel Ha-Galili, R. Makhluf Ben-Yosef (Kasba Tadlah), R.

Mordekhay Mul El-ʿAyn, R. Moshe Ben-Shelomoh, R. Moshe Ben-Zohra, R. Moshe Cohen, R. Moshe Ḥabib, Mulay Ighi, Mulay Inguird, Mulay Tamran, Mul Azadh, Mul El-Bit, R. Nwasser, R. Pinḥas El-Cohen, R. Raḥamim Ha-Yerushalmi, R. Raphael Ha-Cohen (Achbarou), R. Raphael Ish-Yamini, R. Shaul Ha-Cohen, R. Shelomoh Ben-Lḥans, R. Shelomoh ʿAmar, R. Shem-Tov Ha-Mizraḥi, R. Shimʿon Cohen, Sidi Bu-Lanwar, Sidi Bu-ʿAissa U-Sliman, Sidi Ftaḥ Ben-Sliman, Sidi Rghit, R. Sliman Adayyan, Tuqshusht, R. Yaʿaqob Ashkenazi, R. Yaʿaqob Bardiʿi, R. Yaḥya Ben-Yaḥya, R. Yaḥya El-Khdar, R. Yaḥya Laḥlu, R. Yamin Tsabbaḥ, R. Yannay Mul Lmekhfiya, R. Yehudah Ben-Ḥovav, R. Yehudah Ben-Yisra'el Ha-Levi, R. Yehudah Halaḥmi, R. Yehudah U-Re'uben, R. Yissakhar Yisra'el, R. Yitsḥaq Ben-Sliman, R. Yitsḥaq Levi, R. Yitsḥaq Yisra'el Ha-Levi, R. Yonah Daudi, R. Yonah Navon, R. Yosef Bajayo, R. Yosef Ben-ʿEli, R. Yosef Dayyan, R. Yosef Pinto (of Ouarzazate).

4. The scribe who wrote the scroll brought the book to Morocco over the sea on a carpet. It is also called Sepher Tislit of Jerusalem.
5. See L. Voinot (1948, p. 77).
6. R. Hillel Ha-Galili is buried there. One informant reported that rabbis from the period of the First Temple are buried in the cemetery of Tillit.
7. R. David Ha-Levi Draʿ may originate from Spain, but the stories about his *Erets Yisra'el* origin show that no importance is given to historical facts. The importance attributed to the origin from the Holy Land is felt when one informant says that "the saint came from Jerusalem for sure," while another says that "all saints came from Jerusalem."
8. E. Doutté (1914, pp. 208–09) offers a famous list of seven rabbis, which includes: Dâouid Draʿ (R. David Ha-Levi Draʿ), Moûla Ir'i (Mulay Ighi), Chloûmou Bel H'anech (R. Shelomoh Ben-Lḥans of Aghbalou), Rebbi H'abib (R. Ḥabib Ha-Mizraḥi), Moûl el Borj (R. Yitsḥaq Yisra'el Ha-Levi), Sidi H'aiem (Sidi Ḥiyyim) and Rebbi Chemmoûl (R. Shemuel). L. Voinot (1948, p. 64) presents a similar list originating from Demnate that has five saints common with Doutté's list, and in which Sidi Ḥiyyim and R. Shemuel are replaced by Mul Anmay (R. Yaʿaqob Ashkenazi) and Mulay Matil (R. Abraham Cohen).
9. See H. Z. Hirschberg (1965, vol. 1, pp. 17–30).
10. The same story is told by L. Voinot (1948, pp. 55–56), giving the names of seven rabbis: Sidi Cadi Haja (R. Yaḥya Ben-Yaḥya),

Mouley Tamrane (Mulay Tamran), Moul El Bit, Mouley Inguird, Mouley Touabith (Mulay Twabit), Moul El Bordj (R. Yitsḥaq Yisra'el Ha-Levi) and Sidi Khira (R. Ḥayyim). Such stories explain why Jewish saints have Arabic or Berber names.

11. Many traditions related to seven saints are known among Christians and Muslims: see L. Massignon (1950, p. 245); E. Dermenghem (1954, pp. 47–48); F. Jourdan (1983). Groups of seven saints buried at the same spot (*sebatu rijal*) are found in many places in Morocco: see E. Westermarck (1926, vol. 1, pp. 142–43); H. de Castries (1924, pp. 245–304); F. Jourdan (1983, p. 148). Among the Jews, this tradition is found with relation to Ulad Zemmur or the seven Bene-Zmirru, the seven Cohanim of Ait El-Cohen (Imini) and of Ait Bu-Aharon, and the seven Cohanim buried in Mogador.
12. The informants spoke about ten rabbis but usually gave only one name, such as R. David Ha-Levi Draʿ, R. Raphael Ha-Cohen, R. Raphael Ish-Yamini, R. Yaʿaqob Bardiʿi, or partial lists of names. One such list included R. ʿAmram Ben-Diwan, R. David Ha-Levi Draʿ, R. David U-Moshe, R. Ḥayyim Ben-Diwan, and Mulay Ighi; another list included R. ʿAmram Ben-Diwan, R. David Ha-Levi Draʿ, R. Ḥananiah Ha-Cohen and Mulay Ighi; a further one included R. Moshe Cohen, R. Raphael Ha-Cohen (Achbarou), R. Shelomoh Ben-Lḥans (Aghbalou), and R. Sliman Adayyan. During my visit to Marrakech in 1981, an informant named R. Levi gave me the following list of ten rabbis: R. Abraham Awriwer (also called R. Abraham Ha-Cohen Ashkenazi, according to the informant), R. ʿAmram Ben-Diwan, R. David Ha-Levi Draʿ, R. David U-Moshe, R. Eliyahu (Casablanca), R. Ḥananiah Ha-Cohen, R. Ḥayyim Ben-Diwan, Mulay Ighi, R. Shelomoh Ben-Lḥans and R. Yaḥya El-Khdar. In the literature we also find single names, partial lists and lists of ten rabbis. See L. Voinot (1948, p. 56); E. Doutté (1914, p. 209); P. Flamand (1960, vol. 2, p. 41).
13. This is the only list that includes Rashbi (R. Shimʿon Bar-Yoḥay): R. David Ben-Barukh, R. David Ha-Levi Draʿ, R. David U-Moshe, R. Eliyahu, R. Ḥananiah Ha-Cohen, Mulay Ighi, Mul El-Barj, R. Pinḥas Ha-Cohen, Rashbi and R. Shelomoh Ben-Lḥans.
14. Similar traditions exist among the Muslims in North Africa. It is told that Moses and Elijah the Prophet were together in Tlemcen (see E. Doutté, 1900, p. 67). Joshua son of Nun is said to be buried both in Morocco and in Nedromah, near Tlemcen, where his tomb is widely venerated to this day by Jews and Muslims (see R. Basset, 1901, p. 101; A. N. Chouraqui, 1968, p. 5). The Berbers of the

Moroccan Rif claim that Noah's Ark landed there and that Noah's daughter is buried in the region (see A. Moulieras, 1899, vol. 2, pp. 811 and 257).

15. L. Voinot (1948, p. 83).
16. R. Montagne (1924, p. 114).
17. J. M. Toledano (1972, p. 9).
18. L. Voinot (1948, p. 39).
19. We do not know of any rabbi by this name, but Moroccan Jews know him as a *tanna.*
20. He revealed himself in the dreams of some Jews in Sefrou and told them they should not bother to visit him in Israel because he was staying with them, in the mountain called Jebel El-Kebir. See also L. Voinot (1948, p. 52). Another legend of the Jews of Tidili says that R. Shimʿon Bar-Yoḥay is buried in a mountain near their village.
21. A woman dreamed that he was buried near the cave of R. Yehudah Zabali, at Ksar El-Kebir.
22. See I. Ben-Ami (1983a, p. 403).
23. See M. Mazal-Tarim (1939, story no. 53). This is a well-known motif in Jewish literature. It was assigned the number 5842 in the Israel Folktale Archives, in which parallel stories from other Jewish communities can be found.
24. Y. Lewinsky (1961); H. Schwarzbaum (1975, pp. 176–81).

6

SAINTS AND THEIR DISCIPLES

Relationships between a saint and his disciples are complex, sometimes ambivalent. Veneration, blind faith, awe, fear and total compliance go hand in hand with haggling, disagreement, and even menacing threats. Whether the disciple is dreaming or awake, the relationship entails direct speech such as is customarily found among friends: they may rant and rave in the heat of an argument, but usually they arrive at a mutually agreeable compromise.

These different manifestations become apparent when scrutinizing the various forms in which Jews of Morocco address the saints to whom they generally appeal when in dire need. A worshipper of R. ʿAmram Ben-Diwan explained that a person approaches a saint with the words: "We ask of you . . . "; she made it clear that one never says: "Give me . . . !"

On occasion the saint is appealed to as a friend, and there is even a hint that disciple and saint are in league with one another. A disciple of R. Mordekhay Ben-ʿAttar approached him, saying: "If you are on my side, show me how to make a good living." R. David U-Moshe was told: "Oh, saint, if you save me, I'll know that you are mine and I am yours." And R. David Ha-Levi Draʿ was told: "Rabbi, if you let my daughter live and [grow up to] call me father, I vow to serve you all my life—until you send me to Jerusalem."

A follower with a troubling problem may appeal to the saint, pressing him to solve it for him. A young fellow brought a calf to be slaughtered for Mul Timḥdart's *hillulah,* but the calf disappeared. Having fulfilled his vow, the fellow told the saint: "My lord, Sidi Mul Timḥdart! I brought you your calf; now the problem is yours. I promised a calf and it's your business now. You look for it!" The mother of a girl who did not want to marry the man to whom she had been promised appealed to R. Makhluf Ben-Shetrit: "Oh Rabbi, you settle this affair for me!" One evening a female disciple took some women with her to visit R. Ḥananiah Ha-Cohen. When they found the crypt closed, she said: "Oh, R. Ḥananiah, you are ours and we know only you. What will happen to us? Don't disgrace me before these people who want to visit you." Sick people were brought to R. ʿAmram Ben-Diwan and appealed to him: "R. ʿAmram, for life or death!" Their attendants said: "Here is the wise man; either cure him or finish him off!"

Pressure exerted on a saint may even be accompanied by veiled threats. A father said to R. David Ha-Levi Draʿ: "I adjure you to tell me why my sons die!" And a Jew who told the saint a Muslim had accused him of stealing his land said: "Show me how special you are!" The request may even come with an *ʿar,*[1] the threat in this case being obvious. A Jew who had been wronged by a Muslim complained bitterly to R. Aharon Ha-Cohen of Demnate, saying: "If you don't show us one of your miracles with this Muslim, we won't believe in you at all."

Although most appeals to the saints are made orally, on rare occasions they are conveyed in other forms, for example, the letter the caretaker of R. Yehonathan Serero's burial site left on the saint's tomb, asking the rabbi to supply him with provisions for Passover.[2] Stones placed on R. ʿAmram Ben-Diwan's grave and ribbons draped on nearby trees also signify petitions.[3]

Worshippers sometimes tend to identify a person who devotedly tends a saint's shrine with the saint himself and have been known to address their requests to such a caretaker.[4] When this happened to the caretaker of R. David U-Moshe's shrine, his response was: "Do not put your faith in me; believe in the saint."

The saint is perceived as a middleman who mediates between a petitioner and God. Although the request is addressed to the saint, it is clear to everyone that "the saints do no more than ask of God. God gives what they ask for because He cannot refuse a saint." R. Yaḥya Laḥlu's disciples said to him: "We ask of you and you ask of the Almighty, blessed be He."

The attitude toward a saint is always respectful. Jews feel highly privileged to be blessed by the saint—at his home if he is still alive, and, if he is dead, by his descendants or at his graveside. Burial near the saint is also a great privilege[5]; many saints are interred in a consecrated cemetery in Ksar Es-Souk, and local Jews wanted to be buried there too. It was the custom to bury all rabbis who died in Salé near the grave of R. Raphael Anqawa.

While venerating and honoring the saints, their disciples are well aware of their sensitivities and are careful not to offend them. There is a unique set of relationships in which fear of the saints has the upper hand; any offense, even if committed inadvertently, will be punished. This applies to living as well as dead saints, which explains why Jews were always to obey and give donations to R. Ḥayyim Pinto the Younger and R. Meir ʿArama. Doubting a miracle performed by a saint or discrediting his deeds in any way is forbidden. A young man doubted the efficacy of R. ʿAmram Ben-Diwan's miracles, and at night he dreamed that a man called ʿAmram slapped him and sent him to jail. Thereafter he ceased doubting and took great care not to offend the saint. All monies collected for a saint belong to him or her and may not be touched by anyone else. Two children playing a game took money from R. ʿAmram Ben-Diwan's charity box; their mothers, fearing for their lives, hastened to return it. A follower of R. David U-Moshe, who prepared a bull for slaughter in honor of the saint, refused his son's wish to sell it; in a dream he told the saint that the bull deserved to be slaughtered only if it was to be sacrificed for the saint.

Anyone harming a saint's person, grave or disciple will be punished. Saints react severely to Muslims' offenses, which are always construed as being of malicious intent, but they also punish Jewish offenders, even though injury caused by a Jew is considered unintentional. If the punishment is less severe than death, at the saint's discretion it may be commuted in response to the offender's request. A living saint may grant forgiveness upon receiving a contribution, as did R. David Ben-Barukh. A dead saint may be mollified by offerings of olive oil or candles, a ritual meal, or a slaughtering; furthermore, the offender may come with his hands tied behind his back and a knife in his mouth,[6] signifying that for better or worse, he has put himself at the saint's mercy.

An offense against a saint, and the punishment as well, may assume many different forms. A Jew was invited to R. Moshe Ḥaliwa's *hillulah* but was too lazy to go. He began to suffer terrible headaches and found relief only by entering the synagogue with his hands tied behind his back. A Jewish woman went on a pilgrimage to the grave of R. Makhluf Ben-Yosef Abiḥatsira, after which she became pregnant. She did not name the newborn after the saint, and the infant died. The same thing happened with her next child. She named her third child after the saint, and it survived.

Offense against a living saint is also punished, and immediately. The woman of the house in which R. Yehonathan Serero was lodging complained under her breath that the rabbi's feet were dirty. That same night she began to bray like a beast and did not stop until the rabbi pardoned her and gave her his blessing.[7] Another example is that of a man who insulted R. Moshe Ḥaliwa in the marketplace. Before he knew what was happening, he was attacked by flying eggplants.

There are times when the punishment is death, which can be altogether disproportionate to what may have been an unintentional offense. Here again the saint in question may be either alive or dead. Stories about R. David Ha-Levi Draʿ tell of a Jew whose actions were disgraceful, including swearing by the saint in an unjust cause; of a young man who visited the saint and returned on the *Sabbath;* and of another fellow who behaved reprehensibly in a stream not far from the saint's shrine. They say that all these people died soon after. When a woman dismounted to light a candle at the tomb of R. Yitsḥaq Davila on her way to Mulay Ighi, the owner of the animal she rode complained bitterly. He was killed that same night when the house he stayed in was destroyed. It is said that anyone taking the name of R. Raḥamim Eluq in vain will die within the year.

Many traditions tell of saint's curses[8] and the fear generated thereby. Obviously, these refer primarily to real historical figures, particularly to saints who have died only recently. The curse of Ait Naḥmias, for example, was highly dangerous: when R. David Naḥmias traversed the village, everyone was frightened. Once the rabbi was annoyed with a man who argued with his daughter; soon after the man and his whole family died. Whenever R. David Ben-Barukh cursed someone, the curse was realized, so people tended to avoid him. Once, when he was elegantly dressed and visiting Mogador incognito, the Jews received him with lavish hospitality; he complained that they honored his attire rather than himself. When they discovered his identity, they begged his forgiveness and immediately gave him a contribution. A Jew staying at R. David Ben-Barukh's house was taken aback by the rabbi's modest way of life and said scornfully: "So this is R. David Ben-Barukh!" The man lost his sight, and it was restored only after he begged forgiveness of the saint. On another occasion a Jew refused to give him a donation, and R. David Ben-Barukh cursed him, saying that within a year the man would be impoverished—a prediction that came true. In a case involving a Jew and a Muslim, R. Yehudah Ben-ʿAttar ordered the Jew, on pain of death, to pay a given sum of money within three days. Fearing the saint's curse, he paid the Muslim at once. The curse of R. Ḥayyim Pinto the Younger was also very severe: A Jew who broke the rabbi's oil vessel died two days later, and a physician who turned the rabbi out of his house died the following day. The curses of many other saints[9] were also known to be very powerful. Their orders were carried out with alacrity to prevent catastrophe from striking the disciple or his family.

An offense to a saint's caretaker or disciple elicits punishment as if it were an offense against the saint himself. A certain man informed officials that the caretaker of R. David U-Moshe's grave was building a synagogue without permission; the man lost his mind. By the same token, a disciple's curse is considered as effective as that of the saint himself. A disciple of R. Shelomoh Ben-Lḥans cursed a driver who refused to take him to the saint's tomb; the car broke down and would not move until the driver agreed to take the passenger to his destination.

Traditions describing relationships of saints with one another are of particular interest. Living saints go to visit the shrines of dead saints.[10] Saints also reach mutual agreements regarding spheres of influence and patronage in Morocco. R. Ḥayyim Pinto the Younger performed a miracle in Mogador, explaining to R. Pinḥas Ha-Cohen, who was present, that he had exercised his right in the sphere belonging to him and his ancestors, while the area that belonged to R. Pinḥas was Marrakech and Taroudant. R. Pinḥas Ha-Cohen and Baba Dudu, otherwise known as R. David Ben-Barukh the Younger, divided Morocco between them. Alms and contributions collected in the northern section came under the auspices of R. Pinḥas, and Baba Dudu controlled those collected in the south.[11] At least one tradition tells of a saint who died as the result of another saint's curse: R. Yonah Navon cursed R. Ḥayyim Pinto (of Mogador), wishing him a short life. R. Ḥayyim then cursed R. Yonah, who died two days later.

A vow made to a saint when a request is transmitted or granted is of utmost importance. The saint is promised a festive meal; an animal may be slaughtered in his honor;[12] he may be promised an inscribed tombstone, the erection of crypts at his graveside, and other tokens. Barren women or women whose infants have died promise to name a newborn baby after the saint. If such a promise is not fulfilled, the offender risks severe punishment,[13] further evidence of the fear evoked by the saint and the care taken not to provoke him or her. Overcoming great difficulties, a Jew slaughtered two calves for Mul Timḥdart because he had vowed to do so. In a similar situation, a Jew slaughtered two sheep that he had promised in honor of Mulay Ighi, even though the saint appeared to him in a dream and released him from the obligation to slaughter both, as one of them had disappeared. A woman who bore a child due to the intervention of R. Masʿud ʿArama brought him the *seʿudah* she had promised, lest evil befall her infant. A father whose infant was restored to health with the help of Mul Timḥdart fulfilled his vow, twenty years later, to visit the saint's grave.

If one does not fulfill a vow he has made, the punishment is often a relapse into one's previous condition. If an illness is the issue, a person may beseech the saint's help a second time, and the saint may or may not forgive the transgression again. A Jewish physician recovered from paralysis with the help of R. ʿAmram Ben-Diwan but did not keep his vow to slaughter a cow, and the paralysis returned. He went back and begged the saint's help, repeating the vow, but the saint refused to forgive him. A Christian pharmacist from Tangier who had two sick sons prostrated himself on R. ʿAmram Ben-Diwan's grave and promised that if his sons recovered he would pave a road to the grave over which he would build a roof. He did not keep his promise, and his sons sickened again. He returned to R. ʿAmram, promising that if his sons got better he would not leave the site until the road was ready. This time he kept his promise, although instead of a roof he built a spacious covered terrace with columns. It is also forbidden to change a vow or replace it with another one. The Muslim guard at the grave of R. Saʿadiah Dades warned a petitioner, also a Muslim, that he must sedulously fulfill his vow to the saint. When the petitioner gave the saint a smaller donation than he had promised, his mare and colt both died.

Tradition tells that saints never renounce anything they consider due them; they urge people to fulfill their vows, even though the vow may be only in somebody's mind. It is said that R. Makhluf Ben-Yosef Abiḥatsira would appear in people's dreams and order them to fulfill their vows. Once R. Yitsḥaq Ben-Walid appeared in a dream to a woman who had promised to name her unborn baby after him. He warned her to keep her vow, even though her father had just died and the infant would ordinarily have been given the grandfather's name. Fearing dire consequences, she named the baby after the saint. R. David Ha-Levi Draʿ appeared in the dream of a Jew who had promised to build him a crypt; the saint told the man to get up and perform the good deed.

Through dreams the saint addresses his disciples, blesses them, complains to them, or gives them instructions pertaining to himself. R. David Ben-Barukh (Azrou n'Bahamou) would sometimes appear in a dream to one of his female followers and bless her and her family. R. David U-Moshe would appear to the Jew who tended his room and ask God to bless him and assist him in all his undertakings, assuring him that he had nothing to fear. A saint also may occasionally express his or her own state of mind in a dream. Sometimes R. David U-Moshe would appear distressed, a sign to his followers that something was amiss; when he appeared smiling, they knew that all was well.

A saint may complain to his disciples about things they have done to him and, above all, about their inattentiveness to his desires. R. David U-Moshe was known to have asked a disciple whether he would dare sell the bull that had been chosen for slaughter in honor of the saint. He was also known to have told a man who had gone crazy after offending a disciple that he was ashamed of his wife and children because he had performed an act deserving of punishment. Many stories are told about R. David U-Moshe's appearance in dreams of his disciples in Israel to complain that Moroccan Jews have forgotten him. R. David Ha-Levi Draʿ asked his disciples why a crypt was built for all the others but not for him. In a dream, R. Moshe Ḥaliwa informed his son that Jews had ceased visiting his synagogue and thus he vowed they (the Jews) would leave the city. Saints have complained that their graves were not being visited, and sometimes in this way new saints, such as R. Abraham Bu-Dwaya and Mul Sedra, have been revealed.

Saints frequently have personal requests or demands and convey relevant instructions to their disciples, primarily through dreams. R. David Ben-Barukh (of Azrou n'Bahamou) asked that only *paytanim* (cantors), not musicians, be invited to his *hillulah.* R. David Ha-Levi Draᶜ requested a synagogue rather than the paved floor he had been promised; he also told an official preparing to move to Israel who should be given the room that was near the saint's grave. R. Pinḥas Ha-Cohen asked his disciples to light candles rather than give money in celebration of his pilgrimage. R. Hillel Ha-Cohen asked for a second *seᶜudah,* as the first one was impure because a Muslim servant had tasted it. R. Yaḥya Laḥlu told the Jew who headed the Burial Society not to build a gravestone for him. Mul Timḥdart asked to be called Sidi Mul Timḥdart (Master of the Place) rather than by his name. The list of orders, requests and demands emanating from the saints, most often in dreams, is long and variegated,[14] including details about how to prepare a *seᶜudah* or a grave; how, when, and where to hold a *hillulah;* and so forth.

Sometimes an epileptic fit is the medium for transmitting a saint's orders. That was how R. Daniel Hashomer Ashkenazi announced that the abattoir near his burial site had been built over his mother's grave; he asked the Jews to remove it.

During his lifetime a saint usually had an assistant who accompanied him wherever he went, carried his equipment and attended to his needs. When the assistant was a young Muslim, the Jews called him the saint's *ᶜeved* (servant). It is told, for instance, that R. David U-Moshe, R. Ḥayyim Ben-Diwan and Ḥazzan Izzo had such servants. When the assistant was a Jew, he was called the saint's *shaliyaḥ* (emissary) or *shammash* (caretaker). R. Ḥayyim Pinto the Younger had a *shammash,*[15] whereas R. Yosef Abiḥatsira, R. David Abiḥatsira, R. David Ben-Barukh (of Taroudant),[16] and R. David Ben-Barukh (of Azrou n'Bahamou) had *sheliḥim.* Caretakers of saint's graves were also called *shammash* or *shaliyaḥ,*[17] and they had special status in the eyes of the disciples.

Anyone whom a saint helped in time of serious trouble or was expecting a miracle after having made a vow had a special relationship with the saint. A Jew vowed to R. David Ha-Levi Draʿ to be his *shaliyaḥ* if his sick daughter survived. Time and again a follower's testimony includes the term *ʿeved* (servant or slave), attesting to the disciple's total subservience to the saint, much like the attitude of a slave toward his master.[18] A Jew in trouble addressed R. Aharon Assulin thus: "My Lord, perform a miracle for me so that I will be your servant and light candles to you." After he was rescued from the authorities, the head of the Jewish community said to him: "Continue to serve him to whom you are bound like a slave." A Jewish merchant who worshipped R. David U-Moshe once drove to his tomb in a truck carrying tea, a commodity whose private sale was forbidden in Morocco during World War II. Someone informed on the merchant, and he was ordered to appear before the governor. That night R. David U-Moshe came to him in a dream and told him to say that the merchandise belonged to R. David U-Moshe and he, the merchant, was only the saint's servant. The saint also appeared to the governor in a dream and asked him not to interfere with his servant. In another case, an emissary from the Holy Land who was celebrating the Passover festival in R. David Ben-Barukh's home missed his own family very much. The rabbi miraculously showed him his family, and in gratitude the emissary announced that he would henceforth be the saint's servant.

Jews of Moroccan origin continue to use the expression "servant" or "slave" of the saint even after having left the country. A Jew who went on pilgrimage to the tomb of R. Shimʿon Bar-Yoḥay (in Israel) to ask the rabbi's assistance in curing his mortally ill son spoke to the saint as follows: "Ordinarily I come here to pray every year. If my son will be cured, I am your servant. If not, I'll come and set fire to your tomb." Offspring of R. Ḥayyim Pinto visited a wealthy Moroccan Jew who lived in France and asked him for a contribution. He answered: "Everything I have is yours, because I am a servant of the saint, R. Ḥayyim Pinto."

It is interesting that the expression "slave" or "servant" of the saint is used not only in reference to one for whom a miracle has been performed, but also for an individual known to be very close to a saint, usually the organizer of the saint's *hillulah* or an active functionary associated with the saint in one capacity or another. Essentially the title "slave (servant) of the saint" is self-conferred, usually after the saint has performed some special deed on behalf of the disciple or a special relationship has developed between them. A particular saint thus becomes the only or primary saint of his servant, and their interrelationship is on a very personal, invisible level.

Notes

1. See E. Westermarck (1926, vol. 1, pp. 188 and 518 *sq.*): "The assistance of saints is secured not only by humble supplications and offerings, but by means of a very different character: in numerous cases the petitioner puts pressure upon the saint by putting *ʿar* on him."
2. See Y. Benaim (1931, p. 54).
3. The informant said these objects serve as messages or letters.
4. This happens also when the caretaker is a Muslim. In my visit to R. David Ha-Levi Draʿ's shrine in Morocco in 1981, I saw a Jewish woman asking for the blessing of the Muslim guard of the place. In reply to my question, she explained that his blessing is like the saint's blessing.
5. One story tells about a saint who objected to the burial of a certain person near him: R. David Naḥmias's sister was buried near R. Yonah Daudi against R. Yonah's wish, and a snake emerged when they dug the grave.
6. See D. Noy (1964, p. 35).
7. See Y. Benaim (1931, p. 54).
8. One informant said the saints in Israel are more tolerant and do not cause harm to anybody, as sometimes happened in Morocco. Also Muslims believe that the curses of saints are more dangerous than those of ordinary persons: see E. Westermarck (1926, vol. 1, p. 490).
9. Stories tell that R. Meir ʿArama was immediately given what he wanted lest calamity befall the person or his livestock; R. Yaḥya Laḥlu cursed a Jew who said that the rabbi's legal decision regarding his case had been unfair, and the Jew died. It is said that anyone who was cursed by R. Pinḥas Ha-Cohen, even the saint's own son, dried up on the spot. The curse of R. Re'uben Pinto was always carried out. The curse of R. Raphael Anqawa worked instantly. For example, a Jew who had falsely sworn that he had not taken money from an Arab was cursed by the rabbi and immediately went blind. In another instance, when he was judging a court case involving a Jew and a Muslim, the rabbi threatened to curse the Jew, so the Jew immediately told the truth. Officials of the city did not come out to

meet him when he felt that his end was near, and thus R. Saʿadiah Dades cursed the city, saying that there would be more women than men there, and so it was. R. Shelomoh Cohen Gadol was cautioned not to curse the Jews since his curse always came true immediately.

10. R. David Ben-Safet visited the tomb of R. Shelomoh Ben-Lḥans; and R. Ḥayyim Pinto the Younger, in the company of R. Pinḥas Ha-Cohen, visited the grave of R. Ḥayyim Pinto the Elder.
11. A similar geographical division of protected regions in Israel is found in I. Ben-Ami (1977, pp. 90–91, stories no. 2.1 and 2.5).
12. Muslims too "promise to give the saint a present in case his request is granted—to sacrifice an animal to him, to provide his *darbuz* with a new covering, . . . or to whitewash his sanctuary": E. Westermarck (1926, vol. 1, p. 172).
13. See E. Westermarck (1926, vol. 1, p. 173): "If a petitioner does not keep his promise, although his request is granted, he will suffer some misfortune."
14. R. ʿAmram Ben-Diwan was said once to have declared that he preferred stones rather than a gravestone; on another occasion he told a Christian he did not want the roof he was promised, but would be satisfied with a terrace on which his visitors could gather. Many traditions tell of R. David U-Moshe's orders to his disciples: a Jew offended the saint's followers, and was ordered to come to his synagogue with a knife in his mouth, shouting from the entrance to the end. He appeared to a disciple in the daytime, facing the sun, handed him a pick-ax and asked him to build him a grave. The disciple started building the tomb on a Thursday, but it rained very hard. The next day, the sun shone brightly; and he built the grave after the saint appeared to him in a dream and explained that the grave should be erected on a Friday because he had died on a Friday. R. David U-Moshe went into great detail about his room and his *hillulah* in Safed, Israel, and pointed out the exact spot on which to hold his *hillulah* each year, where to place his charity box, where to light candles, how to announce his coming to the Jews of Morocco in writing. He further ordered them not to burn glasses of olive oil but only candles, and to make a curtain for his shrine. He also described all the utensils and cooking for a *seʿudah,* and so on. He also sent a woman to Safed to help with the preparation of the *seʿudah* and asked the people who were preparing it in their house to hold the ritual meal at the site of his dwelling in Safed.
15. Information given by the *shammash* himself, who said that he used to accompany the rabbi everyplace.
16. Information from the *shaliyaḥ's* son.

17. Muslim caretakers of Jewish saint's graves were called "guards."
18. A similar expression exists among the Muslims, but it seems to have a different meaning. See E. Westermarck (1926, vol. 1, p. 186): "Many a saint who is no head of a religious order has *húddam,* 'servants' or followers, whose *ŝēh* he is. . . . The relations between the *seh* and his *hdim* are of a very intimate character."

7

SAINTS AS MIRACLE MAKERS

MIRACLES, WHICH EVOKE AWE AND WONDER, ARE VERY IMPORTANT IN folk religiosity. These extraordinary phenomena signify divine intervention and are tangible evidence of the sanctity of a given person, place or object. Nevertheless, as Huizinga notes, "All life was saturated with religion to such an extent that the people were in constant danger of losing sight of the distinction between things spiritual and things temporal. If, on the one hand, all details of ordinary life may be raised to a sacred level, on the other hand, all that is holy sinks to the commonplace, by the fact of being blended with everyday life."[1] Thus, for one who worships a saint, the miracle becomes, in effect, a daily occurrence.

Moroccan saints perform miracles in many different spheres:[2] they cure illness and control forces of nature; they continue to "live" after death and can become visible to the faithful. The Jews of Morocco, ardent participants in *hillulot,* never tire of relating stories of miracles performed by the saints.[3] The wish for a miracle is ever present, but hope for one naturally increases when troubles loom large, particularly if traditional measures fail to cure a sick person. Hundreds of personal accounts tell of paralytics who retrieve the power to walk, of the blind who recover their sight, mutes who begin to speak, deaf persons who begin to hear, mentally ill whose sanity is restored, barren women who give birth, and so forth.

Most miracles performed by saints pertain to curing illnesses, particularly epilepsy, paralysis, mental illness, infertility, miscarriage, and infant death. Some saints cure all diseases, while others are known to specialize in particular ailments.[4] Epileptics, for example, seek the help of R. Abraham Cohen, R. Daniel Hashomer Ashkenazi, Mul Tazghart and R. Shelomoh Ben-Tameshut. The blind turn to R. David Ben-Barukh, R. David Ben-Safet, R. David Ha-Levi Draʿ and R. Shalom Zawi. At times, sufferers of physical or mental illnesses were roped or chained to a saint's tomb or nearby tree where they spent a whole night—or at least several hours—waiting for the miraculous cure.

Some saints have very specific specializations. R. Shelomoh Ben-Tameshut cured high fever and jaundice. R. Shalom Zawi cured maladies induced by fear. Lalla Safia healed people suffering from weakness. Lalla Luna Bat-Khalifa treated diseased throats with saliva. And R. Raphael Anqawa exorcised demons.

The great importance of progeny in Moroccan Jewry's traditional society explains the frequent appeals to saints in cases of barren women or of families that were childless because of infant mortality.[5] Because modern medical facilities were lacking, particularly in small villages, recourse to the saint and faith in his powers were often the only source of hope in such cases. Several saints, among them R. Abraham Awriwer, R. Abraham Darʿi, R. Abraham Wazana, R. ʿAmram Ben-Diwan, and Lalla Safia, were famous for curing barren women. R. David Ha-Levi Draʿ, Lalla Solica, Mulay Ighi, and Sidi Bu-ʿAissa U-Sliman were known for bringing solace to bereaved families. Women who had miscarriages appealed to Sidi Mhasser.

A baby born after a saint had intervened in one way or another was usually named after the saint,[6] and a special bond was created between them. The namesake then had a lifelong obligation to visit the saint's grave, participate in his *hillulot,* and so forth.

Occasionally, a saint would tell a petitioner that he or she could not cure him or her and would send him or her to another saint.[7] Sick people were sent by Ulad Zemmur to R. Abraham Mul Annes, and by R. Yitsḥaq Yisra'el Ha-Levi to R. David Alshqar. R. Yehudah Ben-Yismaʿel sent a barren woman to Sidi Bu-ʿAissa U-Sliman, who had once referred a Jew who wanted to have only sons to R. Makhluf Ben-

Yosef Abiḥatsira. The caretaker of R. Ḥananiah Ha-Cohen's tomb sent a woman and her sick daughter to R. Shelomoh Ben-Tameshut.

The Jewish saints of Morocco healed Muslims and Christians as well as Jews. R. David Ben-Barukh saved a mentally ill Christian Frenchman; a paralyzed Muslim woman recovered after having been brought to R. David Ha-Levi Draᶜ. Numerous accounts tell of the miraculous cures of Christians who visited the tomb of R. ᶜAmram Ben-Diwan.

A saint can transfer his own healing power to a member of his family, to a disciple, or to a person who took care of him during his lifetime or tended his grave after his death. R. Shelomoh Ben-Yitsḥaq's daughter inherited his healing powers and treated sufferers by touching or spitting on the sore spot. R. Yehudah Gadol Gilᶜad transmitted his healing powers to Lalla Luna Bat-Khalifa, who had cared for him devotedly during his lifetime and tended his grave after his death. A woman fell asleep at R. Yitsḥaq Ben-Walid's tomb and dreamed that the saint gave her a jug; she healed sick people with ointments she put inside the jug. Another woman, under similar circumstances, received a stone from R. Yaḥya Ḥayyim Assulin, with which she cured people.

Because a saint's personal effects were in intimate contact with him, they are believed to possess curative powers. Tradition has it that the clothes of R. ᶜAmram Ben-Diwan are in Salé, and Jews go there and kiss them. Before R. Raphael Anqawa and R. Raḥamim Mizraḥi were buried, people bought fragments of their shrouds at very high prices. To give birth relatively easily, Jewish women would grasp canes belonging to R. Ḥayyim Messas or R. Yitsḥaq Ben-Walid, or would wear belts belonging to R. ᶜAmram Ben-Diwan or R. Yitsḥaq Ben-Walid. A sick person could be cured by putting on R. Ḥayyim Messas's ring.[8]

While still alive, a number of saints became known for their power to heal. R. Moshe Ha-Cohen circumcized a dying child and the child lived; R. Yosef Dahan and R. Moshe Ḥaliwa, when alive, cured the sick by laying on their hands; and as noted above, Lalla Luna Bat-Khalifa's saliva had curative properties.

It is not only at times of illness that the saints are called upon for help. Disciples use their good offices and seek their assistance whenever confronted by a pressing problem. When in danger, particularly during wartime, a Jew might call out to R. David U-Moshe and be saved. A driver who had an accident called upon R. David U-Moshe or R. David Ben-Barukh, and he and his passengers were not injured. A Jew being sued by the Jewish Agency in Israel followed the advice of R. David Ben-Barukh and won the case. Marvels occur that can only be attributed to magic wrought by a saint: locks fell off and a door opened to permit women to enter the shrine of R. Ḥananiah Ha-Cohen or to enable Jews to leave the cemetery where R. Makhluf Ben-Yosef Abiḥatsira is interred. Because of his great faith in R. David Ha-Levi Draᶜ, a certain Jew was able to drink tremendous quantities of wine without getting drunk. A soldier wanted to get home one night, and R. David U-Moshe sent him a car that vanished the moment the soldier reached his destination.

A saint manifests his power in connection with relations between man and wife or in arranging marriages. It is customary to turn to a saint if someone wants to get married or when domestic tranquility is disrupted. A short time after R. David Ha-Levi Draᶜ and Mulay Ighi lifted the spell known as *tqaf*[9] from a girl, she became engaged. R. Ḥayyim Pinto the Younger, R. Makhluf Ben-Shetrit and Mulay Ighi initiated matches or arranged them at the request of petitioners.[10] R. David Ha-Levi Draᶜ and R. David U-Moshe mediated between husband and wife and brought them together. Even merchants appealed to saints to help conclude transactions successfully.

Miracles have been performed not only to extricate individuals from trouble. Saints were sometimes able to protect and save an entire community, *mellaḥ* or city. Here again, no distinction was made between Muslims and Jews. When R. David U-Moshe found all the people of Timzerit gravely ill, he interpreted it as a heavenly decree and gave his own life in return for their recovery. When Buri Khizo was appealed to and a meat-offering was slaughtered in his honor, the saint saved the surrounding area from a typhoid epidemic. Some of the disciples of R. David Ha-Levi Draᶜ were sleeping near his tomb when the roof of the shrine collapsed. Because of his protection, no one was injured.

Many traditions tell how saints saved individual Jews, a *mellaḥ* or an entire city from Muslim attack. One story tells that when hostile bands approached Tillit, stones from the cemetery bombarded them and drove them away. The saint may do more than merely protect Jews from Muslim attack, however: he may intervene for the purpose of improving the attitude of the Muslims.

A saint's tremendous power and complete control over events manifests itself in the punishments he metes out to those who offend him. Most frequently his punishment is directed at Muslims who have desecrated the saint's person or grave, or in some way harmed the Jews. But the Jews, too, may be targeted for punitive action by the saint, particularly if they have been sacrilegious.

Saints possess prophetic powers, and their prophecies always come true.[11] The life of the pasha of Marrakech was saved several times because R. Pinḥas Ha-Cohen foretold plots to assassinate him. When the Jews of Fez were in danger and dispatched an envoy to R. Makhluf Ben-Yosef Abiḥatsira requesting his help, the saint knew in advance why the envoy had been sent to him. During their lifetimes, several saints were renowned for their prophetic powers,[12] and many were known for their ability to prophesy death. R. Raphael Anqawa always recognized signs of approaching death[13] and once took a man he saw in the street, put him to bed, and recited the *shemaʿ* over him. R. Shelomoh Ben-Lḥans foretold the death of R. Masʿud Naḥmias in a distant stable and saw the funeral of R. Mordekhay Ben-ʿAttar in the sky. Some saints prophesied their own death, and many stories in this connection are told again and again.[14]

As I have noted elsewhere, saints often die on Friday—the Eve of the *Sabbath.* When he feels the end is near, the saint makes his preparations. He takes a purifying ritual bath, cuts his nails, wraps himself in his shroud, and recites the *shemaʿ*. Should he be outdoors in a field, a spring may rise nearby to enable him to immerse himself, as was the case with R. David U-Moshe and R. Mordekhay Mul El-ʿAyn. A shroud may come down from the heavens, as it did for R. David U-Moshe. Sometimes the saint descends into his grave by himself, and it closes over him. A saint occasionally makes some final request before his death. R. Yosef Elmaleḥ predicted that he would die in Demnate and asked that they bury him there. Both R. Yosef Bajayo and R. Yosef Ben-ʿEli died in Tabia but asked to be buried in Ntifa. Although R. Isso Ibgui died in Tizi, the village in which he had been born, he asked to be buried in Tazenakht. Mulay Ighi asked the members of the Burial Society to dig a grave for him; he made all necessary preparations, and the grave closed over him. R. Shelomoh Ḥamias foretold that he would be buried next to Mulay Ighi in Ait Rahal, so he went there with his wife; he indeed died and is buried in Ait Rahal. R. ʿAmram Ben-Diwan asked to be buried alongside the tree that still grows near his grave. The Jews asked R. Raphael Anqawa and Ḥazzan Izzo to pray for rain, and they did so, while prophesying that when the rains came they would both die. R. Yaḥya Laḥlu asked to die following the death of a Jew whom he had cursed. R. Shelomoh Ben-Lḥans, too, sought death after hearing that his teacher and mentor, R. Mordekhay Ben-ʿAttar, had died.

While alive and after their death, saints have absolute control over the forces of nature.[15] Their ability to make the sun stand still is legendary.[16] Tradition has it that they always exercise this power on Fridays so that a given activity can be consummated before dark to avoid violating the *Sabbath.* In another context, there is one story of a saint who made the sun stand still on Friday so that the ritual slaughterer could find his knife and slaughter the villager's poultry before the advent of the *Sabbath.* In all other cases the sun stops in its tracks on Friday so that a saint who has died can be buried before the *Sabbath* starts. One Friday the sun shone steadily until Lalla Solica Waʿqnin was buried; then darkness fell suddenly and the *Sabbath* began. The sun miraculously stood still in connection with many saints who predicted their own death.[17]

A saint may halt the sun's progress by word of mouth or by someone close to him—or the saint himself—driving some object into a wall or the ground. Night falls instantaneously when the object is withdrawn. By driving a stick into the ground, R. Yehudah Ben-Ḥovav made the sun stand still so that there would be time to bury R. Mordekhay Mul El-ʿAyn in the Akka cemetery before the *Sabbath.* A wise man was invested by R. Shelomoh Ben-Lḥans with the power to stop the sun's advance by inserting a branch in a wall; this enabled him to finish burying the saint before the *Sabbath* began.[18]

A saint who knows his death is imminent can activate natural forces to prepare his grave. At times, great boulders break away from the mountains and cover him. At other times he unleashes wind and rain storms which testify to nature's sorrow over his death. On the other hand, the storm may signify the saint's ire because a ceremonially impure person presumed to visit his grave.

Water, another natural force controlled by the saints, can be used in the performance of miracles. It is said that R. Yaʿaqob Ashkenazi could turn water into whatever he wished.[19] According to a well-known tradition, R. Yaʿaqob Abiḥatsira sailed over the sea sitting on a mat. While alive and after his death a saint can hold the sea back. Before the King of Morocco, R. Eliʿezer Davila drove a tent peg into the ground to prevent the city of Rabat from being inundated; the floodwaters reached the peg and then receded. When storm waters flooded the Christian and Jewish cemeteries in Mogador, they reached the tomb of R. Ḥayyim Pinto and there they stopped. A saint can keep a river from overflowing its banks; three villages were saved from floods by R. Aharon Assulin, R. Eleʿazar Ha-Cohen and R. Yisra'el Moryossef.

A major role of certain saints in Morocco was that of rainmaker. During a drought Jews would petition a living saint or prostrate themselves on the grave of a dead saint; they slaughtered in his honor and implored him to bring rain. R. Yehonathan Serero and R. Yosef Bajayo acquiesced and prayed, and the rains came. It is said that Ḥazzan Izzo and R. Raphael Anqawa agreed to pray for rain in response to the Jews' petition, but announced that when rain started to fall, they would die. And so it came to pass. R. Raphael Anqawa led the procession to the Jewish cemetery; he was followed by all the Jews and their children, barefoot, their hands bound. At the cemetery they spread ashes over their heads. As rain began to fall, R. Raphael's life ebbed away. Believers visited the graves and slaughtered animals in honor of many other saints[20] to whom they attributed magical rainmaking powers. One particularly impressive miracle was performed by R. Abraham Wazana. During a dry spell he announced to a dreaming woman that there would be water in the river the next day, and so there was.

Many stories are told of springs miraculously created by saints, including R. David U-Moshe, R. Mordekhay Mul El-ʿAyn, and Qayid El-Ghaba. A saint can also restore water to a spring that has dried up. R. Ḥayyim Ben-ʿAttar made water flow in two dry springs that belonged to a certain recalcitrant Jew; the man repented and became religious as a result of the miracle. R. David U-Moshe caused a dry spring near his tomb to fill with water so that parched visitors could quench their thirst at his graveside. Water will also miraculously issue from a saint's tombstone on the day of his *hillulah,* to inform his worshippers that their requests have been granted.

The connection of saints with animals is the subject of many traditions.[21] By order of the sultan, R. Shaul Naḥmias entered a lions' den, stroked the beasts and nothing happened to him. A lion came near R. Shelomoh Ḥamias but dared not touch him. It is said that in his lifetime R. Abraham Wazana extricated a frog from inside a snake that had swallowed it. A dog remained standing at the graveside of R. David Ha-Levi Draʿ during the *Torah* reading and throughout the reading of the *Haggadah* on Passover. The dog died during the Passover week, and its owners buried it wrapped in a shroud.

A saint can retrieve an escaped animal intended for slaughter and can also revive an animal that has died. R. Daniel Hashomer revived a cow that had been slaughtered, in order to return her to her Muslim owners. R. ʿEli Ben-Yitsḥaq brought a cow back to life when two Muslims were arguing over how to divide her carcass.

There is a widespread belief among Moroccan Jews that a saint can assume an animal's form[22] or use the animal as a medium through which to send a sign. Reference is most frequently to doves and snakes,[23] although other creatures are also mentioned. There were always two doves on the palm tree near R. David Ha-Levi Draʿ's tomb. A dove, another bird and even a snake could always be found near the grave of R. ʿAmram Ben-Diwan. Sidi Bu-ʿAissa U-Sliman once appeared in a tree in the form of a dove, and another time in the form of a snake. R. Shelomoh Ben-Tameshut revealed himself in the form of a chameleon, while R. Abraham Cohen appeared as a snake. Many traditions associate R. Shelomoh Ben-Lḥans with snakes (Lḥans means snake): a snake appeared near his grave; his mother gave birth to a snake, and he himself would slough off his skin at night before beginning to study. Two Jews were looking for the spot on which to place R. Hillel Ha-Cohen's tombstone; when they saw a snake come out, they knew exactly where the saint was buried.

Saints are masters of space and can pass from place to place in a single leap. That is how R. Makhluf Ben-Yosef Abiḥatsira went from Tarkellil in the Draa Valley all the way to Fez, after pronouncing the Tetragrammaton. The saint can also instantaneously transport an emissary of his from place to place, usually providing him with a loaf of warm bread to take on his trip. The journey is so rapid that when the emissary reaches his destination the bread is still warm. This was the means of transport used by R. David Ben-Barukh and R. Yehudah U-Re'uben to send emissaries back to the Holy Land, after the saints had settled controversial issues that the sages of Israel were unable to resolve. R. Shelomoh Ben-Lḥans transported an emissary to Marrakech to enable him to see R. Mordekhay Ben-ʿAttar's funeral; in the same way R. Makhluf Ben-Yosef Abiḥatsira sent an emissary to Fez.

When necessary, a saint can produce food for the hungry. Many stories tell of a loaf of bread that was never totally consumed and a *maḥia* bottle that never emptied during the whole night of a *hillulah.* A small portion of couscous was being saved for R. Yannay Mul Lmekhfiya; it was given to Jews who had fled from another village, and not only did they all eat their fill, a portion still remained on the plate.

Tradition tells that saints do not die like ordinary people, but continue to "live" and be active after death.[24] As we have seen, the saint can appear to his followers in dreams, at his grave or in some other place. Every Saturday night R. Ḥananiah Ha-Cohen appeared near his grave. R. Abraham Makhluf Ben-Yaḥya was seen by two Jewish women who had come to light candles in his crypt, and the Jewish caretaker of his tomb saw him in phylacteries and prayer shawl, saying his morning prayers. Anyone suddenly entering the cemetery where R. Shelomoh Bar-Beriro is buried sees a man standing next to a camel, holding a full water-vessel and cup, but the figure vanishes as the intruder comes near. R. Moshe Amselem appears at midnight in the synagogue that bears his name. He thanks his followers for their devotion and stays there to study with them for two hours. People have seen R. Shemaʿyah Cohen and three other saints who were buried in the same place, all dressed in green, with green shoes, walking hand in hand along the road to their crypt.

There are many stories about saints who continue their sacred studies after death, either alone or together with other saints. They read Psalms, study the Talmud; sometimes only their voices will be heard as the saints study together.[25] The Arab guard at the ancient cemetery in which R. David Ben-Safet, R. Ḥayyim Toledano, R. Ḥayyim Ben-ʿAttar and R. Raphael Bibas are buried heard men's voices reading Psalms at ten o'clock in the evening and at two in the morning. On occasion a saint may leave his studies to go to the assistance of a sick person, whereupon he tells his companions that he is too busy to study just then.

There is a belief that a saint's body can be buried in several different places, either in two or more graves or in a grave and somewhere else, such as in a mountain or synagogue.[26]

During his lifetime and after his death a saint may bring about a miracle that enables him to recite the blessing over the wine on the *Sabbath.* R. Yehonathan Serero arrived in a city far from his home and regretted not having wine for the *Sabbath* blessing; suddenly the empty wine jug filled up. Later it was found that the wine had disappeared from his own house that night. Under similar circumstances, a wine glass flew from the house of R. Mordekhay Ben-ʿAttar and on the *Sabbath* Eve landed on R. David Ben-Barukh's table. After his death, a saint can return to his house to sanctify the wine every *Sabbath* Eve, but he will stop coming if his appearance is revealed to anyone outside of the family. Before he died, R. Yosef Turjman told his wife he would come to bless the wine every *Sabbath* Eve and that she would hear his voice but would be unable to see him. He stopped coming when his wife revealed the secret to a neighbor. For a year after his death, R. Shelomoh Ben-Yitsḥaq came to bless the wine in his daughter's house, but he ceased coming when she told a neighbor she heard her father's voice.

Many miracles are connected in one way or another with a saint's grave. It is reported that the ground opened for R. Ḥayyim Ben-Diwan to let him into his grave. The grave of Sidi Sayyid rolled from the Muslim cemetery to the Jewish cemetery. Road-workers were unable to move the graves of R. Eliyahu and R. Masʿud Bar-Mimuna, nor could they dislodge the boulder over R. Shelomoh ʿAmar's grave. Saints frequently object to having a tombstone or marker built over their graves, and any such attempt will be doomed to failure. For this reason many saints have no gravestone.[27]

Many miracles attributed to saints relate to mysterious illumination. It is said that the *shekhinah* descends upon the graves of R. Abner Ha-Tsarfati, Lalla Solica and R. Yehudah Ben-ʿAttar, which are close to one another in the Fez cemetery and are always lit up. Fire descends from the skies to illuminate R. Moshe Ben-Yaʿaqob Ḥayon's grave every Friday, on the first day of each Hebrew month, and on the eve of holidays. Flames from above also illuminate the graves of Mul Terya and Sidi Bu-ʿAissa U-Sliman. The memorial candle lit after the death of R. Moshe Ḥaliwa burned for a whole year without being relit. A light shone from the synagogue in Ashkelon named after R. David U-Moshe, and illuminated an entire room during the blackout enforced at the time of the Six Day War.[28]

Notes

1. See J. Huizinga (1979, p. 151). This description taken from fourteenth and fifteenth century Western Europe fits our reality. See also "Miracle," in *Encyclopaedia Judaica* (1971, vol. 12, pp. 73–81).
2. Similar miracles are performed by Jewish, Christian and Muslim saints: A. van Gennep (1953, tome I, vol. 5, p. 2572); R. Kriss and H. Kriss (1975, pp. 123–24); S. Al-Aflaki (1918–22).
3. As expressed by one informant: "Many miracles did the saints. We live only thanks to the saints and thanks to God." In this chapter a selection of miracles is presented; for a more complete picture of the phenomenon, consult other chapters.
4. See J. Huizinga (1979, p. 165); E. Malka (1946, p. 113). The specialization of the saints is not restricted to the medical field. A. van Gennep (1953, tome I, vol. 6, pp. 2557–609) submits a list of twenty-six national saints responsible for thirteen grape-growing regions in France. E. Westermarck (1926, vol. 1, p. 163): "The miracle-working capacity of dead saints, however wide its scope may be, is often to some extent specialised."
5. J. Gerber (1972, p. 121): "Praying at graves of 'saints' was customary for barren women"; J. Mathieu and R. Maneville (1952, pp. 58–68); I. Ben-Ami (1993b, p. 256).
6. I collected many examples of this widespread custom. Girls too were named after the female saints. The first name of the saint dominated in the region of his burial place, and thus many individuals are named Eliyahu in Casablanca, Ḥayyim in Mogador, ʿAmram in Ouezzane, Ḥananiah in Marrakech, and so on.
7. Muslim saints also send petitioners to other saints. See E. Westermarck (1926, vol. 1, p. 189).
8. This ring was circulated throughout Morocco by the saint's wife. When R. Yisra'el Abiḥatsira, known as Baba Sale, died at the Soroka Hospital in Beersheba, a physician who treated him told me of his stupefaction at the sight of people taking home everything that had been in contact with the saint. The relics of the saints were also venerated by the Christians: see J. Huizinga (1979, p. 161).
9. See I. Ben-Ami (1972, pp. 195–205).
10. The decision of the saint was always accepted. Sometimes a young fellow would claim that the saint appeared to him in a dream and ordered him to separate from his fiancée.
11. S. Cohen (1935, p. 5); E. Westermarck (1926, vol. 1, p. 158).
12. Among the saints known for their power of prophecy were R. David Ben-Barukh, R. Ḥayyim Pinto (Casablanca), R. Menaḥem Cohen, R. Re'uben Azini, and R. Raphael Anqawa.

13. According to tradition of Moroccan Jews, there are 903 signs of approaching death based on Psalms 68:21.
14. The following saints prophesied their own death: R. ʿAmram Abiḥatsira, R. ʿAmram Ben-Diwan, Ḥazzan Izzo, R. Isso Ibgui, R. Mordekhay Mul El-ʿAyn, Mulay Ighi, Mul El-Ḥazra El-Menzura, R. Raphael Anqawa, R. Saʿadiah Dades, R. Shelomoh Ben-Lḥans (Aghbalou), R. Shelomoh Ben-Yitsḥaq, R. Shelomoh Ḥamias, R. Shelomoh Suissa, R. Yaḥya Laḥlu, R. Yitsḥaq Abiḥatsira, R. Yitsḥaq Davila, R. Yosef Bajayo, R. Yosef Ben-ʿEli, R. Yosef Dahan (Tamnougalt) and R. Yosef Elmaleḥ. R. Shelomoh Ben-Yitsḥaq prophesied that his death would occur on a Muslim holiday.
15. See E. E. Urbach (1969, p. 437); I. Ben-Ami (1975b, p. 212).
16. F. Legey (1926, p. 19); E. Westermarck (1926, vol. 1, pp. 152–53): "The saint comforted her by assuring her that the sun would remain in the sky till she was back. So it did; but as soon as she arrived at the palace it suddenly set, and it became dark at once. After this miracle Sîdi ʿĀli ben Ḥámduš was called *gûwad š-šems,* 'the leader of the sun.' "
17. The list includes R. Abraham Amzalag, R. Abraham Cohen Bu-Dwaya, R. ʿAmram Abiḥatsira, R. ʿAmram Ben-Diwan, R. Mordekhay Mul El-ʿAyn, Mulay Ighi, Mul El-Ḥazra El-Menzura, R. Raphael Ha-Cohen, R. Shelomoh Ben-Lḥans, R. Shelomoh Ben-Yitsḥaq, and R. Shelomoh Suissa.
18. I. Rouche (1936, pp. 280–86).
19. Legend says that once R. Yaʿaqob Ashkenazi had a dispute with the Muslim saint Sidi Raḥal, master of the fire. The saints prevented people from using water and fire until their dispute was settled.
20. People went to Ait El-Cohen, R. ʿAmram Ben-Diwan, R. Yaʿaqob Qanizel, and R. Yaḥya Laḥlu to ask for rain.
21. I. Ben-Ami (1989, pp. 33–39); J. Huizinga (1979, pp. 166–67).
22. E. Westermarck (1926, vol. 1, p. 159): "Dead saints may also appear in animal shapes, for example as pigeons or snakes."
23. The Jews were not afraid of the snake in the holy place and the snake would not harm them. A snake that passed over a sick man sleeping by the grave of R. ʿAmram Ben-Diwan was seen as the sign of his cure.
24. This may be the source of the belief that the saints are not always in their graves: thus it is important to leave a message there so that the saint can find it when he returns to the burial site. See E. E. Urbach (1969, p. 440); E. Westermarck (1926, vol. 1, p. 159).
25. E. Westermarck (1926, vol. 1, p. 188): "The dead saints generally live on amicable terms with each other and form a society by themselves."

26. Stories tell that Ulad Zemmur are buried in Safi, Salé, Tiznit, in the *mellaḥ* of Tabugimat, and in Marrakech; R. Eliʿezer Ashkenazi is said to be buried in Tassent and in Banzel; R. David Bel-Ḥazzan is buried in both Mogador and Marrakech; R. David Alshqar—that is, Mulay Ighi—is buried in Casablanca, in the village Ighi, Rabat and Tabia; R. ʿAmram Ben-Diwan is found in Azjen, Salé, Sefrou and near the wall in Ksar El-Kebir; R. David U-Moshe is found in Morocco, Safed and Ashkelon in Israel. E. Westermarck (1926, vol. 1, p. 160): "Some other dead saints are in two graves at the same time."
27. R. Abraham Awriwer, Ait El-Cohen, R. ʿAmram Ben-Diwan, R. Eleʿazar Ben-ʿArakh, R. Yaḥya El-Khdar, R. Yaḥya Laḥlu and others have no gravestone.
28. A similar story tells that the *shofar* blew by itself at *Yom Kippur* in the synagogue of R. ʿAmram Ben-Diwan despite the Moroccan government's order to the Jews not to blow the *shofar* on that day.

8

SAINTS AND THE WORLD OF NATURE

In Morocco many elements of the natural world are associated in one way or another with saints. It is difficult to determine when or why certain trees, bushes, stones, rocks, boulders, springs, waterfalls, rivers, caves and mountains have been consecrated,[1] although they may already have been held sacred at the time of pagan idolatry. In early days they were thought to be inhabited by ghosts and demons, who were eventually replaced by saints. Religious life among the Berbers, who were autochthonous to the region, abounded in myths rooted in the natural world. The Jews, too, may occasionally have participated in such cult rituals, which may help explain their strong ties today to some of those natural sites.

In traditional societies it is fairly common for a religious person to attribute sanctity to certain places. The sacred site, be it stone, tree or spring, is set apart by signs and symbols, and the cosmic significance of such places is clear. The religious ambience and all it encompasses are held sacred, and the special significance of the given natural elements derives from this. The present research has shown that Jews very rarely venerated an object of nature unless it was the focal point of legends concerning actual—or even fictitious—individuals, particularly if dreams are involved. Be that as it may, from the standpoint of religious phenomenology, it is important to note that Jews believed in the individuals associated with such objects and attributed great power to them. It is equally important in this context to note that most of those individuals lived very, very long ago.

Many beliefs relate to stones;[2] in Morocco they were often substituted for tombstones, and candles were lit on them. Traditions tell of great rocks or boulders breaking away from a mountain and burying a saint, which is what happened to R. Abraham Amzalag, R. David U-Moshe, R. Saʿadiah Dades and others. It is told that a cut stone fell on Mul El-Ḥazra El-Menzura; this gave him the name by which he was known: "Master of the Cut Stone." His disciples, covered by stones when the avalanche occurred, were buried there with him.

Stones have been found that mark the burial site of a saint, and tradition explicitly states that the saint is buried there, as in the cases of R. Abraham Makhluf Ben-Yaḥya, R. ʿAmram Ben-Diwan, R. Shelomoh ʿAmar, R. Yaḥya El-Khdar, R. Yehudah U-Re'uben, and R. Yitsḥaq Ha-Levi. It is told that a large rock lay on the ground where R. Eleʿazar Ben-ʿArakh was buried; each time the rock was moved away to make room to build a tombstone, it returned to the same spot. One tradition relates that a stone adorned with a picture of a camel marked R. Abraham Awriwer's grave.

Sometimes saints buried under a stone have been revealed to Jews in a dream. That is the way R. Mimun Elghrabli disclosed to members of the local Burial Society that he was interred under a round stone in the Settat cemetery. A dream revealed R. Yitsḥaq El-Qansi to the Jews of Debdou, after a Muslim woman who saw a light shining from a small stone in the Jewish cemetery called the Jews to come and look at it.

There are times when the saint associated with a stone is not identified with any person, real or fictitious. Cases in point are Mul Tefillin, a large stone near Tamzaourt bearing drawings of a fringed undergarment and phylacteries—*tefillin*—and Lalla Safia, where believers lit candles among small stones similar to paving tiles that were scattered above a large stone. An even clearer case is that of Sidi Mul El-Ḥazra—"My Lord Master of the Stone," in Skoura; a Muslim digging there found candles burning beneath a stone. The holy entity here involves only and exclusively the stone, which is also true of Lalla Qafia, the stone itself being the element bearing the sainted name. It is quite likely that the Cohanim who, tradition tells, are buried around a large rock at Imini and at Tadmout, are figments of the imagination, although one cannot entirely rule out the possibility that at some time long ago, they were real, living people.

Traditions about boulders[3] are very similar to those about stones. Mulay Tamran and Mulay Inguird are buried under boulders, and R. Ḥayyim is interred between two boulders. Pursued by thieves, R. Yaʿaqob Bardiʿi, mounted on his horse, clove a boulder with his stick, went inside the rock and was buried there. A boulder on the site of R. Yoab Ben-Tseruyah's grave bears the rabbi's footprint. There are many boulders above R. Pinḥas El-Cohen's grave. On boulders, too, it was customary to light candles.

Numerous traditions refer to the cairns[4] found in Morocco, where they are known by the generic term *kerkur.* The *kerkur* associated with a saint may take the place of a grave, or it may mark the first place from which the grave is visible, usually an elevated spot where a mountain pass narrows.[5] There are times when the identity of the saint connected with a given cairn is unknown, as in the cases of Lalla Taqerquzt, Tsaddiq Azru and Tuqshusht. There is a cairn in Ait Bou-Hlau, near Ouarzazate, called ʿAremat Avanim—"Heap of Stones"—that oddly enough has no connection with any saint, but was visited by women who believed they were possessed. The women would burn incense on the heap of stones, and if their request to be freed from the magic spell was granted, water gushing from the stones would assume the form of the object that had cast the spell.

Cairns substitute for the graves of the following saints, among others: R. Abraham Awriwer, Mul Bghi Bghi, R. Yaʿaqob Ashkenazi and R. Yaḥya Ben-Yaḥya. At R. ʿAmram Ben-Diwan's burial site many small stones representing petitions left by visitors were placed near the large boulder. This phenomenon of venerating stones identified with the burial ground of saints is well illustrated by the case of a Jewish woman to whom a Muslim showed a heap of stones. Believing that the cairn marked the burial place of the saint R. Raphael Ha-Cohen whom she wanted to visit, the woman lit candles and prayed devoutly over the stones.

Caves,[6] too, feature in many Moroccan traditions. In a way, the cave is a natural expansion of a boulder that has split open; it is the inside of the rock, as it were. One must bend low to enter, if the opening is narrow, and candles are lit inside. Rituals connected with caves are very ancient, and their beginnings are obscure. Tradition has it that R. Ḥayyim Lashqar, Ḥazzan El-Ḥili, R. Yaḥya Laḥlu and R. Yitsḥaq Ha-Levi are all buried in caves.

The identity of the saint in the cave was often unknown, as in the cases of Mul Bab Jemʿaa near Nador, Sidi Mhasser near Demnate, and Mul Jebel El-Kebir[7] near Sefrou. The latter is a very well-known cave in a mountain; it has a wide entrance and attracts crowds of worshippers, Jews as well as Muslims. Some two meters to the left of the entrance is a passageway with a niche containing candles. Two steps on the right lead to a room; to the left, at the end of the passage, there is another room that one must stoop to enter.

Sometimes the local Jewish population used caves as sacred burial ground. Examples include two caves in the village of Tasmesit—Meʿarat Abuqassis and Meʿarat Waʿnono—and Meʿarat Hacohanim in Zerekten. Near the stone marking the burial ground of Ait El-Cohen in Imini are seven holes that gradually widen to enable people to enter and light candles. Unquestionably, the most famous cave is Meʿarat Oufran,[8] also known as the Cave of those Burned (at the Stake) or the Meʿarat Ha-Makhpelah. It is located in a cemetery, and entry is forbidden. There is a story about a sage who was sentenced to death because he went into the cave, while a Jewish shoemaker was given special permission to enter and retrieve a sword the Muslim governor's son had thrown inside; the shoemaker thereby saved the Jews.

There are many mountains in Morocco where, according to tradition, saints are buried. The identity of the saint is often unknown, and he is referred to as Mul Taurirt—Master of the Hill—or Mul Jebel El-Kebir—Master of the Great Mountain. One example is a saint called Mul Aguiga, after the Aguiga mountain in the Anti-Atlas range where he is interred. Others said to be buried in mountains are R. Daniel Hashomer Ashkenazi, R. Ḥabib Ha-Mizraḥi, Lalla Simḥa Ruben, R. ʿObadiah Ha-Levi, R. Raphael Ha-Cohen, R. Shelomoh Ben-Lḥans and Sidi Sayyid. Three saints are said to be buried in the Imi n'Timouga mountain, near Imi n'Tanoute: R. Abraham Darʿi, R. Masʿud Mani and R. Yitsḥaq Ha-Levi. Many boulders, rocks and cairns associated with saints are located at the foot of mountains or on the mountains themselves; saints thus associated include R. Abraham Awriwer, Ait El-Cohen (Imini), R. David U-Moshe, Lalla Safia (Souk El-Khemis),

Lalla Taqerquzt, R. Saʿadiah Dades, R. Shelomoh ʿAmar, Tsaddiq Azru, R. Yaʿaqob Bardiʿi, and R. Yaḥya El-Khdar.

Moroccan Jews also visited certain springs, streams and pools, because water sources near holy graves are also looked upon as consecrated and are believed to possess curative or purifying properties. Hence believers drink or bathe in these waters.[9]

Many traditions tell of a spring that appeared miraculously to answer the needs of a saint.[10] R. Yaḥya Ben-Dossa came to Morocco from Spain at the end of the fourteenth century. One evening on his way to the city of Oujda, he needed water for the ritual washing of his hands. He scratched the ground and a spring bubbled up on the spot. This site, some five kilometres away from Oujda, is known as the Spring of Sidi Yaḥya and is the source of the city's water supply. Elsewhere I have referred to the story of R. Moshe Mimun, who during a severe drought struck the earth with his stick. A spring of fresh water welled up on the spot, and the rabbi revealed that a saintly man named Qayid El-Ghaba was buried there and wanted the Jews to visit him. A spring also gushed up when R. David U-Moshe and R. Mordekhay Mul El-ʿAyn needed water for ritual ablutions before they died. A spring that appeared suddenly not far from the grave of Bent El-Ḥmus indicated her sanctity.

Many saints are associated by tradition with certain springs or are buried near them. Such springs usually become streams or form pools, and these, too, play an important part in rites performed during visits to saints. Worshippers at the Mulay Ighi holy site would bathe in a nearby spring to exorcise evil spirits or cure barren women. There is a legendary belief that the saint purified himself before his death in the waters of this spring. One story tells that there were seven springs at the burial site of Mulay Yaʿqub; each spring was believed to possess curative powers for a different malady. These springs created pools of hot water that no one bathed in — for fear of being burned — until they had recited: *bard uskhun ya Mulay Yaʿqub* (cold and hot, O Mulay Yaʿqub). The sainted Lalla Taqerquzt is associated with a spring that becomes a brook and then a pool which bears her name. There are also springs near the graves of R. Abraham Awriwer, R. Ḥabib Ha-Mizraḥi, R. Shelomoh ʿAmar, R. Yaʿaqob Ashkenazi, R. Yehudah U-Re'uben and R. Yissakhar Yisra'el. Other pools are associated with specific saints. Near Marrakech there is a large natural pool called Kebur Shu which Jews went to for help. There is a large saltwater pool (*miqweh*) near R. Makhluf Ben-Yosef Abiḥatsira into which Jews descended through a narrow aperture; when they would intone "Baba Rabbi Makhluf Ben-Yosef" the water level rose and waves formed. A stream emanating from Sidi Mhasser's cave creates natural pools. Jews and Muslims immersed themselves in them before petitioning the saint.

A stream flows near the Ait El-Cohen graves at Imini, and it is told that non-Jews, too, come to bathe in its waters. It was also customary to take ritual baths in the stream that flowed near R. David Ha-Levi Draʿ's grave when visiting the saint. Pilgrims to the grave of R. Shelomoh Ben-Lḥans used to speak of the amazing landscape and running streams along the way.

Of all natural objects connected with saints, trees[11] are of most vital importance. Many specific trees, growing either above or near their graves, are identified with saints. Strips of cloth, belts, strings, ribbons, hair and other *ex-voto*[12] offerings were customarily hung on the branches, although the trees served mainly as recipients of diseases for which suppliants sought cures. Stones are often found at the base of these trees.

Many saints' names bear the additional general designation Mul Shejra, meaning "Master of the Tree," or they are named after a tree that grows near their burial place. One saint, whose identity is unknown, is called simply Mul Shejra; a very thorny tree grows near his grave. R. Yisra'el Cohen of Tabia is also known as Mul Shejra. Among those saints who bear the additional name of a tree or trees growing at their gravesides are Mulay Ighi and R. Ḥananiah Ha-Cohen, both also known as Mul Shejra El-Khedra—Master of the Green Tree; R. Yaḥya El-Khdar, meaning R. Yaḥya the Green and referring to the many trees on Jebel El-Khdar, the verdant mountain on which he is buried; and Mul Sedra or Mwalin Sedra—known as Masters of the Bush.

It's appropriate to mention here R. David Ha-Levi Draʿ, who is buried near a palm tree from which derive his additional names of Mul Enekhla—Master of the Palm Tree—and Mul Enekhla El-Khdar—Master of the Green Palm Tree. R. Yaʿaqob Ashkenazi is also known as Mul Almay or Mul Anmay, after the tree named "anmay." Mul El-Karma—Master of the Fig—is known only by this appellation. Sidi Bu-Zeggar bears the Berber name for the bush growing at his grave, and Mul Azadh is known by the Berber name for the thorny tree that grows near his burial place. R. Abraham Azulay from Iguenisaine is also called Mul Imitk, the name of a large tree at his tomb. R. Shimʿon Cohen from Ikherkhouren is also known as Tiqi El-Bor, after the trees that grow at his graveside.

Carob trees grow at the graves of several saints, among them Buri Khizo, R. Eleʿazar Ben-ʿArakh and R. Yisra'el Cohen of Tabia. There are loquat groves near the graves of Sidi Harun and R. Moshe Cohen, and fig trees grow at the graves of Mul El-Karma, R. Yehudah Ben-Yisra'el Ha-Levi, Mwalin Bu-Ḥlu (at whose grave there are also olive trees), and Kebur Shu (next to a palm tree). R. Abraham Cohen is buried under a laurel; an almond tree grows from the rock under which R. David U-Moshe is buried; a large tree, similar to an olive, grows over the grave of R. ʿAmram Ben-Diwan. One tradition tells that before he died R. ʿAmram asked to be buried alongside his tree, while another claims the tree grew after the rabbi had been buried at that spot. Jews usually hung bits of cloth, ribbons or gold ornaments on the branches.

Visitors frequently built large fires under these trees, and there are many stories attesting that the trees themselves never burned. A thorny tree grows near the grave of Mul Terya, and legend has it that it is lit up by flames descending from the sky. A tree at the grave of R. Daniel Hashomer Ashkenazi is always green. The large rock on the grave of Mulay Ighi is overarched by myrtle-like shrubbery which never catches fire, despite the many lighted candles set on the rock.

Like rocks and springs, trees associated with saints have acquired special names of their own. The tree at Mul Timḥdart is regarded as part of the saint. The large tree over Mul Tazghart's grave bears the saint's name. Barren women hung charms on R. Masʿud's tree, which is called Lalla Sedira, and then draped the amulets around their necks in the hope of conceiving a child.

Notes

1. "There are many atavistic practices among the Jews and Muslims of Morocco whose origins go back long before the Islamic conquest. Many of those cults center around such natural phenomena as stones, caves, springs and trees. These beliefs seem to have affinities with the ancient semitic polydaemonism that was prevalent in biblical Canaan (e.g. the terebinths of Mamre) and in pre-islamic

Arabia (e.g. the black stone of the Kaʿaba)": N. A. Stillman (1973, p. 260); S. Gsell (1913, p. 243); M. Eliade (1965, particularly pp. 98–137).

2. See E. Westermarck (1926, vol. 1, pp. 56–60, 68–72, 77–79); E. Dermenghem (1954, pp. 141–42); Z. Vilnay (1985, pp. 22–23); T. Canaan (1927, pp. 73–77); A. van Gennep (1909, pp. 20–29).
3. A large rock at the burial place of the Muslim saint Lalla Jamila near Tangier is much frequented both by Muslim and Jewish women: L. Voinot (1948, pp. 39–40). See also E. Westermarck (1926, vol. 1, pp. 68, 72, 77, 78).
4. Cairns or heaps of stones of various types and for various purposes are found in all Islamic countries and in other regions as well. See E. Doutté (1905, pp. 57–68); E. Dermenghem (1954, pp. 141–42); E. Westermarck (1926, vol. 1, pp. 56–62); Z. Vilnay (1985, pp. 22–23); T. Canaan (1927, pp. 73–77); J. G. Frazer (1961, vol. 2, p. 708); A. van Gennep (1909, pp. 20–29).
5. The same phenomenon is found with regard to the *marabouts* in Morocco. See E. Doutté (1905, p. 63–66); W. Westermarck (1926, vol. 1, pp. 58–59): "sometimes a cairn marks the place where a holy man is said to be buried or to have rested or camped, or it is called by a saintly name, as though it were itself a saint."
6. On this subject, see H. Basset (1920); E. Doutté (1909, p. 198); E. Dermenghem (1954, pp. 143–44); E. Westermarck (1926, vol. 1, pp. 72–73); N. A. Stillman (1988, p. 24): "Such practices in popular Judaism are by no means limited to Morocco. Jews in nineteenth century Palestine would spend up to three nights in the cave of Elijah on Mount Carmel."
7. D. Ovadia (1975, vol. 2, pp. 139–40); L. Voinot (1948, pp. 51–52); E. Westermarck (1926, vol. 1, p. 72); N. A. Stillman (1988, p. 23): "The most popular pilgrimage site, however, was not the grave of a particular saint but a cave on a low mountain behind Sefrou's Jewish cemetery. The official name of the hill is Jbel Binna, but the Jews referred to it simply as *z-zbel le-kbir* (the great mountain). . . . In the centre of the base of a cliff facing east is a cave called by the Jews *l-käf* (the Cave) and by the Muslims *kaf l-Ihudi* (the Cave of the Jew)".
8. See D. Corcos (1976, pp. 119–20); R. Boutet (31 March 1936. "Notes sur le judaisme dans l'extrême sud-marocain." *Avenir Illustré,* 11th year, no. 244, pp. 3–5); P. Flamand (1960, pp. 24–32); C. Levy (26 October 1951. "Oufran la Juive." *La Parole*); J. Ohayon (19 February 1931. "Les Martyrs d'Oufran." *Avenir Illustré,* vol. 6, no. 42, pp. 3–4); Vincent Monteil (1948. "Les Juifs d'Ifrane." *Hespéris*

35: 153–54); H. Z. Hirschberg (1957, p. 168); A. Laredo (1954, pp. 126–34); “Les Juifs d’Oufran, la plus vieille communauté du Maroc.” (March-June 1952, in *Cahiers de l’Alliance Israélite Universelle,* No. 63–64, pp. 16–17).

9. See E. Westermarck (1926, vol. 1, pp. 84–89): “In Morocco healing springs are very frequently connected with saint-shrines. . . . There is *baraka* not only in the water of springs but in water generally.” See also E. Dermenghem (1954, pp. 144–45, 148–51); L. Voinot (1948, p. 43).
10. Similar traditions are found among the Muslims: E. Dermenghem (1954, p. 195); and among the Jews in Algeria: I. Achel-Hadas (1961, p. 185). Among the Christians, see A. van Gennep (1947, tome I, vol. 3, p. 1388).
11. Among the Muslims in North Africa, see E. Westermarck (1926, vol. 1, pp. 66–68, 74–77); E. Dermenghem (1954, pp. 136–38); E. Doutté (1905, pp. 89–92).
12. This is a universal phenomenon, particularly widespread among the Catholics. See R. Roussel (1972, pp. 71–74); F. Raphael et al. (1973, p. 14); *Les Pèlerinages* (1960, pp. 22, 51, 57, 59–61, 212, 231, 319); R. Oursel (1978, pp. 99–118).

9

DREAMS IN SAINT VENERATION

Dreams are a most important element in the relationship between saints and disciples.[1] A saint may appear in a dream to someone visiting the saint's shrine or sleeping in his own home. The privilege of seeing a saint in a dream is not granted to everyone: it is considered a mark of special esteem. The saint may make a one-time appearance, using the dream to convey a message or offer a solution to a specific problem. Then again, he may appear time and again, establishing routine contact with an individual.[2] R. David Ben-Barukh often appeared in a certain woman's dreams to give her and her family his blessing. The woman who tended R. Makhluf Ben-Yosef Abiḥatsira's crypt in Kiriyat Gat, Israel, had regular contact with the saint via her dreams. R. Moshe Ḥaliwa appeared in a dream to one of the women in his family whenever she was in distress or pain, and told her what to do. Such routine connections are rare. The two people responsible for organizing the *hillulot* of R. David U-Moshe in Safed and Ashkelon, Israel,[3] maintain that they are privileged to converse with the rabbi, and not only in dreams.

In a dream a saint can cure the sick; if he appears to a sick person who is dreaming while on a visit to the shrine, it means that the suppliant's request for a cure has been granted. A sick man dreamed that R. Abraham Mul Annes struck his legs with a cane, and he woke up cured. A man in pain dreamed that he received a knife from Ulad Zemmur; when the sufferer placed the knife on the source of his pain, he was healed. A paralytic dreamed that R. David Ha-Levi Draʿ told him to get up, and he began to walk. R. Yaḥya Laḥlu passed his hand over the eyes of a blind man in a dream, saying "Look and see!" and the man's sight was restored. Through a dream, R. Mussa Ben-Yishay cured a psychotic man who had been lying near his grave for seven days.

The saint may appear in a sick person's home and heal him there. R. David Ha-Levi Draʿ appeared to a Jew who was going blind and told him his sight would be saved if he put *maḥia* drops in his eyes. R. Shalom Zawi healed a girl who was on her way to visit his tomb and had fallen asleep in a room she had hired for the night in Rabat. Bent El-Ḥmus appeared in a dream to a woman whose knee had become painfully swollen. She told the sufferer to go to a certain spring, and a salve was spread on her legs; the swelling disappeared.

A saint will sometimes give a person a message to be conveyed to a third party. R. David U-Moshe appeared in the dream of a woman who had fallen asleep at his tomb and told her what medicine would cure her husband. R. David Ha-Levi Draʿ appeared in a dream to the caretaker of his tomb and told him to rub oil on the body of a certain sick man; the man recovered. R. Shelomoh Ben-Tameshut told a woman who had brought her sick son to him that she could take him home, for he had regained his health.

A saint can also tell where a necessary medicine can be found. R. David Ben-Yamin told the mother of a sick person that the father of her son-in-law had the medicine the patient needed. In other cases, a saint may announce, through someone else, that he has no cure for a petitioner. R. Daniel Hashomer Ashkenazi asked a woman to tell a blind man sleeping in the crypt at his grave that he had not found a cure for his eyes; however, he would be compensated by good general health and ensured a source of livelihood for himself and his children. There are also instances of a saint telling a person it is in the saint's power to heal someone else. R. Abraham Mul Annes appeared in a dream to tell certain Jews to inform the French governor that the saint could cure his sick daughter. She recovered after spending seven days at his grave.

Saints are very active in dreams associated with childbirth. A pregnant woman will often be visited by a saint in her dreams, or a saint may appear to inform her that she will become pregnant, telling her the infant's sex and the date on which it will be born.[4] R. David Ben-Yamin told a woman that she was pregnant with a son who would be named Yehudah.[5] R. Raḥamim Mizraḥi appeared in the dream of a barren woman and told her he would not cure her unless she brought him bread. After she went on a pilgrimage in his honor and brought the saint a *seᶜudah,* she became pregnant and gave birth to a baby girl. R. Yitsḥaq Ben-Walid appeared in a dream to remind a pregnant woman to fulfill her vow and name her baby after him.[6]

There is always a purpose behind a saint's appearance. He may transmit information about himself, about the dreamer or a third person, or about the community as a whole. A saint can use dreams as a vehicle to reveal himself or to announce to followers that he can be found at a different venue. Thus R. ᶜAmram Ben-Diwan announced that he could be found in Sefrou or near the town wall in Ksar El-Kebir, as well as in Azjen: thereafter the Jews visited all those sites. Other reasons for a saint to appear in a dream may be to ask his disciples to visit his grave or build him a marker, to give orders about his *hillulah,* to remind Jews to fulfill their vows, or to complain because they do not visit his shrine. R. David U-Moshe, for example, appeared to those who tended his shrines in Ashkelon and Safed, both in Israel, and gave them explicit instructions about organizing his *hillulah,* how to invite celebrants, the meat that should be eaten on the occasion, the utensils to be used, the quantity of food necessary and how to distribute it, and so forth. His instructions included forms of punishment for anyone who may interfere with the organization of the *hillulah* as well as a detailed plan for developing the site at which it takes place. He also announced action he was prepared to take against the authorities if they interfered with the building and improvement of the chosen spot.

Moroccan Jews planning to move to Israel asked their particular saint's permission, and approval was sometimes given in dreams. R. David Ben-Barukh appeared to one of his followers to say: "Get up! Leave this place!" To another disciple he indicated in a dream that the man's house would soon be sold. Such dreams were interpreted as signs from the saint that the time had come for them to emigrate. It was through dreams that R. David Ha-Levi Draᶜ and R. Daniel Hashomer Ashkenazi gave their caretakers permission to move to Israel. R. Eliᶜezer Turei-Zahav appeared in a dream to all the inhabitants of a certain village, ordering them to go to Israel. The next day they rushed off to Casablanca to register for emigration. Lalla Miryam showed herself in a dream to the caretaker of her tomb; she complained tearfully that he wanted to go to Israel without her permission. A saint can convincingly dissuade someone from leaving his post at a shrine. Whenever attendants have to be replaced, the saint may announce in a dream who the replacement should be. When the owner of a shrine near a saint's grave leaves Morocco, the saint may appear in a dream to announce who will be responsible for its upkeep thereafter.

If a saint appears in a dream for no obvious reason, it is a sign that the dreamer should visit him as soon as possible. A woman who had no prior connection with R. Yaᶜaqob Ashkenazi had a dream about him, after which she and her husband went to visit the saint's grave and had a *seᶜudah* there. In a dream a saint may reveal where a person can retrieve something that is lost. R. Abraham Mul Annes, for instance, told someone where he could find the body of his son who had drowned at sea. A saint can also bless his disciples in dreams. R. David Ben-Barukh appeared to a worshipper of his grandson and filled the dreamer's basket with bread, after which he never lacked anything. A man may be told in a dream that his death is imminent; R. David Ha-Levi Draᶜ informed an ailing rabbi that he would die within the year but a certain other sick rabbi would recover. The dream may be a vehicle through which a saint comes to the aid of a hungry person. R. Abraham Mul Annes told a sleeping woman to prepare food for a hungry ritual slaughterer who had appealed to him. One young man dreamed that a saint had given him a hint about the identity of the girl who was to be his wife, while another man dreamed that Mulay Ighi gave him a lock of his intended wife's hair. There are stories that R. Pinḥas Ha-Cohen predicted the assassination attempts against the pasha of Marrakech. Similar stories about his grandfather, R. David Ben-Barukh, describe how he told R. Pinḥas in a dream that there was a plot to kill the pasha; he also told him how the attempt would be made. R. David U-Moshe used a dream to teach a prostitute how to tell fortunes with cards, after which she became a righteous woman.

An announcement in a dream may also be relevant for the whole community. Before the Yom Kippur War in 1973, R. David U-Moshe announced that war was imminent; he further indicated when sirens would be sounded to warn the Jews to enter their bomb shelters, and when there would be a cease-fire. R. Yisra'el Moryossef announced that a river would overflow its banks and inundate a village; the Jews gave alms and performed charitable deeds, and when the water reached the very entrance to the Jewish neighborhood, it receded. In similar circumstances, R. Aharon Assulin told the Jews they had nothing to fear because he would halt the flood waters.

A Jewish saint may also appear in the dreams of a non-Jew. A saint may reveal himself to a sleeping Muslim, who then tells the Jews about his dream. A saint told a non-Jew whose life he had saved that he did not want the tombstone the man had vowed to erect for him. R. ʿAmram Ben-Diwan told a wealthy Christian to make a large terrace for his visitors, instead of putting up the tombstone the Christian had promised. A Muslim's dream about a Jewish saint generally pertains to a specific action connected with the Jews, and the saint may use it to transmit a warning or even a threat. R. David Alshqar told the Muslims that if they did not sell a plot on which there was a Jewish cemetery, their children would die. R. Yosef Ha-Galili revealed himself in a dream to a woman who possessed the key to his shrine and refused to give it to the Jews. He warned her that if she did not give the Jews the key, she would suffocate inside the crypt. The neighbor of an Arab woman who had kidnapped a Jewish child dreamed that R. Makhluf Ben-Yosef Abiḥatsira told her to tell her neighbor to return the child to its Jewish mother or the saint would harm her. R. David U-Moshe appeared to the Muslim governor in a dream and warned him not to harm a Jewish merchant who was transporting a prohibited commodity.

It is interesting to consider how the saint makes his appearance in a dream, and in what form his disciples see him.[7] In most cases he appears in the image of an old man with a long beard, and the color white is somehow associated with him. R. Eliʿezer Davila appears mounted on a white horse. Ulad Zemmur is graced with a white beard and wears a *khaza* (Muslim's hat) on his head. R. Abraham Mul Annes appears as an old man with a long cane, a white band around his head. R. David Ben-Barukh appears as a tall, white-bearded man clad in a robe, usually white. R. David Ha-Levi Draʿ looks like an old man with a magnificent face. R. David U-Moshe appears red-faced, in a white gown, his beard reaching his green-belted midriff. Riding on a mare, R. Makhluf Ben-Yosef Abiḥatsira looks like a Muslim *qadi* with something white among his accoutrements. In one woman's dream, R. Abraham Awriwer appeared as a young man in a Muslim hat and long white cotton shirt. Mulay Ighi appeared in a yellow *keffiyeh* (Arab headdress), his face covered with spots. A woman dreaming at the grave of R. David Ben-Yamin saw him as a dead man lying on the gravestone, covered with a sheet; she asked if he was the saint, and he said "Yes."

Sometimes an individual does not dream of the saint himself, but of someone close to him, for example the caretaker or guardian of the saint's tomb. A woman dreamed that the female attendant at the tomb of R. Eliyahu in Casablanca brought her green figs to cure her liver ailment; in another dream a man brought her olives and told her they would help barren women. She bought olives, gave them to women who could not have children, and they conceived. A sick woman and her husband sat at the grave of R. David Ha-Levi Draʿ for a whole year, and then she had a dream of the saint who appeared in the form of his caretaker. He told her to get up and eat lunch and not worry about the evening meal because Jews from El-Ql'ah would bring it and would also invite them to dine on the *Sabbath.* And so it was. A woman strongly attached to R. Ḥananiah Ha-Cohen always dreamed of him in the form of the caretaker of his grave. R. Makhluf Ben-Yosef Abiḥatsira appeared in a dream in the form of the caretaker of his shrine in Kiriyat Gat, Israel, or in the form of a certain man who celebrated a *hillulah* every year in the saint's honor. In a dream R. Makhluf once killed a snake that was threatening the dreamer.

The saint may appear in a dream in the form of someone else who bears the same name. A worried father who had appealed to R. David Ben-Barukh dreamed of a friend named David who told him that in three days his sick daughter would recover. R. David Ha-Levi Draʿ appeared in the form of a sage from Marrakech named R. David Ha-Levi Ha-Laḥmi to tell a dreamer that he did not want his burial site paved, but wanted a synagogue built there instead. A sick man appealed to R. David U-Moshe for help and then dreamed that a relative of his named Moshe gave him a glass of water and he was cured. A boy who doubted the miracles of R. ʿAmram Ben-Diwan dreamed that a man named ʿAmram slapped him and sent him to jail. Occasionally, the saint appears in the form of a man with the same name as that of the caretaker of his grave. A woman who had appealed to R. Shelomoh Ben-Tameshut to cure her daughter dreamed that her brother Meir brought her trays laden with food and told her that her daughter would recover that same night. Meir was the name of the guardian of the saint's tomb. The fact that a visitor named Meir had come to the tomb that morning, bringing a festive meal with him, reinforced the mother's belief that her request had been granted.

Other figures may sometimes represent the saint to whom the petitioner has appealed. A woman with a sick daughter appealed to R. Abraham Darʿi and then dreamed that the saint's wife gave the girl medicine and she was cured. A girl who had lost her mind was taken to R. Yitsḥaq Ben-Walid's grave, where she dreamed of her father-in-law; this was the mark of the saint. In one dream a man white as snow, dressed in black, spread ointment on a child and said he would cure her with the help of R. Shalom Zawi. In the dream of a paralyzed woman, Lalla Miryam assumed the form of a female physician who led her to a spring, telling her to rub the water on her hands and feet; the next day the woman recovered. An extreme case is that of a woman whose children all had died. She appealed to Sidi Bu-ʿAissa U-Sliman, and that night she dreamed that a snake (the saint) gave her mint leaves and a cup of milk. Eventually she gave birth to a son, and he lived.

Notes

1. See Y. Bilu (1987). The phenomenon is also current among the Muslims: E. Westermarck (1926, vol. 1, pp. 60, 85, 159–61, 164–66, 189, 194, 227, 267 and 561).
2. Some people believe it is forbidden to reveal dreams about saints, who may then refrain from reappearing. See I. Ben-Ami (1981a, p. 296, story no. 9).
3. The activities of these two disciples of R. David U-Moshe are described in I. Ben-Ami (1981a, pp. 303–42).
4. When a woman becomes pregnant after appealing to a saint, or a saint appears in the dream of a pregnant woman or her husband, the child shall bear the saint's name.
5. This is an interesting case: here the saint proposes a name other than his own.
6. In that same year the woman's father died; if not for the saint, she would probably have followed the custom of naming the baby after her father.

7. J. Huizinga (1979, p. 161): "Everything contributed to make them familiar and life-like. They were dressed like the peoples themselves. Every day one met 'Messires' Saint Roch and Saint James in the persons of living plague patients and pilgrims. Down to the Renaissance the costumes of the saints always followed the fashion of the times."

10

VISITING THE SAINT: THE *HILLULAH*

PREVIOUS CHAPTERS HAVE FOCUSED ON SAINT WORSHIP AS IT IMPINGED on the daily lives of North African Jewry. The *hillulah,*[1] the mass visit to the saint, however, was set apart; it lifted the worshipper out of his routine pursuits, required extensive preparation, and usually meant spending a week or more away from home.

A Moroccan Jewish family's attachment to a given saint was ordinarily expressed by calling upon the revered figure in times of distress, lighting candles in his name, seeing or hearing him in a dream.[2] If the saint was buried close by it was customary to light a candle at his grave during the day on Friday or on Saturday night.[3] Certain saints were visited on the advent of each new month,[4] while others received regular visits from their own kinfolk. R. Raphael Berdugo's family, for example, went to light a candle at his burial place on the eve of every *Sabbath,* new month, and holiday. A special connection with one saint did not necessarily preclude a relationship with others. Where several saints are buried in the same cemetery, it was customary to visit them all, usually in order of their importance. In Casablanca the first visit was to the grave of R. Eliyahu; in Marrakech R. Ḥananiah Ha-Cohen was honored first; in Fez it was R. Yehudah Ben-ʿAttar. A family whose patron saint was some distance away would often visit the more important saints closer to home. If, for instance, Mulay Ighi's grave was too far away, his devotees would visit R. David Alshqar in Casablanca; those who could not make the journey to R. ʿAmram Ben-Diwan visited the grave of Mul Jebel El-Kebir or lit candles at other sites bearing his name — for example his shrines at Salé and Sefrou, or near the wall at Ksar El-Kebir.

Rather than going to the grave, one might light a candle in a synagogue bearing the saint's name or participate in religious studies there. The particular synagogue might be in another city, as was the R. David U-Moshe synagogue in Mogador; then again, it might have been in the city in which the saint was buried — as in the cases of R. Yitsḥaq Ben-Walid in Tetuan and R. Moshe Toledano in Rabat — or in a town near the saint's grave, as with R. Yaḥya Laḥlu. On their way to or from visits to their own saint, people stopped at the graves of other holy figures,[5] not only to benefit from a supplementary blessing, but mainly to avoid the risk of insulting any saint by ignoring him.

None of the above rites and rituals, however, could compare in intensity and significance with the *hillulah* — the visit to the saint's grave together with a multitude of other worshippers. The *hillulah* was the quintessential expression of the bond between the saint and his venerators. Preparing to set out was in itself an important stage: a celebrant usually embarked on a process of self-purification that included immersion in a ritual bath, cutting his nails, sometimes fasting. The celebrant thus detached him- or herself mentally and spiritually from their ordinary surroundings and began a process of sublimating their soul in anticipation of the encounter with the saint. The hazards of the journey, the brief rest stops at graves of other saints along the way, added to the tense excitement that culminated in the final arrival at the grave of the saint in whose honor the *hillulah* was being held.

A private visit to a saint, outside the framework of a *hillulah,* was usually prompted by some special reason: one went to request his or her assistance or thank him or her for fulfilling an earlier petition. A person sometimes appealed to a saint in someone else's name:[6] a woman prayed to R. David Ben-Barukh to cure a friend of hers, after which the friend made an annual pilgrimage to the saint. A husband asked the members of the Burial Society to pray to R. Yaḥya Laḥlu to give his wife a child; a woman asked her neighbor to light a candle in her name at Ulad Zemmur's grave. Muslims sometimes asked Jews to petition a Jewish saint in their names, and their requests were often granted.

Petitions to a saint related to all spheres of life, although matters involving health and healing predominated. Those who came to be cured usually remained in the vicinity of the grave until their request was granted. In most cases, they stayed seven days. If necessary, they stayed a month or more. One sick woman was known to have remained at the tomb of R. David Ha-Levi Draᶜ for a whole year. When concluding a business deal, the parties to the transaction would visit the saint, swear mutual trust, and drink to a successful relationship. Visits were made in fulfillment of vows or after a saint appeared in a dream. On all such occasions it was customary to light candles at the grave and bring along specially prepared couscous, known as *maᶜaruf.*[7] The dish was prepared at home but the actual cooking was done at the graveside, where the worshippers ate part of it and set some aside for the poor.

Among Moroccan Jews such individual or family visits to saints took place throughout the year, but the mass celebration—the *hillulah*[8]—included additional ritual practices. This most tangible expression of the connection between the saint and his venerators was usually held not on the date of the saint's death—which was often unknown—but either on *Lag bᶜOmer* or in the months of *Elul-Tishri,* toward the end of summer.[9] Families would take to the road, sometimes on foot, sometimes mounted on horses, mules or donkeys. Some graves in the Atlas Mountains could only be reached on foot. In general, it was not until the 1940s that Jews initiated the construction of approach roads and introduced vehicular transportation to the most famous saints.

Pilgrims ordinarily remained at the holy site for seven days, which they summed up in the words *ta irfed sebᶜa ʾiyyam* ([it] takes seven days), although many remained longer, even up to a month. Homage to the saint was not the only attraction of the *hillulah:* it offered opportunities to enjoy the beauties of nature and the pleasure of congenial company in a very special atmosphere. Worshippers tended to prolong their sojourn, loathe to return to normal, mundane cares.

Upon arriving at their destination, families made all necessary arrangements for the duration of their stay. Notables built themselves rooms to live in during the *hillulah;* other affluent people rented rooms. Most worshippers, however, pitched tents. Officials responsible for the sacred precincts superintended the arrangements and helped the visitors settle in. Local Muslims viewed these gatherings of crowds of Jewish pilgrims as opportunities for improving their own economic lot, and they, too, offered essential services, including transportation, foodstuffs and animals for ritual slaughter. Only after these initial preparations were completed did people go to the shrine or tomb to pay homage to the saint.

Although self-purification was mandatory in advance of the journey, if there was a pool or spring near the tomb, worshippers were likely to immerse themselves again before approaching the spot hallowed by the saint himself.[10] It is believed that an impure woman can cause fierce storms. The roof of R. David Ha-Levi Draʿs shrine once collapsed because impure women were present. One woman's menstrual period began during a visit to R. Daniel Hashomer Ashkenazi, bringing on a thunderstorm accompanied by hail and rain. During visits to Mulay Ighi and R. David U-Moshe, a wild hailstorm broke out because there was an impure woman among the worshippers; the storm did not subside until she had gone. Stones fell from the heavens and the earth trembled when an impure woman visited R. Shelomoh Ben-Lḥans. If such a woman approaches the saint, she or a member of her family is liable to severe punishment—even death. One woman who had come to light candles at the shrine of R. David U-Moshe began to menstruate: her life was spared, but she suffered a bad fall at the threshold of the shrine.

Saints are angered by wanton women. Water ceased flowing from R. David Ha-Levi Draʿs shrine when a profligate woman entered. Stones flew through the air and the river overflowed its banks because of belly dancers in a nearby village. When a prostitute approached R. David U-Moshe's grave, rooms and tents collapsed and the air filled with flying rocks. When visiting a saint it was customary for a woman to wear modest clothes, usually a long-sleeved dress reaching to her ankles and a scarf over her head. They were forbidden to use cosmetics: in a dream R. David U-Moshe once ordered a woman wearing make-up to wash her face before visiting him.

At the tomb there was always a group of people reading Psalms. The many ceremonies associated with the *hillulah* included reciting prayers, singing, dancing around the grave, lighting candles, and ritual slaughtering of animals followed by a festive meal—the *seʿudah.* People left bottles of water or olive oil, ornaments, coins and other objects at the tomb overnight, sometimes for several nights. Barren women would leave belts. If a tree grew nearby, streamers, ribbons and kerchiefs would be hung on its branches as *ex-voto* offerings or to receive the saint's blessings. The water or oil would be applied as a cure for illness, and was used either during the visit or later, at home. An ornament that had lain on the holy tomb would be hung around the owner's neck as a talisman, and a barren woman would wear the belt to make her conceive. These various objects signified messages from the devotees to the saint, as did the stones placed on or near a saint's tomb. They are signs of the belief that when the saint's spirit arrives and sees the objects or stones, be it the day of the *hillulah* or any other day, the petitioner will be remembered favorably.

Some of the practices associated with the saint's grave or its immediate environs are reminiscent of folk medicine. The insane, the blind, paralytics and epileptics were roped or chained to the grave or to a nearby tree and kept there at least overnight. Sick children, particularly those who are very young, would be put to sleep on the grave. A sick child recovered after having been cradled on the grave of R. Yaḥya El-Khdar. A mute girl began to speak after lying on R. Yitsḥaq Ben-Walid's grave. The mother of a very sick baby girl placed her on the grave of R. Yitsḥaq Ha-Levi, saying to the saint: "If my baby is from this world,[11] so be it; and if not, I'll bury her next to you"; the saint appeared to the mother in a dream, and the child recovered. A father who put a basket containing his ailing child into the candle niche at the grave of Lalla Solica told the female saint much the same thing; three hours later the child was cured. A sick child's clothing was placed on the grave of R. Ḥayyim Pinto the Younger; the child recovered when they dressed him in those clothes again.

The worshippers fervently believed that contact with anything belonging to the saint or found in his immediate vicinity, has a beneficial effect. The cane belonging to R. Abraham Makhluf Ben-Yaḥya lies near his grave; sick people came to touch it and were cured. People took home water from Mulay Yaʿqub's spring and used it as a curative. At R. Ḥayyim Pinto's grave, soot from candle flames was rubbed on childrens' foreheads, and adults imbibed anything that had spilled over the grave. At the grave of R. Abner Ha-Tsarfati, a sick child's mother mixed a handful of soil with water, strained it and gave it to her son, who drank the potion and recovered his health. A man rubbed his sore eyes with oil intended for ritual candlelighting at R.

Daniel Hashomer Ashkenazi's grave and his eyes were healed. Visitors to R. Yitsḥaq Abiḥatsira's grave poured *maḥia* on the saint's gravestones and then licked it off. Visitors to R. David Ha-Levi Draʿ collected lumps of salt from the area around the saint's grave and use them on Passover to purify food.

It was also customary to give a boy his first haircut at the saint's grave. When a particular saint had been involved in a child's birth or health, the child's first haircut had to be given at that saint's tomb; under ordinary circumstances, however, the ritual could be carried out at any sanctified gravesite. It usually took place when the child was about a year old, although the date was not strictly observed. As the cutting proceeded, the women emitted cheerful ululations and the father prayed for the child's health. A *bar-mitswah* ceremony might also be held during the *hillulah* in honor of certain saints.

Poor people sat near the graves of renowned saints and solicited alms; they were an integral part of the *hillulah's* scene and enjoyed a recognizable status. Some of them went from grave to grave accepting donations from the pilgrims; they were also given food and money by the committees in charge of fundraising in the saints' names. The paupers showered blessings on the visitors for the alms they received, as well as for those they hoped to receive; the visitors themselves seemed to consider charitable acts as part of the *hillulah.*

A most important ceremony held at the hallowed site was the *sheḥitah*—the dramatic ritual slaughtering of chickens, lambs, goats, cows or bulls. In the past, worshippers would bring a live animal with them to be slaughtered next to the grave, its head facing the tombstone. The assembled people would murmur personal prayers pertaining to vows or petitions made during the tense moments while the ritual purity of the animal was being ascertained. When it was declared *kosher,* i.e. ritually pure—meaning the animal was accepted by the saint (and a potentially costly economic setback for the worshipper had been averted)—general relief was expressed in joyous shouting and singing. Some people collected the slaughtered animal's blood to be used in the future as a prophylactic or cure. In those days the ritual slaughterer received no payment other than portions of meat. As the number of animals to be slaughtered increased to several hundred, slaughterhouses were built near the graves of the more famous saints, and special procedures were established. The slaughterer was paid per animal, the meat for the *seʿudah* was set aside, and the hides and innards were put up for sale by the saint's committee. Special customs evolved in connection with slaughtering in honor of certain saints.

Various witnesses confirm that when the slaughter was in honor of R. David U-Moshe, an official functionary would combine the meat with that of other animals, divide it into equal portions, and distribute it among all present. Meat from the first animal slaughtered had to be given to the official in charge. If the pilgrims stayed long enough to require a second slaughter, they were permitted to eat the additional meat themselves. Eating meat that did not conform to the rules, or requesting a second portion on pretense of not having received a first, were punishable offenses. It was also an offense to take meat home unless one had a special dispensation from the saint.

Ritual slaughter was still practiced in the 1970s in honor of R. David U-Moshe in the Israeli town of Ashkelon. The family preparing the *hillulah* usually bought a young bull several months in advance and had it raised by a farmer in a nearby village. Although it was raised together with other cattle, it received more fodder and was given special attention, as befits an animal destined for a saint. The owner came from Ashkelon from time to time to check the bull's development and see that it lacked for nothing; as it grew to maturity, the bull permitted only his owner to approach him with impunity.

The slaughtering itself took place the day before the *hillulah.* The R. David U-Moshe synagogue and surrounding neighborhood buzzed with excited anticipation, because everyone knew that on this the day the bull would be brought to Ashkelon from the village. A group of muscular volunteers was organized to perform the difficult task of roping the powerful animal, getting him on to a truck, and then leading him off and through the narrow entrance into the synagogue. The women accompanied the procedure with jubilant good-luck cries. The Ark and most of the benches of the main hall had been moved aside, and the animal was thrown to the synagogue floor, where the slaughtering took place. The crowd watched the ritual in great excitement, and the blood flowed freely over the floor. From time to time someone came forward, dipped his fingers into the blood and, believing in its curative powers, rubbed it on an ailing part of his body. The ritual slaughterer carefully examined each part of the animal, then raised his right hand as a sign that it was ritually pure. At that point the onlookers burst into loud shouts of joy, and the slaughterer, with some assistants, began to separate the various sections. The liver and spleen were broiled on an open flame, and all those present were treated to a taste. The head, legs and remaining internal organs were put up for auction, while the meat was prepared for the communal meal held after solemn services the following day.[12]

Another important ceremony at a *hillulah* was the public sale of candles and glasses in the saint's name. Large crowds gathered for the auction and the highest bidder was accorded great honor. It was considered a *mitswah*—a virtuous deed—to purchase the first candle; whoever did this was believed to have won a special relationship with the saint. After a certain number of candles had been sold in the patron saint's name, the auction, accompanied by festive singing and dancing, continued in the name of other saints; all proceeds, however, went to the saint in whose honor the *hillulah* was being held. Those who bought candles in honor of other saints usually lived near their shrines or had some special personal connection with them. The auction was accompanied by cries of joy, singing and dancing. Fervent prayers were heard on all sides as a large bonfire near the tomb was fed by burning candles.

The bonfires at a saint's grave on the night of a *hillulah* have given rise to countless traditional miracle-tales. People dancing around the fire could put a hand or head into the flames without being burned; infants and children have been harmlessly passed through the flames, as were sick people who were thereby cured. A mute was thrown into the fire at R. ʿAmram Ben-Diwan's *hillulah,* and he called out to the saint, his power of speech having been restored. A paralyzed woman who was pushed into the fire at R. David Ben-Barukh's grave emerged unscathed and healthy.

Ecstatic moments of devout prayer set the stage for miracles. In their thirst for proof that their requests have been favorably received, petitioners found many different signs which they believed affirmed that their appeals had been heard and granted. One important sign was the saint's appearance before the worshippers on the night of the *hillulah.* He might appear in person—as did Mulay Ighi, who passed by with his wife and told one of the pilgrims that the wishes of all those who came to his grave that year would be granted. The figure of the saint might become visible in the midst of a huge bonfire. It has been said that is how the images of R. Daniel Hashomer Ashkenazi and R. Yehudah Zabali manifested themselves. Celebrants who remained at the grave until late at night sometimes saw the saint, as did a woman at the grave of R. ʿAmram Ben-Diwan. It was dark, and she could not find her way back to her family's tent; a figure appeared, led her to the tent, and immediately vanished.

The saint might also appear to the celebrants in the form of an animal, and such a manifestation elicited great excitement. The belief was that the animal form embodies the saint's spirit, which has come to join the *hillulah* and grant the requests of his venerators. Traditionally, the form assumed was that of a dove or snake, but a saint might also come in some other guise. R. David U-Moshe and R. ʿAmram Ben-Diwan generally appeared as doves, although the latter might also appear as another kind of bird or as a snake. Interpreting the snake as a favorable sign, people were not afraid of it, and they greeted it with loud exclamations of joy. A white dove sometimes emerged from the flames, flew overhead, and disappeared as mysteriously as it appeared. A man who once saw R. Ḥayyim Ben-Diwan in the form of a green bird became very wealthy; attributing the wealth to the visitation of the saint, he built rooms near the tomb and contributed generously to the saint's coffers. Because the devotees equated the presence of an animal or bird with the presence of the saint himself, it was always greeted with clamorous enthusiasm.

Water miraculously emanating from the saint's grave was another sign to worshippers that the saint was present and willing to respond to their requests. If no water came forth, this meant the requests would not be answered. This phenomenon was described particularly in connection with R. Abraham Mul Annes, R. David Ha-Levi Draʿ, Mul Timḥdart and R. Shelomoh Ben-Lḥans, although it has also been attributed to other saints. When this miracle occurred, all those present rushed to sprinkle themselves with the health-giving water. It might sometimes effect an immediate cure — as it did for a man whose son washed him with the water that issued from the tombs of R. Shelomoh Ben-Yitsḥaq, R. Moshe Ben-Shelomoh and R. Aharon Ha-Cohen at Amzouguin.

A saint might also appear, even speak to his faithful, through the medium of an epileptic having a seizure. That was the way Sidi Bu-ʿAissa U-Sliman announced his presence, addressing each and every worshipper who had come to visit him. Other signs of the saint's presence might be a pillar of fire descending from the heavens on the day of the *hillulah* or the saint might make his presence felt in a dream. A venerator might fall asleep at the grave or in a tent or room near by and be cured by the saint in a dream. A dream might also give someone the key to the solution of a problem he had intended to lay before the saint.

In connection with certain saints, customs evolved to help ascertain whether the holy persons had responded favorably to a request. A candle would be lit at the shrine of R. Abraham Awriwer, and if the flame rose straight up, it signified a positive response. With R. Shelomoh Ben-Tameshut, people would throw a stone on the roof over the grave; if the stone did not fall off, it meant the saint would fulfill the request and the petitioner could leave; if the stone fell, the petitioner had to remain there.

The *hillulah* week was unquestionably an emotionally charged, unforgettable experience for the worshipper. He began to prepare himself for the pilgrimage well in advance of the actual departure. During the *hillulah* a sense of oneness knit all the celebrants into a highly motivated religious community with shared beliefs and ideals. The strong emotional warmth enveloping the participants was nourished by repeated praise of the saint and an overwhelming eagerness to internalize and reiterate every word, legend and tradition glorifying the revered figure. The pilgrim avidly listened to, related, and observed everything associated with the object of his veneration. He sensed an almost physical contact with the saint, who materialized at the *hillulah* and talked with worshippers in their sleeping or waking hours. The many prayers offered up in supplication or gratitude purified the pilgrim's soul. He returned home from the *hillulah* conscious of having been imbued with new strength, derived from the knowledge that many others shared his faith, and with new awareness of his saint's greatness and protective power.

Notes

1. See: "Hillulah," *Encyclopaedia Judaica* (1971, vol. 8, p. 945).
2. J. Bénech (1940, p. 187) writes that each Jewish family in Morocco has its own patron saint whose name is written on an internal wall of the house and to whom a lamp is lit all year round.
3. The graves of R. Aharon Ha-Cohen in Demnate, R. Moshe Ḥabib in Toundout, R. Yaḥya Laḥlu near Ksar Es-Souk, and R. Yonah Daudi

in Tikirt were visited on Fridays. On Saturday evenings, visits were made mainly to the graves of saints in large cities like Casablanca, at the tombs of R. Eliyahu, R. David Alshqar and R. Yitsḥaq Ḥadida; in Marrakech at the tomb of R. Ḥananiah Ha-Cohen, and in Settat at the tomb of R. Mimun Elghrabli. Every week the Jews of Fez visited the graves of R. Yehudah Ben-ʿAttar, R. Abner Ha-Tsarfati and Lalla Solica, who are buried next to one another.

4. On the eve of every new month the Jews visited the graves of many saints, including R. David Ben-Safet, R. Yosef Bajayo, R. Makhluf Ben-Yosef Abiḥatsira and R. Moshe Ḥabib.
5. At the *hillulah* of Mwalin Dad on *Lag bʿOmer* 1981 in Morocco I met a pilgrim who told me that he had just finished his one-week pilgrimage circuit. On the first day he visited the graves of R. Ḥananiah Ha-Cohen and R. Pinḥas Ha-Cohen in Marrakech; the second day he visited R. Raphael Ha-Cohen at Achbarou and R. Shelomoh Ben-Lḥans at Ourika; the third day he went to R. David U-Moshe, R. Abraham Wazana and R. Makhluf Ben-Yosef at Taourirt of Warzazate; the fourth day he visited the Muslim saint Sidi Ḥmad el-Khnine, then R. Daoud at Warzazate, R. Eliʿezer Turei-Zahav and Sidi Bu-ʿAissa U-Sliman; the fifth day he went to R. David Ben-Barukh, R. Ḥayyim Pinto and Ulad Zemmur; and on the sixth day his pilgrimage was to the grave of R. Abraham Mul Annes in Azemmour. The route followed in a pilgrimage circuit is also important in other religions: *Les Pèlerinages* (1960, pp. 278–79); F. Raphael et al. (1973, p. 14); R. Oursel (1978, pp. 45–97); P. Barret and J. N. Gurgand (1978, pp. 89–106).
6. The Christians used to pay the pilgrim for this service: R. Roussel (1972, p. 28); P. Barret and J. N. Gurgand (1978, p. 11).
7. The Muslims in North Africa also eat couscous at the graveside of the marabout: E. Dermenghem (1954, p. 153).
8. At the *hillulah* of the most famous saints, thousands of pilgrims were to be found near the graveside. More than one hundred thousand pilgrims were once at the *hillulah* of R. ʿAmaram Ben-Diwan, one informant said, and 17,000 were reported to be there after the time most of the Moroccan Jewry had already left the country (M. Lubelsky, in the newspaper *Herut,* July 10, 1959).
9. Muslim saints are visited on fixed days of the week. At many places there were mass celebrations once a year—called *mûsem* or *lämma*—usually in spring or autumn. See E. Westermarck (1926, vol. 1, pp. 174–76); Catholics celebrate the festival of the saint on the date of his death: A. van Gennep (1949, tome I, vol. 4, pp. 2084–85).

10. A. van Gennep (1914, pp. 41–58).
11. The intention is to check whether the baby has been replaced by a baby-demon. There is a belief in folk medicine that when there is no visible reason for an infant's illness, this is a sign that the demon duplicate of the mother took the baby-person and left the baby-demon in his place. Such an infant is put on the grave of an unknown person: if he cries, he belongs to the world of men and will soon recover; if he does not cry, he belongs to the world of demons and will die. See I. Ben-Ami (1993b, p. 259).
12. This description is based on my personal impression from the ceremony and from information received from people who participated. The ceremony held in 1973 was filmed on behalf of the Folklore Research Center of the Hebrew University of Jerusalem.

11

POEMS AND SONGS OF THE *HILLULAH*

THE *PIYYUT* (LITURGICAL POEM) AND THE SONG CONSTITUTE A VERY important means for expressing the relationship with the saint during the *hillulah* held at the saint's grave,[1] in a synagogue or private house, as well as during every visit to the saint. Through song and *piyyut,* the celebrants articulate their exaltation, love and veneration for the saint.

The liturgy of Moroccan Jews consists of several genres of songs. One is the *piyyut* written entirely in Hebrew and sung exclusively by the men for the purpose of extolling a saint. Sometimes it is composed after the poet has recovered from an illness through the good offices of the saint, has witnessed a miracle or participated in an exceptionally impressive pilgrimage to the saint's tomb.[2] *Piyyutim* of this type are commonly found in manuscript and loose-leaf form, few having been collected or published in anthologies.[3]

Another type of poem is the bilingual *piyyut.* This has alternating Hebrew and Judeo-Arabic stanzas, or begins in Hebrew and switches to Judeo-Arabic in the final stanzas. This type also is usually sung by men, although women generally know the Judeo-Arabic passages.

A third type is the *qasida,*[4] composed entirely in Judeo-Arabic and sung principally by the women to honor the saint. It is characterized primarily by an exciting, energetic rhythm that carries the celebrants away. The men also join, especially when the *qasidot* are ones that would be familiar to anyone who has participated in a *hillulah.*

Ordinarily the *piyyut* and *qasida* are dedicated to a certain saint, though in many songs the names of more than one saint are mentioned. Nearly all of the most illustrious saints have poems and *piyyutim* dedicated solely to them. The songs are sung during the *hillulah* for a specific saint,[5] usually when wine or *maḥia* glasses in his honor are being auctioned. At that time the saint's miracles are praised, as are the advantages gained from drinking wine out of the glass, in the hope of persuading buyers to offer a higher price for the saint's glass.

Certain well-known tunes and poetic forms recur in various different songs. In many songs, especially in the Judeo-Arabic ones, the following stanza is found:

Zekhuto tkun mʿana	[Judeo-Arabic]
Ḥna w-Yisra'el khwana	[Judeo-Arabic]
Hodu l'Adonay ki tob.	[Hebrew]

Translation:

May his merit be with us,
With us and Israel our brethren,
Praise the Lord for He is good!

This stanza may serve either as the finale or the refrain of a song. It combines Hebrew and Judeo-Arabic, as often happens in the daily speech of the Jews of Morocco.[6]

A few of the *piyyutim* and *qasidot,* especially those in Judeo-Arabic, are familiar to and sung by all the Jews. All female informants who were asked to sing songs dedicated to a saint included at least several passages of these songs in their repertoire. My fieldwork revealed a great wealth of songs honoring saints, but it also demonstrated that many such songs have disappeared, largely because of their improvisational nature.[7]

Below is a selection of *hillulah* songs of the various genres.

I. Tsaddiqim el-ʿzaz or "*The beloved Saints*"

This song in Judeo-Arabic by an unknown author[8] is a kind of general hymn of hagiographic poetry. It mentions thirteen well-known saints, although surprisingly some very famous ones, such as Mulay Ighi and R. David Ben-Barukh, are not included.

Refrain:
Ya Rabbi tsmaḥ felli daz
Ya Rabbi tkemmel el-meḥdaz
Ya Rabbi seʿdna ma iʿwaz
Zekhut saddiqim el-ʿzaz.

1. Bdit ntkellem b-ez-zher
U-seddiq el-ʿziz ndker
U-lli telbna-lo iḥder
Ysmo ʿali u-mzehher
Laʿziz Rabbi Yaḥia El-Khdar.

2. Y-allah nemsiw ya laʿbad
Nderbo terqan el-bʿad
U-ntelbo tlibat zdad
U-nzoro saddiqim del-blad
Laʿzaz syadna Mwalin Dad.

3. Saddiq ykun lina snida
U-nziwh min triq bʿida
U-nzoroh zyara zdida
W-yzʿal iyyamna sʿida
Rabbi Eliyahu Mul Dar el-Beida.

4. Ya ḥbabi lukan reto
ʿAzaib saddiq fi ḥyato
Khella elʿezz el-familto
Abyad illi ḥdar fi tfinto
Laʿziz Rabbi Ḥayyim Pinto.

5. Red balk ya khai ma temsis
Fi el-hillula ma terkhis
U-nederʿlik ma tkhellis
Yqbel zyark bla teʿkis
Laʿziz Rabbi Abraham Mul Annes.

6. Y-allah nmsiw ya lkhawa
U-nqablo elʿdab b-el-ḥlawa

U-nzoro saddiq b-es-sfawa
U-lli fih si der yddawa
Zekhut Rabbi Raphael Anqawa.

7. Mazalt nzid f-el-ghnawi
U-nferraḥ qalbi el-khawi
U-ntelb elli nawi
U-saddiq houwa ydawi
Laʿziz Rabbi Shalom Zawi.

8. Msit nzor ya el-khwan
El-saddiq skit b-elli kan
U-rzaʿt b-qalbi ferḥan
Qbel zyarti mul Wazzan
Laʿziz Rabbi ʿAmram Ben-Diwan.

9. Ya l-ḥbab sriw smaʿ
Bas tghfro dnub u-l-khdaʿ
U-zyartna dima tenfaʿ
U-saddiq liha ismaʿ
Laʿziz Rabbi David Draʿ.

10. Ya khai smaḥ fi kul-si
Rah ed-denya ma tdumsi
Ghir saddiqim ma tensasi
U-lhad saddiq temsi
Laʿziz Rabbi David U-Moshe.

11. Waḥd seddiq ya nas
Khella zikhuto ʿla l-sas
U-lli ytelblo f-el-kas
Ydawih deghia men kul bas
Sidi laʿziz Rabbi Pinḥas.

12. Besḥal elli merdo u-heblu
Msaw el-seddiq u-nezlu
El-kissan u-smaʿsaʿlu
Dawahum seddiq men fedlo
Laʿziz Rabbi Shelomoh El-Ḥlu.

13. Ntelbok ya rabbe mulay
Tqbelna had er-ray
Bzahdak nemsiw lʿam ez-zay
U-nʿemlu el-hillula ya khay
Di Rabbi Shimʿon Bar-Yoḥay.

Translation:

Refrain:
O Lord! Forgive what is past!
O Lord! Provide for us in our distress!
O Lord! May our happiness never wane
Thanks to the merit of the beloved saints!

1. I started to speak in my joy
and I shall mention the beloved saint.
Whatever we ask of him he will grant
because his name is exalted and illuminates,
The beloved Rabbi Yaḥya El-Khdar.

2. Come, let us go, o servants!
Let us take to the distant roads
and let us offer up new prayers.
Let us visit the saints of the town,
Our dear one, our master, Mwalin Dad.

3. The saint will be our support
and we shall come to him from far away
and we shall visit him again on the ziyara
and he will make our days happy
Rabbi Eliyahu, the Master of Casablanca.

4. O, my friends, had you but seen
the miracles of the saint during his lifetime,
He conferred his prestige upon his family!
Happy is he who was present at the funeral
of dear Rabbi Ḥayyim Pinto.

5. Beware, o my brother, lest you not go;
Never neglect the hillulah
or forget to pay your vow.
He will receive your visit without delay,
Dear Rabbi Abraham Mul Annes.

6. O brothers, come let us go
and we shall bear the hardships of the road gladly
and we shall be pure at the visit to the saint.
Everyone who is in pain will be cured
By the merit of Rabbi Raphael Anqawa.

7. I shall continue to sing,
To gladden my burnt heart

And request what I crave
And the saint is he who shall cure me,
Dear Rabbi Shalom Zawi.

8. I went on pilgrimage, o my brothers,
I told the saint my affliction
And I returned with a glad heart.
The Master of Ouezzane accepted my pilgrimage,
Dear Rabbi ʿAmram Ben-Diwan.

9. O, my friends, buy candles
To atone for your sins and cheating.
The pilgrimage will always help.
The saint always answers us,
Dear Rabbi David Draʿ.

10. O, my brother, you may give up everything else
Since the world is not eternal,
Only do not forget the saints.
Go and visit this saint,
Our dear Rabbi David U-Moshe.

11. And this saint, o people,
Left us his merit so solidly based
Whoever petitions him through the "glass"
Will speedily be cured of every ill,
Our dear master, Rabbi Pinḥas.

12. Crazy people and mentally ill
Went to the saint and visited there,
Lit cups and candles, and
the saint cured them out of his lovingkindness,
Dear Rabbi Shelomoh El-Ḥlu.

13. We shall petition you, o Lord, our Master.
Pleas accept our prayers.
With your help we shall go next year
And celebrate the hillulah, *o my brother,*
Of Rabbi Shimʿon Bar-Yoḥay.

This is the song in which the largest number of saints is mentioned. Six stanzas begin with the vocative "o," two are addressed to God and four to brothers or friends. This form of direct address is meant to express and emphasize the author of the *piyyut*'s involvement with the group around him. We do not know who wrote this song. However, if all stanzas were composed at the same time, the reference to R. Abraham Mul Annes indicates the early 1940s as the probable date of composition. Despite the uniform style, which makes it seem the work of a single anonymous folk poet, it is not inconceivable that the stanzas dealing with specific saints were added by others. The song has an irresistible rhythm, which has contributed to its wide popularity.

Whether the number of stanzas—thirteen—has a special significance as a formulaic number, or whether it is a common combination of twelve plus one, remains an open question.

II. *Qasida* of the saint's glass auction ceremony[9]

This *qasida* belongs to the category of songs that accompany the auction of *maḥia* glasses in the saint's honor during the *hillulah* at his tomb or in the synagogue. These songs do not have a fixed text, and their structure allows different motifs for each saint.

Had el-kas foq et-tiba
Had el-kas foq et-tiba
U-tiba ʿliha el-hiba
Rabbi ʿAmram mul el-hiba.

Refrain:
Zekhuto tkun mʿana
Ḥna w-Yisra'el khwana
Hodu l'Adonay ki tob.
Had ej-jebel jebel el-Glawi
Had el-jebel jebel el-Glawi
Fih waḥd tbib ka ydawi
Ismo Rabbi Shalom Zawi.

Translation:

This glass is on the lectern
This glass is on the lectern
And the lectern is full of splendor,
The splendor of Rabbi ʿAmram.

Refrain:

May his merit be with us,
With us and Israel our brethren.
Praise the Lord for He is good.

These mountains are the mountains of Glawi
These mountains are the mountains of Glawi
Wherein resides the one who heals and cures
Whose name is Rabbi Shalom Zawi.

III. Another *qasida* of the saint's glass auction ceremony

Khwana Allah yhdikum
ʿel l-flous ma yʿezzbikum
Rabbi David U-Moshe ykhelf likum
Sharbt el-kas wana massi (repeat)
B-zekhut Rabbi David U-Moshe.
Refrain: Zekhuto . . .
Men Meron w-ana ʿla rejlia (repeat)
Zort Rabbi Shimʿon Bar-Yoḥay u-lʿada meqdiya.
Refrain: Zekhuto . . .
Had el-kas b-el-maḥia beida
Zekhut Rabbi Eliyahu Mul Dar el-Beida.
Refrain: Zekhuto . . .

Translation:

My brethren, God will guide you!
Do not worry about money.
Rabbi David U-Moshe will return it to you.
I drank a glass and I go (repeat)
By the merit of Rabbi David U-Moshe.
Refrain: May his merit . . .
From Meron I come (repeat).
I made the pilgrimage to Rabbi Shimʿon Bar-Yoḥay in accordance with custom.
Refrain: May his merit . . .
Our glass is full of white maḥia *(repeat)*
To the merit of Rabbi Eliyahu, Master of Casablanca.
Refrain: May his merit . . .

IV. *Qasida* about Rabbi David U-Moshe

This *qasida* was recorded as transmitted by an informant born in the village of Arba Touggana.

1. Abyad Rabbi David U-Moshe wabyad men zaro
ʿammar el-mal ma ykhta daro.
2. Abyad Rabbi David U-Moshe wabyad men zaro
smaʿa khedra ḥmra fi-daro.
3. Abyad Rabbi David U-Moshe wabyad men zaro
ʿammar el-ʿzara ma-khtaw daro.
4. Abyad Rabbi David U-Moshe wabyad men zaro
ʿammar saddiqim el-kbar ma khtaw daro.
5. Abyad Rabbi David U-Moshe wabyad men zaro
ʿammar kul maḥala ma terta daro.

Translation:

1. Happy is Rabbi David U-Moshe and happy is the pilgrim to his tomb.
Money will never be lacking in his home.
2. Happy is Rabbi David U-Moshe and happy is the pilgrim to his tomb.
A green candle and a red candle illuminate his home.
3. Happy is Rabbi David U-Moshe and happy is the pilgrim to his tomb.
Sons will never cease to fill his home.
4. Happy is Rabbi David U-Moshe and happy is the pilgrim to his tomb.
Great righteous men will never cease to come to his home.
5. Happy is Rabbi David U-Moshe and happy is the pilgrim to his tomb.
Sickness will never strike his home.

V. *Qasida* about Rabbi Daniel Hashomer

Ism el-Lah'nbark b-enhar ub-el-lil
Salamu ʿlik ya Rabbi Daniel
Abyad 'umo wabyad di weldtu
Ait-Shomer hiyya qbilto
Tkun mʿana zekhut torato
Ḥna u-samʿin u-zmiʿ Yisra'el

Endker siman ʿzaibo el-kbar
Tsemʿu u-tsektu ʾntum ya zyar
Rabbi Daniel Hashomer ḥader
Yikun el-waqt mʿa Yisraʾel.
. . . .
Ait-Shomer w-yzor
W-yqra temma mya u-khamsin mezmor
Foq el-qbora di Rabbi Daniel.

Translation:

I shall bless the name of God night and day
Peace be upon you, o Rabbi Daniel!
Happy is his mother who gave him life
The celebrated Shomer family is his clan
May the merit of his great learning be with us
With us, with all those who heed him and with all Israel
I shall mention his great wonders
Listen closely and pay heed, you pilgrims to his tomb
Rabbi Daniel Hashomer is here present
He will be with his people Israel at all times.
. . . .[10]
Visit the tomb of the Shomer clan
And recite the hundred-fifty Psalms
At the tomb of Rabbi Daniel.

VI. *Qasida* about Rabbi David Ha-Levi Draʿ

This *qasida* was recorded as transmitted by its author David Oḥayon, nicknamed Ben-Zuwa. It was composed after the author had witnessed a miracle at the saint's tomb: during a *hillulah* ceremony the ceiling of the synagogue collapsed, but no visitors were injured.

Aziw tsemʿu had el "qassiyya"
Li trat li ana liyya
Li mʿa ez-zmaʿiyya
U-kan sefer fi-yddiya
Nhar el-tnin f-el-ʿsiyya
Fas trat had el "qassiyya"
Teḥt mʿa ed-dnadniyya

U-fekna Rabbi David Ha-Levi dawʿiniyya
Ytemḥa zekher ʿAmaleq
Semʿu had el-klam el-ḥqiq
Ta waḥi makharj . . .
B-zekhut Rabbi David Ha-Levi seddiq
Mulana ʿlina ʿafa
U-duwwezha bla sfa
Ḥit azalna ma-fa
Taḥ es-sqaf d-el-bit u-nas waqfa
B-es-saʿa mulana ussaʿ
B-saʿt dik dgardiʿa
Fekna hadak sbaʿ
Diʾismu Rabbi David Draʿ
Had-siʿmaltu b-femmi
U-lukan anaʾmsemmi
Ma berdliss ana demmi
Myat ras d-el-ghenmi
Ana nesker u-ndakker
. . . u-ntfekker
Rabbi David Ha-Levi zin el-mendar
Di taḥ es-sqaf bihum u-tfekku b-el-ʿmar
B-el *paytanim* zabu sefer m-ghrab
U-kant el-ferḥa f-el-qlab
Nhar el-tnin f-ʿand el-mgharb
Bas taḥo el-khsab
Qeddas di bnadem taḥ
U-ḥetta waḥi ma dzraḥ
Reddo balkum f-had el-klam
U-f-en-nis di-ʿmel mʿana el-*ḥakham*
Zekhuto bas waqfa elʿolam
Ka yziwh en-nas yzoroh f-kelʿam
Zekhuto kbira bezzaf
U-di gheyyet ʿlih ʿamro ma-ykhaf
U-di jaʿando ʿamro ma yzʿaf
El binyan d-es-sla ʿamluh mliḥ
Ta-si ma fih qbiḥ
Waqef ʿlih *shammash* David Oḥayon w-Yitsḥaq Elmaleḥ
Mulana ykhellih sḥiḥ
Qeddas di bnadem taḥ
U-ḥetta waḥi ma dzraḥ
Nteʿmalu mʿana nisim sḥaḥ
Mfih tfekko sḥal m-er-rwaḥ

Huwwa kemmel el-ḥaja
Ha tiᶜu ᶜlih khemsa tiran
Rabbi David Ha-Levi kemmel er-rja
Fel-ḥin jaw *dayyanim* m-ed-Dar el-Beida
U-jaw yferḥo w-yᶜemlo sᶜuda
Yferḥo b-es-sla ej-jdidah
Yfekhum el-*ḥakham* men-had el-qda
El-*ḥakham* ᶜmel mᶜana zekhuto
Ras Yisra'el yifelto
Kul waḥi zᶜafᶜla mrato
Ma fekkna ghir ghetto
Zekhut hadak el-mezian
Ka iziwh en-nas mel-beldan
U-had el-gzerah zrat *b-rosh ḥodesh Ḥeshwan*
U-had el-gzerah tbettelt *b-rosh ḥodesh Ḥeshwan*
El *ḥakham* ᶜmel mᶜana zekhuto
Bas Yisra'el yifelto
Kul waḥi taḥ bᶜremto
Ma fekkna ghir ghetto
Fem el foqi oqfo
Bdaw yzgherto w-yseqfo
Luzeh es-sla ka yḥsafo
Ḥatta f-el-qaᶜel-bit taḥo
Bnadem ma-zal ka yfter
Myat rzal aw kter
Hada b-ettaᶜrizah, Ben-Zuwa b-et-ter
Taḥo f-el-bit ybqa el-ᶜmar
Reddo balkum
Rabbi David Ha-Levi ysbaq qeddamhum
U-fost el-ḥefra oqef ḥatta fekhum
M-el-gzerah di kant zawhum
Mulana yreddkum b-et-tshubah
W-yreddkum el-*Torah*
U-tji l-yshuᶜah daba
Zekhut Rabbi David Ha-Levi kbir et-tebba
M-elli taḥ er-rajel
Kant el mra masi tehbal
M-elli rat rajelha ḥasel
Had el"qassiyya" zbedha David Oḥayon u-Moshe Abergel
Mulana yiᶜtelkum daw f-el-ᶜin
Ta-waḥi ma ykun mghebben
U-*shammash* huwwa David Oḥayon

Had el "qasida" ḫluwwa u-ldida
U-ḥedro fiha Yihud Dar-el-Beida
U-tamanha lira luḥida
Torah ᶜendna ᶜziza
Ḥbiba u-ᶜziza
U-qralhum Rabbi ᶜAqiba.
El-*talmidim* del-*yeshibah*
Zekhut ha-rab Rabbi ᶜAqiba
Zekhuto tkun mᶜana
Ḥna w-Yisra'el khwana
Hodu l'Adonay ki tob
Msa elᶜya nzi ᶜiyyan
U-el-mred ka yrzaᶜ beryan
Had si shufnah b-el-ᶜyan
Zekhut ha-rab Ḥoni Ha-Meᶜaggel
Rabbi ᶜAmram Ben-Diwan
Yifek Yisra'el m-el-ᶜdyan.

Translation:

Come hear what happened to me
To me and to a big crowd
As I held a Torah *Scroll in my arm*
It was a Monday evening
When it happened
I fell and so did the musicians,
But Rabbi David Ha-Levi, the apple of my eye, saved us,
May the memory of ᶜAmalek be wiped out!
Hear these true words!
No one was harmed
Because of the merit of the saint Rabbi David Ha-Levi
Our God saved us
He saved us from disaster
Our hour had not yet come
For though the roof fell in and the people stood there
At that moment our God saved us
In the moment of danger
The "Lion" saved us
And his name is Rabbi David Draᶜ
This is what I have told in my own words
If I did not bear the name of the saint

My heart would not have found the sublime calm
It was necessary to sacrifice one hundred sheep to him
In order to call him up and give him thanks
And we mention his great merit
The handsome Rabbi David Ha-Levi
When the roof fell in and their lives were saved
They escorted a Torah *Scroll with* paytanim *from afar*
And joy was in all hearts
On Monday at twilight
When the columns fell
Several people fell
But no one was hurt
Hear my words!
By the miracle that the saint performed for us
By his merit the world exists
All the year long people make pilgrimages to him
His merit is very great
And whoever calls upon him need not fear
And whoever comes to him does not return home emptyhanded
The building of the synagogue is now beautiful
Without a flaw
And the person responsible was the beadle David Oḥayon and also Yitsḥaq Elmaleḥ
May God bless him with health
Several persons fell
But no one was injured
Great miracles were performed for us
Several lives were saved
He completes everything
In his honor five bulls were sacrificed
Rabbi David Ha-Levi fulfilled the request
When dayyanim *came from Casablanca*
They came to rejoice and hold a seʿudah
At the inauguration of the new synagogue
And the saint saved them from this evil
The saint showed us his merit
So that Israel should be saved
Everyone cared for his wife
We were saved because we called upon him
Because of his lovely merit
People come from all the cities

This calamity was to happen on the First of Ḥeshwan
And at the same date it was cancelled
The saint showed us his merit
So that Israel would be saved
Many pilgrims fell under the ruins
But they were saved because they called upon him
At the door to the second floor they stood
And began to make zgharit *and to clap their hands*
People gathered opposite the synagogue
Until they fell from inside the courtyard
And others were still eating
One hundred people were there, maybe more
One with a drum and Ben-Zuwa with cymbals
And then they fell into the shrine and nothing happened to them
Remember:
Rabbi David Ha-Levi advanced first
And stood in the middle of the building until he saved them
From the calamity which had befallen them.
God will show you the way to repentance
And restore you to the Torah
And salvation will come forthwith
By the merit of Rabbi David Ha-Levi, the great healer
When the man fell
His wife nearly lost her mind
When she saw her husband trapped
This qasida *was composed by David*
Oḥayon and Moshe Abergel
May God illuminate their eyes!
None of you will be sad.
The beadle is David Oḥayon.
This qasida *is sweet and flavorful.*
In it the Jews of Casablanca are present
And its price is one lira
Our Torah *is very precious*
Lovable and dear to all of us
Rabbi ʿAqibah read the Torah
To the students at the yeshibah
The merit of Rabbi ʿAqibah
Will always be with us
With us and with Israel, our brethren
Praise God for He is good
Weariness has gone though I came here weary

The sick person returns healthy
This we saw with our own eyes
The merit of Rabbi Ḥoni Ha-Meʿaggel
And Rabbi ʿAmram Ben-Diwan
Will save Israel from its enemies.

VII. *Qasida* for the auction of the saint's glasses at the *hillulah*

Sri had el-kas (repeat)
As ta tsenna
U-terbeḥ rebḥa el-dida
ʿla zekhut Mulay Rabbi Eliyahu di Dar-el-Beida
Zekhuto tkun mʿana!

Sri had el-kas (repeat)
As ta tsenna
U-Mulah yʿtek di ka tmenna
Zekhut Mulay Shimʿon Bar-Yoḥay ha-tanna.
Zekhuto tkun mʿana!

Sri had el-kas (repeat)
Had el-kas ḥlu fḥal es-sekkar
U-nsriwh mʿend el-ʿattar
ʿla zekhut Mulay Rabbi Mordekhay Ben-ʿAttar
Zekhuto tkun mʿana!

Sri had el-kas (repeat)
Had el-kas mqetter b-er-ris
U-li yirah yirbeḥ w-yʿish
ʿla zekhut Mulay Meir Baʿal Ha-Nes
Zekhuto tkun mʿana!

Had el-kas u-zgharto (repeat)
Nserboh b-zekhuto
Zekhut di Rabbi Ḥayyim Pinto.

Had el-kas mʿammer b-el-limon
U-nserboh fi Rabbi Shimʿon
Zekhuto tkun mʿana!

Rabbi Daniel mul el-hiba
Enti tʿawenna hina
B-el-Lah u-b-es seddiq hina!

Mulay Ighi huwwa sidna
Huwwa sbaʿna u-ʿarna
Yamina aminna!

Rabbi Ḥayyim Pinto huwwa sidna
Yamina aminna
Rabbi Ḥayyim Pinto huwwa ḥbibna!

Translation:

Buy this glass! (repeat)
What are you waiting for?
You will earn a new profit
By the merit of the saint Rabbi Eliyahu of Casablanca
May his merit stand by us!

Buy this glass! (repeat)
What are you waiting for?
Its master will fulfill your wish
By the merit of Rabbi Shimʿon Bar-Yoḥay, the Teacher,
May his merit stand by us!

Buy this glass! (repeat)
The beverage is as sweet as sugar
I shall buy it from the spice merchant
By the merit of Rabbi Mordekhay Ben-ʿAttar
May his merit stand by us!

Buy this glass! (repeat)
Full of maḥia *finely distilled!*
Whoever buys it will reap the rewards and live long
By the merit of the saint Meir Baʿal Ha-Nes
May his merit stand by us!

This glass and its joy (repeat)
We shall drink to his merit
To the merit of Rabbi Ḥayyim Pinto!
This glass is full of lemon
Let us drink to the health of Rabbi Shimʿon
May his merit stand by us!

Rabbi Daniel, the master of the splendor
You will help us
In the name of God and of the saint!

Mulay Ighi is our master
He is our lion and our honor
Our infallible right hand!

Rabbi Ḥayyim Pinto is our saint
Our infallible right hand
Rabbi Ḥayyim Pinto is our beloved!

While the pilgrim drinks, the crowd recites:

Sheteh ha-kol ʿad gemirah	[Hebrew]
Bi-zekhut Rabbi Ḥayyim Pinto	[Hebrew]
Ma tkhelli-fih ḥatta qtera	[Judeo-Arabic]

Had el-kas u-zgharto
Yiserbo Eliyahu ḥatta . . .
Zekhut Rabbi David Ben-Barukh u-zekhuto!

Translation:

Drink it all down
By the merit of Rabbi Ḥayyim Pinto!
Don't leave a drop!

This glass and its joy
Eliyahu will drink until . . .
In honor of Rabbi David Ben-Barukh!

VIII. *Piyyut* by Rabbi Ḥayyim Pinto[11]

Aromemkha ha-El Elohe Yisra'el
Ha-matsil ha-goel mi-deḥi et ragli

Nivhalti me-yir'ah mi-tsur ga'oh ga'ah
Naʿaneti ki amarti matah ragli

Yadekha ʿasuni ve-hem yekhonenuni
Adonay ḥonneni we-heyenna ʿozer li

Ḥay male be-ḥibbah ummatkha ha-qrebah
Odekha va-abarekh otkha le-ragli

Yatsata l-yshuʿah barukh gedol deʿah
Bi ʿanitani ba-mishor ʿamedah ragli

Yishamaʿ qol shiri lefanekha sitri
Atta ta'ir neri tsuri ve-go'ali
Mul qodsho etḥannan betsillo etlonan
Beveto eshtonan ve-hesir kol ḥoli

Ḥalloti ze kammah zakh yashar be-emah
Qoli tishmaʿ lamma ʿazavtani Eli?

Translation:

Exalted are You, God of Israel,
Who rescues and keeps my foot from falling
I was frightened with awe of the Rock
refulgent with His glory
I was answered when I said: "My foot is unsteady"
Your hands made me and they shaped me
God, pity me and help me!
Living God, full of love
You approached Your nation
Yet I shall continue to praise and to bless You
In my footsteps.
You came forward for my salvation,
Blessed is Your great wisdom!
For mercy's sake, hear my prayers:
May my foot rest solidly in uprightness.
Let the sound of my song be heard before You,
My sanctuary!
May You light my candle, my Rock and my Redeemer!
Before His sanctuary I shall plead for mercy
In its shadow I shall find shelter.
Bruised and battered I shall come to His house,
But He will heal my sickness.
I implore you
With fear and trembling, O Pure and Righteous One!
Hear my voice,
Why have You abandoned me, my God?

Notes

1. See A. Shiloah (1992, pp. 164–68); Y. Avishur (1982).
2. A wonderful *piyyut,* in praise of the saint known as Mul Aguiga, was composed by a visitor to the site of his tomb at Aguigal, probably in

the second half of the eighteenth century: D. Hassin (1931, p. 48). For songs in praise of Christian saints, see: A. van Gennep (1949, tome I, vol. 4, pp. 1676–78).

3. Hundreds of manuscripts are found in the Jewish National and University Library, Jerusalem, and in private collections. Haim Suissa (1945. *Yismaḥ Tsaddiq*. Casablanca) is the most important booklet, containing a collection of twenty-five songs and *piyyutim*. D. Hassin (1931), first published at the beginning of the nineteenth century in Amsterdam, contains songs in praise of six emissaries from the Holy Land. See also: H. Zafrani (1977); L. Brunot and E. Malka (1939, p. 276); I. Ben-Ami (1973a, pp. 50–58); E. Hazan (1979, pp. 39–47).
4. See I. Ben-Ami (1971, pp. 1–17); A. Shiloah (1992, p. 189).
5. In L. Brunot and E. Malka (1939, p. 276) there is a song sung by young men only on the occasion of a *hillulah,* to the accompaniment of a mandolina.
6. Like songs in different languages spoken by Jews in other countries, many Hebrew words were intercalated in the songs in Judeo-Arabic sung by the Jews of Morocco. See M. Bar-Asher (1978, pp. 163–89).
7. Nevertheless, new songs in praise of saints are still being composed by Moroccan Jews in Israel. In the Hebrew edition of this book, I included a *piyyut* and a *qasida* in praise of R. Yaʿaqob Abiḥatsira, composed on the occasion of the great *hillulah* held at Ramleh, Israel, in 1980, celebrating the 100th anniversary of his death.
8. This song appeared in a small booklet with Hebrew characters on one side and a transliteration in Latin characters on the other.
9. This and the songs following were recorded in the course of my fieldwork.
10. Line unclear.
11. A *piyyut* published in a very rare single page, with the text in Hebrew on one side and in Latin transliteration on the other. In the middle of the page appears the picture of R. Ḥayyim Pinto the Younger (Casablanca).

12

THE COMMUNAL ORGANIZATION AROUND THE HOLY SITES

The hundreds of saints' shrines, and the religious and social activities connected with them, required a communal organization that would assure the orderly functioning of these sites. It is appropriate to ask whether this need led to the creation of such organization and institutional patterns in North Africa and how they developed. The earliest written information about this appeared in the 1920s, and what preceded this period may be reconstructed on the basis of popular testimony and traditions, as well as from items of information in Jewish and non-Jewish sources.

Undoubtedly, geographical, social and economic needs shaped—to a not inconsiderable extent—arrangements that had long been in existence. It should be noted that the 1930s[1] and particularly the 1940s witnessed the culmination of the development of the physical infrastructure in the vicinity of saints' shrines and access to them; this infrastructure included construction of buildings, services, and access roads. During this period, there was also a remarkable increase in the number of celebrants and in the extent of certain *hillulot.*

Until the French came to Morocco in 1912 and subsequently converted it into a French protectorate, veneration of saints among the Jews was largely a personal and local affair. Numerous saints were interred near small villages and were known only to the inhabitants of the nearest village. A small number of saints had more than local standing, and their graves were visited by Jews from other places. The difficulties of transportation within and between *Blad el-Siba* and *Blad el-Makhzen,*[2] and the poverty of the Jews of the Atlas—the region with the highest concentration of saints' tombs—made it impossible for them to establish large centers for the *ziyara* like those constructed in the twentieth century.

These conditions changed radically in the 1930s. Rabbi Daniel Hashomer Ashkenazi,[3] an unknown saint who became renowned almost overnight throughout Morocco, is an excellent example of this kind of development. The principal factors in this model clearly explain the phenomenon. Here there was an appropriate socio-religious setting that was prepared to assimilate the message of a young man who was saved by the saint and who vowed to honor him. The ordeals of this young man during the war—when the saint protected him—his dreams about the saint, his prosperity and stubborn decision to "build up" the saint by creating the physical infrastructure at his grave, the use of advertising and the concentrated dissemination of tales of the saint's miracles—all these brought about a significant change in the activities connected with the saint's tomb. A similar confluence of factors, with certain changes, recurred at many sites.

The development of holy sites and the increase in the number of pilgrims to these sites generated large sums of money through donations and the sale of *mitswot,* and created a need to manage the activities and finances in an orderly fashion. At almost every site, personal initiative[4] brought about the development of the shrine, and a committee to oversee the saint's tomb would be formed afterward. In time, such committees were formed at every saint's tomb.[5] These committees—generally consisting of a president and other officers, particularly a treasurer—had diverse functions.

The local committee took care of the organization of the *hillulot.* In general there were two *hillulot,* one on *Lag bʿOmer,* the other after *Sukkot.* Wealthy persons ordered rooms to be built; the rest of the celebrants pitched tents, some of which were lent them free of charge and some of which were rented. Sometimes the committee also saw to the paving of access roads to the site and arranged for transportation to the shrine. Each year the committee published announcements and pamphlets inviting people to participate in the *hillulah.* During the week of the *hillulah* the committee was responsible for the maintenance of order. It controlled the sale of *mitswot,* candles, and glasses (of *maḥia*) in honor of the saint, and supervised the distribution of money to the poor and to such functionaries as rabbis, cantors, *paytanim,* ritual slaughterers, guards, and so on. The committees were under public scrutiny, and each year responsible officials handed out a printed sheet with details of the previous year's income and expenditures.

During the period in which the cult of a saint and the pilgrimage to the saint's tomb was strictly a personal and local matter, there was apparently no need for a special body to run such sites. At the turn of the present century, most of the saints' tombs were in a very dilapidated state.[6] According to testimony from the late 1920s, the tomb of Rabbi David Ha-Levi Draʿ, for example, was in ruins.[7] There was no place to sit, and a large heap of garbage covered the tomb. Then a rich Jew who had dreamt about the saint and was saved by him developed the site. He built some ninety rooms, a handsome synagogue decorated in the Arab style, a *yeshibah* for ninety students and an access road. He even distributed letters to all the synagogues extolling the saint.

The local committee was generally in charge of the water and food supply for celebrants during the *hillulah,* and for this purpose it had to appeal to the Muslims of the region for help in selling supplies to the visitors. During and after World War II, when food was rationed, local committees appealed to the French authorities for special allotments of food for the *hillulah.* Each committee concentrated the earnings of the *hillulot* from participants' donations, fulfilling of vows, sale of candles, glasses and *mitswot,* collection of taxes on slaughtering of animals, rental of tents and rooms, and so on. When there was a synagogue named after the saint in another town, it was common for part of the earnings of that synagogue to be forwarded to the committee in charge of that saint's tomb. These funds were usually transferred to the committee during the days of the *hillulah;* occasionally they would be transferred directly to the home of the president of the committee.

Each committee at a saint's tomb reached a formal agreement, which was adapted from time to time, regarding the distribution of earnings from the tomb. These funds included revenues from the *hillulot,* donations by visitors throughout the year, vows in synagogues, earnings from charity boxes from all over Morocco, and so forth. The parties involved in the agreement generally consisted of the local committee of the saint's tomb, committee from the largest town nearest the tomb, committees from villages in the vicinity of the tomb, the Central Commission for the Holy Sites, the inspector of Jewish institutions on behalf of the French authorities, representatives of the Muslim government, and persons who operated on their own initiative at the saint's grave and were therefore influential. Over time, some large communities in whose vicinity there was a saint's tomb—such as Demnate, Marrakech and Ouezzane—began to intervene in the activities at the saint's tomb and demand a portion of the earnings from the local committee.

During the days of the *hillulah,* committee members would distribute flyers to all the visitors. These flyers served as a kind of newspaper in which, for example, were published announcements of new appointments as well as arrangements that had been made for the *hillulah.* This organ of communication also served in the wars between the parties involved in disputes related to the affairs of the saints' tombs. A number of particularly serious disputes required the intervention of French and Muslim authorities before peace was restored among the Jewish officials involved in the quarrel—a fact which detracted from the standing of these committees.

The increase in the number of local committees and the strengthening of their activity led to the establishment of a Central Commission for the Holy Sites and *Hillulot,*[8] in accordance with a government regulation that took effect on April 23, 1947. One of the commission's purposes was to supervise the local committees and determine arrangements to resolve the disputes which arose over the distribution of funds. Members of the commission were appointed for two years by the councilor to the Sherifian government. At the head of the first commission, which consisted of six members, was the Chief Rabbi of Morocco, Rabbi Shaul Ibn Danan. The decisions of the commission, like all the regulations of the Rabbinical Council, required government approval. Although it was appointed in April 1947, the Central Commission did not hold its first session until March 8, 1949. It continued to function for another two years.

At the first session all the members were present, and the issue of distributing earnings from the *hillulot* at the holy sites was the main topic of discussion. Some resolutions were offered and passed but they were extremely unrealistic. Transferring the balance of the revenues from the tomb of one particular saint to another site, for example, was not really practicable. Nor was the expressed intention of educating celebrants and imposing certain standards of behavior upon them during the *hillulah* at all realistic. Anyone who had ever been present at an *hillulah* should have known how impossible it was to supervise the crowds. None of these resolutions was ever carried out. The solution to the problems connected with the *hillulah* required a sensible organization and continuous oversight, neither of which was apparently within the power of the Central Commission, and it disappeared from the scene.

Notes

1. On May 31, 1936, Mr. Yitsḥaq Elmaleḥ presented a request to the French officials for permission to build a road from Souk El-Arba near Demnate to the grave of R. David Ha-Levi Draʿ.
2. *Blad el-Makhzen* was the name of the region dominated by the shereefs and under their rule; *Blad el-Siba*—Land of Freedom—was an independent region, governed by the heads of the Berber tribes and the marabouts. See H. Z. Hirschberg (1965, vol. 2, p. 207). C. de Foucauld (1888), in the chapter of his book dedicated to the Jews, divides them into two groups: Jews of the Blad el-Makhzen and Jews of the Blad el-Siba.
3. See I. Ben-Ami (1973a).
4. At the grave of R. Daniel Hashomer, the initiative came from Mr. Moshe ʿAmar and at the tombs of R. David Ha-Levi Draʿ and R. David U-Moshe from Mr. Yitsḥaq Elmaleḥ.
5. In some towns, societies in honor of and named for the saints were established, as for example the society in honor of R. Yaḥya Laḥlu in Ksar Es-Souk. The members used to come together on Saturday evenings to study Psalms and to celebrate the saint's *hillulah* on the anniversary of his death.
6. See the descriptions of the graves in L. Voinot (1948) and E. Doutté (1909 and 1914).
7. As told by the caretaker of the tomb. See also E. Doutté (1914, p. 212).
8. The Central Commission was designated in French: "La Commission des Sanctuaires et Pèlerinages Israélites du Maroc" or "La Commission de Contrôle des Sanctuaires et Pèlerinages Israélites du Maroc".

13

RELATIONS BETWEEN JEWS AND MUSLIMS IN SAINT VENERATION

An examination of the interaction between Jews and Muslims in the framework of saint veneration brings several interesting aspects to the fore. Although conclusive statistical data about this subject are not yet available,[1] a general trend emerges quite clearly. Jewish as well as non-Jewish evidence confirms that Muslims venerated Jewish saints both overtly and covertly, in some cases even eventuating in the saint's "Islamization."[2] In Morocco, a country where the Jews were a disdained, sometimes persecuted minority, this is a surprising phenomenon and merits investigation. Some Jews worshipped Muslim saints, but these saints were few in number, and traditions can almost always be cited that link these particular saints with Judaism. Such "Judaization" indicates that the Jews did not explicitly acknowledge their veneration of Muslim saints[3]—certainly not to the extent that Muslims acknowledged their veneration of Jewish saints.

This research has uncovered the names of 126 saints venerated by both Jews and Muslims in Morocco. Voinot has mentioned some of them; the rest appear in traditions, tales and legends collected in the present study. The largest group—Jewish saints venerated by Muslims—comprises ninety individuals.[4] An additional thirty-six were worshipped by both Jews and Muslims.[5] Jews visited a few more

Muslim saints[6] as well, sometimes having to do so surreptitiously when Muslims denied them access to a holy site. However, Jews often linked a Jewish tradition to such saints. This trend of attributing a Jewish origin or tradition to Muslim saints was undoubtedly encouraged by the Muslim appropriation of Jewish saints still venerated by the Jews and by the frequent visits of Muslims to Jewish sanctuaries. This phenomenon is the result of centuries of coexistence.

A Jewish saint might be served by a Muslim who acted as his messenger or "slave," took care of all his needs and was constantly at his side. This servant might also happen to be the only person present when his master died, as in the cases of R. David U-Moshe and R. Ḥayyim Ben-Diwan. Additionally a Jewish saint might be revealed by a Muslim, who then informed the Jewish community of the circumstances of the discovery. While ploughing a field a Muslim might turn up a fragment of a Jewish saint's tombstone; the saint might reveal himself in a Muslim's dream or make himself known by some miraculous occurrence, such as a pillar of fire rising above his grave or candles burning beneath a stone. A Muslim who revealed a saint or was present when one died would often become the guardian of the saint's tomb and the beneficiary of certain privileges that remained in his family for generations. Thus, before his death, R. Saʿadiah Dades promised to protect the young Muslim who served him, appointing him and his progeny as guardians of his grave. Many tombs of Jewish saints were attended by Muslims[7] to whom Jewish worshippers gave gifts of food and money. These guardians often witnessed miracles performed by Jewish saints. Among the many stories of such happenings is one about the Muslim guardian at the tomb of R. Ḥayyim Ben-ʿAttar who started to eat *kosher* food after hearing saints reading Psalms at night.

The interaction of Jews and Muslims in diverse aspects of saint worship extended beyond veneration of the same holy individual. Muslim guards who tended the saints' graves fulfilled many different functions: when a *hillulah* took place and the area around the grave was crowded with visitors, the guards and other Muslims in the vicinity were kept busy bringing the Jews livestock, firewood, water and whatever was needed for the traditional feast. On such occasions Jews also hired Muslim servants to perform a variety of other tasks, such as tanning the hides of slaughtered animals.

If the saint was buried in a dangerous or predominantly Muslim area, Jews would hire armed Arab escorts for protection. Some holy sites could be reached only by horse or mule transport, and Jews hired such transport from Muslims. Local Muslims worked on the building of synagogues, tombstones, rooms, and access roads in the vicinity of the saint's grave, sometimes even initiating the construction of lodges which they rented to Jews who came to pay homage to the saint; thus the Muslims profited from the Jews' celebrations and looked forward to them in anticipation of augmenting their earnings. Occasionally some Muslims even carried messages back and forth between the saints in Morocco and sages in the Holy Land.[8]

Muslims usually turned to Jewish saints when they sought healing and their own saints were unable to help them. They would visit a holy site alone or with Jewish acquaintances, or ask a Jew to transmit their request. Many tales are told about Muslims who were cured by Jewish saints and then became devotees of the saint, just as Jews would after a miraculous healing. Some of these Muslims and their families visited the revered figure's tomb annually and slaughtered an animal in his honor. Sometimes the Arabs slaughtered and ate their own meat; at other times they had a Jewish *shoḥet* do the slaughtering and gave the *kosher* meat to Jews.

Many Muslims visited the grave of R. ʿAmram Ben-Diwan. One man who was cured of his paralysis at the graveside jumped into the bonfire burning there and came out unscathed; kissing the tombstone, he gave his crutches to the saint and kissed the stones of the tomb. The family of an Arab woman who had been barren and then conceived after appealing to R. ʿAmram brought the saint great quantities of meat and 80 kilograms of wheat. An Arab soldier in the Sino-Indian War called upon R. ʿAmram, vowing to bring the saint a lamb every year if he came home safely, and he fulfilled his promise. Other Jewish saints cured Arab women of barrenness, restored vision, healed paralysis and epilepsy.[9]

Muslims also appealed to Jewish saints for other purposes than healing. A *qadi,* for example, asked R. Ḥananiah Ha-Cohen to help him find a lost slave-girl, and she reappeared that very night. A Muslim asked Mul Timḥdart to find him a goat to slaughter in honor of a most important holiday; on the way home he came upon a stray goat and appropriated it. Mulay Ighi's Muslim guard also wanted an animal to slaughter; he met a man on the road who gave him a sheep and told him it was his for the celebration.

Jewish saints are known to have saved Muslims' lives and even to have rescued entire villages. An Arab sheikh being pursued by his own men hid behind R. David U-Moshe's tombstone and escaped harm. Every year thereafter the sheikh brought the saint a meat-offering. On several occasions the prophetic vision of R. Pinḥas Ha-Cohen saved the life of El-Glawi, the Marrakech pasha. A Muslim whose ship sank on the way to Mecca was rescued by R. Makhluf Ben-Yosef. R. David Ha-Levi Draᶜ saved members of the Ait el-ᶜAlla tribe when another tribe came to plunder their village; the people of Ait el-ᶜAlla slaughtered a bullock at the saint's grave. Muslims who had come to attack the Muslim town ot Tetuan fled upon seeing lights in the cemetery where R. Yitsḥaq Ben-Walid was buried; the townsfolk realized that it was the saint who had saved them.

Like a Jewish believer, a Muslim believer going to a Jewish saint might be given a sign indicating that his request had been granted. One tradition tells that water issued from the tombstone of R. Shelomoh Ben-Lḥans whenever a truly devout Arab put his hat on it; all those near the grave would splash the water over their faces.

The Muslims of Morocco turned to the Jews and their sages whenever they were confronted by some puzzling or inexplicable phenomenon.[10] They believed that, with the help of their saints, Jews could fathom mysteries. It is relevant to recall here the story of the Arab's camel whose leg could not be pulled out of the ground; when its owners asked the Jews for help and the leg was extricated, the cause of the difficulty was revealed: a stone was found beneath the spot, bearing the date on which R. Abraham Awriwer had been buried. R. Abba Abiḥatsira interpreted two stones that Muslims saw bouncing over the river's surface on a calm day as indicating that there would be seven years of war and famine, followed by seven years of abundance. In wartime Muslims permitted—even invited—Jews to visit the tomb of Sidi Moḥammed U-Belqassem and pray to the saint. Muslims looked to the Jews for help particularly when there was a drought; they would observe their own rainmaking rituals, then turn to the Jews and ask them to petition the Jewish saints for rain as well.[11]

When there was a controversy between a Jew and a Muslim, both sides would bring the dispute for arbitration by a Jewish saint; in such cases both Jew and Muslim would take an oath at the saint's grave. A Muslim once asked a Jew who refused to pay him for some goats to accompany him to the tomb of Mul Timḥdart where they would both make a vow. That night the saint appeared to the Jew in a dream, ordering him to apologize and pay his debt to the Arab, and warning him not to take a false oath at the hallowed graveside.[12] A Muslim and a Jew who argued over a debt agreed to meet and make a vow at the grave of Mulay Matil. The Arab arrived at the shrine first; seeing a snake there, he realized that the saint would protect the Jew. Without making a vow, he suggested to the Jew that they compromise. Arabs involved in disputes with other Arabs sometimes appealed to a Jewish saint and took oaths at his tomb. In Tarkellil Arabs would swear by Bayo (R. Makhluf Ben-Yosef Abiḥatsira), while in Tabia they would place a hand on Mul Timḥdart's grave when taking an oath.

During his lifetime a saint was sometimes asked to arbitrate disputes between Jews and Arabs. In all cases, both parties accepted his decisions, either in fear of his curse or out of respect for his powers. R. Yehudah Ben-ʿAttar and R. Raphael Anqawa, famous as mediators, each settled cases in which Jews had accepted money from Arabs and then reneged on their obligations. After all other authorities—the pasha, the *qadi,* even the king—had decided against them, the Arabs turned to the renowned Jewish sages, who, in both instances, decided in their favor and ordered the Jews to return the money.

The miracles performed by Jewish saints inspired the respect of Muslims, a feeling strengthened by their contact with Jews at the large *hillulot,* where they rendered services to the pilgrims. Muslims displayed their respect and veneration for Jewish saints in many ways: for example, when passing a saint's tomb they would stop to kiss it. Declaring Mul Timḥdart a true saint, some Muslims blessed the Jews in the Lord's name and in the name of the revered saint. When R. Raphael Anqawa ruled in a certain Muslim's favor and refused to accept payment for his arbitration, the Muslim swore that "there is no God but Allah and our lord Raphael is his messenger." During his lifetime R. Raphael won the confidence of many Muslims through the miracles he performed; he also engaged in discussions with them over religious matters. When he died in 1935 his funeral in Salé was attended by thousands, including Muslims, influential Frenchmen, soldiers, a personal representative of the King of Morocco and, of course, multitudes of Jews from all corners of the country.

There have been instances of Muslims adopting specific Jewish practices, although I found no cases of their converting to Judaism or of Jews proselytizing. Eating *kosher* food was the most frequently adopted custom; this would sometimes happen after a Muslim witnessed a miracle performed by a Jewish saint. An Arab guard at the Jewish cemetery in Salé, where four saints are buried, heard disembodied voices reciting Psalms; he recognized this as a miracle and stopped eating non-*kosher* food. Mul Timḥdart granted a request addressed to him by a Muslim. The following day the Muslim lit candles at the saint's grave and said he wished he had been born a Jew; from that day on he forbade Arabs to graze their goats in the vicinity of the grave.

High-ranking officials and other influential Muslims who witnessed a Jewish saint's miracle or recognized the saint's virtues and powers often gave Jews special consideration. This was manifested, among other ways, by assistance in improving the site of the saint's grave and contributing such foodstuffs as wheat, oil, or animals for slaughter at the time of large *hillulot.*[13]

The Muslim populace in general, as well as their rulers, revered certain living saints. R. Ḥayyim Boḥbot was so highly esteemed that even the *qadi* would rise in his presence. When R. Pinḥas Ha-Cohen came to the palace of the pasha whose life he had saved, the guards would stand at attention as if royalty had arrived. The pasha himself would go out to receive him and kiss the rabbi's head and hands. He asked the rabbi to move to Marrakech and presented him with the house of a wealthy Arab. The pasha was in France when R. Pinḥas died, but he returned to Morocco at once to attend the funeral. He even arranged and paid for special transportation facilities to bring the thousands of Jews who wanted to come to Marrakech to take leave of the revered rabbi.

Regrettably, there is also weighty evidence indicating that although some Muslims regarded Jewish saints with respect and reverence, those same saints were sometimes the target of Muslim scorn and contempt. Objects were occasionally stolen from the environs of the tomb, and acts of vandalism or other forms of desecration were perpetrated at the site. Such acts were immediately punished[14] by damaging the offender's property or striking him with paralysis, blindness, or even death. To counteract the punishment, the guilty Muslim had to beg the saint's forgiveness, which was usually granted. Sometimes, when a saint had been outraged, Muslims asked the Jews to intervene on their behalf. In most cases, however, the offender's family would bring an animal for ritual slaughter, promising to do so every year if the saint would rescind the punishment. If an offender appeared on his own behalf, he displayed his total submission by appearing with his hands tied behind his back and a knife between his teeth; he then prostrated himself at the saint's tomb and begged forgiveness. Although the acts of retribution generally filled most Muslims with awe of the Jewish saints, some overcame their fear and even murdered holy individuals. The list of saints who were murdered or chose martyrdom rather than comply with an order inimical to Jewry is long and variegated.[15] There are also tales of Muslims snatching a Jewish saint's body and burying it in their own cemetery in the hope that a measure of sanctity would rub off on them. R. Shelomoh Ben-Yitsḥaq, for example, knew that his death would occur on the date of a Muslim festival, which exposed his body to danger. The Jews therefore made special arrangements to have him buried secretly in the Jewish cemetery.

Muslims occasionally put the powers of a living saint to the test. A sultan tested R. Shaul Naḥmias by locking him in a lions' cage; when the rabbi calmly stroked the lions and remained unharmed, the sultan was forced to acknowledge his saintliness. A king's brother once ordered R. Yitsḥaq Ben-Safet to bring food out to the field for him, and the saint obeyed. It was later discovered, to the amazement of the king's brother, that on the same day some food had mysteriously disappeared from the palace.

Harming a living saint was a most serious offense; such conduct usually cost the offender his life. It is told that every Arab who beat R. David Ben-Barukh in his childhood fell dead on the spot, thereby demonstrating the boy's saintliness. Another story tells that a thief broke into R. Yosef Pinto's home one night and disturbed the saint at his studies. The thief vanished. Only his head remained, and it still hangs there today.[16]

Anyone vandalizing a saint's grave, defiling its environs or stealing objects from the site—which is considered the property of the saint—was looked upon as committing an outrage against the saint himself. Numerous tales are told of Muslims who stole candles, coins, jewelry and other precious objects from tombs of Jewish saints. Others tell of the theft of animals brought as offerings. The saint's reaction is swift and harsh: stolen objects turn into snakes, offenders are blinded or paralyzed. To have the punishment rescinded, the offender must prove his penitence by bringing animals for ritual slaughter in the saint's honor and begging forgiveness.

If the saint agreed to forgive, the blinded offender might recover his sight, the paralyzed person might retrieve mobility. At times, however, the punishment would be fatal. A Muslim stole candles from R. Yaḥya Laḥlu's grave and he disappeared into the ground. Another robber died, and his house was destroyed, after he desecrated the grave of R. Yaʿaqob Naḥmias. A Muslim woman and her sons urinated near the home of R. Yehudah Ben-Baba and refused to clean their mess; thieves stole their flocks and they paid for their misdemeanor with their lives. A peasant died after ploughing near the grave of R. Eleʿazar Ha-Cohen and damaging the tombstone. Others were paralyzed after ploughing near the tombs of R. Abraham Darʿi and R. Abraham Makhluf Ben-Yaḥya. When Muslims came to move R. Eliyahu's tombstone to another cemetery, he made the move impossible by forcing their picks to adhere to the ground; they were unable to transfer the stone until they gave a sum of money to the head of the Jewish community, who then agreed to the removal of the stone.

The immediate surroundings of a saint's tomb acquired an aura of sanctity. Nearby trees were considered sacred; anyone damaging them was severely punished. Some Muslims were paralyzed or even died after sawing branches from trees near the graves of R. ʿAmram Ben-Diwan, R. Daniel Hashomer Ashkenazi, Mul Timḥdart and R. Moshe Wizeman. A Muslim was injured after uprooting a palm tree near the grave of R. Abraham Azulay. The rabbi appeared to him in a dream and told him to bring the tree back and slaughter an animal in the rabbi's honor. The man recovered from his injury after returning the tree and inviting all the inhabitants of the *mellaḥ* to a *seʿudah.* By the same token, no houses could be built or flocks pastured near the burial site. A man who sent his daughters to pasture his animals near the tomb of Ait El-Cohen at Imini met with catastrophe. Sheep grazing near R. David Danino's grave at Demnate were paralyzed and remained so until their owner made a ritual meat-offering to the saint. An Arab began to build a house near R. Daniel Hashomer Ashkenazi's grave, but it was demolished and the Arab died.

As may be seen, any hostile act against a saint, any scornful or disrespectful expression about him or his tomb, elicited severe reprisals. A barren Muslim woman who bathed at the tomb of R. Daniel

Hashomer Ashkenazi was stricken by paralysis. The participants in a wedding procession laughed as they passed the grave of R. ʿAmram Ben-Diwan, and they were immediately paralyzed; they recovered after their families slaughtered in the saint's honor and begged him for mercy. When he mocked Mul Timḥdart, a young man became mute and blind and then died. After a shereef chided the Jews for extolling the virtues of R. David Ha-Levi Draʿ, he could not stop urinating. The shereef pleaded with the Jews to ask the saint for mercy, and after they conducted a ritual slaughtering in the rabbi's honor the shereef recovered. Every year thereafter the shereef himself had a bull slaughtered in R. David's honor.

Jewish saints were an important safeguard against any member of the strong Muslim majority who attacked or maligned Morocco's weak, scattered Jewish minority. The saints protected individual Jews and Jewry as a whole in the face of Muslim threats. When necessary, they also punished Muslim offenders. R. Eliyahu of Casablanca punished a Muslim who threatened to kill a Jew by sentencing him to thirty-six years in prison for the murder of another Muslim. A Muslim who claimed that the land on which the synagogue of R. David Ha-Levi Draʿ stood had been taken from him by a Jew was stricken by illness; for the sake of his health, he waived his demand for the site. Bandits who attacked a Jew on the road lost their eyesight due to the intervention of R. Ḥayyim Pinto Ha-Gadol, and the Jew was saved. A Jew who was threatened by Muslims told them that he was Ḥazzan Moshe Lʿasri's son; his attackers left him alone, fearful of harming a member of that illustrious family. Seeing a Jewess dressed like a Muslim so that she could visit the grave of R. Makhluf Ben-Yosef Abiḥatsira in safety, Arabs locked the cemetery gates, trapping her inside. That night, with the saint's help, the woman pushed the gate and it opened—to the astonishment of the Arabs. One Jewess entered the tomb of R. ʿEli Ben-Yitsḥaq despite the Muslims' prohibition. An Arab informed on her, but she managed to escape through an aperture that opened up in the wall. The informer was burned by the Arabs who had come to kill her.

Saints also shielded the Jews from government officials. From time to time Jewish merchants traded in forbidden goods, and sometimes the authorities were alerted. When this happened, the merchant had only to call upon a saint to have the prohibited commodity temporarily transformed into permissible wares. Thus the power of

R. David Ben-Barukh (Azrou n'Bahamou) turned black pepper into corn, flour, lentils and wheat; the power of R. David U-Moshe turn tea and sugar into corn, wheat and chick peas; ʿarak became water at the bidding of R. Ḥayyim Pinto of Casablanca and oil at the bidding of R. David U-Moshe. One Jew came to a town carrying four cases loaded with forbidden goods. When he was brought before the *qadi,* he stated that the cases were empty; by virtue of the power of R. Daniel Hashomer Ashkenazi, when the cases were opened they were indeed found to be empty, and the Jew was saved. At a time when buying and selling copper was prohibited, R. David U-Moshe saved a Jewish merchant from the police by transforming the copper he was carrying into black pepper, saffron and wool.

The *mellaḥ* of the Jews, too, was protected by saints. There are many examples of saints whose power kept enemies from harming Jews and their residences. Some saints inscribed effective charms, others turned hostile Muslims into dwarves or calmed threatening floodwaters. Some Muslims who were about to attack Jews were turned into columns. Some were killed by a female saint's sword. Others went mad or were immobilized, their legs stuck in sand.[17]

All these and many other tales and legends are part of traditions illustrating the complex interrelationship that prevailed between the Jewish minority and Muslim majority in the framework of saint veneration in Morocco. Some of these traditions may be of an etiological nature, created to explain attitudes and ways of life that crystallized in the course of centuries of coexistence and have been shaped by many different factors. Jews were willing to promote veneration of their saints because it contributed to their survival in an environment that was sometimes hostile. Their self-confidence was also bolstered by the knowledge that they could rely on more protectors than Divine Providence alone. On a practical level, visits to saints—with the resulting intermingling of Jews from different regions in a relaxed, outdoor atmosphere—heightened the sense of Jewish unity and identity. The much-vaunted strength of the saints acted as a deterrent to inimical outside forces. The powerless minority seeking security found a highly effective protective mechanism in the countless miracle tales of punishments inflicted on Muslims who harmed Jews or Jewish saints.

When considering veneration of the same saints by Jews and Muslims in Morocco, the possibility presents itself that improvising appropriate local solutions may be an expression of a way of thinking inherent in human nature. Even if this is so, however, it does not sufficiently explain the phenomenon; the mutuality must be examined in terms of sacred and profane. Veneration of saints is essentially a religious phenomenon nourished by ancient sources and myths. As such, the experience in its unique local form should be investigated within the framework of the history of religions.

The attitude of traditional societies to their homes and sanctuaries is well known.[18] Both Muslim and Jewish societies are basically traditional, and they accepted and shared similar concepts of sacred times and holy places. The large number of Jewish saints in Morocco, the fact that every village venerated at least one saint it considered its own, in effect created a protected territorial continuum within which Jews could feel secure. The chain of saints' tombs encompassed the entire geographical area and gave the Jews their own living space, as it were. Sacred times, too—the *ziyara* and *hillulah* which sometimes continued for weeks—constituted an additional factor that made it possible to carry out the celebrations without fear of disturbance.

Nature and time are invested with a religious dimension respected even in ancient days by both Jews and Muslims. Sacred sites possess laws of their own that must be obeyed by all; violation of these laws always evokes punishment. This religious-traditional outlook characterized both Jewish and Muslim society in Morocco, and encouraged everyone to obey those laws irrespective of religious, social or legal status. Thus it is immaterial that a Jew was a *dhimmi* or disdained and humiliated. The holiness of Jewish saints, particularly when proven to be useful and effective, was itself enough to prompt the Muslims to avail themselves of these saints. Of course, the same applied—although to a much lesser degree—to the Jews' attitude toward Muslim saints. The religious outlook, then, was the framework sustaining the phenomenon of joint saint veneration, together with other factors that abet the manifestation.

With regard to Muslim appropriation of Jewish saints, it should be noted that Jews continued to venerate those saints—or at least to maintain and perpetuate Jewish traditions associated with them. When such a situation was sustained over a long period of time, it sometimes seemed as if the Jews were worshipping a Muslim saint—another example of joint veneration of a saint whom both groups claim as their own.

The feeling of Jewish identity, accompanied by an overall sense of a Jewish mission, and the spiritual uplift inherent in the performance of sacred acts, were vital factors in reinforcing saint veneration among the Jews. It may be that the extensive diffusion of the cult and the great fame of Jewish saints influenced Muslims' attachment to them—and also indirectly affected their attitude toward the Jews. Throughout the Muslim cultural sphere, veneration of Jewish saints is known and accepted. The attraction of Jews to Muslim saints was apparently limited by Muslim denigration of Jews and the Jewish conviction that their saints were superior to Muslim ones.

This appraisal of the mutual relationships prevailing between Jews and Muslims in the framework of saint worship in Morocco offers a model for understanding similar manifestations in the Muslim world.

Notes

1. L. Voinot (1948, p. 51) describes 45 Jewish saints also venerated by Muslims, 14 Muslim saints also venerated by Jews and 31 saints claimed by both Jews and Muslims. It is clear from this report that the Muslims worshipped all Jewish saints described in the book.
2. Even the famous saint R. David Ha-Levi Draʿ was the subject of such a threat: E. Doutté (1914, pp. 211–12). Christians too visited Jewish saints: A. van Gennep (1914, p. 45).
3. Our esoteric approach is in accordance with the theory developed by W. H. Jansen (1965, pp. 43–51). Our material is based only on evidence by Jewish informants regarding their image in their own eyes and how they believed they were considered by the Muslims. An ideal approach would require the study of the subject independently among Jews and Muslims of the same region, but for technical reasons we were unable to undertake such a methodological study.
4. The list comprises the following Jewish saints (with their Muslim designations given in brackets): R. Abraham Awriwer (Sidi Brahim), R. Abraham Cohen (Mulay Matil), R. Abraham Makhluf Ben-Yaḥya, R. Abraham Mul Annes, R. Abraham Toledano, R. Aharon Cohen (Sidi Qadi Ḥaja), R. Aharon Ha-Cohen of Demnate (Sidi Harun or Sidi Mul Lbrakhat), Ait Bu-Aharon, Ait El-Cohen of Amzerkou, Ait El-Cohen of Imini, Ait El-Cohen of Talate, Ait El-Cohen of Tamnougalt, R. ʿAmram Ben-Diwan, R. Daniel Hashomer Ashkenazi (Sidi Denil), R. Daud, R. David Ben-Barukh of Azrou n'Bahamou, R. David Ben-Yamin (Sidi Kherwiʿa), R. David Ha-Levi Draʿ, R. David Naḥmias (Rabbi Dawid Ḥamias), R. David

U-Moshe (Rabbi Dawid U-Mussi), R. Eliʿezer Turei-Zahav, El-Khwatat, R. Ḥabib Ha-Mizraḥi (Mulay Tadot or Nwar-Shams), R. Ḥananiah Ha-Cohen (R. Aminia Ha-Cohen), R. Ḥayyim (Mula Khira or Sidi Khira), R. Ḥayyim Ben-Diwan (Mul Anrhaz), R. Ḥayyim Ha-Mizraḥi (Sidi Ḥiyyim), R. Ḥayyim Lashqar, Ḥazzan El-Ḥili, Imin wa-Mumen, R. Khalifa Ben-Malka, Lalla Miryam, Lalla Rivqah of Bene-Moshe (Sidi Bel-ʿAbbas), Lalla Saʿada Bent-Ashqluḥ (Lalla Saʿada Bint-Esqlakh), Lalla Sol Ha-Tsaddiqah (Lalla Solica or Sol Ḥatshuel), R. Makhluf Ben-Yosef of Kasba Tadla (Sidi Mul El-Qantra), R. Makhluf Ben-Yosef Abiḥatsira (Bayo), R. Masʿud (Sidi Moḥammed ʿAbbud), Meʿarat Oufran, R. Mordekhay Turjman, R. Moshe Ben-Zohra (Mulay Twabit), R. Moshe Cohen (Mul Amegdol or Sidi Tseddiq), R. Moshe Mimun (Saḥib El-Jnun or Sidi Mimun), Mulay Ighi, Mulay Inguird, Mulay Tamran, Mul Azadh, Mul El-Bit, Mul Jebel El-Kebir (Mul Jebel El-Khdar), Mul Terya, Mul Timḥdart (Nwadain), Mwalin El-Gomra, R. Nissim Ben-Nissim of Ait Bayoud, Qayid El-Ghaba (Sayyid El-Yahud), R. Raphael Anqawa, R. Raphael Ha-Cohen of Achbarou (Mul Ashbaru), R. Saʿadiah Dades (Rabbi Saʿadia Datsi), Sepher Tislit, R. Shaul Ha-Cohen (Rabbi Sawil), R. Shelomoh ʿAmar, R. Shelomoh Ben-Lḥans of Aghbalou (Mul Asguine), R. Shimʿon Cohen of Ikherkhouren (Sidi Ikhrakhorn or Tiqi El-Bor), Sidi Abraham, Sidi Moshe (Sidi Mussi), Sidi Mussa of Sous, Sidi Sayyid, Sidi Yaʿqub, R. Sliman Abayu, Tsaddiq Azru, Tuqshusht, Ulad Zemmur, R. Yaʿaqob Ashkenazi (Mul Anmay or Mul Almay), R. Yaʿaqob Bardiʿi, R. Yaʿaqob Naḥmias, R. Yaʿaqob Roshdi, R. Yaḥya Ben-Yaḥya (Sidi Qadi Ḥaja), R. Yaḥya Laḥlu (Abar), R. Yamin Tsabbaḥ, R. Yannay Mul Lmekhfiya (Ait Bu-Ḥlu or Tabuḥalut), R. Yehudah Ben-Baba, R. Yehudah Ben-Yisraʾel Ha-Levi (Mwalin Tassabrant), R. Yehudah U-Reʾuben (Baba Yehuda U-Robin), R. Yehudah Zabali (Sidi Bel-ʿAbbas), R. Yisraʾel Abiḥatsira, R. Yitsḥaq Ben-Walid, R. Yitsḥaq Levi, R. Yitsḥaq Yisraʾel Ha-Levi (Mul El-Barj or Sidi Moḥammed El-Mashzuz or Sidi Moḥammed El-Mukhfi), R. Yonah Daudi, R. Yosef Bajayo and R. Yosef Pinto of Ouarzazate. L. Voinot (1948) describes 55 saints in this group, all included in our list. Nine more saints described by Voinot as claimed by both Jews and Muslims we have unequivocally identified as Jewish saints: R. Aharon Cohen, R. Daniel Hashomer Ashkenazi, R. Moshe Mimun, Sidi Yaʿqub, R. Yaʿaqob Ashkenazi, R. Yaḥya Laḥlu, R. Yannay Mul El-Mekhfiya, R. Yehudah Zabali and R. Yitsḥaq Yisraʾel Ha-Levi. The status of R. Makhluf Ben-Yosef Abiḥatsira, Meʿarat Oufran and Sepher Tislit was unclear to Voinot.

5. This list comprises 36 saints claimed by both Jews and Muslims: R. Abraham Ben-Shuqrun (Sidi Moḥammed Ben-Shuqrun), R. Daud Cohen (Sahul or Sidi Moḥammed Sahlay), R. ʿEli Ben-Yitsḥaq, Ḥazzan of Tirhermine, Irhir Izid, Kebur Shu, Lalla Qafia, Lalla Safia of Agadir, Lalla Taqerquzt, Mulay Sedra, Mulay Tabia, Mulay Yaʿqub, Mul Bghi Bghi (Sidi Bu-Ibrirḥan), Sayyid El-Merhirha (Sidi ʿAbd El-Malk), R. Shelomoh Bar-Beriro, Sidi ʿAbbud, Sidi Belyut, Sidi Brahim (Sidi Braham), Sidi Bu-ʿAissa U-Sliman, Sidi Bu-Dheb (Sidi Bu-Adham), Sidi Bu-Lanwar, Sidi Ftaḥ Ben-Sliman, Sidi Harun of Touggana, Sidi Ḥmad El-Kamel, Sidi Irhrem n'Iduidhen (Sidi Igharm Idwid), Sidi Makhluf, Sidi Mhasser, Sidi Moḥammed U-Belqassem, Sidi Mussa U-Saleḥ, Sidi Rghit (Sidi Rahit), Tsaddiq Kelaʿat Al-Mguna, R. Yaḥya Ben-Dossa, R. Yaḥya Ben-Yosef (Sidi Siyyaḥ), R. Yitsḥaq Ben-Sliman, R. Yosef Ben-Shemaʿyah (Sidi Yussif El-Ḥaj), and R. Yosef Ha-Galili. L. Voinot (1948) cites 31 saints in this category: 22 of them appear in the list above, while 9 others were identified in this study as Jewish saints also worshipped by Muslims; they appear in note 4 above. Lalla Taqerquzt is included by Voinot among Muslim saints also venerated by Jews. More extensive research would undoubtedly lead to the conclusion that most of these saints are Jewish, as I have proven with respect to R. Daniel Hashomer Ashkenazi.
6. Amongst the Muslim saints visited by Jews are: Lalla Jamila in Tangier, a holy rock near the seacoast much frequented by both Jewish and Muslim women desirous of offspring; in Salé, Sidi Bel ʿAbbas and Sidi Bu-Ḥaḥa; in Rabat, Mulay El-Mqi Ben-Moḥammed, Sidi ʿAli Bu-Arḥa and Sidi Makhluf, a Jew who converted to Islam and became a saint among the Muslims; in Ksar El-Kebir, Sidi ʿAli Bu-Gallab, and near Sefrou, the source of Sidi Eli Bu-Srin; in Imidar, in the Western Atlas, Sidi El-Qosh; in the Ansgmir valley, in the Eastern Atlas, Sidi ʿAyyash, which the Jews were allowed to visit only after the French occupation; in Felloush, near Debdou, Sidi ʿAli Belqassem, and in nearby Alouana, Sidi ʿAbd El-Malk; in Tizimi, north of Tafilalet, Mulay Brahim Ben Bu-Lallal. Sidi Raḥal had to be visited secretly because the Muslims forbade the Jews to enter his tomb. This information is essentially based on L. Voinot (1948, pp. 39–47). See also J. Goulven (1927, p. 97).
7. For example, Muslims guards were at the sanctuaries of R. Abraham Cohen, R. Abraham Makhluf Ben-Yaḥya, R. ʿAmram Ben-Diwan, R. David Alshqar, R. David Ben-Yamin, R. David U-Moshe, R. Ḥabib Ha-Mizraḥi, R. Ḥayyim Ben-ʿAttar, R. Makhluf Ben-Yosef

Abiḥatsira, R. Moshe Cohen, Mulay Ighi, R. Saʿadiah Dades and R. Shelomoh Ben-Tameshut.

8. Tradition tells that R. David Ben-Barukh and R. Yehudah U-Reʾuben brought Muslim messengers back from Morocco to the Holy Land in an instant with a still-warm loaf of bread in their hands; further, by pronouncing the Tetragrammaton, R. Makhluf Ben-Yosef Abiḥatsira transferred his Muslim messenger to Fez in a trice.
9. Barren Muslim women gave birth with the help of R. ʿAmram Ben-Diwan, R. David Ha-Levi Draʿ, R. Yaḥya Laḥlu, and Mul Timḥ-dart. R. Aharon Ha-Cohen of Demnate cured a girl of her blindness by passing his hands over her eyes. R. Abraham Cohen healed a paralyzed Muslim, while R. Daniel Hashomer Ashkenazi healed a sheikh's son who had been afflicted with epilepsy. Jews were not always pleased to see Muslims near the saint's tomb. Under no circumstances would they allow Muslims to sleep at the tomb.
10. See Abbé Poiret (1789. *Voyage en Berbérie.* Paris, p. 133).
11. See E. Westermarck (1926, vol. 1, p. 163; vol. 2, pp. 256–86); H. Schwarzbaum (1975, pp. 260–65); F. Legey (1926, p. 126); E. Doutté (1905, pp. 383–89).
12. R. Attal (1978. "Deux légendes rabbiniques tunisiennes," in *Cahiers de Littérature Orale,* no. 4, pp. 186–90).
13. The pasha of R. David U-Moshe's area used to send four sheep to the saint's *hillulah.* El-Glawi, the pasha of Marrakech famed for his generosity, used to visit the tombs of saints such as R. Ḥananiah Ha-Cohen and Mulay Ighi, and send them donations.
14. Punishment for desecration of Jewish holy sites or persons is one of the most popular motifs in Jewish folktales from Islamic countries: E. Marcus (1983, pp. 337–66). For the same motif in Eastern Europe, see: D. Ben-Amos and J. R. Mintz (1970, pp. 301–02).
15. R. David Ha-Levi Draʿ, R. Hillel Ha-Cohen, and R. Yitsḥaq Levi were killed by robbers who demanded their money. R. David Abiḥatsira and R. Yitsḥaq Abiḥatsira sacrificed their own lives in order to save the Jews of the *mellaḥ,* who were in danger of annihilation. They stood directly in front of the cannon but were not killed, so the Muslims tied R. Yitsḥaq to the barrel of the cannon and R. David to a Muslim, in order to kill them. R. ʿEli Ben-Yitsḥaq brought back to life a slaughtered cow over whose meat two Muslims were quarreling; when they saw his miraculous powers, they killed him, buried him in a Muslim cemetery and erected a tombstone. R. Yisra'el Cohen and R. Shelomoh Ben-Tameshut, on the other hand, were killed by Muslims because they refused to have intercourse with Muslim women; see also J. Bénech (1940, pp.

181–84). Sol Ha-Tsaddiqah was murdered for refusing to marry the sultan. Other legends tell that she refused to marry a Muslim or to have intercourse with him, or that she refused to convert to Islam. R. David Ben-Safet was killed by Muslims and buried outside the wall of the cemetery in Marrakech. Sidi Sayyid was murdered by Muslims and buried in their cemetery, but afterwards his grave rolled until it reached the Jewish cemetery. R. Shelomoh Cohen, killed by Arabs, was also buried in a Muslim cemetery. However, a Jewish woman who was living with a Muslim reported this to the Jews, and thanks to the saint, she returned to her own people. Bent El-Ḥmus saved the lives of several rabbis who had been falsely accused of giving Muslims wine; she "confessed" that she had given the wine and was killed in their stead, thus becoming a saint. R. Mordekhay Ben-ʿAttar and R. Mordekhay Ben-Sal were illustrious *paytanim* whom the sultan commanded to call the Muslim worshippers from the minaret of the mosque. Preferring martyrdom, they leaped to their deaths in the courtyard and were buried side by side.

16. F. Legey (1926, p. 8).
17. Other tales tell that R. Aharon Assulin of Fercla and R. Mordekhay Ben-ʿAttar inscribed amulets which kept the enemy from entering the city. R. Eliʿezer Davila once turned into dwarves Muslims who wanted to kill Jews; another time he calmed the sea, which was about to flood the city, while cautioning the king, who was standing at his side, not to harm the Jews. With her sword Lalla Rivqah of the Bene-Moshe killed soldiers of the sultan who had come to attack the Jews. A Muslim who used to beat up Jews went insane thanks to the power of R. Aharon Ha-Cohen of Demnate. Bandits who wanted to attack Jews were paralyzed and stuck in the sand by the powers of R. Yehudah Ben-Shabbat and R. Yosef Zozot. A Muslim woman who lived next to the cemetery in which R. Yaḥya Laḥlu was interred saw a man dressed in green run with a rifle and shoot Muslims who tried to attack Jews on the *Sabbath* Eve. Mul Timḥdart raised a violent rainstorm to keep Muslims from harming Jews; another time, mounted on a white horse, he put the enemy to flight. One night Sepher Tislit took white horses out to fight the Muslim attackers of the city who were mounted on horseback and armed with stones, and he defeated them. A shereef who wanted to harm the Jews by decreeing that they must not blow the *shofar* on *Yom Kippur,* and who also tried to damage the tree of R. ʿAmram Ben-Diwan, paid for both crimes with his life.
18. See M. Eliade (1965); (1969).

14

SAINT WORSHIP AS PRACTICED BY JEWS AND MUSLIMS IN MOROCCO

An understanding of saint worship among the Jews of Morocco is enhanced by an appraisal of the comparable cult developed by North Africa's Muslims who are known throughout the Muslim world for their particularly strong veneration of saints. Such a comparison must point out those aspects shared by Jews and Muslims, and those which are uniquely characteristic of each group. In the absence of a comprehensive theory of Moroccan Jewish folklore, two provisional hypotheses may be posited:

1. By their very nature, the circumstances of saint veneration impose similar cultic manifestations on diverse groups of believers; therefore, the phenomenon ought not to be construed as necessarily the result of reciprocal influence.

2. Pursuant to the theory of reinforcement,[1] different phenomena typical respectively of Jews and Muslims were strengthened by contact between the two groups.

Before comparisons may be drawn, a general description of the nature of saint worship as practiced by the Muslims should be noted. As Goldhizer notes: "Influenced by a variety of factors, some psychological and some historical, the phenomenon of [saint] veneration developed and quickly became entrenched throughout Islam, despite the fact that it conflicted with the Islamic conception of divinity and was not congenial to the Suni spirit; among certain strata of Muslim believers the importance of this cult surpasses the importance of the religious principles themselves and it becomes the quintessence of faith-conscious activity among the masses."[2] Many scholars are of the opinion that the cult of sainthood reached its highest point in North Africa.[3] If there is truth in Bergson's statement that the world is a machine for creating gods, then North Africa can lay claim to over-zealous creativity: the number of saints worshipped there, large as it was already, is still growing.[4]

It seems to me that two facts emerge from an in-depth study of the cult among North African Muslims. First, in many aspects it is surprisingly similar to the cult among the Jews, particularly in its ceremonial-practical dimension and in its devotion to dead saints. These similarities might suggest that Jewish and Muslim cults can be viewed as different aspects of the same phenomenon. The second fact that emerges, however, is that these cults are two distinct and highly diverse phenomena. This becomes absolutely clear upon consideration of the social dimension of the Muslim cultic organization and the specific activities that are exclusive to the numerous North African Muslim religious orders.[5]

The first important point to be noted is that most Muslim saints are venerated during their lifetimes.[6] These individuals are endowed with a divine gift — the *baraka* — a much-sought-after quality they possess to such a degree that people consider them saints. In the forefront of those who have the *baraka* are the *shorfa* or shereefs, descendants of Moḥammed's daughter Fatima.[7] Their number and influence in Morocco is very large, particularly if one includes those who claim they are shereefs.[8] Others who also have the *baraka* are descendants of marabouts, saints who are not shereefs but are otherwise endowed with the hereditary gift. Of course, as with the shereefs, not all descendants are endowed with the same measure of *baraka,* nor will they all become saints: to be sainted a person must possess enough *baraka* to be able to perform miracles. Jewish tradition does not require relationship with a Biblical hero or any other illustrious figure in Jewry; it certainly does not bestow a special religious status, such as that enjoyed by the shereefs with respect to Moḥammed. Nevertheless, in the cases of a few special families headed by such well-known saintly figures as Abiḥatsira, Pinto and Cohen, there are indications that the legacy of sainthood may be transmitted.[9] Their offspring enjoy inherited prerogatives, although not all of them will attain sainthood. Thus although the phenomenon is similar, the proportions are different. While among the Muslims this legacy is the basis on which the religious orders discussed below are founded, among the Jews the manifestation is much attenuated, appearing in only a few families, with no framework that is in any way comparable to that of the Muslim orders.

How, then, does a person become a saint in North African communities? If he is not a direct descendant of Moḥammed, there are certain other proven ways for a Muslim to achieve sainthood while he is still alive and/or after his death. One way is direct transference of the saint's sanctity to another person, who then acquires the *baraka.* In the belief that the saint's holiness is disseminated to his immediate surroundings, the first to receive such emanations is the *muqaddam,* who serves the saint as long as he lives and, when he dies, tends his grave.[10] The saint may also transfer the *baraka* to a devotee, who thereafter may transmit it to his own offspring.[11] Among the Jews there are trustees or officials at the saint's tomb who acquire special status and to whom people turn for help, but the present study found no instances of such officials themselves becoming saints. Even Lalla Luna Bat-Khalifa, who tended to the needs and guarded the sanctuary of R. Yehudah Gadol Gilʿad, did not become sainted by virtue of those deeds, but rather in recognition of her own devout, exemplary life.

One category of Muslim saints that has no counterpart among the Jews comprises warrior-saints—the *Mujahidin*—who fought the Christians in the sixteenth century.[12] Another important group among the Muslims but non-existent among the Jews is recruited from the *mejdub,* mentally ill or deranged people whom Muslims believe are close to God.[13] As with those who claim to be shereefs, the special status and many advantages accorded psychologically disturbed people has produced some odd and not always credible eccentrics. The present study uncovered one such case among the Jews, that of R. Re'uben Azini, whose behavior was considered erratic; nevertheless, he was sainted not because of his peculiar conduct, but because his predictions always came true.

All religions award extremely righteous and ultra-pious individuals with sainthood. This also occurs among Jews and Muslims in North Africa, although again each group evinces different modes of endowment. Among the Muslims, exemplary behavior may endow a living person with sainthood. Among the Jews, however, this would only be a stepping-stone, a significant yet not exclusive element leading to sainthood—and even then only after death. Jews demand unremitting and all-encompassing exemplary behavior. Among the Muslims one finds saints who are thieves, drunkards or sexually promiscuous.[14] This would be inconceivable for Jews.

In both societies sainthood is usually bestowed on a person of outstanding erudition, devotion, and compassion, one who is an extreme ascetic and often fasts for long periods. Jews, however, do not attribute mystic acts to their saints as do the Muslims, who, for example, revere Sidi ʿAbd El-Kader Djilani, who stood on one foot for thirty years, and Sidi Moḥammed Busif, who often submerged himself in water up to his neck for hours at a time.[15] Nor have the Jews adopted the custom so widespread among the Muslims of retiring to a mountain-top to live a solitary life of self-denial.[16]

The most significant and characteristic development among the Muslims is undoubtedly the emergence of the religious orders and their *zawias,* centers of cultic and social activities.[17] They were associated with the Sufism that reached North Africa in the eleventh century, although they did not become significant forces until the beginning of the sixteenth century. Dragué[18] considers such groups of people organized around a living or dead saint as extremely heretical; he condemns the orders as particularistic, sustained as they are by exclusively Moroccan or regional folk traditions.

Each religious fraternity in Morocco is associated with a founder who is a saint. Most of these institutions have established rules and regulations that are binding on their members. The large fraternities are subdivided into smaller centers or *zawias* which, with their subsidiary branches, are also known as *tariqa.* The more important orders opened branches outside of Morocco, sometimes throughout North Africa. Descendants of the order's founder, or others who claimed some connection with the founder, constantly tried to expand the fraternity and strengthen its base through a variety of activities: mediating individual, family or tribal disputes; establishing sanctuaries; protecting wayfarers or residents against attacks from outside; encouraging commerce; conducting weddings; and so forth. Through such activities certain orders acquired political strength that extended beyond their own regions; this in turn elicited vigorous action by the central government to limit the activities of marabouts and fraternities to exclusively religious spheres.[19]

An understanding of these religious orders is a prerequisite for understanding the role of the Muslim saint, who while alive functions within the order and whose activities and authority are defined by his leading position.[20] Praise is accorded the leader of the religious order because of his genealogical connection with the saint who founded the order, and sometimes because of his merit. Association of the Muslim saint with the religious order determined the patterns of his activity and behavior and, in large measure, formed the ideological basis of Muslim saint veneration in Morocco.

Among the Jews, the rituals of saint worship centered around the tombs of dead saints. Although there are cases of people becoming sainted before their deaths,—including R. Yaʿaqob Abiḥatsira, R. Ḥayyim Pinto, R. Pinḥas Ha-Cohen, R. Raphael Anqawa—they are few. Among the Muslims, on the other hand, while worship of dead saints is widespread and important, most cultic ritual focuses on living saints or is practiced within orders run by descendants of a revered founder. This characteristic is very significant, because the link to a living saint will be very different from the connection to one who is deceased. However, in both cases, the saint is close to God and thus a source of benediction to the devotees.

In this context it is interesting to consider the attributes of Muslim saints as described by other scholars and compare them with those of Jewish saints discovered in the present study. Gellner[21] defines the *agurram*—the Berber designation for a saint—as one who is descended from Moḥammed, is visibly a recipient of divine blessing or *baraka,* mediates between men and God, arbitrates between men and men, dispenses blessings, possesses magical powers, is a good and pious man, observes the Qur'anic precepts, is rich, hospitable and generous, does not fight or engage in feuds, and turns the other cheek. Jewish saints do not manifest all these qualities, although they may possess some of them.[22] They mediate between people and God and arbitrate differences between one person and another; they do so in their lifetimes, as did R. David Ben-Barukh and R. Raphael Anqawa, and fulfill similar roles after death when adversaries come to the saint's graveside to seal agreements. They observe all religious precepts prescribed by Judaism and are expected to be generous and loving—although several saints, among them R. Ḥayyim Pinto the

Younger, were better known for their terrible wrath and devastating curses. The most important characteristic of a Jewish saint is his ability to perform miraculous deeds—above all, to bestow curative blessings. The Berbers, too, view a saint's ability to heal as a highly significant quality.

Along with emphasizing his shereef ancestry, an *agurram* will make every effort to publicize the miracles he has brought about, something that would be unheard of for a Jewish saint. The *agurram* lives on the contributions of his venerators and petitioners. His wealth is an indication and function of his success and power, and it enhances his status as an *agurram.* Among the Jews, while certain saints such as R. Ḥayyim Pinto the Younger and R. Meir ʿArama subsisted on alms, they lived modestly, with no thought of flaunting affluence for personal aggrandizement. Moreover, income from contributions to a dead saint is earmarked for the poor who visit the grave or live in the immediate vicinity.

There is an important difference between the two cults with regard to displays of advocacy by the saints. A Muslim saint refrains from taking sides in a fight. This is not necessarily because he is peace-loving, but because partisanship expressed in unrestrained behavior might invite failure and thereby jeopardize his sainthood or influence. A Jewish saint would never be worried about such things.

To summarize, it is evident that a Muslim saint, although presumably endowed—like a Jewish saint—with special qualities that distinguish him or her from other people, nevertheless fulfills certain defined social functions, some of them under internal as well as external pressure or conflict that lead him to succumb to human feebleness like ordinary mortals. Jewish saints are never exposed to such situations and thus do not show such signs of weakness. Hence it emerges that what Jewish and Muslim saints have in common are the very qualities defined by Gellner as the essence of sainthood.

Dermenghem[23] differentiates between "popular" and "serious" saints, both of whom he considers typical of Islam. Popular saints are more prevalent in North Africa; an integral part of local tradition, their actual historic existence is not clear. Obscure, stereotypical figures, they perform amazing miracles: they fly from place to place, sail the seas on carpets, produce rain and so forth. Serious saints, on the other hand, are usually erudite, historical figures specifically treated in hagiographic literature. Popular saints compete with one another, are easily angered and may be harmful. Serious saints are capable of performing miracles, but they do not consider this their major function.

Among the Jews, as well, a few actual, historic individuals have been sainted. There is no doubt, however, that most Jewish saints are what Dermenghem describes among the Muslims as "popular" saints, or else historical persons whose factual stories have been forgotten and long since replaced by fantastic legends.

It is interesting to note in this connection that the Islamic tendency to group saints hierarchically[24] does not exist in Jewry. Fame and veneration of Jewish saints in North Africa was a function of the miraculous deeds they performed: some were more famous and some less, regardless of their genealogy or why they were originally recognized as saints.

According to Goldziher,[25] the qualities enumerated in Islamic literature as characterizing Muslim saints include bringing the dead back to life and the ability to converse with the dead (and with other saints). These saints can also dry up a body of water or walk on water, transform one substance into another, nullify distance, converse with plants and animals, cure sickness, tame wild beasts by talking to them, eliminate time or make it stand still. A saint's prayers are always answered. A saint can predict the future and warn of imminent catastrophe; survive for long periods of time without food and water but also eat unlimited quantities; control natural functions (as in curing a toothache); see things that are happening far away; when necessary, change his or her external appearance and become terrifying. The saint's body is preserved by God and never decays; God destroys anything that may injure the saint. These qualities, most of which also characterize Jewish saints, express an element of belief in the transcendental power of saints, and they are an intrinsic part of the very essence of saint worship, particularly as practiced in the cultural milieu discussed here.

Healing is one of the fields dealt with intensively by both Jewish and Muslim saints. The rhythmically repeated refrain "*Hawwa ja yidawina, hawwa ja*"—"He has come to cure us, he has come"—is probably Moroccan Jewry's most popular verse. It apparently originated with the many visitors who crowded around the saint's grave seeking miraculous cures. "He has come to cure us" encapsulates not only the miraculous healing but the leitmotif of the saint's greatness: at this charmed hour the saint himself appears in response to the prayers of his disciples.

Curing is one of the most important functions of every cult of sainthood in the world. The basic difference between Jews and Muslims in this regard is that among the latter healing is actively undertaken by living marabouts, with dead saints playing a relatively minor role; among the Jews, however, healing was almost exclusively the province of dead saints. As a result, those aspects of healing that rely on the help of a dead saint are fairly similar in both groups, although the proportions are relatively different. Like the Jews, the Muslims, too, turn to saints' tombs for complete cure, for the healing power of a living saint is often limited to certain illnesses. This power is transferable; it can be conferred, for example, on one who has previously been cured of a certain illness or it can be bequeathed to the saint's progeny. In addition, a Muslim saint can pass on his speciality: Sid El-Mandri of Fez bequeathed his ability to cure swellings to his offspring. Dead saints also specialize in curing certain diseases or treating specific conditions, and this phenomenon is similar in the two groups. Jews suffering from nervous disorders went to R. Daniel Hashomer Ashkenazi, while similarly afflicted Muslims went to Sidi Yaḥya of Birmandreis.

Many customs associated with miraculous healing at the sanctuaries are common to Jews and Muslims. Sleeping at the graveside—widely known as *"incubatio,"*[26] a tried and tested treatment—was equally prevalent in both groups. The sufferer slept at the sanctuary until he or she was cured or the saint told them in a dream when they would get better—or sent them to another saint for the cure. *Incubatio* became so deep-rooted a custom that the very act of sleeping at the sanctuary was eventually construed as a remedy. Sleeping near the saint's grave in itself signified an appeal for cure; this applied particularly to the mentally ill, epileptics and those suffering from nervous disorders. Both Jews and Muslims believed that mental and nervous disorders could only be cured by the intervention of saints; relatives therefore brought those suffering from such maladies to a shrine and tied them overnight to the grave or to a tree nearby.

Both Jews and Muslims believed in the principle of sympathetic magic, meaning that whatever is in contact with the sanctuary is imbued with holiness and can help cure the sick. Jews left bottles of water or oil at the grave overnight and then massaged painful parts of the body with the sanctified liquid. Or they left gold and silver jewelry and coins there, and later used them as charms. Muslims did likewise, also attributing acquired magical qualities to ribbons and bits of cloth hung at the holy site. The Muslim practice of treating such ribbons and bits of cloth as well as pieces from the grave's cover as charms for good health that maybe carried off is, on the other hand, an almost unknown custom among the Jews.

Some of the most frequent and important appeals to saints pertained to family affairs. Muslims and Jews both expected the saint to intervene effectively in everything connected with marriage: fertility, sexual problems, protecting infants. Barren Muslim women sought the help of a living saint[27] or visited a dead saint's grave, just as did barren Jewish women. In this sphere sympathetic magic was frequently invoked, including using a belt that had been left on a saint's grave overnight, or picking up a stone or stick that had been near the grave and passing it over a barren woman's stomach.

Jews and Muslims also perceived the connection between saints and animals in much the same way. Lions, snakes and doves are the creatures most frequently referred to by both groups. When any one of these appeared in a place presumably occupied by a saint, it was interpreted as proof of the saint's presence—or at least a sign that a suppliant's request had been granted. In one sense, this seems to confute the fact that the saint and animal are one and the same.[28] Other testimony reflects the belief that saints can appear as animals.[29] Such convictions may derive from a belief in reincarnation or may be an acknowledgement that a saint is so enmeshed with the world of nature that he can control natural forces as he sees fit (and believers bring numerous proofs of this ability). Whichever the case may be, this is a further expression of the close bond between saints and the natural world.

Animals often appear not as guardians of the saint, but to exact retribution for an injury he has suffered. These animals are the medium through which the saint reveals his presence; at the same time, however, they are entirely under his control. The Muslims' Sidi Belyut and Sidi Raḥal and the Jews' R. Shaul Naḥmias are known to have tamed ferocious lions. One of the most famous icons of a saint in North Africa depicts R. Ephraim Anqawa[30] astride a lion, with a snake as reins. The saint's perfect wholeness, then, is expressed not only in his relationship with people, but with animals and the world of nature as well. In this context there is a specific difference in principle between North Africa's Jews and Muslims: Jews did not believe there are sanctified animals who are bearers of the *baraka* (like the marabout-animals referred to by Doutté[31]); for Jews, animals were significant only insofar as they are related to a saint.

The ability to nullify distance is another trait shared by Jewish and Muslim saints. They can instantaneously transport themselves, and others, too, over great distances. Elsewhere in this work I have mentioned the feat performed by R. Makhluf Ben-Yosef Abiḥatsira. A parallel tale is told about Mulay ʿAbd El-Kader, who transported a pilgrim carrying a loaf of bread that was still hot when he reached Mecca. Westermarck[32] tells how saints reputedly transferred holy sites from Mecca to Morocco; no such phenomenon is found among Jews, however.

The saints of both groups can influence the course of natural forces. During a drought, Muslims would turn to a Muslim saint,[33] but as already noted, if they petitioned in vain, they would ask for rain from a Jewish saint whom they thought might succeed where the Muslim had not. (I have not come across any evidence indicating that Jews would petition a Muslim saint for rain.) Both Jewish and Muslim saints have the power to keep a body of water from overflowing and can also make the sun stand still. A Jewish saint always exercises the latter power on a Friday, prior to his death, so that he may be buried before the advent of the *Sabbath.* A Muslim saint stops the sun in its tracks for other purposes, such as to enable a woman to get home before darkness falls.

Jews and Muslims both considered a saint's prophetic ability an important attribute. Muslims ascribe this ability above all to the *mejdub,* psychologically disturbed saints who are approached with questions about the future. Among both Jews and Muslims, saints prophesy on the communal as well as the individual level; they foretell attacks on the *mellaḥ* or village and can predict regional or national conflicts.[34]

Another belief common to both Jews and Muslims is that a saint does not actually die; he or she can reappear in reality as well as in a person's dream. The most frequent reason for a saint's appearance is to save an endangered person or place. In the visions related to the protection of a *mellaḥ* or village, the saint usually appears fully armed astride a white horse, prepared to engage the enemy in battle. The certainty that the saint is guarding him or the *mellaḥ* against the Muslims, as described in so many legends, imbued Jews with a sense of security. Muslims, too, find comfort and security in the saint's protection against hostile tribes or such external foes as the Christians.[35]

After their death Muslim saints, like Jewish saints, meet to study together; people testify that they have seen them engaged in this activity or heard their voices. Among the Jews, such groups are usually small, comprising saints who are buried in the same area. But among the Muslims, they form a council of saints who meet at permanent venues to take decisions affecting the future of the world, or to go on pilgrimage to Mecca together.[36] The present study found no evidence, however, of a Muslim saint studying the Qur'an with an eminent Islamic scholar, the way Jewish saints traditionally study with Elijah the Prophet.

Like the Jews, the Muslims have some saints whom they believe are buried in more than one place. One Muslim saint is called Sidi Taher Bu-Qabrain, meaning "owner of two graves," and a female saint is known as Lalla Azzou Oum-Qabrain. Some Muslim traditions maintain that a saint's body is omnipresent, or that each grave contains only a part of the body, as in the case of Sidi Moḥammed El-Ḥadj, patron saint of Tangier. The notion of a divided body is inconceivable among the Jews, for it would conflict with the Judaic belief in future redemption.

Another phenomenon among the Muslims that is unknown among the Jews relates to the sanctification of objects such as buildings, trees or stones near which a saint has rested or prayed.[37] Visits are made to light candles at these places, even though the saint's grave is not there.

Jewish and Muslim saints have many character traits in common. Both groups are aware that the saint bears within himself a dual power for good and evil with equal potency. Petitioners therefore approach saints of both religions with respect and, to forestall harm, sedulously avoid insulting or angering them.[38] As has been noted, a saint's curse is very severe and can bring catastrophe to a community as well as to an individual. For the Muslims, such a curse can cause a city to fall to the enemy, as Oran fell to the Spaniards after being cursed by Sidi Bel-ʿAbbas Es-Sebti. No Jewish saint would utter a similar curse.

Muslims invoke the *ʿar* much more frequently than the Jews: when they engage in this ritual a saint is obliged to fulfill their requests. Among other things, the prescribed ritual calls for sacrificing an animal, but this is very different from the slaughtering done by the Jews, who sacrificed to a saint in gratitude for an expected or consummated miracle.

Most Jewish and Muslim saints are local, worshipped only by inhabitants of a given village. As their fame spread, they acquired recognition in other villages in the vicinity. When this happens with a Muslim saint, it means that a whole tribe or even several neighboring tribes recognize him. Even if not recognized in other parts of the country, such a local Muslim saint can be highly influential. For example, the Berbers of Tadla submitted to the authority of Sidi Ben-Daud, rather than to the jurisdiction of their temporal rulers.[39] Few Jewish or Muslim saints famous in various sections of Morocco were known and recognized throughout the country as a whole. It is notable in this connection that the national saint of all Maghreb Muslims, Sidi ʿAbd El-Kader Djilani, is buried in Bagdad and never set foot in North Africa.

A vitally definitive aspect of both Jewish and Muslim cults of sainthood in Morocco is the ardent desire, even need, to be in contact with a saint. Belief in the saint gives individuals and communities a sense of security. This great need may explain the diverse ways in which a saint reveals him- or herself; above all it explains the frequency of revelation through a dream. It may also be a factor in the Islamification of Jewish and Christian saints. Among the Muslims, the relationship with the saint is so important that it can lead to a fight over a saint's body or even to the murder of a saint so that he may be given a Muslim burial.[40]

Muslims as well as Jews have family saints with whom they maintain a particularly close association, although this does not prevent an individual or entire family from occasionally petitioning other saints. A city, town or village might also have a patron saint known by both Jews and Muslims as "Mul El-Blad";[41] he dominated and protected the area, and other saints buried in the vicinity were subordinate to him. Local residents invoked the powerful patron saint at every opportunity, often naming their children after him to ensure his protection. In Casablanca, R. Eliyahu was patron saint of the Jews and Sidi Belyut of the Muslims; at Marrakech, R. Ḥananiah Ha-

Cohen was patron saint of the Jews and Sidi Bel-ʿAbbas Es-Sebti of the Muslims; in Fez, R. Yehudah Ben-ʿAttar was patron saint of the Jews and Mulay Idriss of the Muslims.

An interesting phenomenon found among the Muslims but not among the Jews is that of patron saints associated with certain guilds and professions.[42] In Fez, for example, teachers venerate Sidi ʿAli Ben-Ḥrazem, tanners venerate Sidi Yaʿqub ed-Debbagh, hairdressers worship Sidi ʿAli Bu-Galab, shoemakers pay homage to Sidi Moḥammed Ibn ʿAbad, and so forth. Each profession in each city has its own patron saint.

In North Africa there are many anonymous Muslim saints identified only by the appellation "El-Mrabet" or "Sidi El-Makhfi"—"the mysterious." The names and vital statistics pertaining to some of these saints have been forgotten; others, creations of folk tradition, never actually existed. Among the Jews, too, there were some anonymous saints, but with a few exceptions—such as Tsaddiq Azru, the saint of Azrou—the Jews ordinarily identified their saints by name.

With respect to anonymous saints and their sanctuaries, natural elements played a significant role. In this context, too, it is interesting to examine what is common to both groups and what differentiates them. Scholars have written extensively about the large number of natural objects associated or identified with Muslim saints in North Africa. Studies by Doutté, Dermenghem and Westermarck afford numerous examples that enable us to grasp the importance of the phenomenon. It has extended beyond the borders of North Africa and can be found throughout the Muslim cultural sphere. This includes Muslims in Israel, whose attachment to elements of nature has been treated extensively by Canaan.

In broad outline, the phenomenon is very similar among Jews and Muslims. For both groups natural elements found in the vicinity of the saint's grave acquire sanctity due to their proximity to the sanctuary. Stories are told in both cultures about unidentified saints buried near a tree, spring or mountain, and it is interesting to note that many of these saints are revered by both Jews and Muslims.[43]

Certain widespread manifestations among the Muslims are rare among the Jews. To Muslims, for example, trees or stones may designate not only the burial place of a saint, but also a place where he rested or prayed. Jews, on the other hand, always believed that the saint was buried there, even if there was no grave at the site and no details were known. Stones, water sources and trees are often called by a saint's name, as if they were intrinsically holy. Among the Muslims, many stones or boulders and springs bear the names of female saints;[44] trees, regardless of being isolated or at sanctuaries, may also be given names.[45] Female saints named Lalla Taurirt—"owner of the hill"—are very common in North Africa. Although there are stones known by the Jews as Lalla Safia or Lalla Qafia, and the tree near R. Masʿud is called Lalla Sdira, on the whole elements of nature were generally associated with male saints by the Jews.[46]

Muslims attribute sanctity to living creatures, such as fish and turtles, found in pools near the saints. They name and feed them and are careful not to harm them. The present study revealed no similar practices among Jews.[47]

Scholars differ with respect to the essential quality of the sanctity ascribed to natural elements. Gellner[48] distinguishes this sanctity from the usual manifestations involved in saint worship, and he considers it almost an overt form of nature worship. Doutté,[49] too, sees surviving traces of ancient cultic reverence for stones, caves, springs, trees, and so forth, that preceded Islamification, after which certain of the objects were given the names of Muslim saints. Vestiges of ancient rituals may still be found today: at the site of a saint's grave some natural element may be more revered than the saint, as is the tree called Sidi ʿAbd en-Nbi near the sanctuary of Sidi Aḥmed el-ʿAmri on the way to Marrakech.[50] With this in mind, Doutté[51] suggests that the veneration of Lalla Taqerquzt by both Jews and Muslims is the result of a process that took place in several stages, the first of which was effected by the Berber cult of homage to water sources and reptiles. Long ago, when Jews first settled in North Africa, they accepted such cults willingly. When Islam was forced on the Berbers, however, they refused to relinquish ancient traditions. They gave the rites associated with the spring an Islamic cast by calling the source Lalla Taqerquzt, and under this name both Jews and Muslims continued to observe the old rituals. At a later stage, as the demands of Islam became increasingly rigorous, the tradition of "the Seven Saints" was created. It was said that these saints came to pray at the spring, and a sanctuary was built on the spot. Thereafter both Jews and Muslims continued to perform the ritual, but at separate springs. Westermarck,[52] too, cites sources testifying to the existence of an ancient Berber ritual involving stones, mountains, springs, and so on.

Frazer[53] maintain that since antiquity many peoples have worshipped trees and that traces of the cult can still be found in Europe today.

Dermenghem[54] differs from these scholars, suggesting that the reference is not to dendrolatry—tree worship—or worship of water and the creatures that inhabit it. Rather he sees a connection here between the tree or spring and sanctity, a connection represented by the fish in the water. Chelhod,[55] too, sees the attitude toward a tree or spring as linked with its proximity to a holy place, the sanctity accruing from the direct or indirect revelation of a force of saintly character.

Eliade's[56] exposition of the approach that should be adopted with respect to the sanctity of natural elements derives from the dual concept of sanctity of time and place. The place a human being inhabits is the center of the world for him or her and is thus intrinsically charged with holiness. Elements encompassed by the place—such as a tree, spring, boulder, and so on—are holy not because they are near a sanctuary, but because they themselves are integral components of sanctity. As such, they become a sign or symbol of special significance and therefore evoke a special attitude. All of nature is pervaded with religiosity, notes Eliade, but traditional society perceives this religiosity as limited to a given space, beyond which is chaos.

This concept of a sanctified space and all it implies is deep-rooted in Islam. The *baraka* of a living saint permeates his surroundings; when he dies, he comes closer to God and his supernatural powers become stronger. The saint's influence emanates from his grave, the focal point of his power, to the *ḥorm*[57]—the entire vicinity. This explains the great importance, particularly for the religious orders, of both grave and *ḥorm,* not only in the sphere of religious observance, but in everything concerning the social, economic and political life of the village.

Among the Muslims, the holy place in its broader aspect—including the grave, related buildings, and the *ḥorm*—is the scene of many activities other than the *ziyara* with its purely religious connotation. Under the aegis of marabouts, marriages are often performed at these centers. The *ḥorm* offers asylum to fugitives, murderers, thieves. The sanctified area is also a safe place for the temporary storage of agricultural equipment and produce, for peasants may be sure that none will dare touch them. In addition, it is the venue in which arbitration and adjudication of family or tribal disputes takes place, and the scene of the all-important oath-taking ceremony.[58]

Jews, too, promoted belief in the sanctity of the saint's grave and its surroundings, but not to the same degree. None of the activities described above is found among the Jews, although they attributed the same miraculous powers to the sanctuary and followed similar rituals pertaining to sympathetic magic and punishment of vandals. Many stories are told by both Jews and Muslims of the harm that came to an unclean person who went near the grave and to anyone who damaged nearby buildings or trees or tried to pasture flocks there.[59]

The Muslim's strict observance of purity has led them to forbid unclean persons, including Jews, Christians, and often women, to enter their holy precincts. The Jews forbade entry only to unpurified individuals and menstruating women.[60] Although they were not always pleased to have Christians and Muslims visit Jewish saints, Jews had to refrain from protesting because of their status as a religious and national minority.[61] In the visit to saints venerated by both Jews and Muslims, but whose sites were owned by Muslims, Jews had to wait outside, entering the sanctuary only after all Muslims had vacated it. Sometimes they gave the caretaker the gifts and candles meant for the saint. To enter a Muslim-owned sanctuary, Jewish women put on Arab dress.

Some Muslim saints prohibited visits from women, or only allowed them into the surrounding area, as in the Mosque of Mulay Ydriss in Fez. The present study found no such prohibition on the part of Jewish saints, who were visited freely by their female devotees.

The physical surroundings of Jewish and Muslim sanctuaries are very different. The grave of a saint revered by Jews is likely to be either in a remote mountainous area or in a cemetery within the Jewish quarter. It was not until the 1940s that extensive construction work began around saints' tombs; this frequently included crypts and rooms for visitors, and in some instances a synagogue, a *yeshibah* and a slaughterhouse. Throughout the Muslim sphere of influence, the sanctuary is typically built in the form of a *qubba,* a square white-plastered structure with a domed roof. The buildings around the graves of certain famous Muslim saints[62] are elaborately adorned, whereas those erected around even the best known of the Jewish saints were always modest.

Pilgrims visit a Muslim saint only at his sanctuary or at a place specifically consecrated by him. Jews, on the other hand, if unable to get to their own patron saint, visited some other more accessible one.

Many Muslim saints can be visited only on certain days of the week, a restriction no Jewish saint would ever make.

The Muslim *ziyara* always begins with the pilgrims encircling the tomb or *qubba* seven times, counterclockwise. When visiting a saint, Muslims usually bring gifts of money, oil, candles, incense, milk, butter, honey, or an animal for slaughter. These items are given to the *muqaddam,* the caretaker of the sanctuary. If the saint's offspring are still alive, the gifts are distributed among them, with the *muqaddam* also receiving a share. If there are no progeny, the sultan can bestow the right to the contributions on a family of shereefs, even if it is not related to the saint. Sometimes the *muqaddam* leases the position from the sultan for a monthly sum and appropriates the contributions. This is very different from the custom among the Jews, who gave all extra money to the needy.

The Muslim equivalent of the Jewish *hillulah* is the *mussem,* held for several days at the sanctuary once or twice a year, in spring or fall. These festivities are organized by the saint's descendants, the *muqaddam,* or by those who have been given the right to receive the contributions. The *hillulah* of the Jews takes place usually only once a year. Although the major ones are held at the saint's sanctuary, the *hillulah* can also be celebrated in a synagogue, a private home, or even in some other country—as with Jews of Moroccan origin who now have *hillulot* in Israel and in other countries as well. Special committees, made up of people who gave their services gratis, organized the *hillulah.*[63]

The *mussem* of certain Muslim saints—such as Sidi Aḥmed El-Kebir, who is buried some fifty kilometres from Algiers—attracts thousands of celebrants. Many elements are common to both the *mussem* and the *hillulah,* but each group also has its special customs. Jews always lit white candles. Muslims use colorful ones bought at the sanctuary;[64] they light some on the spot, and take others home with them. Burning incense, a widespread custom among the Muslims, was virtually non-existent among the Jews. Muslims use lamps for decoration as much as for illumination, which was not the case with Jews. Although Jews, too, hung ribbons on the branches of trees at the holy place, among the Muslims this *ex-voto* custom is much more widespread, and they festoon every possible spot in the sanctified area: the grave itself, windows, porches, trees, rocks, and so on.

Both groups hold a communal meal at the sanctuary, and they

eat the same traditional dish—*taʿam*—that includes couscous and meat. The food is usually prepared at home but cooked at the site.

Ceremonial slaughtering is an important part of the *mussem:* animals slaughtered include chickens,[65] lambs, decorated cows or bulls, occasionally even a camel. Among the Jews, equal portions of the meat were distributed to all attending the *seʿudah.* The Muslims consider part of the meat to belong to the caretaker of the sanctuary and the rest to be the property of the family that brought the animal. Slaughterhouses have been built near the sanctuaries of the most famous Muslim saints.

For Muslims, the *ziyara* is a time for prayer, singing and dancing, accompanied by the women's joyful *zgharit.* In some places processions are organized: walking, dancing to the accompaniment of instrumental music, and singing, pilgrims converge at the saint's grave, like the processions from Tlemcen to the *mussem* of Sidi Boumedien. Dance has acquired an important place in the Muslim *ziyara.* Groups sometimes dance together, as at the *mussem* of Sidi Aḥmed El-Bernussi in the Fez area, or of Mulay Brahim near Marrakech. Sometimes the women dance alone, and the men dance around them, all holding kerchiefs. A backward and forward movement, accompanied by singing, is typical of the dances executed by the girls. In certain places, horse racing and daredevil feats known as "fantasias" are performed by the men, who, shooting wildly, ride roughshod over a stipulated course while the crowd enthusiastically spurs them on. At the *mussem* of Mulay Idriss from Zarhun, the Ḥamadsha organize a procession, and, dancing in a circle to the accompaniment of the *ghayita* and *taʿriza* (flute and tambourine) they strike their heads with spiked sticks until they actually wound themselves.[66] At the *mussem* of Sidi Aḥmed U-Mussa at Sous, the pilgrims amuse themselves by throwing stones until they draw blood. Another popular game is the *raḥba,* a wrestling bout in which two contestants, standing on their hands, try to overthrow one another with their feet.[67] There were no processions, dancing or cultic games at the Jewish *hillulah.*

An interesting aspect of the *mussem* at several sanctuaries is the free intermingling of the sexes. Throughout the year, the lives of Muslim women are severely restricted, but at these festivities restraint is thrown to the winds; they are not supposed to refuse a man and are expected to confer their favors on anyone who asks. This sexual dimension was altogether absent at Jewish *hillulot.* Nor did the Jews engage in the custom of "sacred prostitution" described by some scholars.[68]

In conclusion, then, along with the similarities, we find many differences in the personalities of the saints themselves and in saint worship as practiced among the Muslims and the Jews. Among the Muslims, the phenomenon, including the nature of the saint or the several types of marabouts, is more extensive and much more complex than among the Jews. The just and righteous marabout acts charitably, lives in holiness, and is close to God. The ascetic marabout renounces the pleasures of this world. There is also the psychologically disturbed marabout, the warrior who participates in battle, the judge and arbitrator who settles disputes among individuals and tribes, the healer, the statesman who deals with political and administrative matters, the sheikh responsible for tribal affairs; and other types as well. In general, a Muslim saint is a living person who plays an active role in society, one who need not necessarily display exceptional moral qualities. The few Jews who acquired the title of saint in their lifetimes did not fulfill analogous functions. They were individuals whose lives were models of exemplary righteous and moral behavior. Because of their virtue and excellence, the community was eager to accept their advice and respond to their wishes, and this endowed them with considerable influence. In other words, the saint did not insist upon obedience. Rather the society around him respected his feelings and sought to satisfy his desires.

It is difficult to evaluate closely corresponding phenomena emerging from adherence to the same cult. Nor is it easy to assess which phenomena are an intrinsic part of the very cult of sainthood and which reflect a reciprocal influence resulting from living in close proximity. It is equally difficult to determine manifestations specific to each group. Nevertheless, it does not seem merely fortuitous that a given custom prevalent among the Muslims is non-existent among the Jews, since each custom rests on a sustaining ideology. Thus greater importance can be ascribed to customs followed by only one group, even if they are not numerous, than to those shared by both groups.

The long and harmonious coexistence of Jews and Muslims in Morocco, their adherence to the same cult of saint veneration, and evidence of the effectiveness of saints within both communities forged the basic framework for the common relevant rituals among

Jews and Muslims. Each group has its own functional way of creating saints, yet the many marabouts and Muslim religious orders in Morocco may have prompted the Jews to create a larger number of saints, thereby enabling Jewish saints to hold their own against their Muslim counterparts.

Notes

1. See I. Ben-Ami (1974b, p. 94).
2. I. Goldziher (1880) was the first to publish important studies for the understanding of saint veneration among the Muslims.
3. Scholars' curiosity and interest in the phenomenon gave rise to many studies. These have been cited in previous chapters when comparing different customs among the Jews and the Muslims. See E. Doutté (1900, pp. 5–6).
4. At the beginning of the century, E. Doutté (1900, p. 13) indicated that maraboutism flourished in Morocco, and ordinary individuals who were thought to have received the *baraka* from God were consecrated as saints by the people.
5. E. Gellner (1969); E. Doutté (1900, p. 17); E. Westermarck (1926, vol. 1, pp. 148–59).
6. P. Shinar (1980, p. 13).
7. J. Chelhod (1964, pp. 188–89).
8. E. Westermarck (1926, vol. 1, p. 37): "The number of shereefs in Morocco is immense. . . . By simply moving from his native place to another district and there pretending to belong to a family of shereefs, a person may both for himself and his descendants gain a title to which he has no claim whatever." See also E. Dermenghem (1954, p. 26); E. Doutté (1900, pp. 44–45).
9. T. Canaan (1927, pp. 53, 302) describes a similar phenomenon among the Muslims in Palestine.
10. E. Doutté (1900, p. 23, and 1914, pp. 310–11); E. Westermarck (1926, vol. 1, p. 42): "The *mqáddmīn* of Mûläi Idrīs' sanctuary in Fez, though they are not shereefs, are even more venerated than the decendants of the saint."
11. E. Westermarck (1926, vol. 1, pp. 41–43) gives several examples of transference of *baraka,* including by means of spitting into one's mouth or by eating from the saint's meal; the transference may occur even without the saint's knowledge or against his will.
12. E. Doutté (1914, pp. 312–13); E. Westermarck (1926, vol. 1, pp. 43–44); T. Canaan (1927, pp. 24, 277.)

13. E. Doutté (1900, pp. 35–36): "c'est pendant sa vie que le ouali s'entend donner ce titre par le peuple; on le considère même comme plus puissant durant sa vie qu'après sa mort. En fait les *bahloûl,* les *medjdzoùb,* les *oualî* vivants pullulent autour de nous dans toute l'Afrique du Nord." See also E. Dermenghem (1954, pp. 29–31); E. Westermarck (1926, vol. 1, pp. 48–49); E. Doutté (1914, p. 5); J. Chelhod (1964, p. 191); T. Canaan (1927, p. 310).
14. E. Doutté (1900, pp. 82–83, 108, and 1914, pp. 188, 239). The Muslims believe it is beneficial to have sexual intercourse with a saintly person: E. Westermarck (1926, vol. 1, p. 198). Muslim women sometimes dream they are having intercourse with dead saints: T. Canaan (1927, pp. 272–73).
15. E. Dermenghem (1954, pp. 27–28).
16. E. Westermarck (1926, vol. 1, pp. 44–45); E. Doutté (1900, pp. 79–80) tells about individuals consecrated as hermit saints in one place, who then left for another place where they lived luxuriously with the alms they received from their devotees. See also E. Dermenghem (1954, p. 27).
17. See G. Drague (1951); M. Morsy (1972); A. Bel (1938); R. Brunel (1926); E. Michaux-Bellaire (1921). Many confreries were not friendly to the Jews: see J. Valadji (1902).
18. G. Drague (1951, p. 112).
19. E. Gellner (1969, p. 78) describes the several services performed by the *agurram.*
20. G. Drague (1951, pp. 106, 117–24).
21. E. Gellner (1969, pp. 74–80).
22. E. Gellner (1969, p. 143): "In the wider or latent sense, sanctity covers all those who claim the appropriate descent. In the narrowest and fullest sense, it covers only those who are highly, respectfully and widely acclaimed and above all *used* as saints by the lay tribes, and who exhibit or are held to exhibit all or most of the characteristics of sanctity on the list."
23. E. Dermenghem (1954, pp. 11 *sq.*). See also J. Chelhod (1964, p. 192).
24. The different titles attributed to the saints in Islam in general and particularly in North Africa—*shurfa* (shereef), *marabout, wali, agurram, mudjahedin, fkir,* and so on—elicit different explanations by scholars. See E. Doutté (1905, pp. 54–56); E. Dermenghem (1954, pp. 21–24); E. Westermarck (1926, vol. 1, pp. 35 *sq.*); J. Chelhod (1964, pp. 189–93); T. Canaan (1927, pp. 272 *sq.*).
25. See I. Goldziher (1880). The list has been reproduced in Kriss and Kriss (1960–62, pp. 9–10).

26. It is called *istikhara* by the Muslims. See E. Dermenghem (1954, p. 132); E. Doutté (1909, pp. 410–14) and (1914, pp. 90, 275). The custom is still practiced by Moroccan Jews in holy places in Israel.
27. E. Gellner (1969, p. 137): "there are the more 'purely' religious or transcendental services offered by the saints. . . . These services may be performed for collectivities or individuals . . . or a woman [may] come to request supernatural assistance to become pregnant." T. Canaan (1927, p. 118) writes that fever and sterility are the two maladies most represented among the diseases for which the help of Muslim saints is requested in Palestine.
28. An exception is R. Shelomoh Ben-Lḥans (Aghbalou), meaning "Shelomoh son of the serpent." Some traditions tell that his mother gave birth to a snake and others that he saved a man's life from a snake. See I. Ben-Ami (1989, pp. 32–34).
29. E. Westermarck (1926, vol. 1, pp. 159–60) and T. Canaan (1927, p. 243) write that dead saints may appear in animal shapes, for example, as doves or snakes. See also I. Ben-Ami (1989, p. 34). For the same phenomenon among the Christians, see A. van Gennep (1949, tome I, vol. 4, p. 1741).
30. Came from Spain to Morocco in 1391, lived in Marrakech for some years and then left for Algeria. He seems to be the first saint consecrated by the masses in North Africa. At his graveside in Tlemcen a major *hillulah* is celebrated every year. See I. Ben-Ami (1989, pp. 37–38); S. Slyomovics (1993, pp. 84–88).
31. E. Doutté (1914, pp. 4 *sq.*) tells about the stork consecrated as a saint both in Morocco and in Algeria, and J. Chelhod (1964, pp. 194–96) about the *baraka,* although a weak one, of doves and horses. See also I. Ben-Ami (1989, pp. 38–39).
32. E. Westermarck (1926, vol. 1, p. 151).
33. Praying for rain at saints' gravesides is a very ancient custom among both Jews and Muslims. See: G. Vajda (1951, pp. 10, 18, 31, 55, 77); A. Ben-Jacob (1973, pp. 29–34); E. Brauer (1934, pp. 366–67). T. Canaan (1927, pp. 219 *sq.*) describes rain processions practiced everywhere in Palestine by Mohammedans, Christians and Jews.
34. Marabouts foresaw the conquest of North Africa by the French. See: E. Doutté (1900, p. 59).
35. E. Doutté (1914, pp. 168, 279).
36. E. Dermenghem (1954, p. 22) writes about "The Council of Saints."
37. E. Westermarck (1926, vol. 1, pp. 49–50); T. Canaan (1927, pp. 50–53).
38. The traditions are very similar in both groups: saints are respected, but sometimes also insulted. See: E. Doutté (1900, pp. 13, 27); E. Dermenghem (1954, p. 133). P. Shinar (1980, p. 13) describes cases

of Berber tribes in South Morocco that treated their marabouts with disrespect because they did not work or fight, and even threatened to beat them when they did not succeed in making rain during a drought. T. Canaan (1927, pp. 246–47) refers to forbearing and irritable saints.

39. C. de Foucauld (1888, p. 52): "Ici, ni sultan ni makhzen, rien qu'Allah et Sidi Ben Daoud."
40. The Muslims killed R. ʿEli Ben-Yitsḥaq when he restored life to a dead cow, and they buried him as a saint in their area. The Jews buried R. Shelomoh Ben-Yitsḥaq secretly, fearing that the Muslims would take his body and bury him in the Muslim quarter. See also E. Westermarck (1926, vol. 1, p. 160); E. Dermenghem (1954, p. 17).
41. The same phenomenon is found in other religions: E. Westermarck (1926, vol. 1, p. 179); E. Dermenghem (1954, pp. 162–63); E. Doutté (1905, p. 14); D. Attwater (1973, p. 148).
42. E. Dermenghem (1954, pp. 163–64). E. Westermarck (1926, vol. 1, pp. 179–81) points out that it is not only respectable occupations which have saintly patrons, and he cites the case of Sidi Qaddur ben Mlek, the patron saint of gamblers. The Catholics too have patron saints for different occupations: D. Attwater (1973, pp. 94, 148).
43. This is the case with Lalla Jamila, Lalla Taqerquzt, Meʿarat Oufran, Mul Jebel El-Kebir, Mul Sedra, Sidi Mhasser, Tsaddiq Azru and Tuqshusht.
44. Among the Muslims in Morocco there are cairns consecrated as Lalla Hsna, Lalla Tignugi and Lalla Nfisa; holy springs known as Lalla Tabakiyut and Zima; and rocks known as Lalla Raḥma U-Mussa and Lalla Tabullat.
45. Many saintly trees are consecrated as Lalla Zineb or Imma Zineb. Most of the names are feminine: Lalla Kheira, Lalla Bathma, Lalla Zarura. See: E. Dermenghem (1954, pp. 138–39).
46. For example, Mul El-Ḥazra El-Menzura, Mul El-Karma, Mul Jebel El-Kebir, Mul Sedra, Mul Shejra, Mul Shejra El-Khedra (R. Ḥananiah Ha-Cohen) and Mul Terya.
47. According to E. Doutté (1914, p. 223), the Jews behaved exactly like the Muslims at Lalla Taqerquzt and immersed their feet in the pond with pieces of bread thereon to feed the saintly turtles in the water.
48. E. Gellner (1969, pp. 284–85).
49. E. Doutté (1914, pp. 221, 275, 318, 369, 389) and (1900, p. 92).
50. E. Doutté (1914, pp. 318–19).
51. E. Doutté (1914, pp. 224–25).
52. E. Westermarck (1926, vol. 1, pp. 77, 78, 83, 84).
53. J. G. Frazer (1960, vol. 1, pp. 144–78).

54. E. Dermenghem (1954, pp. 34–38, 136, 147).
55. J. Chelhod (1964, p. 237).
56. M. Eliade (1965, pp. 21–59) and (1969).
57. J. Chelhod (1964, pp. 229 *sq.*); E. Westermarck (1926, vol. 1, p. 64).
58. The oath as a method for determining the truth or falsity of an accusation is known throughout the Muslim world: E. Dermenghem (1954, p. 167); T. Canaan (1927, pp. 125 *sq.*). E. Gellner (1969, pp. 104 *sq.*) describes the collective oath of the High Atlas Berber society, a legal decision making procedure that requires a number of "co-jurors" to testify—according to a prescribed formula, in a fixed order, and in a holy place—that the accusation is false. Minor issues are sworn at the nearest mosque or holy place, but major issues, defined as those requiring ten or more co-jurors, are taken to the shrine of the igurramen.
59. R. Patai (1942–43, vol. 1, pp. 206–83; vol. 2, pp. 1–64).
60. Both Jews and Muslims forbade prostitutes from entering the holy place, but sometimes the Muslims allowed them to participate in the *mussem.*
61. Muslims and Christians show dislike for the participation of individuals from other faiths in their purely religious ceremonies. See: E. Westermarck (1926, vol. 1, pp. 195–96).
62. Sumptuous shrines were built for Mulay Idriss in Fez, Sidi Bel-ʿAbbas Es-Sebti and Sidi Ben-Sliman in Marrakech, Sidi ʿAbd Al-Raḥman in Algiers and Sidi Boumedien in Tlemcen.
63. Among the Jews, in only a few cases is the *hillulah* organized by the offspring of the saint. These are very modest ceremonies, usually celebrated at home.
64. The ceremony of the auction of candles, so important at the Jewish *hillulah,* is sometimes celebrated by the Muslims, in which case they sell large, colorful candles, beautifully adorned.
65. I. Ben-Ami (1973a, p. 48); J. Desparmet (1935, pp. 178–88).
66. J. Herber (1923).
67. This game, probably of African origin, is known in Northeast Brazil by the name of "capoeira." During my visit to Bahia in January 1979 I had the opportunity to see this cultic game practiced at the festivities in honor of Senhor do Bonfim, the most famous saint of the region.
68. E. Doutté (1914, pp. 188 *sq.,* and 242–44) records the phenomenon in Morocco in connection with the Sidi Rahal women. E. Dermenghem (1954, pp. 212 *sq.*) writes about it in reference to certain North African tribes, describing ritual prostitution as stipulating that men are forbidden to refuse the women, at the risk of incurring the saint's wrath.

15

MOROCCAN JEWRY AND SAINT WORSHIP IN ISRAEL

Among the Jews, worshipper and saint are so closely interrelated that a believer could not conceive of leaving Morocco without soliciting the patron saint's approval, or at least taking leave of him or her. In many cases, worshippers waited for some sign that the saint had released them. Such a sign—or parting gesture—might appear in a dream in which the disciple was told to get up and go to Jerusalem; or one might find a buyer for one's house, by then the sole obstacle to departure. The saint's approval is even more essential in the case of an official involved in organizing the *hillulah.* After most of the Jews of the region had left for Israel, R. Daniel Hashomer's emissary remained behind, waiting for the saint to authorize his emigration. The emissary of R. David Ha-Levi Draʿ, too, waited many years, leaving only after he dreamed that the saint ordered him to go. Lalla Miryam's servant dreamed that the saint complained because he was planning to leave for the Holy Land without waiting for her permission.

There is an element of mutual interest in this dependence. The saint, too, wanted to go to the Holy Land; he sometimes urged his disciples to depart quickly so that he himself could leave. It is said that R. Eliʿezer Turei-Zahav appeared in the dream of each and every villager, ordering them to depart because the time had come for the saint himself to go to his town (Jerusalem) in the Holy Land. R. Makhluf Ben-Yosef Abiḥatsira told the Jews to get ready to go, and he prepared to accompany them, as he could not think of remaining behind in Morocco without his followers.

One might assume that the departure of Moroccan Jewry—most of them for Israel—would have terminated, or at least weakened, their relationship with their saints.[1] Their saint veneration, however, is so deeply ingrained, that there has been a renewal of the phenomenon in Israel. At first, during the difficult years of acclimatization and absorption into Israeli society, only family and home *hillulot* were organized, usually prompted by individual initiative. Then, as time passed, synagogues named after saints began to appear in parts of Israel with large concentrations of Jews from Morocco, and each of these synagogues arranged a *hillulah* for its patron saint. Eventually, it became customary to make public announcements and issue invitations to some of the *hillulot*—such as the celebrations held in honor of R. Yaʿaqob Abiḥatsira in Ramleh, Sepher Tislit in Ashkelon, and R. David U-Moshe in Safed—that eventually attracted crowds of participants from all over Israel.

While a few Moroccan Jews who were direct descendants of saints organized relatively private *hillulot* in their homes, larger centers began to accommodate multitudes of people interested in perpetuating the rites and rituals of saint worship. Communities in Safed and Ashkelon became particularly active: *hillulot* in honor of R. David U-Moshe have been held annually in both towns, with thousands of celebrants participating.[2] They have faithfully reproduced the practices that marked the festivities in Morocco, including ritual slaughtering, prayers, the *seʿudah,* staying overnight at the holy premises, and so forth. In Safed the *hillulah* is celebrated in rooms dedicated to the saint[3] that attract worshippers all year round. In Ashkelon the *hillulah* is held in the synagogue named after R. David U-Moshe.[4] *Hillulot* in R. David U-Moshe's honor are also held in Kiriyat Malakhi, Moshav Zanoaḥ and Netivot. A room in Kiriyat Gat is dedicated to R. Makhluf Ben-Yosef Abiḥatsira;[5] throughout the year Jews go there to light candles and petition the saint, and the *hillulah* is celebrated with large numbers of participants. In Ashkelon a room and synagogue in the name of Sepher Tislit also draw many worshippers.[6] Large *hillulot* are held in honor of R. David Ben-Barukh every year, on the third of *Tebet* in Sdot Mikhah, and in synagogues named after him in Ashdod, Haifa and other places. The descendants of R. Ḥayyim Pinto in Ashdod conduct ramified activities in his honor.

In Sdot Mikhah and Ashkelon, descendants of R. Aharon Assulin of Fercla celebrate his *hillulah* during *Ḥanukkah.* On the 14th of *Tebet* the grandson of R. Abraham Turjman holds an annual *hillulah* in Beersheba in his grandfather's honor. In Jerusalem the offspring of R. Moshe Ḥaliwa enthusiastically celebrate his *hillulah* on the 16th of *Tebet.* The descendants of R. Abraham Wazana in Natanya hold an annual *hillulah* in his honor. R. Abraham Cohen Bu-Dwaya is similarly honored in Kiriyat Shemonah. In Ashdod, a beautiful synagogue was built in the name of R. Shelomoh Ben-Lḥans, and his *hillulah* is held there. Before their immigration to Israel, the worshippers of R. Yaḥya Laḥlu promised to have a *hillulah* in his name on *Shushan Purim* every year (celebrated on the 15th of *Adar* in walled cities, in contrast with *Purim* itself, which is celebrated on the 14th of *Adar* in all other places). A disciple of R. Pinḥas Ha-Cohen who had come to Israel dreamed that the saint asked to be remembered each year, so he holds an annual *hillulah* in his name. Every 15th of *Elul* two families in Moshav Zanoaḥ organize a *hillulah* for R. Daniel Hashomer. In Givat Olga annual *hillulot* are held in many homes in honor of R. ʿAmram Ben-Diwan; a large *hillulah* is also held in a synagogue bearing his name. In Ashdod a *hillulah* is held for R. Barukh Assabagh and also for R. Raphael Moshe Elbaz. In Kiriyat Gat *hillulot* are held in honor of R. Yaʿaqob Dayyan and R. Yosef Dayyan.[7]

There is a prevalent belief that the saints themselves moved to Israel, leaving behind in Morocco only the edifices built in their names.[8] Where they are in Israel is not known, but people are confident that they will reveal themselves in the course of time, primarily the way most of them revealed themselves in Morocco—through dreams. The dream is as effective a conduit in Israel as it was in Morocco; patron saints who were known abroad reveal their presence in Israel by communicating in dreams with their disciples. Many stories are told, particularly about R. David U-Moshe; he not only revealed himself to two disciples in Safed and in Ashkelon, who arranged large *hillulot* in his honor, but appeared in dreams of other people as well. He complained that the Jews from Morocco had forgotten him, and he asked them to visit his room in Ashkelon or Safed.

R. Makhluf Ben-Yosef Abiḥatsira, too, appears in his worshippers' dreams to ask them to visit his room in Kiriyat Gat.

Some traditions tell that a saint passes from place to place in secret ways: while everyone thinks he is still interred in Morocco, his body, in effect, has moved to Israel. The story is told that R. Shelomoh Ben-ʿAttar appeared to a disciple at the graveside of a wealthy man who had died and been buried in Israel. R. Shelomoh informed the disciple that the rich man had been transported to his (the saint's) grave in Marrakech, while the saint himself had moved to Israel.

Saints continue to be created in Israel, and people relish miracle tales about them. The great rabbi of Ramleh-Lod, R. Yitsḥaq Abiḥatsira—also known as Baba Ḥaki and a grandson of R. Yaʿaqob Abiḥatsira—died in a road accident on the 25th of *Adar* 1970. Before R. Yitsḥaq was even buried, his followers were spreading the word that he had died to save the people of Israel from great danger and that his death provided atonement for the sins of the Jewish people. His family organizes an annual *hillulah* in his honor, and Moroccan Jews in particular make pilgrimages to his grave in Ramleh.

An interesting case of a saint created in the new milieu of Israel is that of R. Ḥayyim Ḥuri. He was born on the Island of Djerba, died in Beersheba in 1957 and became a subject of worship, in particular by North African Jews. His devotees make pilgrimages to his grave in Beersheba. Many miraculous cures are attributed to him, and it is believed that he shields soldiers from harm.[9]

The most important saint to emerge in Israel is undoubtedly R. Yisra'el Abiḥatsira,[10] the Baba Sale, another grandson of R. Yaʿaqob Abiḥatsira and the brother of R. Yitsḥaq Abiḥatsira. Baba Sale came from Morocco and settled with his family in the developing town of Netivot, in southern Israel. Numerous miracles were attributed to him during his lifetime, and people came to Netivot from all over Israel as well as from other countries for counsel and blessings. Bottles of water which he blessed were very popular with believers. He died in 1984 and was buried in Netivot.[11] This event initiated a revolution in the practice of saint worship in Israel. One of his sons adopted the title Baba Barukh and provided continuity for the activities in Netivot in honor of his father: he built a *yeshibah,* a synagogue and a sumptuous shrine around the grave, which is visited all year round by Jews from Israel and elsewhere. The large number of visitors is about equal to the number who go on pilgrimage to traditional holy sites in Israel, for example, the tombs of R. Shimʿon Bar-Yoḥay in Meron and R. Meir Baʿal Ha-Nes in Tiberias. Baba Sale's worshippers light candles and submit their petitions to the saint. Bottles of water, now blessed by the son, are available. An annual great *hillulah* is celebrated on the 4th of *Shebat* in Netivot, attended by members of the government, politicians, the Sephardic Chief Rabbi of Israel, rabbis from all over the country and tens of thousands of believers. An annual *hillulah* in honor of Baba Sale with thousands of participants is also celebrated in Beersheba by his grandson, the son of the late R. Meir Abiḥatsira, also known as Baba Meir and renowned for the miracles he performed.

The Pinto family, too, is developing activities related to the worship of its saints in Israel and in other countries in order to broaden its influence among the believers and thus acquire economic and political power. In addition to the *hillulot* in honor of R. Ḥayyim Pinto the Elder and R. Ḥayyim Pinto the Younger, believers visit the grave of R. Ḥayyim Pinto the Younger's son, R. Moshe Pinto, located inside a special edifice erected by the family at the entrance to the cemetery in Ashdod.[12] In 1990, R. Ḥayyim Pinto, the son of R. Moshe, brought the bones of two saints of the family to Israel in a mission that was accompanied by many miraculous events. The identity of the two saints, R. Shelomoh Pinto, the father of R. Ḥayyim Pinto the Elder, and R. Yosef Malka, the son of R. Khalifa Malka, was disclosed by R. Ḥayyim Pinto. He made this announcement during a great *hillulah* organized by him in Kiriyat Malakhi to celebrate the building of a saintly edifice to accommodate the graves of four saints of the Pinto family.[13] Thousands of guests participated in the *hillulah.*

In Israel the saints continue to cure sick people and barren women by the same miraculous means they used abroad. The most important aspect of their activity in Israel, however, seems to derive from that nation's security situation. Today's saint carries a gun, defends borders, informs his disciples when war is about to break out, predicts alerts, orders the people into shelters, and announces an imminent cease-fire or victory. He also miraculously saves soldiers at the front: soldiers tell stories of old men who appear on the battlefield, save them from great danger and vanish. Sometimes the saint heals the wounded and frees captives from prisoner-of-war camps. The day before the *hillulah* in honor of R. David U-Moshe in Ashkelon, the blackout enforced during the Six Day War was lifted; a strong shaft of light suddenly illuminated the central hall of Ashkelon's R. David U-Moshe synagogue, heralding the war's end. A saint can also protect devotees against terrorists: a girl wounded during the attack on Maalot reported having been miraculously rescued by R. David U-Moshe, who also played a major role in healing her wounds. Before the Six Day War broke out, R. David U-Moshe announced to the Jews in Morocco, through his Muslim caretaker, that war against Israel was imminent, but there was nothing to fear because he, the rabbi, was guarding Israel. During the Sinai war in 1956, Jews from Morocco prayed at the tomb of R. Raphael Anqawa, and the saint came to Israel's aid. During the Yom Kippur War, a woman from the town of Migdal Haemek asked R. Abraham Wazana to protect her three sons, one of whom was named after the saint. By grace of Sepher Tislit, some Jews believe, Israel conquered Gaza in the Six Day War.

Jews from Morocco not only have revived the veneration of Moroccan saints in Israel, they eagerly flock to traditional holy places in this country. They visit the Western Wall, the Cave of the Patriarchs in Hebron, the tombs of Rachel the Matriarch in Bethlehem, of R. Shimʿon Bar-Yoḥay in Meron and of R. Meir Baʿal Ha-Nes in Tiberias,[14] the Cave of Elijah in Haifa, the Cave of Simon the Just in Jerusalem and so on. To the Jews from Morocco these sites have a special character and are particularly holy. The *Lag bʿOmer* celebration at Mt. Meron is attended by thousands of Moroccan Jews,[15] many of whom arrive several days in advance, pitch tents and revel in the beauties of nature, as they did during large *hillulot* in Morocco.

At certain holy places in Israel Jews of Moroccan origin are the major perpetuators of cult rituals. This holds true for the worship of Ḥoni Ha-Meʿaggel—a renowned miracle worker of the first century before the Christian Era—who is considered the patron saint of the residents of Galilean Hatsor. His disciples behave toward him as they did toward local saints in Morocco: they visit his cave daily, light candles and read Psalms. It is interesting that his worshippers chose to hold his *hillulah* on Independence Day: Jews come to it from all over the Galilee, as well as from other areas of the country. The choice of date—symbolic of the beginning of the nation's redemption—was intentional. The *Mimuna* (celebrated by Moroccan Jews at the end of Passover) and *Lag bʿOmer* also attract large crowds. Similar customs developed in Yavneh, where the tomb of Rabban Gamliel in a domed edifice downtown is visited daily by worshippers.

Jews from Morocco also visit "new" sanctuaries discovered or "created" in Israel in recent times. For example, in the Moshav Alma, a small village near the Lebanese border, Jews of Lybbian origin developed new traditions around the "rediscovery" of the graves of two *tannaim* buried near the village: R. Eleʿazar Ben-ʿArakh and R. Eleʿazar Ben-ʿAzariah. New tombstones were built—the shrine of R. Eleʿazar Ben-ʿArakh is particularly spacious and decorated. Many miracles are attributed to both saints, and bottles of oil and of earth collected near the graves are sold as healing preparations. The *hillulah* of R. Eleʿazar Ben-ʿArakh was celebrated at the shrine for the first time on the 17th of *Iyyar* 1992 with a large number of participants. Since then prayers are held in the shrine every eve of a Hebrew month.

Two other holy places that emerged in Israel in recent times and attract many believers are the tomb of Dan, son of Jacob, in the old road to Jerusalem, and the grave of the *tanna* Jonathan Ben-ʿUziel in Amuka in the Galilee, in the northern part of Israel. A legend says that this sage, who lived in the first century of the Christian Era, has the power for arranging marriages, and crowds of bachelors of both sexes go on pilgrimage to his grave to request his assistance.

Israel's political leaders, too, have taken into account the attachment of North African Jews, particularly those from Morocco, to the cult of sainthood. During general elections, special appeals to vote for a given party are addressed to this segment of the electorate in the names of specific saints. When certain parties have internal balloting, a saint's name is often invoked to lend support to one splinter group or faction rather than another.

Although there are already many manifestations of intense activity on the part of saint worshippers among Moroccan Jews in Israel, there is little doubt that this is only the beginning of a ramified, multidirectional process; its final outcome cannot yet be foreseen. Saint worship by Moroccan Jews has influenced Israeli folklore and brought about great changes in traditions of pilgrimage and celebration of *hillulot.* Israelis of non-Moroccan origin increasingly visit famous rabbis and miracle workers to receive their blessing; pilgrimages to holy places and graves are organized all year round; busloads, predominantly of Moroccan Jews, include believers from other communities as well; *hillulot* of rabbis and saints from different communities are celebrated in synagogues and community centers. Pilgrimages are organized to holy tombs abroad as well, for example to Morocco, Egypt, Poland and Ukraine. Keen interest in the cult of saints manifests itself in the detailed press coverage of the *hillulot* of Baba Sale and of R. Shimʿon Bar-Yoḥay.

One of the most interesting manifestations of the new tradition occurs in hagiography and folk literature—in the legends, stories and poems praising the greatness and miracles of the saints. Since "In Praise of Ha-Ari," "In Praise of the Baʿal Shem Tov"[16] and collections of Hasidic tales were first published, a new form of hagiographic literature has been created. The number of books and booklets published increases every year, and the same books appear in several editions. Special editions in suitable language with attractive illustrations are printed for children and young people; these are available in bookshops and religious stores as well as at *hillulot* and certain holy places. Indeed, thanks to Moroccan Jews or their influence, the number of hagiographic publications produced in Israel during the last ten years considerably exceeds all that was published in the last two centuries. Such literature can only strengthen the bonds between the Jews, their saints and the holy places.

Notes

1. The Jews who remained in Morocco continue the cult of sainthood, encouraged by the Moroccan government. The official attitude to the Jewish cult of sainthood is expressed by the governments of Egypt, Algeria and Morocco; in a variety of ways they encourage Jews of North African origin to visit holy tombs in their respective countries. In Morocco, *hillulot* in honor of R. ʿAmram Ben-Diwan and R. Abraham Awriwer are organized under the patronage of the government, with the participation of Jews of Moroccan origin coming from Israel and other countries. To underscore their liberal attitude, these governments also invite influential Jews, primarily from the United States, to observe official arrangements that have been made for protecting sites sacred to the Jews. Saint veneration is an important component of the Jewish identity of Moroccan Jews who have emigrated to the United States, Canada or France. In those countries, too, many *hillulot* are held in homes and synagogues. Perpetuation of these beliefs, rites and customs—in

ways specific to each of the new countries of residence—attests to the deep attachment of these Jews to their saints, even at the close of the twentieth century. This connection with saints is characteristic of thirty- and forty-year olds, as well as of the older generation.

2. See I. Ben-Ami (1981a), in which the cult in those two centers is described in detail. Another center was created in Ofakim, through the influence of a married couple, to whom R. David U-Moshe appeared in a dream.
3. Safed is the most important center honoring R. David U-Moshe in Israel. It was created by Abraham Ben-Ḥayyim, a man in his fifties, who was not close to the saint in Morocco but started activities in honor of the saint in Israel after several dreams about the holy man, beginning in 1973. Filled with a sense of mission, he devotes all his time and part of his fortune to the saint. He consecrated his house in Safed to the saint and he and his wife are the caretakers of the shrine. The house has been transformed into an important center of pilgrimage for Jews of Moroccan and other origins, who come from all over the country. A special room has been dedicated to the saint, and believers visit there all year round. They light candles and stay a few hours, or even several nights. The great *hillulah* on the New Moon of *Ḥeshwan* is celebrated in the synagogue and in the courtyard near the house, with the participation of thousands from all over the country. All rituals practiced in Morocco are found here—the ritual slaughter of animals in honor of the saint, the *seʿudah,* auction of glasses and candles in honor of the saint, prayers.
4. The Ashkelon center was created in the 1960s and 1970s by an old man who was close to R. David U-Moshe in Morocco and claimed to have helped build his tomb in Timzerit. After his death, his children continued the tradition.
5. This place was created by a couple for whom the saint performed a miracle in Morocco. After their death, the *hillulah* is now celebrated in the synagogue in Kiriyat Gat named after the saint.
6. See I. Ben-Ami (1983a).
7. This list is certainly not exhaustive, but it illustrates some cases collected in the present research.
8. The informant said the rabbis maintain that the saints are now in Israel, and gave as examples R. Raphael Anqawa and R. Raphael Ha-Cohen. The Jews of Tunisia too believe their saints moved to Israel.
9. See A. Weingrod (1990); S. Houri (1985); S. Deshen (1977); M. E. Haddad (*Beor pney melekh ḥayyim,* Beersheba, n.d.). Another case

of a shrine created in Israel is related by Y. Bilu (1984): a resident of Beit Shean, a small Israeli town, announced in 1979 that he had discovered the entrance to the Biblical Garden of Eden in his backyard, and that Elijah the Prophet had appeared to him in his dreams and had guided him in and out. The place has since then become a pilgrimage center for the local inhabitants.

10. See Eliyahu Alfassi (1985. *Baba Sale—Our Holy Rabbi.* Jerusalem [Hebrew]); Arieh Yehudah Harel (1985. *Light of Israel.* Jerusalem [Hebrew]); David Yehudayof (1985–87. *Baba Sale.* 2 vol. Netivot [Hebrew]).
11. More than 50,000 people participated in the funeral, and believers also came from abroad. A. Bier (1988) describes the holy places in Israel, and, for the first time, the graves of Baba Sale and R. Ḥayyim Ḥuri are mentioned together with the classic, historical holy places.
12. R. Moshe Pinto died on 5 *Elul* 1985. Two years after his death, his sons R. Ḥayyim and R. David Pinto, published a book, *Vehaish Moshe,* describing miracles performed by him. A great *hillulah* is organized by the family in *Elul* in honor of R. Ḥayyim Pinto Ha-Gadol and of R. Moshe Pinto. The family advertises in local and national newspapers and distributes booklets at the *hillulah* praising the saints of the family and telling of the activities of the family in Israel and other countries, including the establishment of *yeshibot* and synagogues in the name of R. Ḥayyim Pinto Ha-Gadol and R. Moshe Pinto.
13. The celebration took place on August 26, 1990. R. Ḥayyim Pinto, the son of R. Moshe Pinto, is the Chief Rabbi of Kiriyat Malakhi.
14. One informant said that she takes her suffering husband to the grave of R. Meir Baʿal Ha-Nes; they stay there for three days, and he goes home in good health. See also M. Shokeid and S. Deshen (1977, p. 98).
15. M. Shokeid and S. Deshen (1977, pp. 93–109).
16. D. Ben-Amos and J. Mintz (1970).

16

CONCLUSION

MANY SCHOLARS HAVE DEALT WITH THEORETICAL ASPECTS OF SAINT worship in the Muslim cultural world, hoping to develop analytical tools that would facilitate a better understanding of the phenomenon. Various methods and approaches reflect the particular theory adopted by each researcher, but since each of them worked within a relatively limited purview, it is difficult to assess the general applicability of their analytical tools.[1] Examination of a phenomenon that is in the process of changing—at the same time that its peripheral framework is changing as well—may eventually nullify the analytical system itself. Thus, for example, Gellner's study[2]—conducted after the independence of Morocco—which shows that the marabouts in the Atlas fulfill a clearly defined social function, is unacceptable to Eickelman,[3] who investigated the same phenomenon several years later.

In studying the tombs of saints revered by the Beduin in Sinai, Emanuel Marks[4] adopted the classical approach of Robertson Smith[5] and found a direct connection between symbols of the social order and models of social behavior. Among those Beduin, the saint's tomb denotes proprietary tribal rights over a geographical territory.[6] In addition, the use of the grave indicates that the tribe's territorial rights are protected by a supernatural power.

Eickelman only partially accepted the "theory of linkage" propounded by Smith, Marks and others. Instead he emphasized the interaction of maraboutism as an ideology with the social order to which it is linked. He submitted that two concepts are indispensable to an understanding of saint worship in Morocco: "obligation" and "closeness,"[7] From Eickelman's perspective, maraboutism is an expression of social activity directly linked to a given context, and this is how he explains the changes that occurred in maraboutism in Morocco after independence. Like many others, Eickelman ignores the religious and folk impulses implicit in this phenomenon. New modes of expression, dictated as it were by a new situation, might certainly be a different manifestation of the same phenomenon.

In a thorough analysis of the role of the marabout-*agurram* in the Atlas as exemplified by the saintly dynasty of the Ahansala tribe, Gellner examined the various tasks of the marabouts against the background of the existing social order. He also called attention to their contribution to the perpetuation of that order. According to Gellner, the functions of a marabout include "supervising the election of chiefs (*imgharen,* sing: *amghar*) amongst the lay tribes, mediating between groups in conflict, acting as a court of appeal in the settling of disputes, providing a sanctuary, working divine blessing, performing miracles, etc.[8] Some of Gellner's assertions are questionable, for example, that the urban society creation of the "healer" parallels the tribal society creation of the marabout. His emphasis on saint worship as a social function, above all with respect to living saints, much diminishes the significance of the phenomenon.

Soon after the publication of Gellner's book, a fascinating study appeared by Morsy.[9] Like Gellner, she stressed the sociological dimension of saint worship. However, using historical and folkloristic methods,[10] she also succeeded in developing an interesting model for analysing a combination of historical, sociological and literary elements that reciprocally illuminate and explain one another.

Dermenghem's study of saint veneration in North Africa, the fruit of some ten years of work, is undoubtedly the most profound.[11] Viewing the cult as a religious phenomenon, he analyzes its overt manifestations from the standpoint of its adherents, associated concepts, objects, holy places and literature. His detailed descriptions, based on personal observation, are most interesting. He succeeded in presenting a clear, well-ordered picture, despite an abundance of data that might have blocked a panoramic view. Fully aware of certain negative, aberrant manifestations, he nevertheless stressed the pure spiritual dimension that animates an individual, sometimes against his will. Someone who comes to a holy place to petition a saint will inevitably transcend his or her "normal" self and undergo an unadulterated religious experience.

The methods described here[12] are not necessarily applicable to the study of saint veneration as practiced by the Jewish minority in Morocco; rather they apply to an independent entity living in its own country, impinged on by countless elements that have no place in the life of the Jews. Hence, saint veneration among the Jews of Morocco must be considered as a totally independent, long-term phenomenon related to Moroccan Jewry's cultural creativity, but nevertheless bearing traces of the Muslim cult of sainthood.

Visits to tombs of saints was a controversial issue among the people of Israel in historical times. Antagonists castigated the custom as a contravention of the stricture prohibiting "prayers to the dead." Protagonists claimed that it is commendable to pray in a place where saints are buried, since the objective of the petitioners is to ask the dead to intercede for them with the Almighty. Maimonides himself derided the custom, maintaining that it was entirely useless. One issue that particularly exercised commentators was whether it is permissible for *Cohanim* to prostrate themselves on the graves of saints, the core of the debate being whether this exposed them to contamination.

Research in the present study reveals that saint worship among Moroccan Jews is unusual in its intensity of veneration as well as in the large number of saints worshipped. Even a superficial comparison with other Jewish communities confirms this assertion.[13] The question arises as to whether, in the absence of specific testimony, it is possible to determine when this cult emerged in Morocco. There is no doubt, however, that the phenomenon is very old, particularly those aspects of it associated with such natural objects as rocks, springs, and so forth.

One of the earliest references to saint worship appears in the manuscript of the twelfth century prayerbook of R. Shelomoh Ben-Nathan of Sijilmassa in Tafilalet.[14] In the fourth chapter the author notes that among the duties imposed on Jews in the month of *Elul* and at *Rosh Hashanah* is "*hada el-mussem el-sherif,*" that is, "going to a saint's *hillulah.*" It should be mentioned that the prayer book is written in Moroccan-Arabic. It is of particular interest that the author made use of two Arabic terms even using the word *ziyara* a number of times in the course of the Hebrew-language prayer to be recited at the saint's grave.

Beginning with the sixteenth century, as a result of both internal and external factors, saint worship among the Jews of Morocco acquired great momentum. At that time there was a conspicuous escalation of maraboutism in Morocco,[15] while in the Holy Land the custom of visiting the tombs of saints grew in popularity as Safed became an important kabbalistic center.

A list of saints and the facts known about them points up several major differences that facilitate classification according to given criteria. One important criterion is whether the object of veneration actually existed or was a figment of the imagination. Saints may be divided into two major groups: those who were real, living individuals and those who revealed themselves through dreams or some other means. The first group—except for a few isolated cases in which some sign of saintliness was manifest at the moment of death or immediately thereafter—includes rabbis and wise men known as erudite, righteous individuals. With respect to this group we are faced with a tantalizing question to which we have as yet no answer: What transformed certain rabbis into saints, while others, who might be more learned, were not sainted, even when none of them was reputed to be a miracle worker? Obviously, the populace decided who merits veneration as a saint: the process by which such a decision was reached, however, is not clear.

Another criterion that may be added to the above qualitative dimension is the quantitative/statistical dimension pertaining to the number of people who worshipped the saint and went on pilgrimages to his or her tomb. Three different groups of saints may be discerned here:

1. Local saints known to and venerated by the residents of a given village. Such a saint may have been connected with a local family. In the course of time, other villagers joined the family in worshipping the revered figure. Conversely, a person may have been directly endowed with sainthood in one of the more usual ways. The local saint was usually celebrated at a limited annual *hillulah,* but his tomb was visited frequently, generally on Fridays.

2. A regional or municipal saint, venerated by people in a num-

ber of villages in the same vicinity, a given region or a whole city. Like the saints in the first group, those in this category, too, are usually buried in the community's cemetery, and the grave was visited more or less frequently.

3. The national saint, venerated by all Jews of Morocco, to whom people flocked from all over the country.[16] Throughout the year these saints elicited devoted observance of activities connected with the *ziyara,* the mass *hillulah* and their complex cultic rituals.

On an individual level, there was no difference in the intensity of devotion accorded each saint. The strength and nature of the personal connection determined its fervour. Saints in all three groups were the objects of great veneration; the ceremonial ritual was a function of the number of believers, not the intensity of veneration.

Most of the saints in the third group—which included R. David U-Moshe, R. Daniel Hashomer Ashkenazi, Mulay Ighi and R. ʿAmram Ben-Diwan—are buried on remote mountaintops or in secluded valleys. Some scholars have interpreted this as the saint's desire for solitude "far from the vicissitudes of life and the importunities of people."[17] It seems to me, however, that this topographical and ecological hurdle demonstrates that someone seeking communion with the saint of his or her choice is ready to go to great lengths, which occasionally involves traveling long distances to inaccessible places. The worshipper thereby performs his first cogitative devotional act, and the inconveniences caused by the saint's geographical surroundings undoubtedly intensify the pilgrim's sense of purpose.

An interesting picture emerges when one examines the distribution of the graves of saints according to geographical regions of Morocco. On the Atlantic coast there are 102 tombs; between the coast and the Atlas Mountains there are 119; in the Mediterranean area the number of tombs falls to 11. There are 21 saints buried in the Middle Atlas; the number of graves of saints rises significantly in the High Atlas, reaching 214; 28 saints are buried in northeastern Morocco and 42 in the southeast. In the Anti-Atlas and the Sous, the present study identified 43 tombs, and in the Draa-Saghro area, 32.

A regional analysis of the cult of sainthood is of great interest. The farther south one goes on the Atlantic coast, the greater the number of graves—the highest figure being in the Salé-Rabat-Casablanca sector, where 57 saints are buried. Mogador, with 23 graves, has the highest number of saints of any of the cities on this coast. The large number of saints buried in Casablanca (18) is of special interest in view of the fact that at the beginning of the century only about 5,000 Jews lived there. The creation of saints in Casablanca in this century is closely associated with the mass migration to that city from the south, primarily from the Atlas Mountains; as a result, in the early 1950s about a third of the total Jewish population of Morocco lived in that city. There are few graves of saints in the northern region of the Atlantic coast, but from the standpoint of saint worship, the proximity to the large center of Ouezzane eased the situation for the population in the north. Out of a list of 29 holy places famous among all the Jews of Morocco, 7 are in the Atlantic coastal cities—a sixth of the total number of saints and about a quarter of the most famous pilgrimage sites.

In the region between the Atlantic coast and the Atlas there is a significant concentration of graves in important cities, the number reaching 44 in Fez-Meknes-Sefrou. The largest number, 48, is in Marrakech, the city with the most graves of saints in all of Morocco; from this standpoint it might be called the "holy city" of Moroccan Jewry. Here, too, the cult of saint worship tended to become stronger in the south. More than a fifth of all saints and ten famous holy sites are found in this area.

The smallest number of saints are buried in the Mediterranean region, where the Jewish population was historically small. There is no famous holy site in the region itself, but people there revered the burial place of R. ʿAmram Ben-Diwan.

In the Middle Atlas there are few sanctified sites. Again, this would appear to be directly related to the small number of Jewish communities in the area. The largest regional center is Beni-Mellal, in which two famous saints are buried.

Most of the graves, over a third, are in the western part of the High Atlas. There is no doubt that the large number of Jewish settlements in the area, together with the conditions typical of Jewish life there—difficulties of transportation and communication, dependence on local and regional authorities, and close contact with the Berber population known for its strong saint veneration—dictated the need among the Jews for saints of their own and motivated each community to establish its independent cultic ritual in homage to a particular saint. The two largest concentrations are in the Demnate-Sidi Rahal-Bou Hallou axis, with 36 saints, and the Ouarzazate-Skoura-Telouet-

Tazenakht axis, with 32 saints. Here again, the farther south one goes, especially south of Demnate, the larger the number of saints. Seven of the important holy sites in Morocco are found in the High Atlas.

Eastern Morocco is adequately represented on the map of holy graves, with 70 saints serving the needs of a Jewish population spread over a large area. In the north the large center is in Debdou, where there are 16 graves, and in the south—on the axis of Ksar Es-Souk-Gourama-Boudenib—there are also 16 graves. Ksar Es-Souk has not only one of the most famous tombs in all of Morocco—that of R. Yaḥya Laḥlu—but also a famous graveyard which, according to tradition, is the burial site of many unknown saints whose revelation will bring the redemption of the Jewish people.

In the region of the Sous and Anti-Atlas, in the southern part of the country, there is quite a significant number of saints, with an important center in Taroudant and vicinity. There are 13 graves of saints there, and another 7 at Tillin. The tomb of the famous R. David Ben-Barukh is in the Taroudant area.

In the Saghro and the Draa Valley area the number of saints' graves, relative to the number of Jewish communities, is large. One of the most famous Moroccan saints, R. Makhluf Ben-Yosef Abiḥatsira, is buried in Tarkellil, in the Draa Valley. Some twelve groups of saints are interred there, most of them members of the same family; these saints are buried together, as in Amazrou, where ten saints are interred in each tomb. Local Jewish traditions relate that until the twelfth century this was an autonomous Jewish realm. Prior to that there were frequent wars between the Jews and the Ḥaratin, descendants of Christian Abyssinians who anteceded the Muslims. Memories of wars and persecutions experienced by the Jews have apparently been perpetuated in the legends that tell of ten saints in each grave. The sanctification of Ulad Siggar—who traditionally "knew how to bring rain"—or the two sisters, El-Khwatat—who all their lives performed charitable acts—can be understood only in the context of the hardships of life in this arid region at the edge of the desert. Traditions concerning Yoab Ben-Tseruyah or giants from the time of Moses find expression in two gigantic graves close to that of R. David Naḥmias.

The correlation between the number of saints' graves and the density of Jewish population in the various regions is important. A superficial survey of the large number of tombs in the big cities (Rabat, Salé, Casablanca, Marrakech, Fez) would seem to indicate a positive correlation between the number of graves of saints and the number of Jews in each place. A more thorough examination, however, reveals that whereas the relationship between the number of saints' tombs and the number of Jews in the Atlas and the South is positive, with the proportion of saints' graves very much higher in relation to the Jewish population, it is negative on the Atlantic coast, in the Mediterranean area and the region between the coast and the Atlas, where there are few graves in relation to the number of Jewish inhabitants. The definitive factor is undoubtedly the large number of settlements in the Atlas and southern areas; only thus can the contradictory trends shown by the present research be understood.

An additional problem is the geographical distribution of Jewish graves visited by Muslims and Muslim graves visited by Jews. Statistically, this phenomenon exists in all parts of Morocco, but it is found more frequently and is more widespread in the southern area, particularly in the Atlas, probably as a result of the proximity in which the Jews and Berbers there coexisted.

A question arises as to whether there is an explanation for the geographical distribution of saints in Morocco and whether it is significant. Does the fact that there are quite a few saints in the south who, according to tradition, were originally from *Erets Yisra'el* mean that, as they traveled from one end of the country to the other, these envoys carried a religious message to remote communities? Or do legends about saints who came to Morocco long ago, and whose arrival in certain areas coincided with the salvation of both Jews and Muslims—as in the case of R. David U-Moshe—strengthen the right of local Jews to live and be buried in that place? If a Jewish saint protected not only the Jews but also the Muslims of a given area, the Jews' right to live there and be buried there acquired a measure of legitimization. This would seem to be the burden of most of the legends and traditions that underscore the salvation of Muslims by virtue of a Jewish saint.

Moreover, to what extent can one refer to the geography of holiness, and what is the significance of the various sanctified stations that have become the objectives of pilgrimages in given geographical areas? With respect to the south, it is altogether clear that the reason most graves of saints are concentrated in this area is directly related to the social and economic situation of the Jews. To a certain extent the presence of sanctified graves was a function of the socio-ethnic and geo-ethnic environment in which the Jewish population lived. The unstable status and insecurity of these Jews, their mountainous surroundings and the interaction with the Berber population, were undoubtedly factors conducive to increasing the number of saints in the area.

A map locating the saints shows there is no "vacant" terrain: the strength of the cult is expressed tangibly in the form of holy graves spread throughout Morocco. The density or paucity of these graves is caused not only by topographical conditions. It is a reflection of historic events and local pressures as well. Jews who were uprooted and moved away were not always able to retain ties with a saint buried near their previous homes. As a result, the memory of certain saints has been lost.

With respect to the ceremonial aspect of the cult, the *hillulah* held at the saint's tomb is without doubt the most important religious and social event of the annual cycle and individual life cycle of Moroccan Jews. It should be borne in mind that in Morocco, during the historic period under discussion here, there were no recreational facilities or institutionalized vacations. The only days of relaxation in natural surroundings were those spent at a saint's shrine immediately after Passover and *Sukkot,* both seasons when the weather is generally clement. The entire family would come along: husband, wife, children, grandparents. There were many reasons behind the family's visit to the saint, over and above renewing and strengthening the bond between them, as expressed in the pilgrimage and *hillulah* at the grave. A barren woman might come in the hope of being enabled to bear children; an unmarried girl might come hoping to find a mate; a husband might seek success in business; there might be need to thank the saint for a miracle he had performed; a child might be given his first haircut beside the saint's tomb in the presence of the entire family, and so on.

Difficulties of transportation in the years prior to the 1930s and 1940s did not deter celebrants from making the pilgrimage. In the absence of approach roads they traveled on donkeys or mules, often covering the last few kilometers by foot. The exaltation experienced by pilgrims as they neared the grave in the natural surroundings typical of these sites undoubtedly overcame any discomfort they might experience.

The *hillulah* brought together people from the most remote corners of Morocco, which meant joyful reunions with relatives and friends. It was a particularly good opportunity for women, ordinarily bound to an onerous household routine, to socialize freely with other women, renew old friendships, and make new acquaintances.

Along with its many positive manifestations, the cult of saint worship was accompanied by certain negative aspects which the rabbis were powerless to fight against.[18]

From recorded testimony and from the general outlines sketched above in chapters dealing with ceremonies pertaining to the cult of sainthood, it is evident that massive efforts were invested in the pilgrimage. They included procuring and preparing food, traveling, walking, settling down at the spot—which frequently involved erecting a shelter, renting a room or pitching a tent, slaughtering, distributing the foodstuffs, selling glasses and candles, lighting bonfires, and so on. At the same time, however, it does not do to exaggerate the importance of the material aspects of saint veneration. The ceremonial dimension, important as it may be, does not outweigh the spiritual dimension expressed in the profound religious emotion experienced by the celebrants.

A study of the phenomena associated with the cult makes one wonder whether cold, rational analysis can possibly evoke their full meaning. Much of the testimony quoted in previous chapters and particularly in Part Two shows the potency of an unadulterated belief in the miracles and powers of the saint, who appears as the numenical instance capable of responding to all of a petitioner's requests. As far as the worshippers are concerned, these are firm, solid elements in which they believe implicitly. The reality inherent in each manifestation of the cult of sainthood is incomprehensible if viewed through the prism of normal, natural reality. The emotional dimension of these manifestations embodies a reality of its own.

The ambiance of the *hillulah,* the special atmosphere permeating the site, and the sense of exaltation in anticipation of a miracle are important religious values that combine to form a deep spiritual experience very much like the experience of prayer. The believer aspires to truth and purity, striving to enter elevated realms that transmute one's material self and mundane daily existence. The experience represents a kind of immersion in a sanctified atmosphere that distills all negative manifestations—such as excessive eating and drinking or wild, unrestrained singing and dancing—and brings the believer unalloyed joy. The famous saying "*Hawwa ja yidawina*"—that is, "Here he comes to cure us," means not only healing the body and soul. It is also a profession of belief in the saint's divine power.

In such a rarified atmosphere of anticipation, it is obvious to all present that the saint will appear. The holy one may be made manifest through some sign—water emerging from the tomb, the sudden appearance of an animal, his image seen through the flames of a bonfire—or may actually appear among the celebrants. The saint's presence is not only a response to the expectations and supplications of the believers. It is a demonstration of the saint's complete identification with all those who have made such great efforts to reach heights of exaltation. Miracles now become self-understood. These heights are expressions of blind faith, of a profound religious experience that fortifies the celebrants' bodies and souls and newly imbues them with the power to withstand the hardships of daily life.

Some major concepts related to the veneration of saints by the Jews in Morocco merit special attention. The convocation at the *hillulah* creates a unique community with values and rules of its own. The social and religious egalitarianism adhered to by the worshippers on these occasions is certainly one of the more noteworthy concepts of the cultic ritual. The strict rules that have been established, for example, with respect to food distribution at the graveside of R. David U-Moshe, exemplify this. At every *hillulah* it was customary to offer much of the food to the public in general, whether it had been brought from home or was prepared from animals slaughtered on the spot. It is a "good deed" (*mitswah*) to offer food, as well as to partake of that offered by others. From a religious standpoint, both giver and receiver profit, for they are thereby performing a religious duty. This opening ceremony is an appropriate background for subsequent events. Although the equality achieved here is primarily of a religious nature, it has repercussions on the social plane as well.

Activities associated with the poor may be considered in the same egalitarian light. The many impecunious people who traditionally came to the *hillulot* accepted contributions unquestionably, just as those who gave considered their giving to be self-understood. It is well to remember that some of the money and food distributed equally among the poor was from the general coffers, that is, deducted from whatever was donated to or collected by the officials.

Some of the sense of equality may have gone by the wayside during the public auction of candles and glasses in honor of the saint; both the first candle and the first glass were sold to the highest bidder. But if we bear in mind that all the money thereby accumulated goes into the general treasury, the auction may be construed as a competition among disciples desiring to honor the saint, a competition that accrues to the advantage of the general welfare. Thus we find that despite the momentary publicity surrounding the highest bidder, his bid is for the good of the public as a whole, and the egalitarian dimension is in no way diminished.

The saint's contribution to these humanitarian activities is a direct function of his importance. A very well-known saint, who attracts masses of people to the *hillulah* as well as frequent visits throughout the year at his graveside, is a blessing for the community where he is interred. Such a community can sustain itself and sometimes even significantly improve its situation. Thus giving to the saint is in effect not only a contribution to a specific class in society, but to the economic and social balance of the community as a whole.

Is this a "system" invented by the impoverished communities of the south to ameliorate their condition? It certainly is a most effective means of bringing help to remote places. Contributions flow from synagogues in the saint's name in large cities, with thousands of collection boxes both there and in private homes; this demonstrates an improvement in fund-raising methods as well as the increased readiness of people to contribute on a regular basis to the saint and to the community near which the saint is buried. Muslims who happen to live in villages near the saint have also benefited from this assistance, particularly during the 1950s and 1960s.

The fact that an entire community is made up of people who worship the same saint creates an atmosphere of social equality, despite differences such as the room of a rich man and the tent of a poor man. Both of them try to be as close to the saint's tomb as possible. As the pilgrims congregate to perform certain rituals that are of vital importance to all of them, the differences among them are obliterated. They mingle freely, greet one another and converse amicably.

The second major concept of saint veneration relates to the all-important covenant that exists between the saint and his worshipper. This alliance can be created in a variety of ways, such as through a dream, a first visit to a saint's grave, a lifesaving miracle, or the saint's intervention to cure an illness. In some cases it may be an extension of an existing covenant between a worshipper's parents and the saint. In this case the relationship is expressed by naming a child after the saint or giving him his first haircut at the sacred tomb.

There are also examples of what may be called a temporary alliance, one created in the wake of a single visit to the saint or after he has given assistance on one occasion. Such a temporary bond often becomes permanent, is strengthened with every miraculous act performed on behalf of the worshipper, and is renewed each year with the visit to the saint's grave on the day of his *hillulah.* The alliance exists even if the worshipper is prevented from actually participating in the *hillulah;* in this case he gives money and candles to a proxy and samples food brought to him from the *seʿudah* in the saint's honor.

When there is an exclusive covenant between a family and a saint, the latter is considered the family's patron; his name often passes their lips. A covenant with one saint, however, does not prevent the family from visiting other saints as well. Such visits are considered meritorious, because they demonstrate a positive attitude to sainthood as a whole. A saint, too, may exhibit a similar degree of tolerance: if he finds himself unable to help, he may send a worshipper to another saint.

When the connection between worshipper and saint is particularly strong, the votary may describe himself as the saint's "servant" or "slave," indicating that the ties between them are more intensive, complex, and ramified than usual. Such ties can be created by the impact of a single event, for example, when a person has been influenced by an experience associated with the saint. Or a special interrelationship may have been forged over a period of time, during which the saint's frequent miracles have transformed an ordinary worshipper into a "slave."

It is difficult to explain the nature and quality of the bond between "slave" and saint, but its overt manifestations can be described. On the one hand, the worshipper has total faith in the saint's protection and identifies fully with him. On the other hand, he does not view his closeness to the saint as a privilege. But there can be no doubt of his great love for and devotion to the saint. He always feels obligated, through carefully organized activities, to spread word of the saint and enhance his name in the eyes of the public. Through conspicuous constancy and devotion, the votary becomes known as one who is particularly close to the saint. Others, therefore, will approach him with requests for help, believing that the saint will respond more readily to appeals transmitted through his "slave."

Another manifestation of the covenant is the concept of the saint's omnipresence in the life of an individual family. The saint's presence is so strongly and constantly felt throughout the year that he acquires something of a tangible daily reality and becomes an inseparable part of the household. If a child trips or falls, a utensil breaks or there is a sudden noise, the husband or wife instinctively calls upon the saint. The special glass or the candle lit in the saint's honor on Mondays, Thursdays, Saturdays, the first of each Hebrew month, and on festive occasions is an additional indication of the tie. The "sacred candle" is a constant reminder of the saint's presence in the house. This concept is obviously an excellent defense mechanism for the Jews: by stressing the constant presence of the saint they ensure themselves of his effective supervision and protection.

The saint, then, is omnipresent, and from this is derived the further concept that he is omnipotent. By his very essence, as well as because of his closeness to God, he can solve any problem that puzzles ordinary mortals. He can bring about miracles through the special forces of nature at his disposal. He is sensitive and responsive to whatever troubles his worshipper believes him capable of assuaging. If assistance is delayed or fails to come, the worshipper understands that he himself or the saint has met with some special circumstance that causes difficulty. The belief that the saint is omniscient and omnipotent is highly important in fortifying the worshipper's certainty that he is safe because the saint is protecting him.

Another important concept of saint worship in Morocco is the *Geulah*—the concept of redemption. Many unidentified saints, some originally from the Holy Land, are buried in Morocco. According to the belief of Moroccan Jewry, when they are identified redemption will be at hand. Revelation of previously unidentified saints can occur in a variety of ways: through dreams, by means of the saint himself, or by means of another saint—and it is vital for the very existence of the Jews. It imposes a crucial function on them: bringing redemption not only for themselves, but for all of Israel. The cult of sainthood, therefore, is not limited to Morocco and important only to its believers there. Rather it signifies complete identification with the religious ideal of the Jewish people and implies a constant effort on the part of all of Moroccan Jewry for the good of the Jewish people. This was the basis for the many links that in the past connected Morocco and the Holy Land. It is also one important explanation for the current worship of saints who were transported to Israel together with Morocco's Jews.

Unlike the other concepts of saint worship discussed above, the concept of redemption is not specifically connected with the life of the Jews of Morocco. But it makes them an integral part of the life and destiny of Jewry as a whole. It is interesting to see how this concept, which has its roots outside the cult of sainthood, filtered into Moroccan Jewry and became linked to saint worship. An awareness that the local system of relationships prevailing between saint and worshippers is part of a larger system of Jewish life fortifies ties on the local level and simultaneously stresses the contribution of the cult of saint worship on the national level. In other words, saint veneration not only brings immediate reward, it bears promise of later reward in the distant future.

In monotheistic religions the cult of saint worship has its origin in a simple idea. Although humans may believe in God, He is usually very far away, altogether unapproachable. The vast distance between God and the devout believer may shape God's attitude toward him or her. The number of people in need of God's help is so great—how can one individual be sure that he or she of all people, will be remembered? Therefore a need emerges for the intercession of a figure whose intrinsic qualities bring him or her close to God, but who nevertheless possesses human qualities familiar to all mortals.

Many questions concerning the essence of religious existence arise in this context. One thing is clear: the saint transcends the role of mediator and acquires an independent entity. It is not clear, however, to what extent the community of worshippers is able to define the relationship between God and the saints.

To summarize, it may be said that the cult of sainthood among Moroccan Jews represents an important and fascinating phenomenon, complex from the standpoint of its content and ramified from the standpoint of its function in daily routine activities. Jews lived in Morocco for many centuries, but they never built monuments or other edifices they could point to with pride. Because of social, economic, cultural and religious conditions, their homes were modest. Their source of pride — in the eyes of the Jews and Muslims as well — was the great rabbis who lived among them and the saints they venerated. Although the gloomy daily realities of Jewish life might irrevocably have sapped their vitality, the saints imbued the lives of those Jews with flavor and purpose, and guaranteed their continued existence.

Notes

1. R. P. Werbner (1977).
2. E. Gellner (1969).
3. D. F. Eickelman (1977).
4. E. Marks (1977).
5. See W. R. Smith (1894). This approach was extended by E. Durckheim (1912), and later by E. Shils (1975).
6. E. Marks (1977, p. 46).
7. By obligation (in Arabic, *ḥaq*), D. F. Eickelman (1977, pp. 10–12) means a system of obligations that binds the parties reciprocally through mutual services; by closeness (in Arabic, *qraba*), in relation specifically to maraboutism, the author's intention is that the saint is close to God and can influence him in favor of the believer.
8. E. Gellner (1969, p. 78).
9. M. Morsy (1972).
10. For methodological study of oral information, see J. Vansina (1973).
11. E. Dermenghem (1954).
12. Reference was made only to methods dealing with the given cultural area. For theories applicable to saint worship in other cultural areas, see C. A. Smith (1976); W. Turner (1974); R. P. Werbner (1977).
13. The lack of studies concerning saint worship in other Jewish communities prevents a profound comparison of the phenomenon. For studies in non-Ashkenazi communities, see A. Ben-Jacob (1973); S. Hayyat (1973); E. Brauer (1948); W. P. Zenner (1965); J. Trachtenberg (1970). For traditions in *Erets Yisra'el,* see Z. Vilnay (1985–86); A. Ya'ari (1962).
14. Y. Tobi (1983. "Rituel de R. Shelomoh Ben-Nathan de Sijilmassa." In M. Abitbol, ed., *Communautés juives au Sud du Maghreb.* Jerusalem: Ben-Zvi Institute, p. 421).
15. E. Doutté (1900, p. 12): "C'est au XVIe siècle que, tout d'un coup, sous l'effort d'une poussé religieuse dont aucun historien n'a encore expliqué clairement la nature et la genèse, le maraboutisme se développe d'une façon extraordinaire."

16. A. N. Chouraqui (1968, pp. 71–79); J. Gerber (1972, p. 121): "Certain graves of 'saints' had only local importance while others were the object of pilgrimage from all over Morocco."
17. H. Z. Hirschberg (1957, p. 152).
18. See Y. Messas (1934. *Mayim Ḥayyim.* Fez, pp. 169–70): "there is no *mitswah* and no respect to saints involved in pilgrimage and in candle-lighting." Beyond the positive or negative fundamental position of the religious institutions with respect to the veneration of saints, there were some practical manifestations opposed by R. Messas, such as travelling in *Sabbath,* eating without blessing, lacking modesty or chastity, excessive use of candle-lighting, and so on. In Israel today and also before its independence in 1948 some rabbis spoke against negative manifestations during the *hillulah* at Meron on *Lag b'Omer.*

1. The tomb of R. Eliyahu, Casablanca

2. The sanctuary of R. 'Amram Ben-Diwan, Azjen

3. The sanctuary of R. Ḥayyim Ben-Diwan, Anrhaz

4. The mausoleum of R. Ḥayyim Pinto, Mogador

5. The sanctuary of R. Abraham Mul Annes, Azemmour

6. The sanctuary of R. Yitsḥaq Abihatsira, Toulal

7. The tomb of R. David Ben-Barukh, Taroudant

8. The sanctuary of R. Abraham Awriwer, Dad near Settat

9. The mausoleum of R.Yehudah Zabali, Ksar El-Kebir

10. The sanctuary of R. Yaḥya El-Khdar, Beni Hmad

11. The tomb of R. Yaḥya El-Khdar, Beni Hmad

12. The mausoleum of R. Raphael Anqawa, Salé

13. The tomb of R. Raphael Anqawa, Salé

14. The tomb of R. Shelomoh Ben-Lḥans, Aghbalou

15. The tomb of R. David U-Moshe, Timzerit

16. The tomb of R. Nissim Ben-Nissim, Ait Bayoud

17. **The sanctuary of R. Shelomoh Ben-Lḥans, Aghbalou**

18. **The grave of R. ʻAmram Ben-Diwan, Azjen**

19. The tomb of R. Ḥayyim Pinto, Casablanca

20. The tomb of R. Yehudah Ben-'Attar, Fez

21. The mausoleum of R. Ḥananiah Ha-Cohen, Marrakech

22. The sanctuary of Ulad Zemmur, Safi

23. The grave of R. David Bussidan, Meknes

24. The sanctuary of R. Yaḥya Laḥlu, Ksar Es-Souk

25. The tombs of Ulad Zemmur, Safi

26. *Hillulah* at the grave of R. Ḥayyim Ḥuri, Beersheba (1974)

27. The sanctuary of R. Yosef Bajayo, Ntifa

28. The sanctuary of R. Abraham Azulay, Marrakech

29. The sanctuary of Mul Jebel El-Kebir, Sefrou

30. The tomb of R. Shelomoh Ben-Tameshut, Marrakech

31. The synagogue in the sanctuary of R. David Ha-Levi Dra‘, Draa

32. The mausoleum of Lalla Sol Ha-Tsaddiqah, Fez

PART TWO

17

THE SAINTS: TALES AND LEGENDS[1]

1. Rabbi Abner Ha-Tsarfati (Fez)

R. Abner was born in Fez in 1827, died there in 1883[2] and is interred next to R. Yehudah Ben-ʿAttar and Lalla Sol Ha-Tsaddiqah.

1.1 "In the name of God and the precious saints, they grant the request of everyone. We go to these saints to plead for things. They are better than the doctors. See! The doctors give pills. That's all! Their [the saints'] medicine is much better. I had a child who was dying, so I said: *I'll go to the grave of R. Abner Ha-Tsarfati.* At twelve noon I went. I said: *R. Abner Ha-Tsarfati, I won't accept any medicine from a doctor or anyone else. I will only accept your medicine. Have pity on me so my child will not die!* I was pregnant and he continued to suckle and that was bad for him. Later in the summer I stopped nursing him and the doctor told me: *Keep nursing him or he will die like a strangled dog.* He told me that he had no chance of living. *Nurse him, but even then it is not certain that he will live.* I said: *No! I won't nurse him.* When the doctor left I went to R. Abner Ha-Tsarfati and said: *I won't accept medicine from any doctor, only from you!* Then I went close to the grave and took a handful of earth. I mixed it with water and strained it through a strainer and gave it to him [the child] to drink until his belly was full, and I rubbed him all over with this water. I covered him with a blanket. After a quarter of an hour I see that he has opened his eyes and his face is as red as a rose and he is sweating, and he said: *Give me something to eat.* Actually he said *Naina,* because he couldn't talk yet. I gave him food and since then he has improved. You see, this shows that the saint is better than the doctor. If you believe in God, He will help you. Look, just the dust of the saint cured him, and the doctor gave him many medicines and they didn't help."

2. Rabbi Abraham Awriwer (Dad near Settat)[3]

R. Abraham is called Mwalin Dad after the mountain on which he is buried. On the mountain there are numerous cairns as well as a spring and a stone with a picture of a camel.[4] According to tradition, R. Abraham was born in the Holy Land and came to Morocco as an emissary.[5] His students are thought to be buried alongside him. He is best known for curing barren women. He is also venerated by the Muslims, who call him Sidi Brahim. His *hillulah* is celebrated on *Lag b'Omer.*

2.1 "One story tells that a Muslim's camel, laden with salt, was passing by. The camel's foot sank into the ground and couldn't be moved. They went to call the Jews. They told them: *You are the experts, get his foot out of there!* When they lifted its legs they found [a stone] with the date of R. Abraham Awriwer. Then they built a marker over it. Every time they wanted to put up a building it would collapse. In fact, there's only a stone."

2.2 "We used to visit his tomb at midnight. Once someone came and said to me: *If you believe, stick your hand inside the tomb where they light candles.* Everyone put burning candles there. I answered: *All right!* I put my hand into the flames. I felt that it was burning as if the skin was coming off. I put my hand on his face, on the face of that Jew of blessed memory. Next day his face was burned and my hands were fine. They weren't burned. That's faith! Somebody else came, put his hand [in the fire]. It hurt him all night, he didn't stop screaming with pain. My innocence did this for me."

2.3 "I'll tell you about Mwalin Dad. Why do they say Mwalin Dad? There were seven brothers. *Mwalin* means 'the owners.' There's a place there with a spring that they call *tagia.* We were there. An Arab started to tease people, saying: *I can jump in and swim here.* They said: *Who can swim here? If you're so brave, let's see you* [do it]!

He jumped in, but he never came back. I saw it with my own eyes. It was Mwalin Dad. I think they celebrate their *hillulah* on *Lag b'Omer.*"

3. Rabbi Abraham Cohen (Tidili)[6]

According to tradition, the saint is buried near a laurel tree. There is no tomb on the site, but there is a shrine for visitors. The saint was also called Mulay Matil until he appeared to a Jew in a dream and revealed to him that his name was R. Abraham Cohen. The Muslims, who also revere him, still call him Mulay Matil. According to tradition, he came to Morocco from Jerusalem in very early times.[7]

3.1 "Once it happened that a Jew had a quarrel with a non-Jew, and he had no promissory note. The minister [judge] told him [the Muslim] that the Jew should go and take an oath . . . and he [the Muslim] said: *I want him to swear to me on [the tomb of] Mulay Matil!* He [the judge] told him: *All right!* The non-Jew told the Jew: *We shall meet there,* and he left for the shrine of Mulay Matil. When he got there, he saw a snake. Its tail was here and it went all around the room. The head went to the other side. It opened its mouth. Before the Jew could get there and take the oath, the non-Jew went down the road [to meet the Jew] and told him: *Come. Give me whatever you want. There is no need to swear an oath.* [The Muslim took the snake as a sign that the saint did not wish the Jew to swear on the saint's tomb because his claim was just.] He went back with him and agreed on a compromise. I also wrote a song about this."

3.2 "A woman from Casablanca was barren and visited the saint. The guard of R. Abraham Cohen, Mulay Matil, came and told her: *If you want to be pregnant, take these stones.* She took them off the grave and put them on her back. By the end of the year, she had a child. It was a miracle."

4. Rabbi Abraham Cohen Bu-Dwaya (Tillit)

This saint is also called R. Abraham Ha-Cohen and R. Abraham Bu-Dwaya. His *hillulah* is celebrated on the eighth (last) day of *Ḥanukkah.* According to family tradition, he came from the Holy

Land as an emissary; upon his arrival in Tillit, he decided to settle there and marry a woman from the Malka family.[8]

4.1 "Before his death, may he rest in peace, at four o'clock on a Friday afternoon, he told them not to leave his corpse overnight. He told them to drive an iron tent peg between the sunlight and the shade, and the sun would stand still until they had finished burying him. And so it came about. He passed away. The members of the Burial Society prepared him. They sent men to dig the grave. They drove the tent peg between the shade and the sunlight, and the sun stood still until they finished burying him. They lit the candles, pulled out the tent peg, and only then did the sun set."

4.2 "R. Abraham Cohen Bu-Dwaya. His brother is R. David Cohen. They told me that when the Jews left Dades to go to live in Israel, two families stayed behind. Arabs came and started to dig up the cemetery. Then he, the saint, as if he were standing in front of them and turning their heads around, did something to them so that they couldn't harm the cemetery. That's what I heard."

4.3 "R. Abraham Cohen Bu-Dwaya. He is called Bu-Dwaya because he had a pipe shaped like a hand, and it was always lit. He came from the Holy Land. He was rich and learned. It fell to his lot to go abroad. He gave his wife a divorce following the religious tradition. He came to Tillit in the Dades Valley where saints are buried since the destruction of the First Temple. He came to Tillit and said: *This is Jerusalem!* He found a place of religious learning and great men. He came with a servant from the Holy Land. He stayed in the town and married a woman from the Malka family. The wisdom of the local men impressed him. He had children in Israel, too. He brought a manuscript with him that is now lost. In Tillit he had five more children. The saint could look at the stars and know who would live and who would die. When his time came, he summoned all the men of the town and told them: *Sit down!* It was the *Sabbath* Eve. They wanted to go home because it was the *Sabbath* Eve, but he said: *No one is going anywhere until they prepare a place for me in the next world.* He told them: *I have to be there before the* Sabbath. *Fix a stick so that the sun will stand still!* They recited the *shemaʿ* and took him to the cemetery. There is a song about this. They held his funeral, and the whole time the sun stood still. When they pulled out the stick, darkness fell. Women who had not given birth or whose children died, went and placed a cow's ear on the grave. He [the saint] told the Jews: *If an enemy comes, stones come out of the cemetery and drive them away!*"

4.4 "R. Abraham Ha-Cohen is called Bu-Dwaya. His sons were also saints. They have *zekhut* [merit]. People were afraid of them, may they rest in peace. They were harsh. We used to help them with money. They would come to the *mellaḥ* and we would give them money because they had merit. We could not say no. When the French entered our town along the road to [the tomb of] R. Abraham Ha-Cohen, they stood still with their hands up. They couldn't move. The officer came and asked and they [the people] said: *It is the saint. Turn around and then you will be able to go on.* R. Abraham Ha-Cohen would take a bottle of *maḥia* and say something and it would turn into water. He would take a *real* and put it on the neck of the bottle, hit it, and it would go into the bottle. He would hit it again and it would come out." [Testimony by the saint's great-grandson, who resides in Kiriyat Shemonah, Israel, as well as by other informants.]

5. Rabbi Abraham Darʿi (Imi n'Tanoute)[9]

R. Abraham Darʿi, who specializes in healing barren women, is buried on the mountain called Imi n'Tanoute near R. Yitshaq Ha-Levi and R. Masʿud Mani. His *hillulah* is celebrated on *Lag bʿOmer.* According to local tradition, the saint was discovered through a dream of one of the villagers, to whom he announced his name. He invited everyone to visit his grave and promised to grant their requests. Upon following the directions given in the dream, the villagers discovered a tombstone. In recent times a shrine was built near his burial place.

5.1 "Nobody knows him, only we from the village of Imi n'Tanoute. Once he performed a miracle for me. My daughter had a white spot in her eye. I used to light memorial candles for the saints to beg for their mercy, but I never took her to the doctor. Once, in a dream, a woman asked me: *Why are you crying?* I answered: *My daughter is sick.* She opened a box and told me that there was *zaʿtar* [savory, a bush with fragrant purple flowers] which I could make drops of to put in her eye. I asked her her name, and she said she was the wife of Rabbi Braham [a nickname for Abraham, the saint's name]. I woke up and told my uncle's wife and she told me that in Mogador there was a woman who had suffered from eye problems and was healed with *za'tar,* water and a little salt."

5.2 "Once Muslims came to plough the place where the saint is buried. They thought: *Why is this saint blocking our way? Let's dig up his grave.* When they started to plough, the ploughshare got stuck in the ground and the farmers were paralyzed. They told them: *This was caused by the Jews alone.* The Jews came and found the farmers paralyzed near the tomb of the saint. The Muslims begged the saint's forgiveness. I saw this with my own eyes. Then the Muslims placed stones all around the tomb and said to the saint: *Ḥazzan! This is your place; no one will dare touch it again!*"

6. Rabbi Abraham Mul Annes (Azemmour)[10]

The burial place of R. Abraham Mul Annes or "The Master of the Miracle" is one of the most interesting examples of a cultic site; during the 1940s[11] it gained great popularity throughout Morocco. Although the cult has flourished in modern times, we are ignorant of many precise details as to how it arose. Tradition tells that the saint is buried in the courtyard of a house in the old quarter of Azemmour. Later, a tomb of sorts was improvised. He is also venerated by the Muslims.

6.1 "We have a saint who revealed himself. His name is Abraham Mul Annes. He was in Azemmour, but he did not reveal himself. When the Jews came, he revealed himself to them and told them: *I am R. Abraham Mul Annes. You must come to me and pay me the honor due me.* The saints appear in a dream to people who are saints like them so that people will believe what they say. So we started to go there, and the Arabs who were there started to bow to us and to honor us, because since the Jews began coming there, they buy fruits and vegetables from them [the Arabs]. They used to say that since the Jews came they really started to live. So they [the Jews] go there, and if water comes out of the tomb, it means that their request has been granted. If not, go home."

6.2 "In Azemmour there is Mul Annes. I used to visit his grave. I'll tell you why they call him that. The Jewish *mellaḥ* was almost empty. The French governor who was in Azemmour, a commander, had a sick daughter, and they couldn't find a cure though they went to many doctors. The saint, seeing that the Jewish quarter was becoming depopulated, appeared to the notables of the community in a dream and told them: *Ask this commander to bring me his daughter to sleep at my grave for seven days and I shall heal her.* They went and told him the saint's request. He answered: *All right. If he will cure my daughter, I shall do a lot.* He brought his daughter, and seven or eight days later she recovered, thanks to God and the precious saint. At first he was not called Mul Annes. Nobody knew him by this name. But since this happened, they call him Mul Annes. The commander every year brings a *seʿudah.* The Muslims and the Jews know him."

7. Rabbi Aharon Assulin (Fercla)

This saint is the master of the place, and the Jews of the area used to visit his grave. Members of his family residing in Sdot Mikhah and Ofakim in Israel still celebrate his *hillulah* during *Ḥanukkah.*

7.1 "He [the saint] performed a miracle for my father. When I was young, in Fercla, the French came and built their office in a village called Tinejdad. The French soldiers used to send Muslims to buy *maḥia* from the Jews. A Muslim comes to my father and says to him: *Give me a bottle of* maḥia! If it was worth a *lira,* for example, he gave him two *liras.* The non-Jew sold it to the soldier. The soldier got drunk, took his rifle and started shooting. He killed non-Jews, soldiers. The authorities didn't know how to catch him. When anyone came close, he would shoot. They threw a hand grenade at him from a distance and killed him. My father asked The Lord to bless him. For eight days he didn't leave the house. [Neither did] the man in charge of the Jews. The first miracle was that the man who drank the *maḥia* was killed. If he hadn't been, he would have told who the Muslim was who had sold it to him, and the Muslim would have told who the Jew was who had sold it to him, God forbid. He was killed. The authorities then came to the Committee of the Jews in Fercla. They didn't ask them who sells *maḥia,* because then they would have had to tell my father's name, but they asked them who made *maḥia* there, and they told him: *We all make* maḥia, *all of us.* This is another miracle. My father was afraid for eight days and he cried out: *O Rabbi Aharon, my Lord!* He cried: *Perform a miracle for me so that I can be your servant and light candles to you. Save me!* The chairman of the Committee came to my father and told him: *Whomever you serve, keep on serving him!* We all agreed. *If the governor had asked* *us who sells* maḥia *in the village, we would have told him it was you.* It was my father who made it. That was his trade. But he asked: *Who makes it?* and not *Who sells it?* So they said: *We all make it.* From then on he (my father) always lights [candles] and greatly honors him [R. Aharon]. He is a great saint. For three days my father and mother fasted because of this."

8. Rabbi Aharon Ha-Cohen (Demnate)[12]

R. Aharon is also called Sayyid Aharon by the Jews. The saint is also worshipped by the Muslims, who call him Sidi Harun or Sidi Mul Lbrakhat, that is, "My Lord Master of Blessings." The Mwalin El-Gomra, a group of saintly *yeshibah* students, are buried on the same site.

8.1 "We do not have any story at all about him [the saint], but I have a story that I heard from a Muslim. When? We wanted to celebrate *Tu b'Shebat* [the 15th day of *Shebat,* observed by eating dried fruits] or something. We had a Rabbi Shimʿon Bar-Yoḥay Society that dug graves and buried the dead. I bought a calf. We took it to the ritual slaughterer and he butchered it. A Muslim came and asked the slaughterer: *Do you know this saint? He is a saint and they* [the Muslims] *call him Sidi Mul Lbrakhat.* He said to him: *You know, a long time ago, so the Muslims say, a family of Muslims came and sat by the cemetery, a bit away from the cemetery. A family came and sat there. They had a young girl who was blind. People made a lot of trouble for her. Once, poor thing, she couldn't take it anymore so she ran away. She walks and walks . . . until she got there. She didn't know [where]. Until she arrived right at the saint's tomb. She sat down and cried. Suddenly she hears a voice, they're calling him from the cemetery:* R. Aharon! R. Aharon! We are waiting for you to come and study in the cemetery! *He said to them:* Forgive me, but tonight I am not coming because I have a guest here and I cannot leave her. *He sat there and spoke to her. He passed his hand over her eyes and the next day she could see. She went back all by herself. Her relatives saw her.* What happened? What happened? *She told them everything. They were so happy, and what honors they showed him! From that day on they honored this place and call it Mul Lbrakhat.*"

8.2 "So that's how we made a Society of Sayyid Aharon Ha-Cohen. We study the *Zohar* [a theosophical work, the most important book of the cabalistic literature]. On Friday we go there. Everyone goes. We have a ritual meal. Once there was a Muslim, may his name be wiped out, who really hated [Jews]. Once two members of the Society left [for home]. There was a ford near [his] fields. He took olive branches and hit them with them. One of them went to the saint to pour out his anger and said: *If you do not perform a miracle for us on this Muslim, we will not believe [in you] or do anything!* So what happened to him [the Muslim]? As soon as he got home, he went crazy. He stayed that way for three days."

9. Ait El-Cohen (Imini)

Ait El-Cohen were also called Ait Cohen, Seven *Cohanim* or just *Cohanim.* Their *hillulah* was held twice a year, in the month of *Tebet* and on the first of the month of *Elul.* According to tradition, these *Cohanim* came from the Holy Land. Their identity is not known. They are also venerated by the Muslims.

9.1 "On a mountain around half a kilometer from Imini, seven *Cohanim* are buried, so it is told. This is a very ancient burial place. It is said that they came from Jerusalem. They were rabbinical emissaries. They were sent to bring donations to the Holy Land. So when their *hillulah* is held in *Tebet* or on the first of *Elul,* everyone loves to participate in this *mitswah*—men, women and children. Everyone loves to carry a jug of water on his shoulder all the way to the saint. They bring calves and sheep and slaughter them there. They come to beg for mercy, for instance, if someone has no children, barren women. . . . People are granted whatever they ask for. The Arabs would also bring cows, goats and sheep there for an offering. Sometimes, when there was no rain, they would come to us to beg us to slaughter a calf at the graves of the *Cohanim* so that it would rain, because they had no irrigation there. I myself can testify that on Friday nights I often saw Arabs going to the [Imini] river to bathe, change their clothes, bring candles and light them. I often went there with Arabs. The place is always lit up with candles."

10. Rabbi ʿAmram Ben-Diwan (Azjen)[13]

R. ʿAmram Ben-Diwan is one of the most celebrated saints of the Jews of Morocco; people would flock to his grave from every corner of the country. According to tradition, he was born in Hebron and came to Morocco at the beginning of the eighteenth century as an emissary from the Jewish community in the Holy Land. He is buried close to the Azjen cemetery, near the city of Ouezzane.[14] There is no tomb there, only rocks and a wild olive tree. The Muslims called him Ben-ʿAmram and would also visit his grave. Muslim leaders honored him and helped defray the costs of the *hillulot,* celebrated by the Jews three times a year: on *Lag bʿOmer,* on *Tu bʿAb* (the 15th of *Ab*), his memorial day, and on the first of *Elul.* Even now the Jews of Morocco continue to celebrate his *hillulah* in Morocco[15] and in Israel. According to tradition, R. ʿAmram is the father of R. Ḥayyim Ben-Diwan; father and son came to Morocco together.

10.1 "I went to Ouezzane, to R. ʿAmram Ben-Diwan. They [the pilgrims] slaughter and have tents, and they stay there seven days. All the people and those who made vows. He [R. ʿAmram] also used to help the Muslims. I myself once took an insane Christian woman there. She used to get up in the middle of the night to murder her father and mother. I took her to him [the saint] and she stayed there with me for seven days. She was insane. The demons grabbed her from underground. They would order her in the middle of the night to get up to murder her father and mother. Every night they slept with fear. They went around with her to all the saints. I said to her: *Look, I'm going to Ouezzane. Come with me.* So she came with me. We stayed there seven days, and she was more at peace when she went away from there. She no longer got up at night with knives. Before this, the French woman said that someone would come and tell her to kill her father and mother. When the saint cured her, no one came to tell her this. She slept soundly. We prayed for her, in Arabic, and we thank God that she felt more at peace. After someone recovers, he vows to make a *seʿudah.* He says: *Here is a* seʿudah *for you, O my lord saint!* They invite people, they bring a band and lots of drinks. Sometimes doves go out, and that is a sign that the saint has answered us. Sometimes when a bird comes out, they say that this is a sign that the saint's soul is in that bird or dove in order to answer people. I never saw this, but they even tell about the snake, that if it comes out, they give a *zgharit.* They give a *zgharit* until the whole world shakes. They say: *Look, the saint has answered us!* No, no one is afraid of the snake. He doesn't hurt anyone. He goes out, stands up, sticks out his tongue, and dances. And the people give a *zgharit* until he goes back to his place. The tree with the flames under it day and night was not burned. The tree was always green. It was never burned and it never lost its color. Boxes of candles burned under it. Everyone who came to visit hung something on the tree. One person hung a rag, another a ribbon. They say that this is so that God will grant their request. It's like writing a note and putting it in the place of the pilgrimage. We didn't know how to write, so we would hang up this ribbon . . . we would leave bottles of water for a whole night and sometimes for seven days. Afterwards we would drink the water or rub it on our bodies. Sometimes we would take it in the morning and return it in the evening. There were two bottles, one we would leave and the other we would use. We would give some of this water to neighbors who didn't go there. And if someone wanted to leave oil there overnight, he could. He could also rub it on his legs if he had rheumatism, for instance. It heals. We would put jewels of silver there and then wear them around our neck or put them in a bag. It is the saint's medicine."

10.2 "Once there was a wicked shereef who hated Jews. He came to cut his [the saint's] tree, and we were present. Twenty Arabs came with saws in their hands. The shereef pitched a tent on the spot and sat down. They passed around tea to the people, and he sent someone to cut down the tree. They were all injured. Some lost hands, others lost legs, and someone died. Not one was left. Then the shereef left the place quickly on his horse. He was afraid he would die, too. He arrived in Ouezzane and began to tell how the Jews had performed miracles. He came to vent his anger on the Jews there. Then the shereef of Ouezzane, who liked Jews, told him: *It is the* Sayyid [the Saint]. *You went to harm him and he avenged himself on you.* He said to him: *You, you have exactly one year to live!* He told him: *What do you expect? If anyone harms the Jews, God avenges Himself on him. He is a* sayyid, *how dare you go and cut down his tree? What do you have against him?* Everyone stood around gaping. He stayed quiet until the Eve of *Yom Kippur.* On the Eve of *Yom Kippur,* he told the Jews that anyone who blew the *shofar* would go to prison. But in the synagogue of R. ʿAmram, the *shofar* was blown even though no one blew it. People heard it and so did the policemen who came to inspect the synagogue. Then they took Yosef A. to prison. The poor fellow hadn't even been there. The police went to the shereef and told him: *We heard it!* He asked: *Who?* They said:

They have no one but Yosef A. He said: *Put him in prison!* On the Eve of *Yom Kippur!* Then the people went to Daniel, who was an important man, and told him: *What is this? He didn't blow the* shofar, *but they took him to jail.* He [Daniel] went to Mulay El-ʿArbi, the shereef who liked Jews, even though he was a Muslim. He told the shereef: *I am leaving this city because Mulay ʿAli and Mulay Aḥmed rule so unjustly and unfairly.* He [the shereef] asked him: *You did not blow the* shofar? He said: *Sidi, we did not blow it; the police lied.* He asked: *But what if God blew the* shofar? So he immediately summoned the police and told them to release him [Yosef A.], because the shereefs Mulay ʿAli and Mulay Aḥmed were his grandsons. He said to them: *If God acts righteously, then He did it, and if not, do as you please.* That night Mulay Aḥmed [who had forbidden the blowing of the *shofar*] went to sleep in his palace and he never woke up. They went to see how he was and they found him dead. Everyone got up, even the Jewish women mourned him, and his mother used to say: *All this was because of the injustices he did to the Jews.* Then the Jews had some relief."

10.3 "They tell that once a [Muslim] wedding procession passed by and they started to mock R. ʿAmram Ben-Diwan. They stayed just as they were. They were all paralyzed. Then they started to weep. Their relatives came from the village and brought a cow for slaughter. They slaughtered her near the head [the anterior side of the tomb] of R. ʿAmram and then they could move."

10.4 "I believe that God is One, and our masters the saints only ask things of God. When they ask God for something, He gives it to them, because God cannot let the saint go away empty-handed. His tears fill up a pool, and God gives him what he asks for. Many sick people go to the saint. And he would help them. If a person passes by—since there are seven worlds and a world beneath us—and if he has stepped on someone [a demon], it causes epilepsy. Then they go to someone who writes [an amulet] because the doctors cannot help. They go to the saint, tie the hands of [the sick person], and he prays, begs, and weeps, and if God grants his request, he becomes new [healthy]. And if not, he dies. Sometimes they pass through the flames and aren't burned. Many barren women go [to the saint]. R. ʿAmram left his belt, which is in the hands of Makhluf Seruyah. Every woman who wore it had an easy delivery, because in those days there was no doctor, only this belt. They would take the belt and put it on the woman's head and everything would go smoothly. The ancestors of Seruyah got it and passed it on from generation to generation. A woman who has her period cannot enter. She can go as far as the cemetery, but cannot go inside. Because it is in the fields and she can make her request from outside. The Lord may grant her request; if not. . . . The Jews in our town of Ouezzane were terrified of these things. Under no circumstances can a woman with her period go to R. ʿAmram. Even in the synagogue, no woman from Ouezzane goes there to light candles. These are the women of Ouezzane. I know nothing about the others."

10.5 "On the grave of R. ʿAmram there is nothing but stones. It is because of his modesty, because R. ʿAmram was very humble. On the place where he is buried there is a large stone next to a tree and many small stones next to it. So people say that the large stone is his grave. And the small stones—they say that everyone who passed would weep by a small stone and ask, with the small stone in his hand, and say: *R. ʿAmram, do thus and so for me, it is like a letter. If you are here, here is your stone, and if you are not here, when you come you will see it!* And so they leave stones. Many people did this and that is the reason why there are many stones there. The saint is not only in Ouezzane, he is also in Paradise, and only sometimes can you manage to catch him there. You can't always catch the saints in their place. You don't know whether they are there or not. That's why I take a stone and say what I want and say: *Behold, I am writing the letter to you and leaving it here!* Then when he comes from the Paradise to his grave, he finds the "letters" there and reads them. And then someone comes to you in a dream, but it is not he."

10.6 "If there was some great trouble, we would go to pray at his tomb. I remember how once, when I still lived there, all the Jews of the place went to R. ʿAmram, and then the Arabs came and said to us: *Our pleas have not helped and now you go and ask your saint!* That day, we didn't even get back from R. ʿAmram's before it started to rain and we came home drenched."

10.7 "I myself took [to the saint] someone who had been hit by a policeman and couldn't walk anymore. Then they said to me: *Ḥabib, you take him to R. ʿAmram!* I hired a donkey—he [the sick man] lived in Casablanca—I hired a donkey and put two sacks on him. On one side I put him and on the other side I put stones. I took him and I went from Casablanca to there. This was eleven years ago [1963].

There were buses but no one wanted to take him. So I went into the saint's shrine with him and tied him up with ropes, so he wouldn't move, and I threw him next to the saint and said: *Here, oh saint! Either cure him or finish him off!* Blessed be He and blessed be His name! He did not sleep that night until his leg had healed. The saint did not come to him in a dream but sent a snake which crawled over him. The people saw the snake but it did not touch anyone. In the morning I found that he was fine. In the morning he could already stand up and afterwards he started to walk."

10.8 "They say that R. ʿAmram Ben-Diwan is from the Holy Land, and that his son got sick and went blind. His son was R. Ḥayyim Ben-Diwan. He had always wanted to take him to the Cave of the Patriarchs at Hebron. Every Friday, R. ʿAmram would take a sum of money and give it to the guard without saying a word to him. Several Fridays went by until one day the guard asked him: *I want to know what you give me the money for.* He told him: *I want you to know that I have a son thus and so and I want to take him inside the Cave of the Patriarchs and beg for mercy on him!* Then he said: *Come this Friday when the Arabs are entering to pray, and then I'll let you in.* That Friday he did just as he was supposed to do. He admitted them. But then he went to the Arabs and told them: *There is a Jew here with his son entering the Cave.* So the Arabs said to him: *If we find the Jew and his son, then that will be all right, but if we don't, then whatever we meant to do to them, we'll do to you!* Then the son of R. ʿAmram entered and he could see, and he asked: *What graves do I see here? What is here?* He came close to them and his eyes were open. Three men came out to them—Abraham, Isaac and Jacob—and held their hands and brought them in through one gate, and they found themselves in Ouezzane. The Arabs came and did not find anyone, so they took it out on that Arab."

11. ʿAsarah Be-Kever (Amazrou)[16]

The name means "ten in the grave." According to tradition, ten persons are buried in each grave. It is forbidden to enter the site.

11.1 "In Amazrou there is a cemetery near the village. There are graves there and they say that in each grave there are ten persons. They say that once there were pogroms and many Jews were killed, so they buried ten people in each grave. At last, nine were left and they didn't know what to do. Then an angel in white appeared and asked the gravediggers what they were waiting for. They told him. He agreed to be buried with them so that they could close the grave. The gravediggers took a ritual bath first, cut their nails, and purified themselves."

12. Rabbi Daniel Hashomer Ashkenazi (Arba Touggana)[17]

R. Daniel Hashomer is one of the saints most venerated by Moroccan Jews; they flocked to his shrine every day of the year. He is known especially for his miraculous cures of mental illnesses. According to tradition, he came from the Holy Land to Morocco in early times. He is also venerated by the Muslims, who call him Sidi Denil. In various places in Israel, Moroccan Jews continue to celebrate his *hillulah* on the first of *Elul.*[18]

12.1 "I was sick for three months with something like typhus. I don't remember. I couldn't talk or walk. My father of blessed memory took me to this rabbi [R. Daniel Hashomer]. I had barely reached there when I got well. I opened my eyes and asked my father for some food. We spent two nights there. I felt good and I wasn't sick. I was twelve or thirteen years old, and in my joy at getting well, I told myself: *Oh, Lord, when I grow up and have a good job. . . .* I vowed that I would come [back] to this saint."

12.2 "The Muslims were afraid of him [the saint]. No Muslim who cut off a piece of the tree there or did something [bad] lasted long. A year ago one [a Muslim who injured the saint] died. The Muslims are afraid of him. They say: *This* shomer [the Saint] *is tough!*"

12.3 "When I was in Casablanca, I was inducted into the French army [probably the Foreign Legion], and I came home five years later. I got married. I bought a store and sold things there. People used to go to the saint's tomb. I also decided to go. Then I remembered that I had made a vow to build a house at the sanctuary. I made up my mind and I went. At that time, Arabs worked in the cemetery of this saint. It was an ancient cemetery. I went over to one Arab and told him that I was interested in building a house there. He answered: *What do you need?* I said: *Stones!* I brought cement and tiles in order to build there. I started to build. The Muslims began to dig the foundations. I asked them if they found a stone with anything written on it to bring it to me.

That same day a Muslim suddenly brought me half a stone. On it was written: *Mar Moshe Ben-Moshe bi-shnat 5200, be-ḥodesh Iyyar* [Mr. Moshe the son of Moshe in the Hebrew year 5200 in the month of *Iyyar*]. That's what was written there. I told these Muslims that whoever found the other part of this stone would get 100 reals. . . . An Arab brought me the other part. I glued it to the first part. I built this tomb and put this marble there. I built a house with all the amenities. I affixed a piece of marble to the house with my named carved in it. . . . It was in 1944. The *qadi* came there. The Muslims invited him. They fixed the boundaries [of the shrine]. . . . Afterwards I had to organize the *hillulah* at the shrine, but I didn't know where to start. . . . A certain rabbi said to me: *Let us write letters to the cities telling them that we are celebrating the* hillulah *in the month of* Elul. *And let us tell them about all the saint's miracles.* . . . I went to the members of the committees of the communities of Casablanca, Fez, Rabat, Es-Saouira, Marrakech, Beni Mellal and Settat, and we wrote about all the miracles that R. Daniel Hashomer of blessed memory had performed. And we also fixed his *hillulah* on the first of *Elul* each year. We sent letters around to all the cities to invite large numbers of Jews to visit the saint's shrine. I went to the *qadi,* informed him that we had fixed the *mussem* in the month of *Elul,* and asked him to notify all the villages in the vicinity that anyone who had cows, eggs, and poultry should bring them [to] sell because it was the first [*hillulah*] and the Arabs did not know about it. I went to Casablanca and printed tickets for an allowance for the poor. . . . When the first truck from Casablanca arrived, I told the people about setting up a committee for the shrine. I told them that only volunteers would be considered. All the people were glad. People also came from the other cities. We set up a committee of thirteen people including myself. I told the people that they would work for the sake of Heaven [without pay]. . . . I addressed the women: *Ladies, is there anyone among you who wishes to work for the sake of Heaven? It's not work, it's just welcoming visitors! How? . . . Give* maḥia *to everyone who comes. And hand out the tents!* I also brought an electric generator and hung up lights. . . . The women were in charge of the reception. Everyone who came received a *zgharit* and a glass of *maḥia* to gladden his heart. . . . At the Evening Service I requested that the Jews not quarrel with the Muslims . . . because we had come to the saint so that he would cure the illness of each one of us, and so that the Muslims would always remember us [favorably] and would help and serve us. . . . Next day was the first of the month. The *pqidim* [officials] each had his own job to do. Everything went very smoothly."

12.4 "Everyone who suffers from epilepsy is cured there. Once they brought a girl from Meknes or Fez and she recovered instantly. That night the image of the rabbi appeared. For three hours his image appeared inside a flame. Not only I but thousands of other people saw it. The saint, may he rest in peace, had a beard and wore a *qawaq* [scarf] on his head."

12.5 "There was a man who was a shepherd. At that time people told him that this saint was not important. He went and found burning candles and other valuable objects on the saint's tomb. He took them. Suddenly daylight turned into the darkness of night, and he didn't know where to go. Wherever he turned he saw darkness. His family and friends started to look for him. They looked for him but didn't find him. They began to shout and to tell everything that had happened to him. They came to our master, the saint, and they slaughtered on his tomb. Only then did this Muslim see the light of the sun, and he left."

13. Rabbi David Alshqar (Casablanca)[19]

According to tradition, R. David Alshqar is Mulay Ighi, one of the most illustrious saints in Morocco. His *hillulah* is celebrated on *Lag b'Omer,* but the Jews visited his tomb every day of the year, particularly on Saturday night. The Jews call him Mul El-Blad, "Master of the City." Tradition has it that he came from the Holy Land.

13.1 "We have a big cemetery, and the first one [of the saints who are buried there] is R. David Alshqar. He came only as a traveler. The place where he is was an Arab's orchard. He died and they buried him there. Afterwards he showed himself, and then the Jews began to bury their dead there and to visit the place. If there was a *hillulah* or the first day of the Hebrew month, they would come and ask the Arab guardian to light a candle at the saint's tomb, but they did not enter because the place belonged to the Arabs. The owner of the orchard was an Arab, and if anyone died they buried him in that cemetery. When the owner of the orchard died, the Jews bought the place."

13.2 "In the Casablanca cemetery which was on the rue Krantz, they celebrated the *hillulah* of R. David Alshqar on the day of the *hillulah* of R. Shimʿon Bar-Yoḥay. He is Mulay Ighi, who is buried in Ighi, near Zerekten. He is not buried in Casablanca, but they used to celebrate his *hillulah* there. If anyone has vowed to visit his [Mulay Ighi's] grave or bring a votive offering to the people studying in the saint's shrine, but cannot go to Zerekten because it's too far away, or because it is difficult to travel to Marrakech and from there walk to Mulay Ighi, then he can bring it to the Casablanca cemetery. There was a room there in which members of the Burial Society, as well as *yeshibah* students, recited Psalms for the repose of the saints. Then they would pay the pledge or make a *seʿudah* or give to charity. They light candles there. There was a legend that a man or a woman dreamed that whoever couldn't go to the saint's tomb could come to the Casablanca cemetery, and with the help of the rabbis and students offer up a prayer for the saint's repose, distribute the gifts, the votive offerings which he had vowed, and the *seʿudah.*"

14. Rabbi David Ben-Barukh (Azrou n'Bahamou)[20]

R. David Ben Barukh, also known as R. Daud Ben-Barukh, R. David Ben-Barukh Ha-Cohen, R. David Ben-Barukh Ha-Cohen Azzogh (the Great) and R. David U-Baruk, is the most celebrated member of the Ben-Barukh Ha-Cohen family.[21] His grandsons, the brothers R. Barukh and R. Yamin Ha-Cohen, and his great-grandsons, the cousins R. David Ben-Barukh (Baba Dudu) and R. Pinḥas Ha-Cohen, are also well-known saints. The *hillulah* of R. David Ben-Barukh is celebrated on the 3rd of *Tebet.* In various parts of Israel it is still celebrated in private homes as well as in synagogues named after him. The Muslims venerate him as well.

14.1 "Every year I went to R. David Ben-Barukh. I used to take my wife. In the beginning there were no rooms. Once we all slept in one room. I saw how crowded it was, so I gave orders to the caretaker and he built me a large room. I had everything there: beds, an oven. . . . My grandfather was the one who built the boundary around the shrine. My grandfather is buried there, next to him [the saint]. The Arabs killed him. We had many fields there. When I grew up I wanted to see the area, so we would leave Casablanca every *Ḥanukkah* and stay there about ten days. We had family there and we stayed with them."

14.2 "I used to go to him and ask for his blessing and celebrate his *hillulah* every year. I made a vow. He performed many miracles. A great saint. Once a rabbi came as an emissary from the Holy Land to collect alms. He arrived at the saint's house on Passover Eve. R. David Ben-Barukh was wearing a *khil* [a modest woolen garment]. He [the emissary] asked: *Where is R. David Ben-Barukh?* He said to him: *Why do you want him?* He answered: *I want to spend the festival with him.* He said: *I am he. Welcome!* The saint, may he rest in peace, took him to his home. He took him to the bath house. He gave him clothes. He rejoiced with him on the night of the *Seder* [a ceremonial dinner held on the first night of Passover that includes the reading of the *Haggadah*]. The candles were lit, the cups were ready for the *Seder,* when a tear fell from his [the emissary's] eyes. The saint said to him: *What is it?* He said: *I miss my home.* He [the saint] did like this [gestured] with his hand. The emissary fell asleep and arrived at his [own] home. He [the saint] told him: *Wake up! Here is your wife. Here are your children. Here is everything!* The rabbi said: *You really are a saint! I am your servant!* This is what I heard from people who were at the saint's shrine."

14.3 "The family of R. David Ben-Barukh, may he rest in peace, came from Oufran. A cruel Muslim shereef oppressed the Jews of the *mellaḥ* of Oufran in the Tiznit region. That is where the family of R. David Ben-Barukh, which is descended from Aaron the priest, comes from. R. Barukh [the father of R. David], may he rest in peace, left the place and is buried in Mogador. They ran away from the village. R. Barukh lived in a village called Imin n'Taga, north of Tiznit. He had a young son named David. The shereef slapped him. The skeikh had a son the same age as David. The two youths began to play, when suddenly David hit the Muslim boy and he was swallowed up by the ground. The terrified Muslim came to R. Barukh and said to him: *If you want to remain here, I shall leave, and if you leave then I shall stay.* The rabbi, may he rest in peace, left the place and bought a house in Taroudant."

14.4 "They tell how R. David Ben-Barukh, when he was a boy, sold needles in the street. Once an Arab came along and wanted to twist his neck in the marketplace of Taroudant. All he [the boy] did was turn around and the Arab fell down on the spot. The same happened to the second, the third, the fourth. . . . According to what they told me (I wasn't there myself), people went to the *mukhtar* [head of the village] and told him that the son of the saint did such and such. He summoned his [the saint's] father, R. Barukh Ha-Cohen, who said to him: *My lord, I know nothing.* The *mukhtar* said to him: *I have a slave whom I bought at a high price and I want to do an experiment on him.* The *mukhtar* ordered the slave to strike David's hand. The slave hit him and instantly fell down and died. After that the people knew the great virtue of the boy."

14.5 "At one time there were two hundred rabbis studying the *Torah* and the *Talmud* here in Jerusalem in a *yeshibah* near the Temple. They came upon a problem in the tractate *Baba Metsiʿa,* which they could not solve. None of them could. R. Shelomoh Naḥmias, a native of Marrakech, told the head of the *yeshibah: There is only one man who can solve this problem.* He asked: *Who is it?* He answered: *R. David Ben-Barukh from Taroudant.* He asked: *Is it nearby?* He told him: *It takes a year to get to Morocco.* So they hired a Muslim named Moḥammed from the Old City of Jerusalem. They hired him for a year, six months there and six months back. He went via Egypt, and on the very day the six months were up, the Muslim arrived in Taroudant. He started asking where the rabbi lived, and everyone told him: *Keep going!* He asked where the house of the Ḥazzan Ben-Barukh was. He came to the road with the orchard of R. David Ben-Barukh, a large orchard. He [the saint] was wearing his red garment, with his mattock on his shoulder. It was after he had watered [the orchard]. The Muslim came up to him and asked where the house of R. David Ben-Barukh was. The rabbi asked him: *Where have you come from in search of him?* He answered that he had come from far away, from the *yeshibah: I've brought him a letter.* The rabbi asked for the letter. The Muslim said that he would give it only into the hand of R. David Ben-Barukh. The rabbi told him that he himself was the rabbi he sought. He took the letter, and on the way home he read it. He wrote down the solution. He gave him [the Muslim] a loaf of bread weighing one kilogram, and said: *Take it and return to Jerusalem. Here is some food for your journey.* The Muslim replied: *Oh, Ḥazzan Barukh! I arrived here after six months' travel!* He told him: *Do not be afraid! Get up!* The Muslim got up, put the bread into his basket, and set out. That moment the Muslim found himself inside the Temple [in Jerusalem]. He couldn't believe his eyes. He still had the loaf of bread. He went to the *yeshibah.* All the sages stood up and cried out at once: *Why, Moḥammed, didn't you go yet?* He replied: *You are not* *sages. There is someone wiser than you. Come and see the bread that he gave me from his own house.* They took the letter and read the solution. They divided the bread amongst themselves and thought that the solution was a good one. May he rest in peace. R. David Ben-Barukh was the one who did this for the sages of Jerusalem."

14.6 "I saw someone dancing on the fire, and nothing happened to him or his clothes. He was right in the fire, and he shouted several times: *Viva R. David Ben-Barukh!* He was happy and afterwards he went out of the fire and nothing had happened to him."

14.7 "Everything is according to faith. There are many sick people who go there for seven days. They call it: *It 'takes' seven days at R. David Ben-Barukh's!* Then, may his merit sustain us and all Israel, they come home healthy. Sometimes there is a woman who can't become pregnant, so she says: *I'll go to R. David Ben-Barukh's and sit there seven days until he sends me home and then I'll be pregnant!* Sometimes there is a person whose children die young. He says: *If I have a child this time, I'll take him and give him his first haircut at the tomb of R. David Ben-Barukh, and I'll name him after the saint.* And there are people who don't succeed at something, and there are people who want to form a partnership, so they say: *Let us go and make a toast at the grave of R. David Ben-Barukh, and you won't cheat me and I won't cheat you, we shall be one heart!* There are many reasons why people go [to the saint] and it is all according to their faith."

14.8 "Once there was a *goy* in Paris who owned a big factory. He had a son and daughter. The daughter was married and the son was crazy. Then the father died, and his son-in-law, his wife and the crazy son were left. Everything was in the hands of the son-in-law. Then one of the workers saw the owner of the factory crying. He said to her: *What's wrong?* She answered: *My poor brother is crazy, and how much money he has! I can't stand it. He destroys everything we have at home. He hits us!* Then the worker said: *Listen, I am a Moroccan from the city of the saint R. David Ben-Barukh. If you will just believe me, go there with your brother and he will return healthy to France.* She spoke with her husband and he summoned the Jew. The poor fellow had not been back to visit his hometown in Morocco in eighteen years. He said to him: *Come, is this what you told my wife?* He answered: *Yes!* He asked him: *Can you travel [with us] because we do not know where the saint is buried?* He offered to take him and give him a month's wages, and they would cover all his expenses. They took him. When they wanted to board the plane, the crazy man disappeared. They couldn't find him. There were only ten minutes before takeoff. Then the poor Jew cried out: *With the help of God and the help of R. David Ben-Barukh, wherever this sick man may be, bring him to us!* Suddenly the man appeared from under the plane. They took him and arrived in Casablanca. From there they traveled to Taroudant and from Taroudant to R. David Ben-Barukh. They tied him with ropes at the saint's grave. The *paqid,* Mr. Knafo himself, and the Jew from Paris tied up the sick man at the grave and began to shout: *R. David Ben-Barukh! R. David Ben-Barukh!* Then the sick man said to them: *Why did you tie me up?* They answered that he was crazy. He said he was not crazy. He himself shouted: *R. David Ben-Barukh!* He began to cry out on his own. They cut the ropes. He said to them: *Why did you tie me up?* They replied: *Because of your sickness.* He answered that now he was as normal as they were. What did he [the brother-in-law] do? They didn't know how to make a *seʿudah.* He said to them: *Gentlemen, I come from France. I do not know what we have to do according to your custom.* They told him that a sheep had to be slaughtered. He said to them: *One sheep is not enough!* He asked them: *How many poor people are there here?* They said that there was a village one-and-a-half kilometers away from the shrine. They went and called all the poor people of the village. He invited them to come at such and such a time. He asked them approximately how many poor people there were. They told him that were about fifty poor families. He said to them: *All right!* He figured five kilograms of meat per person, five of semolina, and five of sugar, and multiplied by the number of poor people. They figured it out and he gave them the money, and they did everything. They returned to Paris and the Jewish worker who had brought them got a two-month vacation."

15. Rabbi David Ben-Barukh (Taroudant)[22]

This saint is usually called by his cognomen, Baba Dudu, or R. David Ben-Barukh Ha-Qatan [the Younger]. He is the great-grandson of R. David Ben-Barukh (who is buried in Azrou n'Bahamou), the son of R. Barukh Ha-Cohen (who is buried in Taroudant), and the cousin of R. Pinḥas Ha-Cohen.

15.1 "I'll tell you about R. David Ben-Barukh. My father, Ḥayyim O., was his servant. He would accompany him on all his trips to the villages and would return with him to the city of Taroudant. Once, the day before Passover, they came to the city of Taroudant. My father, of blessed memory, said: *Listen, I must set out tonight!* The saint answered: *How can you? At night there are no caravans to accompany you.* My father insisted. In the end the saint consented. He said: *Look at that window over there and see what a Jew from Amizmiz left there.* My father went to the window and found a pair of shoes and ten reals hassani. The saint gave my father the money and said to him: *You know that there is a Muslim from your village who went to the Tuesday market. He is with his caravan. He will accompany you. Join up with him. He bought seven calves. Don't be afraid!* He was very much afraid of setting out on the road. He went to that place and found the Muslim with his calves. The Muslim said to my father: *The saint sent you?* My father said: *No!* My father asked him to get ready to set out. The Muslim was afraid. He replied: *Why should we risk our lives and set out at night? The bandits can steal our property.* My father answered: *Come, let us set out, and I shall be responsible for what happens!* After they had gone several kilometers, armed bandits met them but they were all paralyzed. They couldn't use their weapons. The Muslim was astounded and said to my father: *Now I know that it was the* ḥazzan [the saint] *who told you to come to me, to set out at night.* They continued on their way and arrived the next day."

16. Rabbi David Ben-Safet (Marrakech)

The full name of the saint is R. David Ben-Safet Ha-Levi. Ben-Safet is apparently a cognomen, derived from the toponym Ben-Sfat (from Safed). He is also called El-Khdar (the Green) and Sidi Mul Tsor (the Master of the Wall). He is buried outside the wall of the Jewish cemetery of Marrakech. His burial place was visited by pilgrims not only from Marrakech and its environs, but also from distant locales. His *hillulah* was celebrated at his grave on the eve of the first day of every Hebrew month. His descendants now live in Israel.

16.1 "I'll tell you about this beloved saint. He sold silver items in the streets of the Arab quarter. A Muslim woman asked him into her house, hit him over the head, and killed him. She buried him near her house, behind the city wall. The Jews started to look for him, and the beloved saint put his hand out of the wall and showed himself to them. That is why he is called Sidi Mul Tsor. He put out his hand and showed himself."

16.2 "A rich man from Fez took R. David Ben-Safet to a wedding. The saint rode on a mule and died there in the home of the rich man. It was prohibited to bury him in the Marrakech cemetery because of the king, so that he [the king] would not die. Every barren woman would give birth. Every blind person was able to see. Everyone who had any request whatsoever would go there, even without a *seʿudah.* He would tell them, in dreams: *If you have nothing to bring as a* seʿudah, *just bring a potato and that will be enough for a* seʿudah, *and I shall grant your requests!*"

16.3 "One of the saint's friends once had a dream. He used to go to light my grandfather's lamp in the Latana Street [in the *mellaḥ* of Marrakech]. Every time he came he would ask my daughter to tell him how the saint died. One night he had a dream. He was in a field and a woman was removing the dust from the trees with a white towel. He asked her: *Who owns this orchard?* She answered that it belonged to R. David Ben-Safet Ha-Levi. He asked her to show the saint to him. He went and found the saint sitting at a spring holding a golden cup in his hand. He asked him: *Ḥakham! Tell me how you attained this rank!* He answered: *I died young, but because I had intended to observe all the commandments, the Lord, blessed be He and blessed be His name, credited me as if I had actually observed them. Now I dispense medicines to the sick!* He asked the saint how he had died. He answered that when the rich man took him to Fez, they put the Evil Eye on him. He was born in Marrakech, and was called El-Khdar because when he entered the slaughterhouse, no animal he slaughtered was ever *taref* [ritually unfit for consumption]."

16.4 "R. David Ben-Safet once went to visit the grave of R. Shelomoh Ben-Lḥans, and on his way back, when he got to Bab Hmad [Hmad Gate, one of the gates of Marrakech], he fainted. They tried to revive him, but they couldn't. He passed away. There was a custom and also a decree of the sultan that it was forbidden to bury a body in the cemetery if the person had died outside the city. Masses of Jews came and organized a great funeral for him and buried him outside the city wall."

17. Rabbi David Ben-Yamin (Beni Mellal)[23]

R. David's *hillulah* is celebrated on *Lag bʿOmer.* He is also venerated by the Muslims, who call him Sidi Kherwiʿa.

17.1 "I was deathly ill when I was about twenty-six. I couldn't eat. They gave me up for lost. I was vomiting all the time. My mother decided to take me to sleep at the [tomb of the] saint R. David Ben-Yamin. And then, at night, the saint came to my mother in a dream and told her: *Your cure is in the house of the father of your son-in-law. That is where his cure is!* She went there and told him: *The saint told me thus and so.* He knew how to write [an amulet] but, since the death of his son, he had vowed not to have anything to do with folk medicine. But then he told her: *Get an eggplant, an egg, and salt and small scales.* She brought them to him. He weighed the salt and the egg and ordered her to put them under my pillow overnight and then to weigh which was heavier. He told her, but now I don't remember which, if one was heavier than the other . . . I would live, and if the other was heavier, there was no hope. Next day I got up and began to eat with a very hearty appetite. I wolfed down everything until people thought that I was eating like this because I was in danger of dying. I got fantastically well and since then I haven't had any problems whatsoever."

18. Rabbi David Bussidan (Meknes)[24]

R. David Bussidan, born in Zawia and died in Meknes, is also known as R. Daud or R. Daud the Great. He lived in the sixteenth century and was revered as a saint during his lifetime.

18.1 "R. David Bussidan died a long time ago. Originally he came from Jerusalem. He lived on carob, one piece in the morning and another piece in the evening, only to keep body and soul together. He would say Grace over the carob and give thanks to God. Once he had a guest from Jerusalem itself. In Jerusalem they lived under carob trees. They didn't have a thing. They had water [a spring] nearby. May they rest in peace. Once a guest and his wife came to spend the night with him [R. David]. They brought a hen and a chick. The next morning they [left and] forgot them. The hen was left walking around. She laid many eggs and had many chicks. She filled the place with her chicks. What could he [the saint] do? He sold and bought sheep which had many lambs. Later, the guest came back.

He [the saint] asked: *Where were you?* Once people had faith and blessings. No longer: *You left a hen, now go and sell what there is.* He said: *Very well, but it must be divided fifty-fifty.* He [the saint] said: *Absolutely not! It's all yours!*"

19. Rabbi David Ha-Levi Draᶜ (Draa)[25]

R. David Ha-Levi Draᶜ is one of the most popular saints among the Jews of Morocco. His shrine,[26] which is situated some fifteen kilometers west of Demnate, attracts thousands of the faithful every year.[27] He is often called Dawid Draᶜ, Mul Enekhla (Master of the Palm Tree) or Mul Enekhla El-Khdar (Master of the Green Palm Tree). According to many traditions, R. David came from the Holy Land.[28] He is also venerated by the Muslims, who call him Mul Draᶜ (the master of Draa).

19.1 "I was the first *shammash* [caretaker] of this saint's shrine, may he rest in peace. Only the Jews of Demnate knew about him. They were the first. My sons all died in infancy, may you never know such tragedy. I took my youngest daughter and said at the tomb: *Oh, R. David Draᶜ Ha-Levi! Let this little girl live! I vow to serve you until the day you send me to Jerusalem!* May he rest in peace. My daughter was born in Marrakech and she lived."

19.2 "One time I was sick. I couldn't stand up. I went to R. David Draᶜ. I stayed at his grave for a year, and by virtue of his powers I recovered. I stayed there a whole year. My husband visited me on the first of every [Hebrew] month. He would bring me meat for *sheḥitah.* There was a *yeshibah* there where students studied. I stayed there a year until we had nothing left. Everything was gone, and we didn't even have anything to buy for the *Sabbath.* That night he [the saint] appeared to me in a dream in the form of David Ben-Zuwa. The saint said to me: *Get up and eat lunch and do not worry about supper. Jews will come from Kelaa and you will eat with them!* Jews came who knew my husband. We spent the *Sabbath* with them and they gave us money. From the day I had the dream I started to walk and stopped having the pains. Before that I had been to doctors. God help those doctors! I wore a cast three times and it didn't help. Only the saint helped me. How did this happen to me? Once after I was married I quarreled with my husband and spilled water near the drain in our house in Casablanca [if done without prior warning, this act is thought to offend the demons who live there, rousing their wrath against the offender]. We lived there near *Otsar Ha-Torah* [a Jewish school]."

19.3 "At first we did not know him [R. David Ha-Levi], and we went there only because of the dream: In 1928 a person named Shimʿon Malka from Berrechid had a dream. He told us and then we went there. We were afraid, but there we found R. Yitsḥaq Malka, the collector for the Fund of R. Meir Baʿal Ha-Nes. He had come to the *mellaḥ* of Draa. I said to him: *Stay with us for the* Sabbath—because we were very much afraid. He told me that in the *mellaḥ* they had given him five reals so that he would spend the *Sabbath* with them, but that if I would give him ten reals, he would spend the *Sabbath* with us. I told him: *I'll give you forty reals!* This R. Yitsḥaq had come from Tiberias to collect donations for [the Fund of] R. Meir Baʿal Ha-Nes. He came to the *mellaḥ* of Draa, which is about two kilometers from the shrine. We spent the *Sabbath* with all the Jews of the *mellaḥ.* When I got there, there was nothing but his grave. There was a palm tree and people buried there their dead. I built over ninety rooms there."[29]

19.4 "In 1930 I was mortally ill, and the doctor said there was no hope for me. At that time R. Shimʿon Abiqassis, who [later] did the proofs of the book by R. David Ha-Levi, was staying in my house. R. Yitsḥaq Malka and R. ʿAbbu were also staying with me. At that time R. Yaʿaqob Toledano was *dayyan* in Tangier, and he was looking for antique books, and so was R. Moshe Ḥay Elyaqim, who was from Tiberias and was *dayyan* in Casablanca and the master of R. Yaʿaqob Toledano. Then I slept and dreamed that someone brought me a text, a book, and there were many holes in it, but the writing was still intact. He said to me that this was the work of R. David Ha-Levi, and he said that he was R. David Ha-Levi. I asked him: Ḥakham, *where are you from?* He said he was from Jerusalem, that he had gone to Spain and from Spain he had come here. I started to perspire profusely and then, when I woke up, I told my wife to give me a little soup to drink and—*I will tell you the dream!* I woke up the sages who were staying in our house and told them the dream. Next day, the doctor came to examine me and he said that I had been saved from death, and then I got well. I went to the synagogue of Ben-Saud, where I met R. Moshe Ḥay Elyaqim. I told him my dream and then he took a letter out of his pocket. He told me that R. Yaʿaqob

Toledano had found the work of the saint inside a chest that had been buried in the ground in Fez and he was asking five hundred pounds sterling for it. I told him to buy it from him. The book looked just the way it had in my dream. I had five hundred copies of it printed. I left this book [the manuscript] in a chest in my house, and the money just poured down from Heaven. In 1951, R. Yaʿaqob Toledano came specially from Jerusalem to tell me that he wanted to put it [the manuscript] in the National Library, so I gave it to him free of charge. Since the book left my house, things have been going downhill. At one time they wanted to give me six thousand dollars for it, but I didn't want to sell it. I built some ninety rooms. I built a very beautiful synagogue with decorations in the Arab style, and there was also a *yeshibah* there with ninety students. And I also built roads to the shrine. There were four *mellaḥs,* and I fed them. I used to bring boys from the villages and make a *bar-mitswah* there on the day of the *hillulah.* He [the saint] was not known to the Jews outside the area. Only after we circulated letters to all the synagogues did they start to come from Casablanca, Marrakech. . . . I used to go there four times a year: after Passover, after *Sukkot,* on the first of the month of *Elul,* and on *Shabuʿot.* The Muslims also visited his tomb and said that he 'showered favors.' "

19.5 "They say that there was a Muslim, a shereef, who said to the Jews: *Why do you praise this saint so highly? Is he the only one in the world? What's all the fuss about?* They, the Muslims, consider him a saint. Suddenly this shereef began to urinate. Urine flowed out of him all the time. Wherever he was, he urinated. He was a great shereef. He went to the Jews of Demnate and begged them to ask for mercy on him. He brought a black ox, a sack of semolina, twenty kilograms of oil. The Jews slaughtered the ox, made a *seʿudah* and asked for mercy on this shereef. The next day the shereef recovered. And that's why we delay the time of slaughter of our own animals until the shereef's black ox is slaughtered. Every year we would first slaughter the ox of the shereef and only afterwards did we slaughter our own. He would come early because he was afraid that he might be late. This is what he was ordered to do every year."

19.6 "I recall one thing about R. David Levi, may he rest in peace. My father was still alive. Once he had pains in his eyes. In the village where we grew up in Morocco there were no doctors. My father was in danger of going blind. Suddenly a man appeared to him in a dream and said: *I am R. David Ha-Levi. Take a drop of* ʿarak *and drip it into your eyes!* My father woke up that night and put the drops of *'arak* into his eyes. The next morning he got up cured! And I remember that my father fasted while he walked to the saint's tomb fourteen years ago. I am now fifty-two years old."

20. Rabbi David Naḥmias (Tazda)[30]

R. David is one of the most famous of the members of the Ait Naḥmias. Some members of this family of saints enjoyed regional popularity. R. David is the father of R. Yosef Naḥmias, a renowned teacher of Marrakech. R. David's *hillulah* is celebrated in the month of *Elul.* He is also venerated by the Muslims, who call him R. Dawid Ḥamias.

20.1 "R. David, I remember him from when I was still a boy. He wore a *qawaq* [a kind of headcloth] and a *zukha* [a long robe buttoned in front]. He was tall. Who could pass by if R. David Naḥmias was there? Women were forbidden to kiss his hand. They couldn't even touch him with their hand. Only bow to him. . . . In our village he only had to go by and you were afraid!"

20.2 "The Ait Naḥmias [family] is dangerous! Their curse is very dangerous. Once an uncle of my father quarreled with R. David Naḥmias's daughter (they were married). He was rich. His name was David Perets. He quarreled with her, and then R. David came and he was also furious with him. Afterwards he died. His son Yosef died and also Eliyahu, another son, and even she (the wife) died. All four in a single month! Also the poor mule was paralyzed in the lower part of her body. I saw it myself! The Ait Naḥmias are very dangerous!"

21. Rabbi David U-Moshe (Timzerit)[31]

Visitors from all over the country flock to R. David U-Moshe's tomb every day of the year. According to tradition, he came from the Holy Land. His *hillulah* is on the first of *Kislew* and is still celebrated in many places in Israel. He is also venerated by the Muslims, who call him R. Dawid U-Mussi.

21.1 "The saint came to our city of Tazenakht. He went to Tanil, to Tamstint. They [the Muslims] call him 'The Sheikh of Amerzan.' He arrived in Tamstint on a Friday. He went around to all the villages—the whole world—to collect money for the poor of the Holy Land. When he had finished collecting the money, he came to the village where he is now buried. There he found six or seven *mellaḥs* where Jews lived. Every village has one, two, three or four *minyanim* [pl. of *minyan,* the quorum of ten adult men required for holding liturgical services]. He went to all of them. He arrived there on a Friday, he and his servant. The servant was born and grew up in his house in the Holy Land, and he [the saint] taught him. He was a Muslim Arab, black, a servant. When the saint arrived, he found that all the villagers were ill. All of them—Jews, Muslims—all were dying. The saint arrived and said: *Lord of the world! What shall I do? Listen! I came to collect alms for the poor, and I came here and found everyone dying!* A heavenly voice said: *You will annul the decree of all these dying people, Arabs and Jews!* And he said: *I accept. My death in exchange for the lives of others!* He went to our cemetery, went inside, and sat down. Angels came down from the sky. A spring gushed forth, may he rest in peace. His shroud came out. Everything came out: his shroud, his ritual bath. He put on his shroud and saw that his grave was ready. He went down into his grave. Only his servant was with him. When he had gone down into his grave and disappeared and all the [heavenly] messengers who buried him had gone, the servant began to cry: *Ya Sidi! Ya Sidi!* [Oh, my master! My master!] The mountain [near the grave] is like a tarboosh and underneath it was something like a pipe. Here is the river bed and there is the stone. A stone which had been up above came down, and the one which had been down below went up, and they met at the place where the saint was buried. The servant returned to the village. He found that all the people who had been sick were running around [had recovered]. You couldn't find a single sick person! They said: *Where is the saint they said had come? Where is the saint they said had come?* The servant told them: *He is dead!* They said: *Either you produce him or we'll kill you!* Arabs crowded around him, Jews crowded around him. They wanted to kill him. He told them: *If you believe in God and you know your cemetery, I'll show you where the saint is. You have signs and you know where your cemetery is.* They said: *We know!* Then he said to them: *Let us go!* He went with them. He said: *Here is your cemetery. Are there stones there?* They said: *No!* He said: *Here is the hole that the stone rose out of!* The place that the stone rose out of was big enough for two hundred people. The one that came from below came like a tractor until the stones covered the saint like so and hid him. They asked him: *Where is the* ḥakham? He said to them: *He is here. This stone is above his head. If you want to sit, sit. If you want to kill me, kill me!* They said: *Alik l-aman! [we believe you!].* They didn't touch him. They took him and treated him hospitably. My forefathers, my family, went to Jerusalem with him, with the servant, and stayed there. They went with him in order to see the saint's house. And they came and said that the saint's house is in Talpiot, in Jerusalem. They went with him and took the money that they had collected. Immediately after his death, he [the saint] appeared in a dream and said to them: *This is what you must do all your lives!* From generation to generation we have continued. Each one brings a calf or poultry. In God's name and in the name of the saint, they gather and do [what the saint commanded]."

21.2 "People came from Azemmour. People came to visit there but there was no water to drink at the shrine. They complained bitterly. There was a little spring, but it wasn't enough. They said: *Oh saint! We need water!* And the water started to flow in the spring. Drink as much as you want. There was a *seʿudah,* in the name of God and the saint. And I had no more *maḥia.* It was all gone. I had only a bottle. I put on my *djellaba* [long robe] and went into the shrine. I put the *maḥia* under my arm and said: *Oh, saint! I don't want people to despise me. I have nowhere to get any [more* maḥia*]. Give me a glass of yours!* I poured. *Give me your glass!* I poured . . . until they didn't want any more *maḥia.* The bottle was as full as before. Full! As if they hadn't touched it. A miracle of the saint! The same thing with the bread. I put it down, it was all gone. They said to me: *What good is one slice of bread for all these people, for all the servants of the Lord? What will you do?* I told them confidently: *Don't worry!* I put it aside, covered it, and said: *Look, take as much as you like! Just let me take it and divide it up among the people!* I cut and gave, cut and gave until the people got tired and didn't want to eat. And the slice [of bread]? It was [the same] slice!"

21.3 "I've been at the shrine of R. David U-Moshe many times. The women throw gold or platinum rings and there isn't even a guard there. And no one dares to take anything. All night long on the night of the *hillulah* at the tomb. The idea is that the rings will absorb the holiness of the saint. They take them back the next day. Once something happened. A girl took a ring and her hand 'dried up' [became paralyzed] instantly. Her hand stayed closed until the treasurer [of the shrine] came and asked the saint to forgive her, and then her hand opened. It was a great miracle."

21.4 "According to tradition, in the Holy Land all the pious people and the *yeshibah* students live on alms. Ten men went to collect alms for the poor, including R. ʿAmram Ben-Diwan, his son R. Ḥayyim, R. David U-Moshe, Mulay Ighi, R. David Ha-Levi. . . . The saint [R. David U-Moshe] wanted to reveal himself. He appeared to an old man in a dream and told him: *I am so and so, buried in such and such a place, and the sign is there, straw scattered around. Where the straw is, that is where my grave is. But I command you [Jews] not to finish the place [build a shrine over the grave]!* The old man was from Morocco, from Agoim, the village near the [grave of the] saint. So he went and saw, and on that day the saint revealed himself with visible miracles no one can doubt."

21.5 "One time the Muslims wanted to kill their sheikh. He fled to the Jewish cemetery. There was a stone [there]. The Muslims started looking for him among the graves, but they didn't find him. They left. Three days later, these Muslims changed their mind about killing the sheikh. They said: *This sheikh never did us any harm. Let us look for him again and reinstate him!* R. David U-Moshe, may he rest in peace . . . when they came . . . the sheikh stood up. They asked him: *What happened to you?* [The sheikh replied:] *Here is this saint. If you had killed me, none of you would have returned home [alive]. And he saved me when I came to him!* The sheikh vowed that every year he would bring an ox to slaughter at the tomb of the saint and would offer up a *seʿudah.*"

21.6 "I used to visit his tomb. I was the *shoḥet* there at the saint's [shrine]. One time a man came who had no sons. He made a *seʿudah,* slaughtered something, a sheep. While he was sitting with the rabbi there, a snake came out and went toward his wife who was sleeping nearby. This was during the day, not at night. The snake came out. The husband was afraid. This rabbi told him: *Don't be afraid. It is the saint who has come to cure your wife!* The snake went back to his place. His wife woke up and told how she had dreamed that the saint sent her a snake. She dreamed and saw the snake. The saint told her that this snake would take from her everything she had [her barrenness] and she would have a son. And she did give birth to a son! This man went to visit the tomb of R. David U-Moshe every single year. [Once] when the boy was ten years old, after the *seʿudah,* he and his father went down to the village called Agoim, near the shrine. There is a road there. There were many trucks there which came to take away soil that contained copper. . . . There were about thirty big trucks that had come there to load up. When these trucks start to leave the place, no one can go down to the road because the trucks take up the whole road. There was a long convoy of trucks. The first one that left honked and honked his horn. This boy (I was there), this boy was run over. The truck drove over him. His father screamed and practically died of fright. The truck stopped, the boy got up and ran to his father, and he didn't have a scratch on him. I saw it with my own eyes. It was a great miracle. He went back to the saint's shrine and told them. He told them that the saint had given him a son and had saved him."

21.7 "In the shrine of R. David U-Moshe, when the Six Day War broke out, the Muslim guardian had a dream about the saint. The same night that the war was supposed to break out in Israel, he had a dream in which seven horses went out from this place and galloped across the sky. He went to Casablanca and told the members of the Jewish community committee that the saint had come and told him that war had broken out in Israel, but there was nothing to fear because the saint was protecting the country."

21.8 "From the month of *Tebet* until Passover, I used to travel to Casablanca in order to bring money for the poor from the members of the committee who were in charge of the shrine. So I brought money on the eve of the festivals of *Sukkot, Pesaḥ* and *Rosh Hashanah.* Every poor person would receive his own envelope with the amount he was supposed to get. This was the money that had been collected at the shrine. It all went into one fund, the fund for the poor of the seven villages."

21.9 "Once the mule of a Jew from the village of Ouarzazate was dying. They wanted to throw it to the dogs. A Jew named M. B., of blessed memory, told the Jews that if they would give half the price [of the mule] to R. David U-Moshe, the mule would live. And so it was. The mule recovered, '*b-el-Lah u-b-sidna*' [by the grace of God and of our master]. With the money they built a room [in the sanctuary]."

21.10 "Once a Muslim found himself in the saint's shrine, and he said something against the Jews. He went blind. But every time he looked toward the saint, he could see, and when he looked toward his house, he couldn't see a thing. When he got tired, he appealed to the saint and promised that every year, on the day of his *hillulah,* he would bring two bundles of wood. On the *hillulah* he brought the wood. The Jews wanted to pay him, but he told them everything that had happened to him. Another Muslim stole something from the holy place. Every time he tried to walk toward his house, a snake barred his way until he got tired and returned what he had stolen. He begged the saint's forgiveness and mercy."

21.11 "In the shrine there was a green tree growing out of a stone. It was an almond tree. It is the custom to cut a boy's hair [for the first time] when he is one year old. We weigh his hair and donate money of the same weight as the hair so that we can put the hair into an amulet for the boy to wear. You have to do it. The same for girls, "*b-el-Lah u-b-sidi!*" Anyone who can't do it brings a *seʿudah* and goes on his way."

22. Rabbi Eleʿazar Ben-ʿArakh (Iguenisaine)[32]

22.1 "R. Eleʿazar Ben-ʿArakh, one of the earliest *Tannaim* [illustrious teachers quoted in the *Mishnah,* the section of the *Talmud* consisting of the core of the oral law compiled by R. Yehudah Ha-Nasi], is buried near us. So it has been told from the time of my father, of blessed memory. They told the following story: R. Eleʿazar Ben-ʿArakh came to a rich Jew from Casablanca in a dream and asked him to build him a marker. He was buried beneath a carob tree. People used to come on pilgrimage to the place and light candles. When the Jew dreamt this, he saw him, and he [the saint] asked him to build him a marker, so that he would see his merit. The rich man was a guest of my father. He asked them: *Is R. Eleʿazar Ben-ʿArakh buried near you?* They said: *Yes!* He asked them: *Do you know his permanent resting place?* They said that they had heard from their forefathers. They took him to his [the saint's] grave. He arrived. He asked them to remove the stones from the site so that he could build on top of it. The workers came. All day they worked, from morning to night, and managed to roll away the rock that had covered the place. They rolled it to the *wadi,* which was more than a thousand meters away. That night they did not manage to build, so they thought they would start building the next morning. They brought the bricks and building materials. In the morning, when they came to build, they found the rock back in its place. It had come up from the *wadi* and returned to the spot. They were amazed. They didn't know what to do or how to do it. They said that if the saint did not want them to build, what should they do? Again they tried to roll away the rock, and the next day they found it back in the same place."

23. Rabbi ʿEli Ben-Yitsḥaq (Imi n'Tanoute)

R. ʿEli was murdered by Muslims after he had performed a miracle for them. They then started to venerate him as Sidi ʿEli U-Yitsḥaq. His burial place is in Muslim possession and Jews are forbidden to visit it.

23.1 "He is buried in our town. Muslims came and slaughtered a cow and started to fight over her. He passed by and saw them fighting. He asked them: *How much will you give me if I bring this cow back to life?* They skinned her and put all the pieces together. The rabbi gave the cow a kick, pronounced the Divine Name over her, kicked her and said: *Get up!* The cow got up and began to run around. When they saw this, they took the rabbi and slaughtered him, buried him and built a marker over him. It was R. ʿEli Ben-Yitsḥaq and he became Sidi ʿEli U-Yitsḥaq, as the Muslims call him. Once I asked the rabbi of our town, R. Abraham Ben-Lulu. They used to send him questions from the Holy Land and he would answer them all. They told me that the rabbi, R. ʿEli Ben-Yitsḥaq, went up [to Heaven] body and soul and the Muslims built a marker over his grave. When I asked R. Ben-Lulu if I could visit the tomb of R. ʿEli Ben-Yitsḥaq, he said that since the saint went up [to Heaven] body and soul, there is nothing to visit."

24. Rabbi Eliʿezer Davila (Rabat)[33]

R. Eliʿezer was born in Salé in 1711 and died on the 3rd of *Adar,* 1761. Though he did not live long, he was renowned as a scholar during his lifetime and wrote many works, including the posthumously published *Magen Giborim, Maʿayan Ganim* and *Milḥemet Mitswah.* A synagogue and a street are named after him in Rabat. He is buried in the old section of the cemetery.

24.1 "Once, may he rest in peace, the sea almost flooded the city of Rabat. R. Eliʿezer Davila went to the king and told him: *My* *lord, you know that the sea is about to flood the city of Rabat.* The king went with him. With his own eyes he saw that this was about to happen. So the saint took his stick and stuck it in a certain place, and the waves did not go past the saint's stick.[34] Then the saint turned to the king and told him: *Beware! Do not harm the Jews!*"

24.2 "They say that he made the sea stand still, may he rest in peace. His stick was buried near the gate to the *mellaḥ*. Whenever someone came in, he kissed it. My son's wife was pregnant, and my son said to me: *Mother, if I have a son, I shall call him Eliʿezer!* I answered: *Mazal Tov!* [Congratulations!] A daughter was born and after her a son, and we called him Eliʿezer. In his dream, the saint appeared on a white horse. He [my son] asked him [the saint] what he was doing there. He answered that he was guarding the place. That is how my son dreamed of him, because he was praying in the synagogue named after R. Eliʿezer Davila."

25. Rabbi Eliʿezer Turei-Zahav (Tamaarouf)[35]

The saint is also called R. Eliʿezer Ben-Yerushalayyim. On *Purim* all the Jews of the area used to visit his grave and celebrate his *hillulah.* According to tradition, he was an emissary who came to collect donations for the Holy Land and supplied the residents of the area with *tsitsit* (the fringes of entwined threads worn by Jews on the four corners of the prayer shawl called *tallith*), and *tefillin* (phylacteries). He is also venerated by Muslims.

25.1 "R. Eliʿezer died in our village. When we were getting ready to go to Israel, the Zionists came to our village to register us, but we did not wait for them. The saint came to each one of us in a dream and told us: *Arise! Until now I took care of you. Now it is time for me, too, to go up to my city. I cannot remain here!* Each day he would come to someone else. Everyone was afraid. We went and were registered and went to Casablanca. We left all our property. One Jew left around two hundred cows and buildings, too, behind and fled to Casablanca. Not a soul was left. We were all afraid. We did not even wait until we had sold our property, because of the dream about the saint, may he rest in peace. If he said something in a dream, the next day it came true. May he rest in peace. We were afraid. We all trembled. That same Jew was afraid too. He fled with his sons; he left them in Casablanca, returned to the village, sold all his property and only then did he go to Israel."

25.2 "He is a saint who came from the Holy Land. He passed away in Tamaarouf and is buried there. [If] a person comes who is unclean, impure, he cannot enter the cemetery where this saint is buried. One Friday we were invited to someone in the village when we heard that a person had entered this cemetery, and a strong wind blew up and threw him to the ground. When the people of the village came to see him, they treated him and found out that he had been unclean—this man should have taken a ritual bath before going in to visit the grave of the saint. I was present and I saw with my own eyes. The villagers had warned the man beforehand and told him that he had to be clean and pure, and that before entering the cemetery he had to take a *tebilah* [ritual bath]."

26. Rabbi Eliyahu (Casablanca)[36]

R. Eliyahu is one of the most celebrated saints in Casablanca, indeed in the whole region. His family name is unknown. He is called R. Eliyahu Ha-Cohen, Mul Dar-El-Beida (Master of Casablanca), or Qandil El-Blad (Illuminator of the City).

According to tradition, R. Eliyahu came from the Holy Land. He appears in the Tidili list of ten rabbis who came from Israel to Morocco. The saint Lalla Saʿada, believed to be his wife, and the saints R. Yitsḥaq Qoriat and R. Masʿud Oḥana are buried near him. All four saints were buried in a place called El-Bḥira, near the Marrakech Gate in the heart of the modern city, before their remains were reinterred in the new cemetery in Ben-Msik, in the suburbs of Casablanca. There are many traditions relating to the transfer of the saints' remains to the new cemetery, where a magnificent structure was erected over the grave of R. Eliyahu.

26.1 "We used to go to R. Eliyahu. He was buried in the old cemetery near Bab Meraks [the Gate of Marrakech]. Above his shrine there was a synagogue, and seven students were buried near him. Later on they moved him to the new cemetery. They opened his grave and moved him because they [the Moroccan authorities] wanted to demolish the place and build a road."

26.2 "R. Eliyahu Ha-Cohen is buried in Casablanca. They once wanted to build, but whatever they put up was destroyed. One *Sabbath* morning I dreamed I saw a Jewish woman named ʿAisha, who was the caretaker of the shrine [a dream about the caretaker of the shrine is considered a dream about the saint]. She brought me green figs and said: *What's the matter with you? Everyone who eats these green figs is cured of pains in the liver.* I didn't believe it. I had another dream in the afternoon. I saw someone enter my house with a donkey, bringing olives, half white and half black. He said to me: *Why don't you want to give olives for barrenness? Get up and give them olives. I am giving you this remedy!* Next day I went and bought olives. A woman who hadn't gotten married yet [came to visit me]. I thought: *Let's put this saint to the test. If I give her the olives and she gets married, I'll know it's true!* She took an olive and that same week, her fiancé came and they were engaged. She had a child. Another Jewish woman came from Ouezzane. After six years of marriage, she still had no children. She came to try the olives and she had a child. And there were many [cases] like them."

26.3 "All the Jews know about this saint. In 1958, the authorities wanted to transfer his grave to the Ben-Msik cemetery in Casablanca. He had been buried there [in the old place] for many years, and the authorities requested permission from the Jewish Community Committee to move his grave [the saint was buried on the ground floor of the building that housed the Committee]. The members of the Committee asked the authorities for a lot of money. The Muslims refused. They sent the workers to move the grave. Many people saw this with their own eyes. When the Muslim came to dig with his pickax, the pickax got stuck in the ground and he was paralyzed. He couldn't move; he was like a tree stump. The foreman went to the Committee and told them what happened. They sent ten *yeshibah* students. The minute they started to read from the Psalms, the Muslim was released. For two days he had been glued to the spot. The same authorities came to the president of the community and told him that they needed the saint's burial place for paving a road. The Committee demanded a huge sum of money. They paid it. That night the saint, R. Eliyahu, appeared to the head of the Jewish community in a dream. He told us this himself in the synagogue. The saint said to him: *Now that you have sold me for money, I cannot take revenge. If you had not taken money from them, you would have seen what punishments I would have inflicted on them. Then you would have seen the* *heroic strength of the saints!* The head of the community also told us how the saint had appeared to him in a dream. With this money, a large marker was built in honor of the saint in the new Ben-Msik cemetery, and Jews came from all the cities to visit his tomb. I heard that there was a woman who went blind. Her husband took her to the saint. He tied her hands, and she cried the whole night. She slept, and the next morning, when she woke up, she was well. This was a great miracle. A great miracle!"

26.4 "I was cooking an omelette to take on the pilgrimage to the tomb of R. Eliyahu. I didn't want to go. I asked my husband to take the omelette. The taxi driver was waiting downstairs and he was in a hurry. I told my husband to go and I would come later. When I said this, I dropped the hot omelette on myself and the oil burnt me. It was because I had told him that I didn't want to go to R. Eliyahu. I went to the drugstore and bought some ointment and then I went by taxi to R. Eliyahu. I was in great pain. I slept there and R. Eliyahu in his [rabbinical] robes stood next to me [in a dream]. With the help of God and the help of the saint, I saw him with my own eyes. He said to me: *I shall make a medicine for your hand. Do not go to a doctor. But next time, do not tell your husband that you do not want to go to R. Eliyahu!* I went home. I bought some ointment and it helped me a lot. It was a miracle!"

26.5 "A Jewish woman went blind. They shut her up in the *Makhzen.* The next morning she got up and she could see. She said that the saint R. Eliyahu had appeared to her in a dream. It was she who first mentioned the name of R. Eliyahu. R. Eliyahu told her to say that he was R. Eliyahu and that it was he who had cured her, and that was why she had come out with healthy eyes. Then the members of the Jewish community committee and the notables each donated money and they built the cemetery. They built a gravestone for the saint, and above the shrine of R. Eliyahu they built a synagogue. May he rest in peace!"

27. Rabbi Ḥabib Ha-Mizraḥi (Ait Ourir)[37]

Also called R. Ḥabib and R. Ḥabib El-Mizraḥi. Tradition has it that the saint came from the Holy Land, arriving in Morocco in early times. He appears in two lists of rabbis who came from the Holy Land to Morocco to convert the local population. He is also venerated by the Muslims, who call him Mulay Tadot, after the acacia tree at his tomb.

27.1 "I know someone named R. Ḥabib El-Mizraḥi in Ait Ourir, and he is very dear. He did not have many visitors. Only very few, because he was very far away, on a mountain, and it was very hard to get to him. All he has is a little shrine, and over his grave there's no marble or anything. It is in a corner like a niche. It is around seven kilometers away, inside the mountain. We would go on foot or ride on a horse or mule. In the same place there is a cemetery of Ait Ourir. His pilgrimage is held on Tuesdays. There is a market held on Tuesdays, and people who come to the market take this opportunity to go to the saint. There was no *paqid,* but there was an Arab who took care of the place. They didn't make a *hillulah* for him, because he was unknown, which was a pity, because if they did arrange the place properly. . . . The Arab lived close to [the tomb of] the saint, and he accompanied everyone who came to the saint, stayed with them and gave them water, and they would give him a little money. This Arab used to say: *What bad luck I have that the Jews don't come to this saint; otherwise I could be rich like the other* pqidim!"

28. Rabbi Ḥananiah Ha-Cohen (Marrakech)[38]

R. Ḥananiah is buried in Marrakech and is considered the patron saint of the city. He is also called R. Ḥaniniah, R. Ḥinaniah Ha-Cohen, Rabbi Aminia Ha-Cohen, or Mul El-Shejra El-Khedra (Master of the Green Tree). According to tradition, he came from the Holy Land to Morocco with his brothers, R. Moshe Cohen and R. Raphael Ha-Cohen. The Muslims also visit his tomb.

28.1 "R. Ḥananiah is in the Marrakech cemetery. They come to him on pilgrimage from all over Morocco. Everyone who comes to Marrakech has to come to R. Ḥananiah. Everyone who wants to swear an oath says: *Dkhalt-ʿalik b-er-rbi Ḥninia!* [I adjure you in the name of R. Ḥninia!] He is the saint we have in Marrakech. He has a shrine with doors. Every Saturday night they go to the cemetery and pray there. Three-four hundred people come there every Saturday night. People who love the saint. I myself have been there some three hundred times. They sell glasses [of *maḥia* in honor of the saint] there. They don't open the doors [of the room] until they sell all the glasses. There was a man who was the caretaker there. His name was Mordekhay Naḥmias, and he leased the room from the committee. He gave the committee money and they distributed it to the poor. The things [glasses, candles] of the saint were sold at a very high price. They sold the rights during two periods: from *Sukkot* to *Pesaḥ* and from *Pesaḥ* to *Sukkot*. People would bid to buy the room. There was one man named David Elzgar. He and Naḥmias would bid, each one [bidding] higher than the other. But a lot of money is also made from the sale of glasses, and they also charge for opening the door of the shrine. When they open the door, they sing: *Pitḥu-li shaʿare-tsedeq* [Open to me the gates of righteousness!] [Psalm 118:19]. R. Ḥananiah is a great lion!"

28.2 "My son is called Shalom Ḥananiah. My first sons were all stillborn. I asked my wife to go to Marrakech to give birth, and I asked her that if she has a son, she should let me know and I'd name him Shalom Ḥananiah. And that's what happened. She went to Marrakech. She had a son, and the first son was named Shalom Ḥananiah. We had him circumcised and we stayed there for three months, and then we went back to Casablanca."

28.3 "Once there was a *qadi.* His servant girl ran away because he hit her. She ran away. They told the *qadi* that if he wanted to find his servant girl, he could bring oil and a *seʿudah* to R. Ḥananiah. He came, took off his headdress and shoes, brought a jug of oil, gave some money and said: *Master, please tell me where my servant girl is!* We then used to spend seven days at the tomb of R. Ḥananiah. At night, we saw the servant girl coming. Her feet brought her to the tomb of R. Ḥananiah Ha-Cohen. We were lying there. She came in, and we told her: *You scared us! Why did you come?* She answered: *I am the* qadi's *servant girl. He hit me and my feet brought me here!* They called the *qadi,* and in the morning he came and fetched her. He said: *There is no one like your God. Oh Jews! Peace be upon you!*"

28.4 "I'll tell you a story about R. Ḥananiah. I knew him [visited his tomb]. There was a woman who would go to his tomb only in the evening. One night they locked the room with two locks. She went with her two daughters and three other women. They told her the room was closed. She told them: *Wait, I'll open it!* She called out: *Oh, R. Ḥananiah! We are no strangers! You are ours and we know only you! And what will become of us? We have only you!* The door began to move. She kept saying this for half an hour. She said: *Do* *not shame me before these people who want to visit you now!* The room opened. The locks fell to the floor, and they entered and stayed until morning."

29. Rabbi Ḥayyim Ben-Diwan (Anrhaz)[39]

According to tradition, he is the son of R. ʿAmram Ben-Diwan and came from the Holy Land. His *hillulah* is held on *Lag bʿOmer.* He is also venerated by the Muslims, who call him Mul Anrhaz.

29.1 "R. Ḥayyim Ben-Diwan, the son of R. ʿAmram Ben-Diwan, is buried in our village. He came as a young man to collect money. He came with his servant. He came to a stream called Ouirgane. There the earth opened up and he went inside, may he rest in peace. His mule and servant were left outside. The servant went to the Muslims. May he rest in peace, he immersed himself in the stream [for ritual purification]. He came back up and buried himself. A large rock came and covered him. This is what the people told us. The daughter of the rich man, Yeshuʿah Corcos of Marrakech, came. She built him a grave marker and would come to visit his tomb."

30. Rabbi Ḥayyim Pinto (Mogador)[40]

R. Ḥayyim is a member of the illustrious Pinto family, from which many saints have sprung. He is usually called R. Ḥayyim Pinto Ha-Gadol (the Great, the Elder), to distinguish him from his grandson of the same name, who is also known as R. Ḥayyim Pinto Ha-Qatan (the Younger). Born in Agadir, he moved to Mogador at the age of ten. There he died at a ripe old age on the 26th of *Elul* 5605 (1845). During his lifetime he was renowned for his erudition and for the miracles he performed.

R. Ḥayyim Pinto is famous throughout Morocco, and two books with stories extolling his miracles and deeds have been published.[41] He is the most illustrious of the saints of the Pinto family—which included his father, R. Shelomoh Pinto; his son, R. Yehudah Pinto; and his grandson, R. Ḥayyim Pinto Ha-Qatan. His descendants now reside in Ashdod, Israel, and actively promote a wide variety of activities in perpetuation of the memory of R. Ḥayyim and his grandson.

30.1 "In his house [in Mogador] there is a jug. They take oil from this jug and give it to women. They also take oil from the *ner* *tamid* [Hebrew for eternal light, a lamp in honor of the saint] and rub it, for instance, on a hand, if it hurts. Wherever they rub in the oil, it gets better. On the night of the *hillulah* there would be no room to sit down. Only the poor who came got a lot of money, three or four hundred reals each. People would light a lot of candles at the tomb, until their smoke reached the sky. They put the soot [of the candles] from the tomb on the children's foreheads. They pour water on the tomb and drink it. That's the medicine. They cut the hair of many children there. Whoever wants to cut his child's hair, takes him there, bringing cakes. They cut the children's hair there so that the saint will pray for them and bless them. They say to the saint: *Look, this child is yours! Every* hillulah *I shall bring him to you!* And they donate something in honor of the saint. Some people give chickens or a sheep."

31. Rabbi Ḥayyim Pinto (Casablanca)[42]

R. Ḥayyim Pinto is a popular saint. He was active in Mogador and Casablanca. He died on the 15th of *Ḥeshwan* 1937 in Casablanca, and is buried in the old cemetery there. He is the son of R. Yehudah Pinto and the grandson of R. Ḥayyim Pinto, who is buried in Mogador.[43] He is sometimes called R. Ḥayyim Pinto Ha-Qatan (the Younger), to distinguish him from his grandfather. Jews go on pilgrimage to light candles at the saint's house in Casablanca.[44] R. Ḥayyim's descendants in Israel perpetuate the cult.

31.1 "About fifty years ago [1924], R. Ḥayyim Pinto was saying the *Birkat Ha-levanah* [the blessing of the New Moon]. When he finished the blessing, he told the people who were with him: *What did we say in the blessing? Ke-shem she-anaḥnu meraqqedin. . . .* [As we dance toward thee, but cannot touch thee. . . .] *I promise you that some of you will live to see the day when man will go up to the moon and dance there!* The people who were with him asked: *How can such things come about?* He told them: *It will happen!*"

31.2 "He had a sacred custom. He would collect money from people and distribute it among the poor. When he finished distributing the money, he would always wash the kerchief [in which he had collected it]. Once they asked him why he did this. He told them that the worst filth in the world was money. *So I wash the dirt out of my kerchief!* Although he lived off the money we used to give him, he would say: *This money is dirt!* He had another sacred custom. He would go into the house of some poor Jew every day and ask: *What have you made to eat today? I want to eat some of what you prepared!* We all know what a poor person eats—vegetables with a slice of bread and that's all, or bread with tea and a salad. The saint R. Ḥayyim Pinto of blessed memory sat with them and ate their bread and made them happy, and would take his leave blessing them. He did not always like eating at the tables of the rich and said that the *shekhinah* and the blessing are present at the tables of the poor more often than at the tables of the rich. He would say that belief in God was gotten from a life of poverty and want rather than from a life of luxury."

31.3 "I saw the miracles of R. Ḥayyim Pinto in Casablanca. I had a son who used to have fits. Sometimes such fits that they would say he was dead. Finally they told me I had to take him to R. Ḥayyim Pinto. He was two years old. What did I do? I couldn't take him so I took his clothes [and put them on] the shrine. I made a *seʿudah.* I dressed him in those clothes, and since then he has been healthy. Now he is married and has children. He hasn't had any fits since then."

32. Rabbi Hillel Ha-Cohen (Rabat on the River Draa)

According to local tradition, R. Hillel was an emissary from the Holy Land, who was robbed and then murdered by Muslims. It is told that he was only eighteen years old at the time of his death. He was buried on the site of the murder, and the faithful have visited his grave ever since.

32.1 "I distributed rations in a town in Draa called Mezguita, which is about 140 kilometers from Ouarzazate. In 1942 I went there to distribute rations to the Arabs. I settled in a place where there was an army camp. There are a lot of villages there, one called Aghdz, another Aslim, another Rabat, another Tamnougalt, Auriz. All these villages are located at the beginning of Draa. We asked someone which rabbis they have here in the cemetery. He told me: *There is a rabbi called R. Hillel.* One day we had nothing to do. I told my friend Elqayam David: *Let's go there on pilgrimage!* We went and found stones, and a place where people lit candles and oil, but nothing else. Just a few big stones, one on top of the other, and they were all blackened. We sat down. My friend said to me: *Look, let's volunteer,* *let's build this grave!* I told him: *All right!* When we got back, we sent [people] to Marrakech. They brought us bricks, cement and whitewash. We took all the building materials there by car. We brought an Arab and two friends, and we didn't know how to build it. This rabbi is called R. Hillel. Nobody knows how to build the tomb. To the right or to the left. We start to think. We say to the Arab: *Come, let's have a glass of tea and rest a bit. Then we'll see how to build the tomb!* We sat down. Suddenly a snake crawled out to his full length. The Arab saw it and told us: *Listen, Jews! I saw a snake. I'll go with a stick. If he runs away, I won't say anything. If he doesn't run away, I'll make a mark at its head and a mark at its tail, and that is where the tomb of R. Hillel will be!* He took a stick and stood up and we watched him. He walked over to where the snake was sleeping and made a mark at its tail and a mark at its head, and the snake did not budge. As soon as the Arab stopped making the marks the snake left straight away. We didn't know where to. When we heard what the Arab said and we saw what he did, our hair stood on end and we were filled with the grace of the saint. We were glad we understood how to build. The Arab took three days to finish the work. A month later, a Jew came from the village of Aslim with his [diseased] eyes. He arrived exactly the month he first couldn't see a thing because he had gone blind. He came to R. Hillel and removed his clothes, dropped them on the floor. He started to shout: *R. Hillel, do not let me stay blind! I beg you night and day to help my eyes!* He sat there seven days and returned with his eyes altogether healthy. Now his eyes were not sick at all, and before that he would look and could not see a thing. That is what his wife told us. She came and said to us: *You should live and be well! And may the Lord help you because of this tomb of R. Hillel! My husband slept there for seven days and now he can see!* The old Arab [who had helped build the tomb] told how the rabbi had come from the Holy Land with his two animals. There were [religious] books on the animals, and he used to go around collecting contributions. I don't know if this was true. Where did he come from? They say that he was a *ḥakham* from Jerusalem. When he arrived there, they say, he met up with Arab robbers. They took the animals and killed the rabbi, and the servant from the villages who was with him ran away. When they heard that the rabbi was dead, the Jews came from these villages and buried him. They say that this was about 600 years ago. This village is over 1,000 years old."

32.2 "Our master, R. Hillel, is buried in the Mezguita region. There is one woman [now] here. . . . They used to hold a *seʿudah* for him every year. They had a Muslim housemaid. When they prepared the meal, they gave her some of the *seʿudah,* because she was their servant. [People] came there. No one dared touch this food, as if they thought it was a dead beast of the Muslims. They asked the people to eat, but they all said they couldn't. The food just stayed there. That night, he [the saint] appeared in a dream. He told them that the *seʿudah* was unclean and that they must prepare other food. If they did not, their blood would be upon their own heads. They asked the housewife. She said that everything was *kosher* and added that she had given some of the food to the Muslim maid. That decided it. They had to throw all the food away and prepare another *seʿudah.*"

33. Rabbi Hillel Ha-Galili (Gourama)

According to local tradition, R. Hillel came from the Holy Land.

33.1 "Near our town there was a cemetery from the time of the destruction of the Second Temple in Jerusalem. All of them [sages] are from the Holy Land, from the time of the destruction of the Second Temple, but nobody would go into the cemetery. But he [the informant's guest] said: *I'm going in!* My husband and our rabbi, too, told him: *They say it's forbidden! They say we must not go inside!* He said: *I'm going in! Let's see what happens!* Honestly, his foot took only [one step], I don't know who took him and threw him from here to there. We laughed so much. He said it just happened to him that way [and added]: *Now I believe!*"

34. Idbud Fassin (Assaka)

A group of seven saints, sometimes also called Ait Idbud Fassin.

34.1 "Idbud Fassin. They are seven great saints, but only three of them can be visited on the ground below. Four of them are on the mountain. No one can visit them. Anyone who goes up never comes down. It is just like the story about the Cave of Makhpelah. His father of blessed memory [the father of an informant from Tiznit] would go there every year and slaughter sheep and cows. Every year. The town of Assaka is small, and the people were very poor. He would slaughter there for all of them and divide it up among them. They were good Jews. There was an Arab who once went to steal candles. He stole them and his hands got stuck and he couldn't move. Along came a man called R. Abraham. He said to him: *Tell me, what did you do?* It was the rabbi of Assaka. He said: *Tell me what you have done and we shall release you!* He said: *I took the candles from there!* He said to him: *Now get up and return them!* [He said:] *But I can't move!* [The rabbi said:] *I say to you. Get up!* It was already three or four days that he couldn't move. He took the candles. Somehow he managed to get up and return them, and then all the Arabs gathered and apologized. His mother [of the same informant from Tiznit], I remember, could have only daughters. She said: *I'll go there on pilgrimage!* My father slaughtered a bull. I remember that day. The whole town ate and some was left over. When they had finished eating, he gave them more. . . . His mother went there and she was pregnant. Suddenly a snake appears right in front of her! Somebody comes. She started screaming: *A snake! A snake!* It rose up right in front of her. When she turned around, they told her not to move. The snake wiggled and continued on its way. The rabbi told her: *You will have a son! You will have a son!* And she did! She had a son, Abraham. We used to go [to the saint] after *Lag b'Omer.* It was really something. They would start in the morning, on foot. Uphill. They would walk two or three days."

35. Kever Navi (Mogador)

Kever Navi (Tomb of a Prophet) is a small tomb in the cemetery of Mogador. According to one tradition, the occupant is the infant son of the saint R. David Bel-Ḥazzan, who is also buried in Mogador. The saint was called Navi (Prophet), because he could speak from the day he was born.

35.1 "In the cemetery in Mogador there is the Navi, who spoke on the day he was born. He is the son of R. David Bel-Ḥazzan. He was born, and that very day he spoke. He said: *Give me the clothes to wear!* So they called him the Prophet. He didn't live long. His mother was called Lalla Rachel. He put on the clothes, lived for three days, and died. That's what people told me. He was born and he spoke, and his mother was afraid of him. His mother is buried at his side, near R. Yaʿaqob Bibas and R. Yaʿaqob Elmaleḥ.

36. Rabbi Khalifa Ben-Malka (Agadir)[45]

R. Khalifa, probably born in Tetuan, died in Agadir, where he is interred in the old cemetery. His *hillulah* is held on the 3rd of *Elul.* A very wealthy man, he was the author of the books *Kaf veNaqi* and *Qol Rinah.* The Muslims also visited his tomb.

36.1 "R. Khalifa Malka . . . was very rich and very righteous, a Kabbalist and wonderful poet. . . . The Jews of Agadir tell how, on *Yom Kippur,* seven ships laden with goods came to him, and the captain came for his orders once, twice and then a third time. He [the saint] said: *Lord of creation, the vanities of this world want to distract me from worshipping you! May it be your will that [the ships] all sink!* And he was left a wretched pauper. They used to call them the ships of R. Khalifa Malka. And the rich man, R. Moshe Ben-Yaʿaqob Gedalia, from Amsterdam, used to send him monthly [financial] support. He suffered the tortures of the righteous. His only son was killed on his wedding day. Even after his death he was not spared suffering. It is now [1975] some ten years since the government decided to transfer his grave. They delivered a great eulogy in his honor, and on that day declared a public fast in Agadir. Over his grave they built a splendid marble shrine."

37. Rabbi Levi Ben-Levi (Boujad)[46]

The saint is buried in the old cemetery outside the town. According to tradition, R. Levi's father passed away while his mother was pregnant; the newborn infant, therefore, was named after his father. His *hillulah* is celebrated on *Lag bʿOmer.* He is also venerated by the Muslims.

37.1 "R. Levi Ben-Levi, R. Yehudah Qadosh and R. Yaḥya Ben-Yaḥya are buried in the old cemetery. The Arabs turned the cemetery into a cultivated field, but when they tried to plough those graves, miracles occurred and the saints appeared to them in their dreams. So they left the graves alone and all acknowledged their holiness."

37.2 "The saint was born in Boujad and passed away there. His brothers, R. Yitsḥaq and R. Shelomoh Ben-Levi, are buried alongside him. When he died, chains came down from the sky and raised him up to Heaven. Three date palms grew by virtue of his merit, and that is why he is called Mul Enekhla. If we want to request something, we call upon R. Levi Ben-Levi, Master of the Date Palm. In Boujad, we had saints whose graves we visited: R. Yosef Gabbay, R. Eliyahu Demnati, R. Yaḥya Ben-Sliman, Bu-Izzo Elbaz, R. Hodi, the father of Bu-Izu, R. Yissakhar Seluq, R. Shelomoh Asbaᶜ Boḥbot, R. Shelomoh Ben-Lḥans and R. Yaḥya Ben-Yaḥya, who is also called Mul Enekhla."

38. Rabbi Makhluf ᶜArama (Skoura)

R. Makhluf is a member of the saintly family of Ait ᶜArama. One tradition maintains that the saint is buried in Imerhane.

38.1 "Yes, I remember them from when I was a little girl. My father took care of his tomb. He was the one who built the tomb. The tomb was low, almost level with the ground. The son of R. Masᶜud ᶜArama was R. David ᶜArama. He was in Casablanca. They were great sages and would write [amulets] for people. People would visit their grave and make a *seᶜudah* there. If someone had a problem, he went to the saint to ask him to help. Once, on a *Sabbath* Eve, when we were children . . . that Friday nobody had visited the cemetery [a serious breach of pious custom]. The Muslims saw that the whole cemetery was lit with flames. They came to tell us. They thought we were having some kind of celebration there. They came and asked the Jews: *What's going on in the cemetery? We saw all the tombs lit up!* That Friday no one had visited the cemetery, but the Muslims came and told us that all the graves were lit up. This I remember. The Jews went and saw that all the graves really were lit up with cans of olive oil. They couldn't get near the cemetery. No one dared to do anything near the saint's grave, because if anyone dared, something terrible happened to him. It was sure to. I still remember that, when I was a little girl, the Muslims wanted to do something there and something happened to them. I don't remember exactly what, because I was just a little girl."

39. Rabbi Makhluf Ben-Yosef Abiḥatsira (Tarkellil)[47]

According to some traditions, R. Makhluf came to Tarkellil from Tafilalet. His family is said to have originated in the Holy Land. His *hillulah* is on the 1st of *Tebet.* His son, R. Eliyahu, is buried next to him. He is also venerated by the Muslims, who call him Bayo. In

Israel, R. Makhluf's *hillulah* is celebrated in many places, but particularly in Kiriyat Gat, where the saint has a shrine which is thronged with visitors all year round.

39.1 "I bathed in his *miqweh.* The village was near Ait Attab, where there were people who looted the villages and then ran away. The saint came, may he rest in peace, and said: *I shall take upon myself one half of the city!* And he did. When he would approach a place, strong winds would begin to blow and stones would fall, and they [the robbers] could not come near. So they never harmed Tarkellil. They built a shrine over his grave which was inside the city. There is a *miqweh* there, where they immerse themselves for ritual purification, and there is also a synagogue. To enter the *miqweh,* you have to go through a pretty narrow opening, down one or two steps, and you can't see the end of the *miqweh.* The water is salty, like the ocean. And when you're in it and say *Baba R. Makhluf Ben-Yosef!,* the level of the water rises and waves form, and no one knows where the water comes from. Afterwards, they give a little money to the Arab woman who lives there. After the Jews emigrated to Israel, the Arab woman lived there. She took care of the place even while the Jews were there. The sheikh of the Arabs made her caretaker of the place, and that is how she makes her living. Women, too, go there after purifying themselves."

39.2 "Here is another story about R. Makhluf Ben-Yosef. He [his shrine] was left alone in the village [after the Jews left for Israel], he and three *Cohanim.* One night, the remaining Jews went to sleep near his tomb, so that he would show them what to do. He told them: *Arise! I, too, shall go [to Israel] with you!* A Jewish woman from their area slept at our place and told us this. The next morning they got up, sold their belongings to the Muslims, and left. He [the saint] told them that he was going, too. He also came to Israel. He told them: *Do you think that I shall remain here? I am going too!* He came here [to Israel] to help our soldiers."

40. Rabbi Masʿud Naḥmias (Marrakech)[48]

The saint is buried beyond the city wall. He passed away outside the city of Marrakech. According to the burial customs in Morocco, he was interred near the wall with other people who died outside the city.

40.1 "The saint passed away in Ntifa at the beginning of the century. According to our custom, he could not be brought for burial in the cemetery in Marrakech, because then the sultan would die. My father, who was the head of the Burial Society, went to Ntifa forty days after the saint passed away. He went to take the body. No one dared come close. My father opened the tomb and saw that the body was still warm. They left. On the way they ran out of gasoline. My father called on the saint for help and so they got to Marrakech without gasoline. My father told me this."

41. Meʿarat Oufran (Oufran)[49]

Meʿarat Oufran (the Cave of Oufran) is also called Meʿarat Ha-Nisrafim (the Cave of the Burned Ones) or Meʿarat Ha-Makhpelah (Cave of the Patriarchs). According to tradition, it is forbidden to enter this ancient cemetery. In 1792, fifty Jews were burnt at the stake here. They all became martyrs, the foremost among them R. Yehudah Ben-Naphtali Afryat. The Muslims also used to visit the holy place.

41.1 "[To get] to Oufran you have to go from Agadir via Tiznit. Many saints are buried in our cemetery. No one may enter the center of the cemetery because it is sacred. We only bury [our dead] around it. Some say the place has existed since the destruction of the Second Temple, and some even say since [the destruction of] the First Temple. The emissaries who went to collect alms used to come from here, from Jerusalem. They would fast and purify themselves [in a *miqweh*] so that they could enter, and even then they would not have the right to go in. They tell of a certain sage who fasted and purified himself. They tell me he went into the center and they [the saints] came to him in a dream and said: *We are giving you just enough time to get back to your own place!* They gave him time to get home and then he died."

42. Rabbi Mimun Elghrabli (Settat)[50]

This saint is buried in the ancient cemetery of Settat. The Jews used to visit his tomb every week at the close of the *Sabbath.*

42.1 "R. Mimun Elghrabli. I don't know where he came from, whether Marrakech or Casablanca. R. Mimun revealed himself as a stone. His grave disappeared. In the cemetery, only one round stone was left. Whenever people passed by, they asked themselves: *What* *kind of stone is this?* He appeared before the members of the Burial Society of Settat and told them: *I am R. Mimun Elghrabli. Now you must build [a shrine] over me and prepare a* seʿudah! We built [a shrine] over him and every Saturday night we used to visit his grave. Maybe it was twenty or thirty years ago [the interview took place in 1973]."

43. Rabbi Mordekhay Ben-ʿAttar (Marrakech)[51]

R. Mordekhay Ben-ʿAttar is one of Marrakech's greatest rabbis.

43.1 "I heard that R. Mordekhay Ben-ʿAttar hid a talisman so that if the enemy should come to the Jewish neighborhood, he would not be able to get in. Even when the Arabs want to come in, they turn back as if their feet had swelled. When people pass the gate, they kiss the marble. That's where the talisman is that I told you about. I remember that when people came to buy things . . . on Sunday. When you went through the gate, you would say: *R. Mordekhay Ben-ʿAttar, if you are on my side, open the way for me to make a good living!* You pray at the wall. You go inside and you see people who have faith. You say: *How much does this cost? And that? Give me this and that!* He answers: *All right!* You go into the *medina* [old city] of the Arabs. I'll show you what luck is. One time I went to Marrakech after Passover. I went in to the rabbi [prayed to the saint] there. [Later on] I went into the store of Yitsḥaq N. and said to him: *How much does this cloth cost?* It was silk that the Arabs would buy for their wives to wear on important days. He answered that one meter cost thirty-eight reals. I thought: *I'll rest today and tomorrow God will have mercy on me!* I went into the house of an Arab who was sick. Just then he opened his store. I asked how he was feeling. He said he was sick. I said I was sorry to hear that. . . . I saw that he had silk. He was asking fifteen reals per meter. I bought seven hundred meters from him. I put it on my mule and went to Yitsḥaq N. He told me that one meter costs now forty-one reals and I told him that I'll sell it to him for thirty-eight reals. I gave him all the fabric I had. I remember this, and it was all because of the power of R. Mordekhay Ben-ʿAttar, may he rest in peace. Then that Arab asked his father about the silk, and told him that he had sold it for fifteen reals. He told him: *Too bad God didn't take you! I was sick . . . and you have ruined our house!* He told him that it now costs forty. . . . Every time I go to Marrakech, I must pray to the one who is buried near this gate, may he rest in peace. He's the foremost among the Jews. If a merchant tells you: *We swear to you by R. Mordekhay!* you can believe him. That's it. And not just the Jews. You say to him: *By the life of your father and of R. Mordekhay Ben-ʿAttar!*"

44. Rabbi Mordekhay Mul El-ʿAyn (Akka)

The name of the saint is connected with a spring near his tomb. He is buried alongside R. Yehudah Ben-Ḥovav. According to tradition, he came from the Holy Land.

44.1 "They say that they [R. Mordekhay Mul El-ʿAyn and R. Yehudah Ben-Ḥovav] came to collect alms. They came on a Friday and had another three days' walk to get to Akka. They were in a field. Then R. Mordekhay said to R. Yehudah: *I'm not well!* That is, he was going to die. He took the stick from his hands and stuck it into the ground, and a spring welled up. He was dying and asked him [R. Yehudah] to start reciting the *Shemaʿ*. Then R. Yehudah took the stick and stuck it in and said: *God, do something so that he will not die this way in a field. Please answer our plea!* R. Yehudah Ben-Ḥovav told: *He said that he would grant our request until we would arrive and die in the* mellaḥ *of Akka.* Only this saint [R. Mordekhay] bathed in the water there and they were in Akka. The sun had begun to set when he drove his stick in, but it did not set until they reached Akka. They buried him there. And R. Yehudah Ben-Ḥovav stayed in the village until he passed away and was buried alongside him [R. Mordekhay]. The Jews of Akka told me this when I was there."

45. Rabbi Moshe Ḥabib (Toundout)[52]

R. Moshe Ḥabib is also called R. Moshe El-Mizraḥi. According to tradition, he came from the Holy Land.

45.1 "We would always visit the tomb of R. Moshe Ḥabib on *Sabbath* Eve. We would light candles near his tomb. The whole village. His original name was R. Moshe El-Mizraḥi; we call him R. Moshe Ḥabib. He came from Demnate. From Demnate he came to Toundout, where he passed away and was buried. It is the custom to go on pilgrimage to his tomb. We built his tomb and we visit it, in the name of God and the saint. The whole village visits his tomb. He came to us in a dream and told us that the Muslims were going to dig up the bones of the dead in order to burn them and work magic for their flocks, so that the sick sheep wouldn't die. When they [the Muslims] got to the cemetery, they saw two tall horses that reached up to the sky, and they couldn't get in to the place! In the name of God and the saint! We used to visit his tomb and light candles on it every first of the month and Saturday Eve. Someone guarded the place. Some people stayed there seven days. We used to make ritual meals. We would bring bread that we had baked in the oven, chicken soup, and whatever we could—sometimes couscous, too. At *Ḥanukkah* we brought doughnuts."

46. Rabbi Moshe Ḥaliwa (Marrakech)

R. Moshe Ḥaliwa was born in Beni Sbih in Draa, where a synagogue and a *yeshibah* are named after him. His *hillulah* is celebrated on the 16h of *Tebet* and is still observed by his descendants in Israel.

46.1 "Once there was a rich man and he was very proud. He said: *I do not want to go to the* hillulah! He said: *I will not go to the* seʿudah! This was in our town, in Marrakech. And then this man who didn't want to go to the *hillulah* recited the Evening Service and went home. He told his wife: *I have a headache!* She said: *It's because of R. Moshe Ḥaliwa, because you did not go to his* hillulah! He said: *I have sinned! I have acted perversely!* He came home and wanted to go inside. He didn't recognize it and he didn't hear. He called out: *Where's the door?* He couldn't get in. *The door! Where's the door?* What did he do? He went home and brought a rope. He said to his brother: *Tie my hands behind my back. Tie me up and drag me to the shrine of R. Moshe Ḥaliwa!* He tied him up with his hands behind his back. He brought him up to the building. He saw the door and went in. He took a bottle of *ʿarak*. He drank it down. He got up and danced and was merry. After that, he came [to the shrine] until he died recently in Beersheba. That was a year and three months ago [the interview was held on January 19, 1974]. He came here several times. He only had to hear of the *hillulah* of R. Moshe Ḥaliwa, wherever it might be, and he would come."

47. Mulay Ighi (Ighi)[53]

Mulay Ighi is one of the most widely venerated saints among the Jews of Morocco. His shrine is visited by pilgrims every day of the year, but especially during his *hillulah* on *Lag bʿOmer.* Some traditions identify him with R. David Alshqar, buried in Casablanca.[54] Those who could not get to Ighi (some 100 kilometers from Demnate) visited the grave of R. David Alshqar in Casablanca. Mulay Ighi is also called Mul Shejra El-Khedra (the Master of the Green Tree) after the bush that grew near his grave and never caught fire from the candles lit by the faithful.

According to tradition, Mulay Ighi came from the Holy Land to Morocco in very early times. He appears in lists of seven or ten rabbis who came to Morocco to convert the gentiles or collect donations for the Holy Land. He is openly venerated by the Muslims and honored even by the Muslim leaders.

47.1 "Mulay Ighi is buried in a field. There is, let's say, a wall from here and a wall from there, and he is buried there with many other sages. They say he is from Jerusalem. He did not come from these villages. There were ten sages, and each one went out to a different place in order to collect alms. They say about Mulay Ighi that he went to the village of Zerekten, which is some ten kilometers from his burial place. He went to the people of the city and of the Burial Society, and said to them: *Come with me!* He said to them: *Dig here!* They dug. They say that he went down to the river and immersed himself [for ritual purification]. He put on the shroud and told the grave to close up, and the grave closed itself. Whoever goes there always has his wish fulfilled. Anyone who is sick or a woman who does not give birth, they go there. He was a sage from Jerusalem. He went out with R. David Ha-Levi Mul Draᶜ, R. ᶜAmram Ben-Diwan, and R. Ḥananiah Ha-Cohen. This happened a long time ago, long before I was born. But at that time there were also people who came as emissaries of R. Shimᶜon Bar-Yoḥay, R. Meir Baᶜal Ha-Nes and Rachel Immenu (Rachel the Matriarch). . . . I remember when I was a little boy, sages on mules would come with their servants and take alms. Our ancestors told us about his [Mulay Ighi's] burial place. The Arabs would also come there. If, for example, an Arab was passing near the place, he would come to the saint and kiss him [his tomb]. They knew he was a Jew. They tell how an Arab had nothing with which to celebrate *Aᶜid el-Kebir* [a great festival celebrated forty days after the small festival that closes the fast of *Ramadan,* the ninth month of the Islamic calendar]. He was the guardian of the shrine. He said to him [the saint]: *See, I have nothing to celebrate with!* In the evening he was wandering around. He met a man who said to him: *Take this sheep! It is yours!* And another story. Two thieves stole a mule and a carpet belonging to a Jew from Marrakech. They took the mule and put the carpet on it. They rode on it all night. But at dawn they saw that they were still in the same place they had started from. This happened in our own times. . . . People who go there, stay there three or four days. . . . There are people who put a bottle of oil on the grave or a gold earring. People put it there and afterwards take it back with them. But there are thieves in Taghmat, a little village near [the shrine of] Mulay Ighi. They steal things from there. Candles. They are poor."

47.2 "Mulay Ighi is also buried in a place far away. . . . His name is R. David Alshqar. In that place there are some seven Muslim villages. They called the place Ighi. His grave is near Zerekten. Nothing is built, but there is a large stone there with a plant like myrtle growing on it. They call it *imitk.* The plants shade the stone. They light many candles there, sometimes two hundred boxes, and these plants never catch fire. The *imitk,* may he rest in peace, is as green as mint. After *Sukkot* we always went on pilgrimage there. At one time as many as 40,000 Jews would come. The man who was in charge of everything was called Shalom Buskila and he is buried there. He was the *shoḥet* and the president of the *Ḥebrah* [*Ḥebrah Qaddishah*—the Burial Society]. He received the money for the slaughtering, and people entered only with his permission. . . . No one can go up to him [the saint] without first taking a *tebilah* [ritual bath] in the spring. A bit farther on is a waterfall. A woman who cannot bear children goes there for a *tebilah.* She says: *Oh, Mulay Ighi!* And then she makes her request of him, and then she gives birth. She's bound to! A woman who has her period must not be there. Her husband must not take her with him. The women are very much afraid. It has happened many times. If she goes when she has her period, she returns and not eight days go by before she gives up the ghost to the Creator!"

47.3 "Over his grave is a tree. They did not build a room over him. There is only a tree. In Morocco it never happened that Muslims attacked the Jews. They were afraid of the saint. The Muslims also visited him and they were afraid."

48. Mul Jebel El-Kebir (Sefrou)[55]

Mul Jebel El-Kebir (the Master of the Great Mountain) is also called Mul Jebel El-Khdar (the Master of the Green Mountain). The saint is buried between Sefrou and Bahloul, near the Sefrou-Fez road, in a mountain cave with a wide opening. Two meters to the left of the opening is a passageway. Next to it is a sort of depression in which candles are lit. To the right, two steps lead to a room, and to the left is a room one can enter only by bending low. This cave is known as *Kif el-Yahud* (Cave of the Jew); it is visited by Muslims as well as Jews. Which saint is buried there is not known. According to various traditions, it is R. Shimᶜon Bar-Yoḥay, the Prophet Daniel, or R. ᶜAmram Ben-Diwan.

48.1 "We used to go to the one called Mul Jebel El-Kebir the Saint. We would light candles and pray to him. No matter why we went to him, he would help us. His grave has opened inside a great mountain, and that's why they call him Mul Jebel El-Kebir. He told them: *I am here!* He appeared to a great rabbi in a dream and told him: *If anyone wishes to come on a pilgrimage to me, I am to be found there!* We would travel from Fez to Sefrou and climb high up until we got to the mountain to visit him. After he told the rabbi: *I am in such and such a place,* they set up a spot there for lighting candles and places to sit and sleep. A person would go there with a sickness and return healthy, even the deaf and dumb. He would grant everyone's wishes. Whoever goes there, says: *Oh, Sidi Mul Jebel El-Kebir! We entreat you; we have come to beg of you, have mercy upon us and cure such and such a disease!* Yes, we saw a mute who hadn't spoken for years start to talk. God freed his tongue, and he began to talk normally. By the grace of God and the saints! On *Lag bᶜOmer,* thousands would come from all the towns. There water flowed from the wall. It would make a little puddle, and people would rub that water on themselves. The Muslims would also come and bring whole boxes of candles. They lit them inside the cave until the people sweated."

48.2 "In Sefrou we had R. ᶜAmram Ben-Diwan and R. Shimᶜon Bar-Yoḥay. To get to R. Shimᶜon we climbed a high mountain. We used to go on pilgrimage to R. ᶜAmram. We would call upon R. ᶜAmram. A long time ago people dreamt that he told them he was with them and that he was in their mountain. We don't remember, because it wasn't during our lifetime. He told them that he was in their mountain if they wished to visit him. R. Shimᶜon told them: *If you do not wish to visit my grave [in Meron, in the Galilee], I am in your mountain!* So they said that this was the mountain of R. Shimᶜon and the mountain of R. ᶜAmram."

49. Mul Sedra (Ksar Es-Souk)

Mul Sedra or Mwalin Sedra—"Master(s) of the Bush"—is buried near R. Yaḥya Laḥlu and Mul Terya.

49.1 "Mwalin Sedra. They were not known [to the Jews]. A Jew, a neighbor, tells that he dreamt that he went to visit the tomb of R. Yaḥya Laḥlu. As he was climbing up to the burial place, some people stood in his way. They asked: *Where are you going?* He said: *I am going for a visit [to a saint].* They answered: *Why don't we merit your visiting our grave? We are Mwalin Sedra, the Masters of the Bush!* From then on, people began to visit the grave of Mwalin Sedra."

50. Mul Tefillin (Tamzaourt)

Also known as Great Rock, Mul Tefillin (Master of the Phylacteries) is a rock with drawings of fringed garments and phylacteries. Pilgrimages are made to the site.

50.1 "Mul Tefillin. I was there [visited the place]. He, the precious saint, died there while he was praying. His phylacteries remained near him. His name is not known. All they found were his *tefillin.* He was praying, and then he went, body and soul. His *tefillin* were left behind. They found the *tefillin* as well as his date [of death]."

51. Mul Terya (Ksar Es-Souk)

Mul Terya means "Master of the Light" or "Master of the Lamp." It is a tree near the tombs of R. Yaḥya Laḥlu and Mul Sedra, which sometimes appears to be illuminated at night. The saint is also venerated by the Muslims.

51.1 "In Ksar Es-Souk there is Mul Terya, a tree, where we light candles. Near R. Yaḥya El-Ḥlu. It is a very thorny tree. Every evening flames come down from the sky and light up this tree and also the burial place of R. Yaḥya El-Ḥlu. Jews and Muslims visited his tomb. Everyone had his request granted."

51.2 "Mul Terya. They said that all through the *Sabbath* they used to see a lamp [shining] on his tomb. *Terya* is the lamp that is lit in a glass filled with olive oil. It is lit in the synagogue. It is special for the saint. In the synagogue they called these memorial glasses *terya.* In El-Ksar there were families called Lʿasri and also Shitrit, Sabbag,

Oḥayon and Levi, but no Cohen. There were no *Cohanim.* A few came, but they didn't do well. They say that the *Cohanim* do not fare well there. I heard of one who died childless and lonely there."

52. Mul Timḥdart (Tabia)[56]

According to local tradition, the saint hailed from the Holy Land. His *hillulah* is celebrated on *Lag bʿOmer.* Jews come from all over Morocco to visit his tomb. The Muslims also venerated him openly. They called him Nwadain, 'the Saint of the Jews.' The name Mul Timḥdart seems to imply that the saint was a school teacher.

52.1 "I once heard that an Arab had sold goats to a Jew, as many as he wanted, but the Jew denied it. The Arab said to the Jew: *You know, we have no contract or anything. I ask only two things of you: Come [with me] to your Jew, to the saint. God is true! You will not take an oath on a Torah scroll or phylacteries. Come with me to your* ḥazzan! That night the rabbi [the saint], may he rest in peace, came to the Jew in a dream and asked him to give the Arab his money, and beg his pardon. *If you come to take an oath [false] on my grave, you know what you will get!* Finally the Jew went to the Arab in the company of two other Jews. He pleaded with the Arab. The Arab said to him: *Now you are telling the truth. Give me half the amount and you take the other half. I only wanted to believe that your rabbi is a saint, that he is true and his words are the truth!* May he rest in peace."

52.2 "I know [the shrine of] the saint Mul Timḥdart. If a man is mortally ill and his legs are paralyzed, and he goes there and sits there seven days, he will stand up on his own two legs and go home. We used to pierce the ears of the sheep with an awl [probably to mark them as the saint's untouchable property] and say: *Oh, Mul Timḥdart!* Then we would release them to graze until the time came to slaughter them. The sheep scattered, grazed, and nothing would happen to them. That's what we did to all the sheep intended for other saints."

52.3 "Sidi Mul Timḥdart! There was a wall which was built and he was revealed. A woman had an epileptic seizure and called out his name. And then they built him a shrine and a place for lamps and lighting candles. They called him Sidi Mul Timḥdart."

52.4 "Whoever wanted to emigrate to Israel went to visit his grave, and in that way the saint could free him to go to Israel. There was a man named A. T. Today he lives in the south of Israel. He got to Casablanca and something [bad] happened to him. He went back to the village and asked the saint to free him. He offered up a *se'udah* and emigrated to Israel."

53. Rabbi Nissim Ben-Nissim (Ait Bayoud)[57]

R. Nissim is buried on the summit of a mountain named Jebel Lakerya, a place that could be reached only on muleback. According to tradition, he came from the Holy Land to collect funds in Morocco. His *hillulah* is celebrated on *Lag b'Omer.* Muslims also used to visit his tomb.

53.1 "There is a *ḥakham* near Mogador, R. Nissim Ben-Nissim, buried in Ait Bayoud, an Arab village. There's a courtyard there. The Arabs don't claim him for their own. I have a daughter who came here some months ago from Morocco. She told me that there's a guard in the courtyard. She went there with about a hundred people who came from Casablanca to spend the *Sabbath.* She told me that on Saturday night, when they wanted to open the shrine, one of them bought the key [the right to open the shrine] for a million francs. They sold candles for a hundred thousand and a hundred and fifty thousand francs. It wasn't even his *hillulah,* they just went there on a *Sabbath.*"

54. Rabbi Pinḥas Ha-Cohen (Marrakech)[58]

R. Pinḥas Ha-Cohen, also known as R. Pinḥas Khalifa Ha-Cohen Azzogh or Baba Pinḥas, was a member of R. David Ben-Barukh's family. R. Pinḥas died on the 14th of *Tebet* 5712 (January 12, 1952).

54.1 "R. Pinḥas Ha-Cohen Azzogh is in Marrakech. In the name of God and the saint, he is alive and active. If something was supposed to happen to someone, his grandfather would appear in a dream and tell him: *Such and such will happen to him, he will die or something will happen!* He told [a prophecy] to the pasha of the city and saved his life. On the day our beloved [saint] died, the pasha also died. I celebrate his *hillulah* because of his great virtue. I work only for the sake of good deeds. I dreamt about him. I know him. He performed countless miracles. Once they wanted to destroy Marrakech and kill the pasha. He [the saint] went to him that morning and told the pasha: *Watch out! If you drink this coffee, you will die!* The pasha asked: *What are you saying?* [Rabbi Pinḥas said]: *I told you. Your maidservant wants to kill you. They are there outside and they are planning to kill you!* [The pasha] told him: *All right!* [R. Pinḥas] told him: *Here comes a cat!* He called the cat. He gave her a little of the coffee and she lay down dead at his feet. That was it. In the name of God and the saint! The saints have performed many miracles. We are alive only by their virtue and the virtue of God. R. Pinḥas! I knew him and prayed to him. His miracles were greater than he. His grandfather would come and tell him things [in his dreams] about other people. Then he [the saint] would come to these people and tell them: *Arise! Such and such will happen to you!* And, may God preserve us, if he cursed anyone, he would dry up [die] instantly! Yes! His [own] son! He told him: *Do not get married!* His son wanted to marry a girl from an unworthy family. His son told him: *I want to marry only her!* He [the rabbi] told him: *Go!* He died. There is no one like R. Pinḥas!"

54.2 "Once, when the pasha of Marrakech was involved in a quarrel with the king of Morocco, they plotted to kill him [the pasha] in the mosque, to stab him in the back with a knife in the Kutubya Mosque. The pasha had armor against bullets, but not against a knife. R. Pinḥas went to him on Thursday and told him: *On Friday you go to pray with the king, but they are plotting to kill you!* The pasha did not go the next day; he sent a cousin who looked like him. He dressed him in his clothes and promised to guard him so that nothing would happen to him. The cousin came to the mosque. When he wanted to bow down, someone came and tried to stab him in the back. They seized him. The cousin told them: *I am not the pasha!* Immediately the pasha's bodyguards who were from the Zaian tribe arrived. That same day, everyone who had been in the mosque got what was coming to him. When the pasha came to deal with the king, the pasha promised to remove him from his throne, and so he did."

54.3 "R. Pinḥas's son and his wife used to come to our home. Every time they came to Casablanca they stayed in our house. R. Pinḥas's son and his wife. His son Shimʿon and his wife stayed in our house. I have his picture. His wife was Simy Tangi. R. Shimʿon told me about something that happened to his father in Fez. Once he went to Fez. He [R. Pinḥas] went to Fez because he and Baba Dudu were brothers, and they divided everything so that there would be no quarrels. They divided up Morocco [for purposes of collecting alms]. R. Pinḥas got the north and Baba Dudu the south. Then R. Pinḥas of blessed memory went to Fez to collect from the alms boxes. He arrived in Fez, may the memory of the saint be a blessing! The Jews of Fez received him handsomely and joyfully. The following day he was sitting with his host. Next door to his host's store was the store of a Muslim, a highly respected man. What did he do? He asked the Jew to let the rabbi come with him to his house for a few hours, and he promised to bring him back. The Jew said: *All right!* and asked R. Pinḥas to go with Monsieur [the Muslim] and he would be responsible. The Muslim led him through some remote places, until he brought him into a house. He called his mother and children and wife and they all kissed the rabbi's hand. He brought him inside, led him downstairs. R. Pinḥas was afraid. The Muslim told him: *Do not be afraid, master! Eventually I shall tell you everything!* He took him into a room where he found an ark and a *Torah* scroll. He said: *Listen, master! There is a lot of money here for you. We are waiting for one of you to come and take it. It all belongs to R. David Ben-Barukh! All the money! Every time the alms box fills up, I guard the money. All the money that you see [is meant] for R. David Ben-Barukh. When I asked them who you were they said that you are the grandson of R. David Ben-Barukh. We are Jews!* Only he was afraid of the Muslims [because] he was a forced convert. . . . It was R. Shimʿon, the son of R. Pinḥas, who told me."

54.4 "I'll tell you about R. Pinḥas Ha-Cohen Azzogh. R. David Ben-Barukh was his grandfather. He was born in Sous. Here is his biography. He studied in Sous and used to ride around to all the villages and cities on his mare to collect alms. He arrived on his mare in Marrakech with his servant. The first time I came to Marrakech I found the *mellaḥ* full of pious Jews studying the *Torah,* performing the *mitswot,* fasting and all. There was even a rabbi standing at the gate to the *mellaḥ,* examining every Jew who went in or out to see whether he had said his prayers. All he had to do was examine your hand for the marks left by the straps of your phylacteries. Anyone who did not have these marks had to go back inside. He stood near the arched gate, which was named after Baba R. Mordekhay Ben-ʿAttar. And so R. Pinḥas came to collect alms in Marrakech and wanted to spend the *Sabbath* with the rich man, Yeshuʿah Corcos. On Wednesday he entered Marrakech. On Thursday the pasha's policemen told him that a Jew had a beautiful mare, which he [the pasha] should take [for himself]. He told them to go and bring the mare. They came to Yeshuʿah and told him the will of the pasha. Yeshuʿah Corcos told them that they could come to his stable and take whatever was there, but must not touch his guest's mare. It was the pasha Ḥadj El-Tami. He [a policeman] told Yeshuʿah: *Send men to take the mare!* Yeshuʿah replied: *You send them!* He called R. Pinḥas to go and appear before the pasha. The pasha wanted to sell his mare. R. Pinḥas answered that she was not for sale and [said]: *Go and fetch her!* The pasha immediately sent his police to fetch the mare. When they opened the stable where the mare was kept, they found that the stable was full of snakes. They were afraid because the snakes wanted to swallow the messengers. They came back. The pasha asked them: *What happened?* They told him about the snakes. The pasha came in person. R. Pinḥas and Yeshuʿah Corcos remained at the pasha's house. The pasha arrived. He went in and saw snakes everywhere. He went back to speak with R. Pinḥas. He asked him where he was from. R. Pinḥas replied that he was born in Sous. The pasha invited him to come and live in Marrakech. The rabbi refused. The pasha told him: *Look, I am returning the mare. Go through the city of Marrakech and [choose] whatever house you like: I shall give it to you!* On Sunday the rabbi went to look for a house. He went back to the pasha and told him which house he liked best. It was the house he lived in until his dying day. A rich Arab lived there. The pasha sent messengers to tell the tenant to leave. He left. He gave him [the tenant] a different house instead of this one. That week the rabbi came to live in Marrakech. This was the miracle."

55. Rabbi Raḥamim Mizraḥi (Rabat)[59]

His *hillulah* is celebrated on the 1st of *Adar.* A synagogue in Rabat is named after him.

55.1 "In Rabat there is R. Raḥamim Mizraḥi. He came to us from the Sahara. He had an iron leg and limped. The children of the *mellaḥ* used to pick on him and bother him because of this leg. They would throw stones at him. He fell down. He came to Rabat. He was a *kabbalist.* They gave him a room. This was a room belonging to the Jewish community. He never married because of his leg. Once, on the *Sabbath* Eve, ʿAmram Zaguri came to me at nine o'clock to ask me to come with him to keep watch over a dying Jew, who had one leg and was named R. Raḥamim. I understood. We went together. We sat next to R. Raḥamim as he lay sick and dying. He died as if he were fighting with his Creator. He had a knapsack full of books. All manuscripts. So I said to ʿAmram Zaguri: *ʿAmram, tonight he will have a good and blessed night. It is certain that he [R. Raḥamim] is a great saint. His passing is special!* I saw his forehead shining as if the *shekhinah* of God had come down on him! His face was red. In the room there was a small lamp which didn't illuminate anything by comparison with the bright light that came from the face of R. Raḥamim. It lit up the room for us. At eleven o'clock, it seemed like daytime rather than nighttime. The room was all lit up. All the walls glowed. A neighbor came to ask who had lit a light on the *Sabbath* [a forbidden act] and who was with us. And this was the *shekhinah* of God, as if a white sheet had been laid over him. I asked ʿAziza, the neighbor: *Who lit the light?* She said it wasn't she. She even got angry and said: *What? Do you think that I would light a candle? I'm a very religious woman!* And I said to ʿAmram: *Look!* My hair stood on end. We read "And the Lord is in his Holy Temple" and the Song of Songs. R. Raḥamim was breathing through his nose and mouth; his eyes were shining and a sheet of light was spread over him. ʿAmram told me that he couldn't read and that this was the first time he had seen such a thing. Next morning, I went to a *paqid* of the Burial Society and told him: *Sheikh Daud! This* ḥakham *is great!* We saw a white sheet spread out over him. At first we didn't notice the signs of death on him, because there was only a feeble lamp there, until suddenly a great light appeared in the room. Then all the Jews of Rabat began to come to the dead man's house. They were all called to come and to participate in the funeral. They all come to give him honor. Jews came all the way from Port Lyautey, they came from Oran in Algeria, and they all said: *B-el-Lah u-b-sidi [in the name of God and of the saint], with God's help and the help of our Master, viva R. Raḥamim Mizraḥi!* They all marveled at the miracles of the saint, blessed be he! What can I tell you? The pieces from his shroud were sold for a thousand francs each. Every barren woman keeps a piece as a talisman. Our sheikh cut up all the shrouds of the rabbi. We brought other shrouds. We cut fourteen meters into pieces and sold them. That day we collected one million francs! The two of us, ʿAmram and I, who had been present as the rabbi lay dying, we were appointed to sell and to collect the money. ʿAmram said to me: *Yitsḥaq, we've collected a lot! Let's take some of the money for ourselves!* I scolded him and said: *How can we take the money of the rabbi? He is a great saint!* The privilege of burying the rabbi was sold for one hundred fifty-six thousand reals. The privilege of lowering the head was bought by Prosper, a rich merchant of Rabat born in Algeria. He asked that only he should buy it. R. Moshe Ben-Walid and R. Masʿud Tsabbaḥ were still alive at that time. It was they who lowered the rabbi into the grave. Prosper A. bought the privilege, but let the two rabbis lower the body. They took off their shoes and lowered the rabbi. Three days later I went to Mr. A. and got the money from him. I gave it to Mr. Berdugo, who was the president of the community. Sheikh Daud Boḥbot asked me to invite the officials of the Burial Society to a general meeting. I was a member of the Burial Society for fifty-two years in Rabat. That night there was a meeting. The *paqid* of the Society came. Each one gave some money. He welcomed everyone. In the end, they decided to give ʿAmram and me thirteen thousand francs. ʿAmram wanted to give the money back because it wasn't enough. I scolded him because I had worked without pay, and you can't return money [to the Society of] R. Shimʿon Bar-Yoḥay. We built a tombstone and a shrine near R. Eliʿezer Davila."

56. Rabbi Raphael Anqawa (Salé)[60]

R. Raphael (1848–1935) was known for his wisdom and erudition. The Jews considered him a saint during his lifetime; Muslims and Christians also respected him greatly and sought his assistance. Jews from all over Morocco as well as representatives of the Muslim and French governments attended his funeral. He was the author of numerous works on the Talmud and religious law.

56.1 "During his lifetime people went to him, but they were afraid of him. It was a kind of mystery. When I was a boy studying in the *yeshibah* and he would come there, I used to kiss his hand. I remember that once I told my mother: *The hands of R. Raphael are not like the hands of a human being. They are like silk. It's like getting a short circuit.* She said: *He is a holy man! It is good that he gave you his hand. There are some people to whom he does not give his hand!* R. Raphael always asked the principal of the *yeshibah* how I was getting along in my studies. R. Raphael was the head of the *yeshibah* for the whole world. Whoever had trouble with any word would ask him, and he would explain it."

56.2 "They say that his curse works immediately. Once there was a *goy* who lent a Jew three hundred reals. Three years later the Arab needed his money and asked the Jew to return the loan. The Jew denied that he had received money from him. The Arab went to complain to the pasha. He told him he was ready to swear by Muḥammad that he had lent the Jew this sum of money. The pasha asked him if he had a note or any witnesses. The Arab had neither a note nor witnesses. The pasha told him that he could not rule in such a case. So he went to the *qadi* and the *qadi* told him the same thing. He went to the governor and his reply was the same. The poor fellow, who really needed the money, went home in tears. Suddenly he met a respectable-looking gentleman, an Arab, who asked him: *Why are you crying?* He said: *Look, no one can save me. Not the pasha, not the* qadi *or the king!* He asked: *What happened to you?* He said: *A Jew took my money and refused to return it to me!* He said: *Why did you go to the king [the governor in the name of the king]? Go to R. Raphael, the Chief Rabbi, and he will get you the money from heaven or from earth. Just go to him, but kiss him!* The Arab went and found R. Raphael praying. He removed his hat and kissed the saint's foot. He told him: *I am a* goy, *but save me in God's name!* The Arab told him the whole story. The rabbi said to his servant: *Go and call this Jew!* The Jew came and R. Raphael told him: *Return the money!* The Jew refused. The rabbi told the Arab: *Go now and return at three this afternoon!* He told the Jew to go but to come back at one o'clock. The Jew came back with his daughter and swore on the money. R. Raphael asked him: *Did you really not take it?* He said: *Yes!* He [the saint] said: *If you really did not take the money, then may you be blessed; but if you did take it, you will go blind!* His daughter was named Esther. Her father took her hand and said: *Oh, my eyes!* He went blind. It happened right then and there. I was not present. I was told this story, and I saw him later as a blind man. He started to cry. He went to the rabbi. The rabbi said to him: *Once the bullet is shot out, it cannot be returned to the barrel. That's that! I cursed and now nothing can be done!* Except that he gave him his blessing and gave him understanding too. Indeed he used to sell spices in his store and could find everything. You could give him a bill and he would know how much money it was. He could tell the difference between all the coins. He remained blind to the end of his life. He swore he had not taken the money and was certain he was telling the truth. And he [the saint] put a curse on him. From that time on, he [the saint] stopped doing this [cursing]."

56.3 "R. Raphael was some rabbi! No other rabbi could match him. They didn't call him rabbi the way they now do. They called him 'The Angel Raphael.' You will see his picture, at the bottom it says: 'The Angel Raphael Anqawa.' That's what he was like when he died. He died on the Eve of the *Sabbath,* and I was standing beside him. First of all, you could not recognize his body. He had the *shekhinah* which is indescribable. He did not have the face of a dead man or a dying man at all. He was breathing, his mouth was red, and his hair was white. When the *Sabbath* was over, people came from all over, rabbis from France. We were three kilometers from the cemetery. The cemetery was crowded, and all along the way the road was full of people. The year he died, he had foreseen it. It was a drought year. There had been a drought for two or three years, and the Arabs believed that only the Jews could save them from the drought. If they prayed, there would be rain. So they came to R. Raphael and told him that he must pray and he must walk barefoot to the cemetery with his people. R. Raphael replied: *If I pray for rain, my life will be over. You will have rain, but I shall be lost!* That is the way it is. It is a decree from Heaven. He said: *God will protect you, but I shall be your expiation, and not only I but many others will go!* So he went up with us. It was really painful to see. When the saint felt that his end was near, he said to them: *Gentlemen, I do not want a splendid funeral nor a sumptuous tomb. I want a simple stone, a modest burial!* Since he had many medals, a French army brigade wanted to march in his funeral. So two notables held two pillows with the medals. After them came a group of seventy or eighty Muslim notables, including the king's officer, since the king was forbidden to participate in a funeral, and all of them wore white. After them came a group of Christians of all ranks, followed by Jews in groups—a group from Marrakech with a *shofar* and reciting lamentations, a group from Casablanca, a group from Ouezzane, from all the cities. . . . At the ritual ablutions, only six rabbis could wash him. Not everyone could come in. They sold pieces of his shroud for thousands of francs.

Everyone wanted a piece, for good luck. In the cemetery, people paid fifty francs for every stroke of the shovel. For filling a sackful of earth, each paid fifty francs, and fifty for emptying it, a hundred and fifty francs. I remember that the grave was dug for eighty thousand francs at the time. There were eulogies. R. Moshe Elyaqim Ḥay, a rabbi from Israel, spoke in Hebrew. . . . We wanted to bury him in a place we call '*Yeshibah shel Maᶜalah*' [the Heavenly Abode]; there they [the dead] are all righteous people. It is an ancient burial ground. R. David Ben-Safet, R. Ḥayyim Toledano, R. Ḥayyim Ben-ᶜAttar the First, and R. Raphael Bibas are buried there. . . . They took him to a new area where they buried him. Over the tomb they built a dome, open on all sides, and they made a special place there for the candles."

57. Rabbi Raphael Berdugo (Meknes)[61]

R. Raphael Berdugo (1747–1822) was a member of an illustrious rabbinical family that included his grandfather, R. Moshe Berdugo, his father, R. Mordekhay, and his brother, R. Yequtiel. He was the author of numerous books. His *hillulah* is celebrated on *Lag bᶜOmer.*

57.1 "R. Raphael lay in his grave for many years. When [in 1823] the king wanted to use his burial place, they removed the saint's bones and buried him some place else. That was when they found that his shroud was still white. It was R. Raphael Berdugo. He is the grandfather of R. Yehoshuaᶜ Berdugo, who was a judge in the religious court."

57.2 "R. Raphael Berdugo used to study the *Torah* at night in the basement of his house. He kept his legs tied with a rope so that if he started to doze, he would wake up and not miss his *Torah* studies. A long time ago my parents lived in the same house. I remember, when I was little, that no one dared come near to the courtyard of R. Raphael Berdugo. I remember that R. Yehoshuaᶜ would come to visit the grave of his grandfather, R. Raphael, and light candles every *Sabbath* Eve, [Jewish] holiday Eve and first of the month. In the basement, too, a candle was always burning. Any female neighbor who came to us was forbidden to go down to this basement. They celebrated his *hillulah* on *Lag bᶜOmer.* It was the custom to go to the cemetery and take along a *seᶜudah.*"

58. Rabbi Raphael Ha-Cohen (Achbarou)[62]

According to tradition, R. Raphael came from the Holy Land to Morocco together with his brothers, R. Ḥananiah Ha-Cohen and R. Moshe Cohen. His *hillulah* is celebrated twice a year, on the eighth day of *Pesaḥ* and the eighth day of *Sukkot.* The saint is also venerated by the Muslims, who call him Mul Ashbaru.

58.1 "There are no more saints in Morocco. They've all disappeared. All you see is their shrines. They themselves are in Israel. Many rabbis have said so. They said that R. Raphael Anqawa, R. Shimʿon Bar-Yoḥay and R. Raphael Ha-Cohen are here, though they don't know where. Nobody knows. It's a big secret, but people say they are here."

58.2 "We had R. Raphael Ha-Cohen in our town, and we used to ride to him on animals. There was this naive Jewish woman. She went to a man [a Muslim] who rented animals. She said to him: *Take me to Rabbi Raphael!* She gave him money. He had an old animal. They went on a Friday. They were halfway there when he saw that the animal did not have the strength to walk any further. When they got to the tree which is called Shejrat Mul Argawi—that's where the Arabs who are coming from the direction of Marrakech sit and rest and make tea, and then continue on their way—and he saw that his animal was exhausted, he told the woman: *Get off! Look, here is the* ḥakham! He unloaded her things, and she started to light candles on the stones where the Arabs heat their tea. And she says: *Sidi El-ʿziz [My Beloved Master]! Heal me! See how I have come to you!* And she prays and he [the Arab] was laughing to himself. He stayed there with her over the *Sabbath.* She asked him: *Where are all the people?* And he answered that on that *Sabbath* no one had come. On Sunday, as they were about to go home, she lit candles and prayed. On the way to Marrakech, he laughed the whole time, and whenever he told this story, he laughed his head off. He made a joke of it, but her pilgrimage was accepted because of her faith, because she thought this was the saint. In Marrakech, he used to ask the people: *Who wants to go on pilgrimage to Shejrat Mul Argawi?*"

58.3 "When R. Raphael Ha-Cohen's time had come, late one Friday afternoon, he commanded the sun to stand still. It stood still until his grave had been dug. He sewed his shroud, went down to his pool and immersed himself. He put on his shroud and entered his grave. The grave closed over him. Only one lone Arab saw him as the grave closed. When R. Yaᶜish Dahan, my mother's grandfather, may he rest in peace, passed by, the Muslim asked: *Jew! Do you know where your master is?* He answered: *Where is our master?* He answered: *Come, and I'll show you! Here is the place!* He dug down and found a [marker with a] date [of death]. He went and informed the local Jews and they built a tomb for him. We proclaimed throughout the town that a rabbi named R. Raphael Ha-Cohen had been discovered. The Jews began to visit his tomb."

59. Rabbi Raphael Moshe Elbaz (Sefrou)[63]

R. Raphael (1823–96) was a renowned and prolific poet, the author of many works. He was the cousin of the saint R. Abba Elbaz, who is also buried in Sefrou. His *hillulah* is held on the 22nd of *Tammuz.*

59.1 "Every visitor to his tomb had his request granted. R. Raphael Moshe Elbaz was the uncle of my mother-in-law. Her father was R. Shelomoh Elbaz [the informant is mistaken: R. Raphael had two brothers, R. Bezalel and R. Eliyahu]. One time, my mother-in-law's mother asked her to bring a pot of tea to her father. She took it. A tongue of flame came out of the top story [of the house], and she fell down the stairs and was sick for three months. This happened because as she went up the stairs, she found the *shekhinah* descending on the room where the two brothers were studying. The *piyyutim* of R. Raphael Moshe Elbaz are famous everywhere."

60. Rabbi Saᶜadiah Dades (Cheriaa)[64]

On the site of his tomb is a large boulder with a carob tree near by. There is no inscription. According to tradition, R. Saᶜadiah came to Morocco from Spain four or five hundred years ago, at the time of the persecutions. He is also venerated by the Muslims, who call him R. Saᶜadia Datsi.

60.1 "There was also R. Saᶜadia Datsi. He came to Tetuan [the informant must have meant Melilla, the town closest to the saint's tomb]. When he arrived, he went up to a youth and told him to go to the community leaders and tell them that so and so has come and was going to die, and he wanted them to do what had to be done for him. The youth went and told them, but they said they did not know any such person. Then he cursed them, saying that their women would be many and their men few. . . . And in fact the women there reached the age of forty without finding anyone to marry. Then he came to an Arab and asked him to take care of him. He said: *I'll show you what I can do!* He held the shroud in his hands and immersed himself in the tears that fell from his eyes. He told him that a strong wind would come and blow a large rock which was near there, and the rock would close his [the rabbi's] grave. He told the Arab that his house would burn down, but warned him to remove his property and family, so that they would be saved, and then it would be seen [proven] how great he was in the eyes of God. He commanded the Arab to do one more thing. When anyone came to visit [his grave], he should take only one *dirhem* [silver coin] from him and no more, otherwise he would forfeit the blessing. He had promised the Arab that it [the saint's blessing] would remain with him and his descendants."[65]

61. Sepher Tislit (Tazenakht)[66]

Sepher Tislit—*Torah* Scroll of Tislit—is also called the Tislit Scroll of Jerusalem. According to tradition, it originally came from the Holy Land. Its *hillulah* is celebrated on the first day of the month of *Ḥeshwan.* The scroll was brought from Morocco to Israel and is presently in a synagogue in Ashkelon, where Moroccan Jews continue to celebrate the traditional annual *hillulah.* In Morocco, Muslims too would appeal to Sepher Tislit.

61.1 "Sepher Tislit is from our village. It is a small scroll. They say that once Muslims came to the synagogue where the Scroll was. A Muslim broke open the door and went inside, then the door closed behind him. All the doors of the synagogue closed. The Muslim opened the Ark and took the scroll's silver "apples" [*rimmonim*-shaped ornaments] and the money from the alms box. When the Muslim tried to get out, he found all the doors locked. He went back to the Ark to return what he had stolen and the door opened. When he tried again to get out, the door closed. In the morning, he got out and ran away to the oven [which stood near the synagogue]. Someone came [in a dream] to the beadle of the synagogue and told him: *Take wood and light the oven!* The beadle brought trees and wooden boards and thought: *What does this dream mean?* When he brought the trees, the Muslim stood up and said to him: *I did such and such,* *but now have mercy on me!* From that day on, the Muslim was paralyzed. The Jews went to the Muslim head of the village and told him that they had decided to leave the village because of what that Muslim had done. The sheikh asked the messengers to bring the Muslim. When they found him, his legs were paralyzed. They brought him in a basket. The sheikh asked him: *Why did you do it?* Then the sheikh told the Muslim to bring a sacrifice to the saint. They brought a sheep, but at the last moment that Muslim died. It was because he had opened the Scroll."

61.2 "There is a lot to tell. Sepher Tislit performed many miracles. I was born in Tazenakht. The date of the *hillulah* is on the date when it arrived there, the first of the month of *Ḥeshwan.* This Scroll of the Law, our forefathers tell us, was from the time of the destruction of [the Second Temple of] Jerusalem [70 A.D.]. The *ḥakham* who copied it sat in a *miqweh* and wrote it out. The enemies, the Philistines, took his son away from him. On the day he completed the Scroll of the Law, they returned his son to him. He pronounced the Holy Name in full and arrived in the village next to ours. It is called Tislit. Our ancestors went to buy it. They spoke with him [the *ḥakham*], agreed on the purchase and wanted to pay him, but he suddenly disappeared, and there was no one to pay. It [the Scroll] is passed from father to son, and it performed many, many miracles. Something was missing [in the Scroll]. They sent it to Jerusalem with R. Masʿud Wizeman from Marrakech. The sage who corrected it died at the end of the year after he finished sewing it [the parchment]. Once the enemy, the Muslims, entered the city [Tislit]. He [the Scroll] went forth and defeated them. Many miracles!"

61.3 "One time there was a war among the Arabs, that is, between two villages. So in our village some Arabs offered up a sacrifice to Sepher Tislit and defeated the other village. From that day on, they always burn candles to Sepher Tislit. Arabs light candles for Sepher Tislit, Arabs from our village, and they honor him. What can I tell you? The Scroll was in our synagogue. The Muslims would enter the synagogue and light the candles and honor him, even more than the Jews."

61.4 "Before we wanted to immigrate to Israel, it was sunny and very hot. As they were taking it [Sepher Tislit] out of the Ark, it suddenly turned the whole world upside down. No one could see where he was going. It was pitch dark. The Arabs didn't say a word to us. On the contrary. Arabs wept and brought candles to the synagogue. To this day they take care of the synagogue. There are still [the interview was held in 1976] two families there. The Arabs even built [a wall] around our cemetery so that no one would come close."

61.5 "My father told me that this Scroll was written long ago by someone from the Holy Land. The one who wrote it spent forty days and forty nights in the *miqweh,* and he wrote it [without stopping] until he finished it. He wrote it in the *miqweh* until he finished it! They placed it inside a new synagogue to pray to it. An Arab came and stole it. He took it abroad and sold it to Arabs. There was an Arab who knew my grandfather. He came and told him: *Do you want me to sell you something that the Jews pray to?* He [the grandfather] thought it must be phylacteries or a prayer shawl, so he said: *All right! Bring it to me!* He told him: *It is something that I cannot bring here to you. Come and see it first!* He took him. He found a Scroll. When he saw that it was a Scroll of the Law, he opened it and read the words and found inside it a letter which he [the scribe who had written the scroll] had written: *So and So wrote it in such and such a place, in the* miqweh. . . . He stayed there forty days and forty nights until he wrote it. And when he had written it, he put it inside a new synagogue, and someone came and stole it. . . . My grandfather bought it from him. My father's grandfather, not actually my grandfather. It goes from generation to generation."

61.6 "The one who wrote Sepher Tislit was the Baʿal Shem Tov. My whole family is from there, from Tazenakht. When he [the Baʿal Shem Tov] arrived on the Eve of the *Sabbath,* he gave it [Sepher Tislit] to the Wizeman family. They are rich. On the Eve of the *Sabbath,* when the Baʿal Shem Tov arrived from abroad, he came to the village and wrote this Scroll. He said: *I must leave this Scroll with the rich Wizeman family!* He came to a place where there is a rock they call Tislit. That is the name of the rock. He called his servant and told him: *Go and tell the Jews that they should come to take it [the Scroll] from here, and that they should invite me for* Sabbath. *And this is their* Torah *Scroll!* The servant went to tell the village. They came to the place but did not find the saint. All they found was the Scroll and a letter. It was addressed to the Wizeman family. So they took the Scroll, and every year they celebrate the *hillulah* in its honor."

61.7 "Every year the sheikh gave an ox for the *seʿudah* of Sepher Tislit. He had to give oil, flour, a sheep or an ox. He makes a donation for every *hillulah.* From that day on, every time a Muslim wanted to go on a journey, he would pass by and leave something next to Sepher Tislit in the synagogue. And as he passed, he kissed the walls of the synagogue where Sepher Tislit is."

62. Rabbi Shalom Zawi (Rabat)[67]

R. Shalom Zawi died on the 29th of *Kislew* 5572 (1812) and is buried in the old part of the cemetery of Rabat. A synagogue is named after him in Rabat. In its courtyard are several rooms for pilgrims and there are many places for lighting candles.

62.1 "R. Shalom Zawi is in Rabat. I experienced a great miracle there, too. One time I went out of my house in the morning and I saw a naked black man whom people had stripped. I was afraid. I went outside, I saw, and I was afraid. This happened right after I gave birth to my daughter. I couldn't walk. I was afraid that the black man would run after me. From that day on, I had it [my sickness]. There wasn't a professor or doctor who didn't examine me, and with every medicine that I took, it was just as if I had taken it and poured it down the toilet. I turned blue because I saw something that frightened me. I couldn't talk. I had a daughter, but I did not know whether I was married or if I had a daughter. I didn't remember anything and I didn't know anything. One evening, my husband finished studying and I suddenly had this attack. I couldn't feel myself. Then the neighbors came running to take care of me. That same evening, my husband saw that I was slowly turning purple. He said to me: *Please, call on a saint!* I cried out: *Oh, R. Shalom Zawi!* My poor husband was sitting at my side. He took me and put me in my bed. The next day it was R. Shalom Zawi's *hillulah.* So the poor man [my husband] took me to Rabat and left me there in the care of a Jewish woman, who for a modest sum accommodated Jews who came to visit the saint's grave. He went and bought fruit, wine and oil and took them to the woman because there were five of us. She lit the oven and made food for us. They all ate, but I couldn't eat. The people asked my mother why I wasn't eating or moving. She told them that I was sick. She [the woman] gave me a bed, and gave my brother a carpet. There were at least three people in the room. It was in the synagogue named after R. Shalom Zawi. It was fantastic. I called upon the saints and they answered me! In the evening, when I had fallen asleep, I saw a sage [in my dream], and he says to me: *Arise, my daughter, and go home! He who took it, has taken it [the illness], and he who left it, has left it!* This is what I heard. I woke up. I spoke with my father. He washed his hands and said to me: *Wait! I shall tell you my dream!* He told me that R. Shalom Zawi had told him: *Go home, because he who took it, has taken it [the sickness], and he who left it, has left it!* He got up joyfully and took his belongings and his children, and we all went to the cemetery. We held a *seʿudah,* made a contribution, and from that day on I got well. I don't know why I called the name of that saint. I did not know him, but I had heard about him. I called upon him because my remedy was in his hand and this shows his miracles. I visited there one other time when I was getting ready to move to Israel. I was there. Again I thanked the saint. You have to thank even people for a favor, so why not a saint? This is what happened and it was miraculous."

63. Rabbi Shelomoh ʿAmar (Beni Mellal)[68]

According to tradition, the saint came to Morocco from the Holy Land on behalf of the community. The Muslims also visited his tomb.

63.1 "He was buried under a large rock on the mountain, and under it runs a spring. Once they wanted to pull that rock down in order to pave a road. Whenever anyone tried to touch the stone, his tool would fly back. They brought tractors. It didn't help. When the Muslims became independent, they wanted to uproot that stone in order to pave the road. Then they decided to leave it where it was, because they said it was impossible to touch the tomb of the saint."

64. Rabbi Shelomoh Ben-Lḥans (Aghbalou)[69]

Also called R. Shelomoh Belḥans or R. Shelomoh Bel-Laḥnesh, he is one of the saints most widely revered among the Jews of Morocco, particularly in the south. His name means "Son of the Snake," and many traditions linked with the saint center on the motif of the snake.

According to tradition, he came from the Holy Land to Morocco in ancient times. His name appears in the lists of Demnate which mention seven rabbis who came to Morocco to convert the gentiles to Judaism. An early tradition from Tazart says that R. Shelomoh

Ben-Lḥans is the brother of R. Ḥayyim Lashqar. R. Shelomoh is also venerated by the Muslims, who call him Mul Asguine.

64.1 "A woman who had her period was forbidden to go to the saint. This happened to me. I went to R. Shelomoh Ben-Lḥans. On the *Sabbath* Eve I got my period, I and two other women. That night rocks fell from the sky and the ground shook. Then we left the saint's shrine and stayed outside. Also a woman who had intercourse with her husband could not go there until she had done *tebilah.*"

64.2 "I was at R. Shelomoh Ben-Lḥans. We were there, and I saw this [a miracle] with my own eyes. We were on a *ziyara* at the tomb of the *ḥakham,* and there were many people singing and dancing at the grave. Suddenly someone got up and said to us: *The saint is with us! Right in this room!* Then we saw how the saint's grave was filling up with water as if someone had spilled a bucket of water on it. The people cried out for joy, and everyone came and took a little water and rubbed it on his face. The people told us that this was a sign that the *ziyara* of everyone who was there at the time had been accepted. The next day we had a great celebration because of the miracle which we had seen with our own eyes. There is a room there with two doors, and his grave is on the right-hand side, built of cement covered with marble. People come from Marrakech to Ourika. They stop there, and the Arabs know that we are coming to the saint. They hire out animals. One person hires out a donkey and another one a horse. You load your belongings on the animal and ride around eight kilometers into the mountains on very difficult roads. Some people now go there by car. The road is very winding and dangerous, but by the grace of God and the saint, no one was ever hurt. There was never an accident. He [the saint] is on the mountain, and there is an orchard below. When people want to rest, they go down there and spread out rugs. They eat and drink there, play and laugh. At the saint's [tomb] they read from the *Torah.* Some people read the *Torah* and others laugh and play to honor the saint. There is no cemetery there, only his grave. People come mostly after *Sukkot,* but also after *Pesaḥ* and *Shabuᶜot.*"

64.3 "Why do they call him Ben-Lḥans? They say that once there was a snake that wanted to bite someone and he himself caught it. The saint is an Ashkenazi Jew who came to Ourika and died there. He came from Jerusalem. They [the saints] are all from Jerusalem."

64.4 "Why did they call him Ben-Lḥans? They say that the saint's mother had been barren. She became pregnant and gave birth to a snake. This snake used to crawl around all day outside and in the evening he would leave his skin and come to his mother. That is why they called him R. Shelomoh Ben-Lḥans. At his tomb the prayers of people are accepted. I cannot tell you any more about these things because I am afraid that something will happen to me in the night, and I live alone."

64.5 "I remember that one time I was reading the Psalms at his grave when suddenly a big snake crawled out. He appeared out of nowhere. No one left or moved, and it stayed until we finished reading Psalms, until dawn, and then the snake went back into its hole. That is the way the saint shows himself. If the saint accepts the visitor's plea, he makes water flow. If no water comes out, the person's plea has not been accepted."

64.6 "The saint came from the Holy Land with his servant. They came on horseback. They came to collect alms. In every city they would spend a *Sabbath.* When they came here, he died. This [Ben-Lḥans] is his surname. Why? They came with two horses. He left them not far from the slaughterhouse. The *qadi* wanted to take the two horses after he [the saint] died. When they came to take them, they saw that snakes had tied the two horses so that it was impossible to move them. They couldn't take them. They came to tell the *qadi.* The *qadi* said to them: *Summon the Jews!* When the Jews came, the snakes turned into ropes. Since then they called him R. Shelomoh Ben-Lḥans. Without this surname of his, the Muslims would have taken the saint and made him one of theirs. This happened 430 years ago. Before, water would come out of his tombstone, but since they built, water comes out of the threshold of the synagogue."

65. Rabbi Shelomoh Ben-Tameshut (Marrakech)[70]

R. Shelomoh Ben-Tameshut or R. Shelomoh Tameshut was an illustrious rabbi from Marrakech. He was a contemporary of the eminent R. Yitsḥaq Deluya. R. Shelomoh was murdered by Muslims.

65.1 "R. Shelomoh Ben-Tameshut, may he rest in peace, mastered *aslai* (epilepsy). Whoever suffered from this disease was brought and tied with ropes to the tomb, until he was cured. I myself suffered from this disease. I was afraid. In the *ḥeder* (Jewish primary school) someone hit me. I was afraid. He hit me on the head. I was ten years old at the time. My mother took me to the grave of R. Shelomoh Ben-Tameshut. They tied me up and, praise be to God and the saint, I got well. I stayed tied up there seven days. I was my mother's only son. They gave me food to eat. On the last night [the saint] came to my mother in a dream and said to her: *Take your son! He is healthy!* We made a *seʿudah.* We brought poor Jews and my father handed out poultry, pies and rolls."

65.2 "If anyone has the sickness they call *ḥemma* [jaundice], all they have to do is go to him [the saint] and sleep there three days, and he will get well. He is buried in the Marrakech cemetery. He has a room. The sickness is caused by fear. I once got this sickness from fear. The yellow went into my eyes and I got this sickness. I stayed three days at R. Shelomoh Ben-Tameshut's. I slept there and my father slept with me. During the day I sat and people came one after another. Yes, in Marrakech, the cure for jaundice is to go to R. Shelomoh Ben-Tameshut."

65.3 "I had a fever. I went to the tomb of R. Shelomoh Ben-Tameshut. People told me that if you throw a stone on the roof above the tomb and the stone stays there, it is a sign that your request has been granted, and if you throw a stone and it falls off, it is a sign that the saint does not grant your request and wants you to stay with him longer. When I threw the stone and it stayed on the roof, I left the tomb and got well. I was sick, and no doctor could cure me until I went to R. Shelomoh Ben-Tameshut, I and my sister's sons. Every morning we threw a rock onto the roof of the mausoleum and each time it fell down, until it stayed up there and then we came back."

65.4 "I know only the saint named R. Shelomoh Tameshut in the city of Marrakech. He was very handsome and instructed students in the *yeshibah.* After his studies, he would take a basket, put gold and silver rings into it, and go to the Arab markets to sell them. Once he went and the king's wife saw him from her window. She told her servant: *Among the Muslims and our kings we have no one as handsome as this sage. Bring him in!* [He came in]. She said to him: *I have something which I must tell you, although it is forbidden me to tell you!* She told him: *Listen! I am the wife of the king. If you do what I tell you, all well and good; but if you do not, I shall cut off your head!* He told her that he was a rabbi, and he knew what punishment he would suffer if he did this thing. She wanted him to sleep with her. *God forbid!* he told her. She threatened to call her servants, who would hack him to pieces. He told her: *I do not care! Whatever you want to do, do. It is forbidden for us!* Finally he did not agree to anything. The servants of the king took him and hacked him to pieces. The saint's wife waited for him until midnight, until morning, but he did not come. She said: *This is bad!* She was surprised because until that day he had never been late. She went to the members of the community committee and told them about her husband. The second night, R. Shelomoh came to her in a dream and told her: *You do not have to do anything. You will see where I am. They cut me up in the king's house, where ministers sit, and they quartered me!* His wife went to the president of the Jewish community. [He] went to the king and said to him: *My master, the king, every day our rabbi goes to sell gold and silver jewelry to the ministers. And he came to his wife in a dream and told her that he had been hacked to pieces!* They quartered him. The king answered that the Jews just wanted to give the Muslims a bad name. The president answered: *We shall make a search, and if we do not find the body of the rabbi, you can cut off our heads!* They went in and searched in all the rooms and did not find him. What did the saint do? May his virtue protect us! From the place where he was buried, he put out one hand. They saw it. They dug down and removed the rabbi, just as his wife had dreamt it. The king sentenced all the members of his household, even the animals, to death by burning, and he called the street *Derb Aḥriq* (the Street of Fire)."[71]

66. Sidi Mul El-Ḥazra (Skoura)

Sidi Mul El-Ḥazra means "My Lord Master of the Rock."

66.1 "Once a man was busy irrigating his field. He started digging out a rock that was stopping the flow of the water. He hit it and hit it until he dug out the rock, and then underneath it he found burning wicks. He stopped digging. He went to the local Jews and told them: *What are you sitting around here for? Come see! One of your saints is buried near here!* It was a Muslim who had been digging. People went to see and saw burning wicks everywhere. Since then he [the saint] bears the name of the rock. They call him Sidi Mul El-Ḥazra and visit the site."

67. Ulad Zemmur (Safi)[72]

Ulad Zemmur (the sons of Zemmur) are also called Ulad Zmirru, Ulad Ben-Zmirru, Ulad Bene-Zmirru and Bene-Zmirru. According to tradition, they were seven brothers who were interred together.

This is an interesting example of a family of Spanish exiles, about which there is a great deal of documentation and historic detail.[73] Highly influential in Moroccan governmental circles as well as in the Jewish community, they became legendary. Their burial ground serves as a cultic site for the people of Safi, as well as for the faithful who come from all over Morocco to visit the tomb. The Ulad Zemmur are also venerated by Muslims.

67.1 "I always visited their graves. Our forefathers told us that they were not dead, but that they were living under the ground. The ground opened and swallowed them up. They would say to everyone who visited them: *Go! Your request has been granted!* Everyone who sat at their grave for seven days and seven nights would have his request granted. All the Jews of the city flocked to it."[74]

67.2 "I was born in Safi. They are seven saints who were buried in the same grave. There is a large mausoleum, and Jews from all the cities flocked to it. Even from outside Morocco they would come on pilgrimage to the tomb of the Bene-Zmirru. They came to visit and their prayers were granted. There was a Jew who was at the point of death. The doctors said that it was impossible to cure him. He came and held a big *seʿudah,* and people ate it for seven days. On the seventh day someone appeared to him in a dream, wearing a *khaza* [a kind of head covering], bearded, and carrying a knife. He said to the Jew: *Strengthen yourself with this knife! Put it on the diseased spot!* He did so, and the next day, when he woke up, he told his father that he no longer felt pains in his body and that he was healthy. [It was] on the seventh day of the *seʿudah.* Every Jew who was born in Safi knows this story. That sick Jew did not live in Safi. He came there from a distant city."

68. Rabbi Yaʿaqob Ashkenazi (Sidi Rahal)[75]

The full name of the saint is R. Yaʿaqob Naḥmias Ashkenazi, also called Mul Almay or Mul Anmay. He appears in the lists of seven or ten rabbis who came from the Holy Land to Morocco. He is also venerated by the Muslims.

68.1 "R. Yaᶜaqob Ashkenazi is called Mul Anmay. May he rest in peace, he quarrelled with a shereef called Sidi Raḥal. They say that this Sidi Raḥal was the master of fire. If he called to it, the fire would blaze up. And R. Yaᶜaqob Ashkenazi, Mul Anmay, was the master of water. If he called to it, whatever he wanted the water to turn into, the water would turn into. One day they quarrelled. Our fathers tell us this. This one of ours, R. Yaᶜaqob Ashkenazi, stopped their fire and they stopped us the water [here the informant seems to be mistaken, because it must have been R. Yaᶜaqob who stopped the water]. Within a short time, everyone began to die, some from fire and some from thirst, because there was no water. Afterwards, they made peace. One restored the fire and the other restored the water. May they rest in peace! For this reason they call him Sidi Raḥal. He is also important to the non-Jews. Between him [his tomb] and the cemetery of the Jews, it is about one kilometer. We pass him [his tomb] but the Arabs don't let us [go inside]. For example, if someone had no boy child and then a boy was born, they tell him to go on pilgrimage to Sidi Raḥal. They go, but they go in secret. For instance, if you have friends, you ask them to stand guard while the one with the baby boy goes inside to visit [the saint], so that he will live."

68.2 "Mul Anmay is one of the Ten Martyrs (according to tradition, ten rabbis slain by the Romans). Ten who left Jerusalem to collect alms and take them back to Jerusalem. For the poor. They died on the way. Each one was away two or three years. One died in a certain place and was buried there."

69. Rabbi Yaᶜaqob Naḥmias (Tazda)

Also called Sayyid Yaᶜqob, R. Yaᶜaqob Naḥmias is buried in the local cemetery with other saints from the same family, among them R. David, R. Yosef and R. Masᶜud Naḥmias. The Muslims also used to visit his tomb.

69.1 "May he rest in peace. The French wanted to pave a road through his tomb. As the engineer came to start work on the mountain [the rest of the story is unclear]. . . . The Arabs, for example, if they just let their sheep graze on his mountain or when they take candles from there, in less than a day, both he and his house are gone. In Tazda, nobody can enter the cemetery of the Ait Naḥmias. People are afraid. There are only saints there. At night, if you go by the place, you start trembling. I myself went past the place."

70. Rabbi Yaḥya El-Khdar (Beni Hmad)[76]

R. Yaḥya El-Khdar (the Green) or R. Yaḥya Lakhdar is named after the mountain on which he is buried, Jebel El-Khdar. It is one of the most developed holy sites in Morocco, with a large synagogue, many houses, a bakery, and other services. The saint has no tombstone. According to tradition, he is buried on the left side of the entrance, under a small mound where there are three hearths for lighting candles. His *hillulah* is held on the day of the *Mimuna* (festival celebrated by Moroccan Jews at the end of Passover) and on *Lag b'Omer.* According to one tradition, R. Yaḥya is the brother of R. Eliyahu from Casablanca; another tradition says that he came from the Holy Land.

70.1 "Around the sanctuary there were many trees. At the end of Passover we would go there. We would spend the whole night singing and dancing. They would slaughter sheep and roast them. They would hang the sheep and put it in the oven. They would drink a lot, too, as at weddings. Once my son ʿAmram was paralyzed. Whenever anyone touched him he would fall down. He was one year old. He stopped talking. I took a vow to visit R. Yaḥya El-Khdar. The father of F. took me there. I took the boy and laid him on the tomb and said to the saint: *Oh R. Yaḥya El-Khdar! Remove from me this illness of the child!* From then on he got well. I gave him his first haircut there. We stayed there eight days."

70.2 "R. Yaḥya is buried in Beni Hmad. They say that once the Muslims came suddenly to attack the Jews. They always hated the Jews. When R. Yaḥya El-Khdar saw that the Muslims wanted to kill him and abuse him, he lifted a large stone and went under it. There are no buildings near his tomb. The slave [a Muslim] wanted to murder him. The saint took the stone and recited the *shemaʿ*. The Jews now visit his grave in Beni Hmad. The slaves [the Muslims] entered the Jewish quarter. Several were killed and several fled. He, the saint, did not want them to abuse him and defile him. He took this stone, recited the *shemaʿ* and hid himself under the stone. It was a large stone. They used to light candles on it. There are no houses or anything there. Visitors that come to the *hillulah* have to stand on the grass. The Muslim women bring water in jugs. The whole area where he is buried is green. The saint pronounced the Divine Name in full and hid under the stone."

71. Rabbi Yaḥya Laḥlu (Ksar Es-Souk)[77]

R. Yaḥya Laḥlu is also known as R. Yaḥya El-Ḥlu. The Muslims call him Abar. Jews from all over Morocco, as well as Muslims, visited his grave. According to tradition, he came from the Holy Land to Morocco in early times. His *hillulah* is celebrated on *Shoshan Purim* (the day after Purim).

71.1 "Many people come to our *mellaḥ* in order to spend the night in the shrine. They say that Jews lived here who came after the destruction of the Temple. They found graves there from 1,500 years ago. Sometimes, during drought years, they appealed to him [the saint] for help. They would go and bring an ox from the Burial Society, and after they slaughtered it, it would rain. We used to distribute the roast meat to the members of the Burial Society. We built a tombstone over this spot and the next day we found that it was all in ruins. The saint appeared in a dream and told the president of the Burial Society not to build. He asked him not to build a tombstone, and so it has remained without any building. We celebrated his *hillulah* on *Purim,* because he died on *Purim.*"

71.2 "R. Yaḥya Laḥlu. In the time of the First Temple—because our *mellaḥ* existed since the First Temple. . . . Once two Jews came to him to try their case. He was a teacher as well as a cantor. Nobody knew of his powers. They did not know that he was like this. He was modest. Two Jews brought their case to him. He judged their case and pronounced sentence. One of them said that this was no sentence and he did not accept the sentence. He [the saint] told him: *You may not believe me, but I have pronounced the sentence of the Holy One, blessed be He, and there is no appeal!* The Jew did not accept this and said that it was not a just sentence. The rabbi told him: *If I have not pronounced a just sentence, then tomorrow they will carry your bier or mine!* He told him: *If I have not pronounced the sentence of the Holy One, blessed be He, I shall die tomorrow, and if you do not believe, you will die tomorrow!* The next day, at that same moment, it was heard in the city that the man had died. The Jew who refused to accept the rabbi's sentence died. They told the rabbi that the Jew had died. The rabbi was grieved. He thought, why did he cause his death. His curse had been accepted, may God protect us! From that moment he began his ritual immersion. He told the Jews of the *mellaḥ: Tomorrow, no one shall leave the* mellaḥ, *and if anyone does leave, I shall excommunicate him! But why?* they asked him. *There are some people that have to travel!* He told them: *Tomorrow no one shall leave this place! Tomorrow all of you must be here!* He did not tell them what would happen the next day. The next day, at that same moment, he began his ritual immersion, changed his clothes, and prayed. All the Jews of the *mellaḥ* came and asked him: *What is going on?* He told them: *Sit down!* They sat down. He asked them to recite the *shemaʿ* for him. They were stunned. They did not believe it. He adjured them to recite the *shemaʿ*, and he added: *You will hear two words from me. If I stay in your hands, then I shall stay in your hands and you shall bury me here, but if not, follow my shadow. On the place where I am standing, bury me!* They recited the *shemaʿ* and suddenly chains descended from the sky, and he was instantly taken up. Immediately they followed his shadow, and close to the *mellaḥ* the ground opened up and he entered. They said: *Our master, Mul Terya, Mul Terya* [the Master of Light, the name of the tree which grows near his tomb and which sometimes glows mysteriously at night], *our master, R. Yaḥya Laḥlu!* They called him El-Ḥlu [the Sweet] because of his righteousness, because of his good deeds, and because he was lifted up to the Holy One, blessed be He. This story is told in every generation. This happened in the time of the First Temple."

71.3 "There was a Jew from Oujda whose legs were paralyzed. He was seen by all the doctors. They told him that only R. Yaḥya Laḥlu could cure him. This Jew came there to spend the *Sabbath* at the home of a wealthy Jew named Ḥayyim Shetrit, of blessed memory, a rich man who sold tea and sugar wholesale. He called the president of the Burial Society, who was named Bu-Setta ["the Owner of Six," because he had six fingers on each hand and six toes on each foot], and told him: *Give me ten men from the Burial Society to escort this Jew who wants to visit the tomb of R. Yaḥya Laḥlu!* He asked them to beg for mercy from R. Shimʿon [Bar-Yoḥay, patron saint of the Burial Society], that he should heal him, since all the doctors could do nothing more for him. The Jew from Oujda took a sheep with him to the tomb, a barrel of wine, and sixty liters of *maḥia.* We went. There were fourteen of us from the Burial Society. I swear it's true. There were fourteen of us, and we started to recite Psalms and chapters from the *Zohar.* Then we held a *seʿudah.* The president of our Burial Society told us: *Members of the Society, all of you must drink all the* maḥia; *anyone who leaves one drop in his glass will be beaten by all seventy-two members of the Burial Society!* Everyone raised his glass and said: *To the joy of R. Shimʿon, our master!* I also drank a bottle of *ʿarak.* We drank. He started to pour out wine. We drank. The president of our Society announced: *Say "To the joy of R. Shimʿon" and drink up, everyone!* This president of the Burial Society raised his hands and said: *Our master, R. Shimʿon, and our master, R. Yaḥya Laḥlu, this man asked me, we ask you, and you ask the Holy One, blessed be He! Take this paralyzed man and raise him up!* Just then he turned to the paralyzed man and said to him: *Stand up!* The sick man stood up and walked back with us. We had taken him to the saint on an animal, with one of us holding him on the right and another holding him on the left. On the way back, he walked on his own two feet."

71.4 "Once Muslims came to attack us in the *mellaḥ.* They ran and stood beside the grave of R. Yaḥya Laḥlu. Their sheikh was not with them. Afterwards someone came and asked them: *What do you want to do?* They answered that they wanted to attack the Jews. He warned them about their saint [the saint would protect the Jews]. On Friday night they planned to attack us. We were sitting on the roofs of our houses. That night the Muslim watchmen did not come to guard the *mellaḥ.* A Muslim woman told us later—she lived near R. Yaḥya Laḥlu—the Muslim woman told us she saw with her own eyes someone dressed in green running back and forth, with a rifle and shooting right and left. All the Muslims ran away. Before we immigrated to Israel, we fixed a rule that we will continue to celebrate the *hillulah* of R. Yaḥya Laḥlu every *Shoshan Purim.*"

71.5 "One time a Muslim woman, the wife of the governor Suliman, was ill. She had tried every remedy. Her husband once came to us on the day of *Ramadan* [the ninth month of the Islamic calendar], and said: *Jews! Your saint appeared to me in a dream and I asked him to pray for my wife to recover!* I filled a glass with *maḥia* and gave him some to drink. He refused. I asked him to drink. He drank and his wife also drank, and since then she began to give birth. When she gave birth, she got proud as if nothing had happened to her. She had a son. The father traveled to Rabat. He told us that every night people came to him in a dream and asked him to pay his debt. Once he came to us and asked to call the Jews together. He brought a sheep. We slaughtered it and made a *seʿudah.* He named his son after the saint. The Muslims complained to him [about this]. He answered that thanks to the Jews his wife recovered and bore a son. There were many miracles."

72. Rabbi Yannay Mul Lmekhfiya (Bou Hallou)[78]

Also called Mul El-Mokhfiya, this saint is buried with R. Mussa Ben-Yishay, and the two are known as Ulad Bu-Ḥlu. His *hillulah* is held on the 25th of *Shebat.* According to tradition, he came from the Holy Land. The Muslims, too, worship him.

72.1 "They say that once there was a saint called R. Yannay Mul Lmekhfiya. That's what he was called. Why? Once Arabs attacked the Jews. The Jews fled the village of El-Medin to the neighboring village of Bou Hallou. That night, the rabbi of the town of Bou Hallou was studying in the *yeshibah,* and his family was at home. They had made couscous for their evening meal. They ate and left him a plateful. The rabbi's daughter went and told him. He asked her: *What did you eat?—Couscous.—Did you leave anything?—Just a plateful for you!* He said to her: *Let in people ten by ten, and they shall eat. I told you, let them in ten by ten!* They all had plenty to eat. That's why they called him R. Yannay Mul Lmekhfiya."

73. Rabbi Yehudah Ben-ʿAttar (Fez)[79]

R. Yehudah is popularly called R. Yehudah El-Kebir (R. Yehudah the Great) or Rabbi El-Kebir (the Great Rabbi). He was born in the month of *Elul* 5415 (1655) and died on the 19th of *Siwan* 5493 (1733). He was already considered a saint during his lifetime. He is the patron saint of Fez. The Muslims also visit his tomb.

73.1 "In Fez we had three saints, one alongside the other: Lalla Solica, R. Abner Ha-Tsarfati, and R. El-Kebir Ben-ʿAttar. One next to the other. We would go to them every week because it was close by. We did not even have to go by car. There was always a brilliant light which came down over their tombs. The great sages who stayed there to study until late would see these things. We only went there and came home. They used to say that the *shekhinah* descends on these three graves."

73.2 "This is a story from Fez from two hundred years ago at the time of R. Yehudah Ben-ʿAttar of blessed memory. Any sentence that was passed by the rabbis during his lifetime that did not have his signature was invalid. Once there was a Muslim who bought fruits from a Jew for two thousand reals. A year later he brought the money to the Jew. The Muslim asked the Jew for his note, and the Jew said that he would look for it and send it to him. The Muslim trusted him. He thought that since he knew the Jew and they had been doing business for many years, the Jew would not cheat him. To make a long story short, six months later the Muslim came and bought more produce. He asked the Jew to give him the old note which he had already paid. The Muslim bought produce for four thousand reals and the Jew said that he would give him the note when he paid the four thousand reals. The Muslim paid and the Jew gave him the note for two thousand reals. Some time later, the Jew sued the Muslim for four thousand reals. The *qadi* summoned him and told him to return the four thousand reals to the Jew. The Muslim replied that he had already paid, but the Jew claimed that he hadn't. They went before the king, Sidi Ḥmad, Mulay Aḥmad (two hundred years ago). The case was transferred from the *qadi* to the king, and the king ordered the Muslim to pay the Jew four thousand reals, otherwise they would sell all his land and he would be left penniless. When the Muslim realized the danger he was in at the hands of the king, he brought the four thousand reals, gave them to the Jew, and was silent. The Muslim began to weep. He came to the Jew, begged him to have mercy and they would divide the money fifty-fifty. Many days and years went by. At that time there was no supreme court except for the decision of the king. The king made his decision and that was that. The Muslim almost went crazy. Every month he would come to town and talk with the merchants of the city. He would ask them to find the remedy [a solution]. He announced that he would give half the money to whoever would show him what to do so that the Jew would return him his money. This went on for a year. One day he met a merchant. He asked him: *What do you have against so and so?* He answered: *What do I have against so and so? He took four thousand reals from me. I paid my note twice over!* He told him: *Do you want to get your money* *back?* The Muslim answered: *I'll do whatever you tell me to!* He told him: *There is a rabbi by the name of R. El-Kebir Ben-ʿAttar. It is he who shall judge your case and without him [there is no justice]. . . .* He went to R. El-Kebir, may he rest in peace. He lived alone. He studied *Torah* in a cellar and afterwards would go to sleep in his house. A synagogue was built over this cellar, and R. David Elbaz of blessed memory used to pray there. That is where our master, R. Yehudah Ben-ʿAttar, was. He studied and tried cases there. He was sitting there when they brought him the Muslim. The Muslim told him: *Oh,* Ḥazzan! *Act for God's sake!* He told him the whole story. He said: *So and so, I used to pay him interest. I paid the note, and he sued me, and the king decided that I must pay him, so I paid him again!* He added that he was not so much sorry about the money as about the fact that the Jew had cheated him. The rabbi asked him to be seated. He called his servant and told him to summon "so and so." The rich man came. The rabbi spoke with him, and he [the Jew] said that he was telling the truth. The rabbi asked the Muslim to come back in two weeks. When the two weeks were up, the rabbi summoned the Jew who had said that he would not pay. The rabbi, may he rest in peace, told him: *Do you know what? Let us divide the money in half. You will get half and the Muslim will get half!* The Jew answered: *Rabbi, if you want to haggle, I accept!* The Jew spoke [admitted] the truth, and according to our *Torah,* if someone makes a partial admission he must pay the whole. The rabbi told the Jew: *Bring the Muslim four thousand reals, otherwise he* [*you;* the impersonal form is used to avoid giving offense] *will die in three days!* When the Jew heard the rabbi's curse, he paid up. When the Muslim received the money, he said: *The Jew [the rabbi], the brother of the Jew, has judged me justly, while the king, a Muslim like me, judged me unjustly!* He went to tell the Muslims: *Arise, my brothers! Whoever does not convert to Judaism, may he die!* He told them that their master, the king, had rendered a false verdict and he had to pay, whereas the Jew, who was a rabbi, judged him justly. He brought butter, a sheep and wanted to give the rabbi a gift. The rabbi, may he rest in peace, told him: *Even if you yourself turned into a sheep, I would not take even a* gersh [coin of little value] *from you!* He told him that according to Jewish law, the *Torah* must never be sold for money, because we die for the *Torah* and study it, but we never sell it, and he would not take a bribe. He added that if the Muslim ever wanted to buy anything from a Jew, he should first come to the rabbi, and he would tell him which were the honest merchants with whom he should do business. The name of R. Yehudah Ben-ʿAttar is known throughout the world because the king of the land unjustly tried a case of fraud while the rabbi had administered justice."

74. Rabbi Yehudah Ben-Baba (Tagounit)

According to tradition, R. Yehudah Ben-Baba's son, whose name is not known, is buried at his father's side. The saint is also revered by the Muslims.

74.1 "Once a Muslim woman moved her bowels near the saint's house. So did her sons. The woman who took care of the place came over to her and asked her to clean it up. The saint came to the caretaker to warn her. In the morning she went to the Muslim woman to ask her to clean and whitewash the place. If she did not do it, something bad would happen to her. The Muslim woman refused. Early next morning, the woman's sons were killed by gunshots. She went out to the pasture with her flock, and they [the animals] were taken from her. Then she came to beg the saint's mercy, but he said: *No!* Every month the Muslims make a *seʿudah* [for him]."

75. Rabbi Yehudah Zabali (Ksar El-Kebir)[80]

Despite clear evidence that a Jewish saint is buried there, the Muslims claim that it is the grave of a Muslim saint, whom they call Sidi Bel-ʿAbbas.[81] According to R. Yosef Benaim (1931), it is likely that R. Yehudah Zabali died in 1780.

75.1 "R. Yehudah Zabali is buried in a courtyard, and over him [his tomb] is a *yeshibah.* On the night of his *hillulah,* he comes out. His image appears in the fire. My mother of blessed memory, before the *hillulah,* used to go with another Jewish woman to whitewash the room. People dreamt that R. Meir Baʿal Ha-Nes was buried near the tomb of R. Yehudah Zabali. There are little stones there, and on these stones they light candles. One man dreamt that near the wall R. ʿAmram Ben-Diwan was buried. They showed him the spot [in the dream]. They dug there and found a sapling, which had grown and grown until it became a large tree that covered the place."

75.2 "In our city we have a courtyard in the name of R.

Yehudah Zabali. Inside the courtyard there is a nail on which he [the saint] hung a chicken that laid one egg every day. People lived in this courtyard, but there was a niche which no one would come close to. Only on Fridays a certain Jew would collect candles and light them there. Anyone who does not want to go to the tomb of R. Yehudah Zabali goes to the courtyard. The nail and the string are still there. Whoever wanted to get married would go to that courtyard. If a woman was unclean, she was forbidden to enter. If she did enter, her children or her husband would die, because the place is sacred. They also make *se'udah* there."

76. Rabbi Yisra'el Cohen (Tabia/Tilouine)

This saint is also called Mul Shejra (Master of the Tree) or R. Yisra'el Mul Shejra El-Khedra (Master of the Green Tree), because of the trees growing by his tomb. According to tradition, R. Yisra'el was killed by Muslims for refusing to have sexual intercourse with a Muslim woman.

76.1 "People go to R. Yisra'el Cohen on foot. We used to walk from Tabia in the morning. People would spend the whole day there and return in the evening. It wasn't the custom to spend the night there, because it was in the desert, and there were only Muslims there. R. Yisra'el Cohen was burned to death by the Muslims. A Muslim woman wanted him to sleep with her. He said: *No!* She said: *If you do not want to, we'll burn you to death!* He replied: *Then burn me!* She burned him. He made known his last will to the Jews. The Muslims were going to burn him to death. He asked that the Jews gather his ashes and place them in his robe, and put it on a mule and walk behind it without speaking to it. Wherever the mule stopped, that was where they must bury him. The Jews followed the mule and it stopped outside the village, in the place where Muslims lived. They buried him there, and carob trees grew up near his tomb, one at his head and one at his feet. When one is bowed down it leans on the other above the tomb. Anyone suffering from an illness visits the tomb, cuts a piece of cloth from his clothing, hangs it on the carob tree, and goes home healthy. They buried him in a field. The Muslims used to go to the tomb to put out the candles that the Jews lit, and take them. The saint made them all go insane, from the oldest to the youngest. When they realized this, they stopped, and every time they see Jews going to the tomb, they ask: *Are you going to the saint? May God help you!* People would visit his grave. They would bathe in the river that flows near the tomb. The men would fish there. We women would prepare the fish and stay there until the evening and then go home. In the name of God and my master! When I came to Israel, I dreamt that I went to visit his grave. I told the people: *Let us go and visit the grave of R. Yisra'el!* They told me that it is far away. I answered that it was not far away, and that we could get there. We arrived there and went under the carob trees. We visited his grave, in the name of God and my master. There's a big shaded area there."

77. Rabbi Yitsḥaq Abiḥatsira (Toulal)[82]

R. Yitsḥaq is the younger son of R. Yaʿaqob Abiḥatsira, the founder of the great dynasty of saints Abiḥatsira. R. Yitsḥaq was born in Boudenib in the Tafilalet region. He was murdered by Muslims on the 14th of *Shebat* 5672 (1912) in the village Beraka, at the age of thirty-six. He was renowned for his prophetic ability as well as for the miracles he performed while still a youth. R. Yitsḥaq Abiḥatsira is also venerated by the Muslims.

77.1 "Once there was a Muslim sheikh who wanted to kill R. Yitsḥaq Abiḥatsira. He took him out to be executed. The Jews of the *mellaḥ* went with him. The rabbi told them: *Return to your homes! I shall be the expiation for the Jews! I shall give my life for them!* The Muslims put him into the barrel of a cannon. They tied him to it. When they fired it, his soul ascended to heaven like a dove."

77.2 "One time there was no rain in Morocco. The rainy season had passed. If, for example, it would begin in *Ḥeshwan,* then we were already in *Kislew.* Then people came to him, Arabs and also Jews. They asked him to pray for rain. He told them: *All right! In a little while there will be rain. Never fear!* They said to him: *No! We must have it [now]!* He went outside, raised his eyes to the sky, and before the people could get home, it started to rain very hard. . . . All the Arabs respected his parents, and they all knew that he was a saint."

77.3 "In Toulal [there is] R. Yitsḥaq Abiḥatsira. You have to go on foot some eight kilometers. There was a *mellaḥ* in Toulal. They used to celebrate his *hillulah.* Even now Jews went there from Jerusalem. A year ago they went via France to celebrate his *hillulah.* The Arabs paid them the greatest respect in the world. They honor them.

There is a permanent Muslim guardian. They have faith! An Arab had a son who had something wrong with him; he was mentally retarded. So they brought him to the tomb of the rabbi and had him sleep there alone. The next day they came to see the boy. They found him safe and sound. This really happened about forty or fifty years ago. In recent years Arabs come and bring goats and sheep, slaughter them, and bring ovens. Not only on the day of the *hillulah,* but also on other days. I remember that once there was a *hillulah* on a Sunday, like last year, and we went from the town of Erfoud. All the people. Everyone who had a car or didn't have a car. They rent a bus and everything. All night they go there, and in the morning people sit down and sing, drink, eat, and roast meat. They slaughter [animals] all day and all night."

77.4 "R. Yaʿaqob [Abiḥatsira] had only one wife. May he rest in peace! Once in Tafilalet—this was told to me by Baba Sale [R. Yisra'el Abiḥatsira, one of the last saints of the family, who died in Netivot, Israel, in 1984], my rabbi. . . . Once they wanted to bless the *Birkat Ha-levanah* (the blessing of the New Moon). This was in the time of R. Yaʿaqob, his father. But just on that day there was a cloud [over the moon]. If they would not recite the blessing that evening, then the blessing could not be recited at all. They prayed the Evening Service, and R. Yaʿaqob stood with the sages, his sons, and the congregation, but R. Yitsḥaq was not there. After the Evening Service they waited. R. Yaʿaqob said to them: *Where is Yitsḥaq, my son? Where is he? Bring him here!* They said: *He's a bit drunk!* He told them: *Never mind! Bring him here!* He came. The father said to him: *How does it look to you, Yitsḥaq? Shall we have to forego the Birkat Halevanah tonight?* He [R. Yitsḥaq] said to the moon: *Aren't you ashamed of yourself? Here are my father and the congregation, and you are all covered up?* That is what he said. The cloud blew away and the moon came out and they said the Blessing of the New Moon. R. Yaʿaqob said to them: *Do you see? His drink [even when he is drunk] is better than you!* He only drank a bit."

77.5 "That same year the rabbi [R. Yitsḥaq] died, he came to Boudenib. We lived in Boudenib. Baba Sale used to come there also. When he [R. Yitsḥaq] came, he started to ask the people where Beraka was. He did not die in Toulal, he's just buried there. When he was in Boudenib, he asked where Beraka was. The people did not understand why he was asking about this place. But he knew that he would die there, may he rest in peace! He asked: *Where is Beraka?* When he went there, may he rest in peace, he parted from his caravan and went on ahead with his servant and donkey. They went on ahead. When they walked ahead, he was seized and stabbed with a knife. He died instantly. When he was in Boudenib he asked where Beraka was. When he died there, the people realized that the rabbi had known where he would die. They took him from there to Toulal. He died in an open field. There were no people. In Toulal there were Jews. Beraka is not far from Toulal."

78. Rabbi Yitsḥaq Ben-Walid (Tetuan)[83]

R. Yitsḥaq Ben-Walid (1777–1870) is the author of the celebrated commentary, *Wayyomer Yitsḥaq*. His *hillulah* is held on the 9th of *Adar*. The Muslims also visit his tomb.

78.1 "In Tetuan we have R. Yitsḥaq Ben-Walid. There is still a synagogue named after him and his library is there. [The interview was held in 1974. In 1978 the library was transferred to the Jewish Quarter in the Old City of Jerusalem, where it serves a *yeshibah* named after the saint.] Also his cane and phylacteries are all in his house."

78.2 "I'll tell you what I heard from the members of his family. Once the Muslims were about to go into the city in order to attack the Muslims who lived there. Tetuan was 'The Little Jerusalem.' That's what they called it. When the Muslims came, R. Yitsḥaq was already dead and buried in our cemetery. When they came, there were lights in his cemetery. Then the Muslims ran away. They ran away. He performed this miracle for them. They were about to attack the Muslims of the city and, of course, they would have attacked the Jews, too. The Muslims of Tetuan were like the Jews of Tetuan. The Muslims realized that it was he who had performed this miracle. Jews as well as Muslims would visit his tomb. They came from Alcazar, bringing candles to light, and all kinds of food and drinks."

78.3 "In our town of Mazagan there was a woman named Nana who could cure sick people. I saw people who knew her and had been given quite complex treatment by her sometimes. They say that she went to pray at the tomb of R. Yitsḥaq Ben-Walid of blessed memory. She fell asleep at the tomb, and in a dream she saw the rabbi telling her: *Take this jar and every remedy that you put into it will be successful!*

When she woke up she found a small jar. In this jar she would put all kinds of ointments and powders that she could use for cures. Before she treated a wound she would say: *Oh, R. Ben-Walid! May your hands precede mine!*"

79. Rabbi Yitsḥaq Ha-Levi (Imi n'Tanoute)

R. Yitsḥaq is buried on the mountain Imi n'Tamouga, inside a cave. There is a narrow entrance through which the Jews crawl. R. Masʿud Mani and R. Abraham Darʿi are buried near him. His *hillulah* is celebrated on *Lag bʿOmer.*

79.1 "R. Yitsḥaq Ha-Levi is buried near a mountain called Imi n'Tamouga. I went there on pilgrimage with my brother-in-law, to the tombs of R. Yitsḥaq Ha-Levi and R. Masʿud Mani, the saints who revealed themselves on that mountain. They appeared in a dream to some people and asked them to visit them there. My brother-in-law visited there. He couldn't see, and it was difficult for him to read a book. He asked me to go with him. We went on horseback. We got there and he started to read. He cried out with joy: *Look! I can see now!* He couldn't see in one eye. I said: *Mazaltov (congratulations)!* Afterwards, we went home."

80. Rabbi Yitsḥaq Yisra'el Ha-Levi (Bzou)[84]

Tradition has it that this saint—better known as Mul El-Barj, Mwalin El-Barj or Mulay Burja—came from the Holy Land. He appears in the lists of seven or ten rabbis from the Land of Israel who came to Morocco to convert the *goyim.* R. Yitsḥaq is also very popular among the Muslims, who call him Sidi Moḥammed El-Mashzuz or Sidi Moḥammed El-Mukhfi.

80.1 "Sidi Mul El-Barj is buried in Bzou. He [his tomb] is in a field, and people take him offerings of meat. A rich man came and made him a building and he showed himself. A spring flows out of his tomb. And when he grants a request, he shows that through signals of water. The water flows from over his tomb. Once a Jewish woman went and asked him for a remedy. Then he told her that he didn't have her remedy and he sent her to R. David Alshqar, and there she found her remedy. Once a *goy* came and peed on the site. As he peed, he got paralyzed and he couldn't stop peeing. Afterwards they brought a cow there. He begged and only after that did he get up, and since then the Arabs can't do anything bad there. And every year they would bring sheep and cows and have the Jewish slaughterer butcher them, so that it [the meat] would be *kosher.*"

81. Rabbi Yosef Bajayo (Ntifa)[85]

R. Yosef Bajayo is also called R. Yosef Abujayo, Ajayo, Abajayo and Ben-Ajayo. According to tradition, he was a rabbi from the Holy Land who came to Morocco to collect alms. He died in Tabia in the 1920s and is buried in Ntifa. He is also venerated by the Muslims.

81.1 "R. Yosef Bajayo was from the Holy Land. They drew lots and it was his turn to go to Morocco to collect funds. He came to us and took care of the *bar-mitswah* celebration of many boys. Afterwards he went away and returned to us. One time we had a drought. He prayed and it rained. He was the guest of R. Shelomoh Ben-Ḥammu, who was the mayor of the town [the president of the Jewish community]. I'll tell you about his merit. He told the people that he was going to Tabia where Mul Timḥdart, may he rest in peace, is buried. He told them that he was going there to collect alms. He left and told them, when he was midway in his journey, that his death was approaching. He asked to wash his hands and recited the *shema*ᶜ. Then they wanted to bury him in their village, but when they tried to lift him up, they could not. They sent to us in Ntifa [to announce the saint's death]. The people of Ntifa went to get him, because he had ordered them not to bury him there [in Tabia], but in Ntifa. And he, may he rest in peace, ordered this because there are sages there. The Jews of Ntifa went and lifted him up with their hands. That same day the skies opened up and there was rain and lightning. They gave him the ritual ablution, may he rest in peace. I named my son after him because my [first] sons were stillborn. I called him Yosef Ḥayyim Elmaleḥ. We used to celebrate his *hillulah,* and when my son grew up he did the same. That same night [that the saint was buried], he went up to heaven, body and soul. A Muslim woman called Saliḥ saw this. He was lifted up. He disappeared, ascended, may he rest in peace. Next day the Muslim woman said that the rabbi had gone to Jerusalem. That night I dreamt that a stream was flowing beneath him. When he died, all the Jews mourned him. That whole month they slaughtered no animals [for meat]. The stores were closed and they blew the *shofar.* Now, when they come to visit his grave, a stream suddenly flows next to him and whoever was sick when he came, goes away healthy. Whoever came with paralyzed legs, walks. I myself was afflicted in my arms and legs. When I slept in his shrine, water gushed out. I washed my arms and legs. Next day I returned home healthy."

81.2 "Aside from R. Yosef Bajayo, I don't remember the name of anyone else in Ntifa. But people would go to visit the tombs of other saints, under the stones. But I don't remember their names. R. Yosef Bajayo is first-rate. The others are not familiar to me. They were great sages, but they do not measure up to the saint, R. Yosef. R. Yosef had the spirit of prophecy. He thought that Tabia was not a fit place for him to be buried in. He asked for a more respectable place. People came from Casablanca, from Marrakech, and from all kinds of places. There was even one man, an Arab named Jilali, he had a bus in Casablanca. When he would come, he would give the rabbis money so that they would bless him there. He was always successful. Once he was in a traffic accident and nothing happened to him. My father told me that R. Yosef died in Tabia but he gave an order that they should bring him to Ntifa. They brought him on Saturday night. They were strong men, faithful sons of faithful fathers. They asked R. Shimʿon Bar-Yoḥay to help them. They were like horses. They didn't mind walking, not like the people of our day who can't, so they only go by bus. There was one Jew who could walk forty or fifty kilometers just like that. He had strength."

82. Rabbi Yosef Zozot (Tamzaourt)

According to local tradition, R. Yosef Zozot was born and died in Tamzaourt. He is buried near his uncle, R. Shaul Zozot, who is also venerated as a saint.

82.1 "Once a caravan was attacked by fourteen bandits who wanted to steal from it. They called upon R. Zozot and they [the bandits] were all paralyzed. The families of the paralyzed men sacrificed cows and pleaded with the saint, and only then did he free them."

Notes

1. The reader will no doubt note the peculiar style of the tales. The author is well aware of the unclear passages, hiatuses, repetitions,

digressions, and non sequiturs, as well as ambiguous uses of phrases such as "he said" and "he answered." These are the results of the author's exact transcription of spontaneous interviews with his informants. I have retained some of those idiosyncrasies in the English translation, but have preferred to keep the prose as grammatical as possible, rather than attempt a precise rendition of the often distracting style in which the tales were told.

2. Y. Benaim (1931, p. 18); D. Ovadia (1974–77, vol. 2, p. 141).
3. Y. Benaim (1931, p. 12); J. Goulven (1927, pp. 93–94); J. Lasri (1978, p. 167). Concerning the meaning of the saint's name, see A. I. Laredo (1978, p. 373).
4. J. Goulven (1927, p. 93) gives a very detailed description of the place. On *Lag bʿOmer* 1981 a great *hillulah* was celebrated there with the aid of the Moroccan government and the Jewish community. It is notable that many improvements have been introduced: a road has been built to the nearest town, Settat, about 17 km away; the grave is in a big room that serves as the entrance to the synagogue, and many rooms have been built for the pilgrims who visit the place all year round.
5. The informant said the rabbi was one of the Ten Martyrs—the term used to designate ten rabbinical emissaries who came to Morocco from the Holy Land to collect alms. His list includes R. Abraham Awriwer, R. Abraham Mul Annes, R. ʿAmram Ben-Diwan, Bene-Zmirru, R. David Ha-Levi Draʿ, R. David U-Moshe, and so on.
6. H. Z. Hirschberg (1957, p. 155); L. Voinot (1948, p. 68).
7. According to L. Voinot (1948, p. 68), Mulay Matil appears in the Demnate list of seven rabbinical emissaries who came to Morocco from the Holy Land in very ancient times.
8. Every year a great-grandson of the saint celebrates the *hillulah* in his honor in Kiriyat Shemonah, Israel.
9. This may be the same R. Abraham Adarʿi cited by Y. Benaim (1931, p. 18), who lived in the eighteenth century.
10. N. Banon (1981, p. 372).
11. D. Corcos (1976, pp. 227–28) describes how the saint was "invented" through a dream and how the place became very popular in the 1940s, attracting flocks of visitors from nearby Mazagan and especially from Casablanca; J. Alfassi (1981. *The Community of Azemmour.* Netiv ha-Lamed He, pp. 24–26 [Hebrew].)
12. According to P. Flamand (1952, p. 108), the *hillulah* of the saint is celebrated in mid-January. R. Aharon was known for his miraculous cures of snakebite: E. Mauchamp (s.d., p. 178). The Arab guardian of the shrine in the old cemetery of Demnate told me in 1981 that

the saint is known for helping spinsters and that Muslim maidens too come to stay there overnight in the hope of becoming engaged.

13. See E. Aubin (1904, pp. 489–90); Y. Benaim (1931, p. 102); L. Voinot (1948, pp. 49–50); J. Lasri (1978, pp. 28–30); J. Goulven (1927, pp. 96–97); N. Banon (1981, p. 372); A. Elmaleh (16 *Iyyar* 1946. "The *hillulot* of *Lag b'Omer,* the *hillulah* of R. 'Amram Ben-Diwan in Morocco." *Hed Hamizraḥ,* pp. 6–7 [Hebrew]); Alegria Abitbol (22 May 1930. "Un pèlerinage à Ouezzan." *Avenir Illustré,* pp. 5–6); L. Conquy (January 1932. "Les miracles du pèlerinage d'Ouezzan." *Paix et Droit,* 12th year, no. 1, pp. 9–10; J. Elhadad (June 1957. "Le Saint d'Ouezzane, Rabbi Amram ben Diouane." *Cahiers de l'Alliance Israélite Universelle,* no. 109, pp. 5–7); M. Haloua (June 1953. "La Hiloula d'Ouezzane." *Information Juive,* no. 45); E. Haymann (18–24 May 1973. "Pèlerinage à Ouezzane." *Tribune Juive,* no. 225, pp. 16–17); E. Michaux-Bellaire (May 1908. "La Maison d'Ouezzane." *Revue du Monde Musulman,* vol. 8); S. H. Pinto (12 June 1930. "Le pèlerinage à Ouezzan." *Avenir Illustré,* pp. 7–9); Y. D. Semach (1 June 1928. "Pèlerinage à Ouezzan." *Univers Israélite,* 83th year, no. 37, pp. 301–02); Y. D. Semach (March 1937. "Le Saint d'Ouezzan, Ribbi Amram ben Divan, et les saints juifs du Maroc." *Bulletin de l'Enseignement Public du Maroc,* no. 152, pp. 79–99); "The Zadik of Ouezzan (from Moroccan Jewish Folklore)" (*Alliance Review,* vol. 6, no. 23, p. 8 (June 1951)); "Un pèlerinage juif au Maroc (Ouazzan)" (*Univers Israélite,* 66th year, no. 9, pp. 272–73 [11.11.1910]); *Bulletin Mensuel de l'Alliance Israélite Universelle* (1910), pp. 98–99.

14. Other traditions tell that R. 'Amram is buried in Salé where a shrine bears his name (J. Goulven [1927, p. 97]), and in Sefrou and Meknes.

15. The pilgrimage today is under the patronage of the Moroccan government, which takes care of advertising and organizing the event. I participated at the *hillulah* there in *Lag b'Omer* in 1981 with many Jews of Moroccan origin who came from Israel and other countries as well. The place has undergone significant development. At the entrance there is a large sign with the name and words praising the saint in three languages—Arabic, Hebrew and French. The saint is buried under a cairn about three meters long. A large synagogue and several pavillions are found nearby.

16. The informant's family originates from Amazrou and he himself visited the place as a child. See also I. Ben-Ami (1982b, p. 96).

17. See I. Ben-Ami (1973a); L. Voinot (1948, p. 29); J. Lasri (1978, pp. 49–52).

18. This date was established by Moshe A., the informant who told stories 12.1 to 12.3. The inhabitants of Arba Touggana celebrated the *hillulah* of R. Daniel on the 15th of *Elul,* and this tradition continues to the present in the village Zanoaḥ near Jerusalem.
19. According to Y. Benaim (1931, p. 26), J. Lasri (1978, p. 71) and F. Legey (1926, p. 4), the saint is buried in the village Ighi, while other traditions say he is interred in the old cemetery of Rabat and in Tabia.
20. Y. Benaim (1931, p. 26) says the rabbi died in 1761; L. Voinot (1948, pp. 77–78); E. Mauchamp (s.d., p. 180); J. Lasri (1978, p. 44); S. Y. Benaim (1980) describes a great *hillulah* celebrated from December 20–24, 1979, in Azrou n'Bahamou, north of Taroudant, in the Sous area inhabited by the tribe Raḥla. Some traditions tell that R. David is buried in Meknes and in Marrakech.
21. This family of saints was renowned in Morocco. One tradition tells that it originates from the Oufran area, which R. Barukh—R. David's father—left for Taroudant. The exact relationships among the several members of the family are still unclear.
22. The picture of Baba Dudu is well-known among Moroccan Jews and appears in the books of J. Lasri (1978, p. 46) and N. Banon (1981, p. 374).
23. According to J. Lasri (1978, pp. 101–05) the saint revealed himself to a Jewish woman in a dream and announced that he is buried there near his wife; L. Voinot (1948, p. 57) describes the place outside the walls of Beni Mellal and adds that the Muslims call the rabbi Sidi Kheroua after the name of a tree found near the grave.
24. Y. Benaim (1931, p. 26).
25. Y. Benaim (1931, p. 26); L. Voinot (1948, pp. 65–66); J. Lasri (1978, pp. 146–47); E. Mauchamp (s.d., p. 178); E. Westermarck (1926, vol. 1, pp. 195–96); N. Banon (1981, p. 374); E. Doutté (1914, pp. 208–13); P. Flamand (1952, pp. 108–11); J. Bénech (1940, p. 187). One tradition says R. David is brother to the saints R. Yehudah Ben-Yisra'el Ha-Levi, R. Yitsḥaq Yisra'el Ha-Levi and R. ʿObadiah Ha-Levi.
26. The grave is found about fifteen kilometers west of Demnate. A picture of the place appears in E. Doutté (1914, p. 208). A very detailed description of the sanctuary at the beginning of the century is given by L. Voinot (1948, p. 65), but the situation changed in the 1930s and especially in the 1940s, when the site was much improved. In my collection I have a postcard with the picture of the saint, a palm tree and a mountain in the background.
27. In the original Hebrew version of this book I have described the

income and expenditure at the saint's shrine during the years 1928–46, which illustrate the ramified activities at the sanctuary.

28. J. M. Toledano, in the preface to the book *Sepher Ha-Malkhut* (1931, Casablanca), attributed to R. David Ha-Levi Draᶜ, claims that the saint came to Morocco from Seville at the time of the Expulsion from Spain. Other authors as well as popular traditions attribute the saint's origin to the Holy Land.
29. Told by Y. Elmaleḥ, of Casablanca, who was most active in everything concerning the Jewish sanctuaries in Morocco, both personally and on behalf of the National Committee of the Organization of the Jewish Communities.
30. L. Voinot (1948, p. 80) tells that the saint came to Morocco a long time ago, in contradition to our informant, who claimed to remember the saint from his infancy.
31. In the present research I have collected more than 175 stories about this saint. See I. Ben-Ami (1977, 1980c and 1981a); Y. Bilu (1978); L. Voinot (1948, p. 81); J. Lasri (1978, pp. 38–41); N. Banon (1981, p. 374).
32. This is a very interesting tradition about the "existence" of the grave of this *tanna* in Morocco. It is not known when the dream described in the story occurred. Independently from this tradition, Libyan Jews of Moshav Alma have recently "rediscovered" the grave of R. Eleᶜazar Ben-ᶜArakh near their place in northern Galilee. They built an impressive shrine and celebrate the *hillulah* there on the 17th of *Iyyar.*
33. Y. Benaim (1931, p. 22); J. Goulven (1927, pp. 91–92, 153–54); J. M. Toledano (1972, pp. 270–71); H. Zafrani (1972, p. 246); J. Lasri (1978, p. 87); N. Banon (1981, p. 373).
34. Another tradition tells that the stick belonged to the saint's grandfather. J. Goulven (1927, p. 92) describes the miracle of the sea and says that it happened in the year 1755.
35. According to L. Voinot (1948, p. 77), the saint died in 1905. He always dressed in leather and had the gift of prophecy. Both Jews and Muslims visited his grave seeking his aid to cure diseases.
36. Y. Benaim (1931, p. 21) says that nothing is known about the saint's life; N. Banon (1981, p. 373) affirms that the saint died in 1806 and that his *hillulah* is celebrated in September. I remember as a child in Casablanca that pupils would visit the grave of R. Eliyahu to request the saint's help before school examinations.
37. L. Voinot (1948, p. 71) gives a very detailed description of the burial place situated about 400 meters from Ouar ech Chems, in the Zat

valley inhabited by the Mesfioua tribe. See also E. Doutté (1914, p. 209).

38. Y. Benaim (1931, p. 42) says that the saint has a great reputation among the Jews in Morocco. His grave is considered very ancient. Nothing is known about his origins or his life; L. Voinot (1948, pp. 52–53); N. Banon (1981, p. 374); J. Bénech (1940, pp. 181, 188–89); E. Mauchamp (s.d., p. 182). F. Legey (1926, p. 36) presents a picture of the sanctuary and adds that women used to fasten rags on the olive tree by the saint's grave in the belief that their troubles would be attached to the tree and later dispersed by the wind.
39. J. Lasri (1978, p. 143) affirms that the saint is buried in the village Tagadirt n'Bour, near Anrhaz; L. Voinot (1948, p. 74) describes the place, situated not far from Agueni, at the Ouzguita. The nearest *melláḥs* are Imarhira and Tagadirt n'Bour. One tradition tells that the saint is the brother of R. Moshe Cohen.
40. See I. Ben-Ami (1975b); Y. Benaim (1931, p. 38); P. Flamand (1960, vol. 2, p. 45); N. Banon (1981, pp. 374–75).
41. M. Mazal-Tarim (1939); A. Ben-Attar (1961. *Sefer Shenot Ḥayyim.* Casablanca [Judeo-Arabic]). Most of the stories I have collected in the framework of this research are identical to stories in these two books. I have therefore preferred not to repeat them here.
42. The inscription on his grave says: "Died on October 20, 1937, at the age of 73 years"; J. Lasri (1978, pp. 137–39) presents a well-known picture of the saint; N. Banon (1981, p. 373).
43. The Pinto family is a very famous family of saints. The two sons of R. Ḥayyim Pinto, the renowned R. Raphael (Baba Raphael) and R. Meir (Baba Meir), were mourned by the Jews when they were killed by a Muslim in 1980. They were buried in the cemetery in Ben-Msik, not far from the grave of R. Eliyahu.
44. The house is in Commandant Provost Street, no. 36. In my visit there in 1981, I found a loose page in poor French describing how after Baba Raphael and Baba Meir were killed, the family intended to close the house, a site of pilgrimage for believers. However, in view of the many requests from devout followers and particularly in view of the last request of Baba Meir, it was decided to keep the house open for visitors.
45. Y. Benaim (1931, p. 80) says R. Khalifa lived at the time of R. Eliʿezer Davila; N. Banon (1981, p. 375); J. M. Toledano (1972, p. 22); L. Voinot (1948, p. 49).
46. J. Lasri (1978, pp. 174–76).
47. L. Voinot (1948, p. 82). R. Makhluf seems to belong to the famous Abiḥatsira family, but the exact relationship is not known.

48. Y. Benaim (1931, pp. 84–85). R. Masʿud is probably the son of R. Yaʿaqob Naḥmias Ashkenazi.
49. See chapter "Saints and the World of Nature," note 8; Y. Benaim (1931, pp. 26, 29, 58, 114); M. Mazal-Tarim (1939, pp. 50–52). The saints R. Yehudah Ben-Naphtali Afryat, R. Shelomoh Ben-ʿAbbu and R. Yaʿaqob Ben-Shabbat, as well as many rabbis, are buried in the Cave of Oufran.
50. J. Lasri (1978, pp. 156–58).
51. Y. Benaim (1931, p. 87).
52. P. Flamand (1960, vol. 2, p. 46).
53. Y. Benaim (1931, p. 26); J. Lasri (1978, p. 71); P. Flamand (1952, p. 108); E. Mauchamp (s.d., p. 178); F. Legey (1926, p. 4); J. Bénech (1940, p. 187); L. Voinot (1948, p. 64).
54. Other traditions tell that Mulay Ighi is the cousin of R. David Alshqar and the brother of Sidi Rghit.
55. L. Voinot (1948, p. 51); A. Mograbi (1968, p. 70); D. Ovadia (1974–77, vol. 2, pp. 139–40; vol. 3, p. 83); N. Stillman (1973, p. 260; 1988, pp. 91–92).
56. J. Lasri (1978, pp. 42–43) tells two stories about Mul Timḥdart: according to the first, the saint revealed himself in a dream of a Jew, saying that he was buried in Tabia; the second tells that the rabbi and his students died while praying in the cemetery for the local population's relief from cholera.
57. I. Ben-Ami (1980a); D. Corcos (1976, p. 284); L. Voinot (1948, p. 53); J. Lasri (1978, pp. 91–93); N. Banon (1981, p. 374).
58. N. Banon (1981, p. 374). One informant said that the rabbi had come from the Holy Land.
59. J. Goulven (1927, p. 92) tells that R. Raḥamim came from Tetuan or from Iran and had a wooden leg. After his death, this leg was kept in the synagogue for some years as a holy relic to be kissed by female visitors. The director of the Jewish school brought this custom to the attention of the Chief Rabbi of Rabat, who ordered that the leg be removed.
60. Y. Benaim (1931, p. 108); A. Elmaleḥ (12 September 1935. "Rabbi Raphael Incaoua." *Avenir Illustré,* p. 101); Y. D. Semach (30 May 1935. "Rabbi Raphael Encaoua." *Union Marocaine,* and 6 September 1935. *Univers Israélite,* 90th year, no. 553, p. 810); "Pèlerinage de Hilloula au cimetière de Salé sur la tombe du Grand Rabbin Raphael Encaoua" (*Noar,* no. 3, p. 9 [June–July 1946]); "Le Grand Rabbin Raphael Encaoua" (*Afrique du Nord Illustré* [November 25, 1928], p. 9). A picture of the saint appears in

J. Toledano (1982. *Le temps du Mellaḥ.* Jerusalem, p. 82), and on a postcard in our private collection.

61. Y. Benaim (1931, pp. 106–07).
62. L. Voinot (1948, p. 75); J. Lasri (1978, p. 177); E. Mauchamp (s.d., p. 177); P. Flamand (1960, vol. 2, p. 47); N. Banon (1981, pp. 373–74).
63. Y. Benaim (1931, p. 107); D. Ovadia (1974–77, vol. 2, p. 310). According to the *Encyclopaedia Judaica* (vol. 6, p. 572), R. Raphael "was a talmudic scholar, kabbalist, poet, and scientist. He wrote many works, including *Halakhah le-Moshe,* responsa (Jerusalem, 1901); *Shir Ḥadash,* poems (Jerusalem, 1935), and *Eden mi-Kedem* (Fez, 1940). Still in manuscript are many of his writings including *Kisse ha-Melakhim,* a history of ancient kings and of the Jews."
64. L. Voinot (1948, pp. 53–54); R. Bendahan (15 May 1956. "Hilulá en Melilla: una ingente multitud visitó la tumba de Rebbi Saadia Edaty." *Luz.* Tanger, vol. 1, no. 5, p. 16).
65. This story explains why the saint is not buried in Melilla as well as the relationship between the saint and the Muslim family that has guarded the grave for generations. See L. Voinot (1948, p. 54).
66. E. Mauchamp (s.d., pp. 181–82); L. Voinot (1948, p. 84); I. Ben-Ami (1983a).
67. N. Banon (1981, p. 373); J. Goulven (1927, p. 92).
68. L. Voinot (1948, pp. 56–57); J. Lasri (1978, pp. 165–66).
69. Y. Benaim (1931, p. 119) says the saint was very famous in Morocco and that he came from the Holy Land as an emissary; E. Doutté (1914, pp. 22, 209); E. Mauchamp (s.d., p. 180); L. Voinot (1948, p. 72); J. Bénech (1940, p. 187); N. Banon (1981, p. 373); A. Seluan (1968. "L'Helloula de Salomon Bel Lahnech à Ourika." *Maroc Tourisme,* no. 49, pp. 33–35).
70. Y. Benaim (1931, p. 117); J. Bénech (1940, p. 181–84).
71. Parallel versions of this story are told by Y. Benaim (1931, p. 117), D. Noy (1964, pp. 63–64) and J. Bénech (1940, pp. 181–84).
72. Y. Benaim (1931, p. 31); E. Doutté (1914, p. 383); P. Flamand (1960, vol. 2, p. 44); J. Lasri (1978, p. 131); F. Legey (1926, p. 156). L. Voinot (1948, pp. 47–48) gives a very detailed description of the grave and its surroundings. Other traditions that we collected tell that Ulad Zemmur also are buried in Salé, Tiznit (south of Agadir), Marrakech and in the *mellaḥ* of Tabougimt.
73. D. Corcos (1976, pp. 306–09, 315).
74. Another version of this story is told by Voinot (1948, p. 48), who adds that the Ulad Zmirru were Jews from Granada who immigrated at

the time of the great persecutions. The head of the family, R. Abraham Ben Zmirru, went first to Fez and then in 1499 moved to Safi. Although no graves were built, people say that R. Abraham, his six brothers and his sons are buried there.

75. Y. Benaim (1931, p. 68) gives his name as R. Yaʿaqob Naḥmias, a sage from Demnate, descendant of R. Masʿud Naḥmias, but on p. 119 gives the correct name R. Yaʿaqob Ashkenazi; L. Voinot (1948, pp. 20–21) describes the grave and says that the Jews call the saint R. David Ashkenazi or R. Shemuel Ashkenazi; P. Flamand (1960, vol. 2, pp. 41–43).
76. The grave is in the Mzab region. Other traditions tell that R. Yaḥya El-Khdar is buried in Demnate, between Settat and Demnate or at Wad-Zam; Y. Benaim (1931, p. 63); J. Goulven (1927, pp. 93–95); N. Banon (1981, p. 374).
77. Y. Benaim (1931, p. 62); L. Voinot (1948, pp. 36–37); J. Lasri (1978, pp. 64–67).
78. I. Ben-Ami (1975c); L. Voinot (1948, p. 27); P. Flamand (1952, p. 108).
79. Y. Benaim (1931, pp. 46–50); J. M. Toledano (1972, p. 192).
80. L. Voinot (1948, p. 19) gives a detailed description of the place; Y. Benaim (1931, p. 52).
81. The same name is attributed to Lalla Rivqah of Bene-Moshe and to the Muslim patron saint of Marrakech.
82. N. Banon (1981, p. 374).
83. Y. Benaim (1931, p. 76); N. Banon (1981, pp. 374–75); L. Voinot (1948, p. 53).
84. E. Doutté (1914, p. 209); J. Lasri (1978, p. 68); N. Baron (1981, p. 374); L. Voinot (1948, pp. 23–24).
85. J. Lasri (1978, pp. 120–21).

18

HOLY WOMEN: TALES AND LEGENDS

FEMALE SAINTS WHO WERE AS HIGHLY REVERED AS THEIR MALE COUNTER-parts merit separate treatment. Certain great, wise women—even prophetesses—appear in the Biblical and Talmudic-Midrashic literature. Some of them eventually elicited the highest veneration among Jews both in *Erets Yisra'el* and the Diaspora. Renowned women from the Biblical period include: Adam's wife Eve, Sarah, Rebekah, Rachel, Leah, Bilḥah, Zilpah, Seraḥ (daughter of Asher; buried in Persia), Dinah (daughter of Jacob), Jochebed (mother of Moses), Zipporah (wife of Moses), Miriam, Elisheva (wife of Aaron), Job's wife (buried in Syria), Deborah the Prophetess, Ḥuldah the Prophetess, Ḥannah (mother of Samuel), Jael (wife of Ḥeber the Kenite), Ruth the Moabite, Queen Esther, and Em I-Kabod. Famous women from the Talmudic era are: Ḥannah the mother of the Seven Sons; the wives of R. Judah Ha-Nasi, of R. ʿAkiva, of Shammai, of R. Ḥoni Ha-Meʿaggel, of R. Shemaʿyah Ḥasidah, of R. Shimʿon Bar-Yoḥay, of R. Ḥananiah Ben-ʿAkashyah, of Ḥalafta, of R. Joshua of Sikhnin, of R. Ḥanina Ben-Dosa, of Abba Saul; Shammai's daughter-in-law; and the mothers of R. Shimʿon Bar-Yoḥay and of R. Krospedai.

The Jews' unique high regard for women as exemplified in the stories of the Matriarchs, sometimes generated widespread popular veneration and created special situations which no longer prevailed after the Talmudic period. No female figure arose thereafter who was widely venerated. Lalla Sol Ha-Tsaddiqah, recognized and revered by the Jews of Morocco and abroad in the nineteenth century, was an outstanding exception.

Among the Biblical figures, the fame of certain women indubitably stemmed from their unusual holiness, from deeds they are known to have performed or those that legend attributed to them. Others became famous because of their illustrious husbands. The connection with a male figure has conspicuous practical manifestations during the Talmudic period, when the name of the female saint is sometimes unknown and she is identified only as "wife," "mother," "daughter" or "daughter-in-law" of. . . . A few women were nevertheless awarded particularly high status and esteem; these include the Matriarchs, Seraḥ daughter of Asher, and Queen Esther.

As part of the current renewed interest in pilgrimages organized by various groups in Israel (synagogues, community centers, societies for the encouragement of pilgrimages, and so on), the graves of female saints now have many visitors. It is interesting to note that in addition to organizations that arrange trips to the graves of saints in general, certain women's groups arrange visits for women only, and only to the graves of female saints.[1] From the standpoint of popularity, Rachel's tomb near Bethlehem has received the greatest publicity. It is the best known site today, as it was in the past, among Jews both in Israel and in the Diaspora. Many anecdotes and commentaries stress Rachel's concern for her sons and her intervention on their behalf with the Almighty. One of the customs associated with the graves of saints, and above all with Rachel's tomb, is to encircle the grave with a silken thread and then tie the same thread around a sickbed as a get-well charm. It may also be tied around a virgin's stomach to ensure that she will marry, or around that of a barren woman who hopes to give birth.

In countries where both Jews and Muslims revere numerous saints, one might expect to find many female saints. With the exception of Morocco, however, this expectation is not borne out. The present study netted the names of twenty-five women whose graves are visited and who are the objects of a certain amount of veneration. Usually called Lalla, Imma or Bent, they represent close to four percent of all saints worshipped by the Jews of Morocco. The variable stature of different holy women parallels that of male saints. Lalla Sol Ha-Tsaddiqah, for example, is revered nationally—not only by the Jews of Morocco, but by Jews abroad as well. Other female saints are recognized in specific regions, sometimes only by the inhabitants of certain villages—or even by no more than a few families. Lalla Sol Ha-Tsaddiqah and some others are highly respected not only by women, but also by men who recognize their power and greatness. Nevertheless, the typical process by which several obscure male saints acquired country-wide renown generally did not operate in the case of holy women. Only a historic event or an impressive achievement, as in the case of Lalla Sol Ha-Tsaddiqah, could make a female saint nationally famous.

Contrary to tradition for male saints, *hillulot* are seldom celebrated in honor of holy women and synagogues are not built in their names. Pilgrimage of several days, as it was known in Morocco, to the shrines of male saints, did not occur to the sanctuaries of female saints. It seems that the relationship of the devouts with the female saints was more of a personal character, manifested by visits to the sanctuary to petition the saint, when all the known rituals of prayer near the grave, candle-lighting, *se'udah* and so on, took place.

The central problem is to find a satisfactory explanation for the existence in Morocco of an extensive cult of female saints venerated by men as well as women. The traditional affinity for famous women characteristic of the Biblical and Talmudic periods was undoubtedly a contributory element, but it is not solely responsible for the phenomenon. If it were, we should also find extensive veneration of female saints in other centers of Jewry (outside of Persia). It is common knowledge that the Babylonian custom of permitting women to study the written Bible held sway in Spain. The Sephardic Jewess was much more involved in community life than was the Ashkenazi Jewess. Many poems written by Jews in Spain are in praise of women. But this, too, fails to explain the Moroccan phenomenon: there were no cults of holy women in other Sephardic communities, such as those in Salonica or Constantinople. Significantly, the Jewish women in Morocco, like the Sephardic women in the Jewish Diaspora, played an active role in ceremonies and festivities of the cycle of the year. They were also very important participants in nuptial and bereavement ceremonies, for which they created almost all known secular poems and *romances*.

The intense involvement and participation of Moroccan women in everything connected with the cult of sainthood and pilgrimage, as well as in the creation of a voluminous body of poetry and the creation and propagation of an extensive hagiographic literature, undoubtedly laid the groundwork for the burgeoning of female Jewish saints. In addition, the existence and great popularity throughout North Africa of a number of female Muslim saints no doubt afforded an appropriate background for such development. The strong cultural interaction, characteristic of relations between Jews and Muslims in North Africa on other levels, was felt in this sphere, too. The case of Cahena, the Jewish queen of Berber extraction who lived at the end of the seventh century, is a legendary example of cultural exchange.[2]

The outstanding features of female saints from the Biblical and Talmudic periods also play a part here. Some female saints are known by virtue of their connection with a male saint; these include Lalla Saʿada, wife of R. Eliyahu, and Lalla Kherwiʿa, wife of R. David Ben-Yamin. On the other hand, the fame of Lalla Sol Ha-Tsaddiqah—attributable to her martyrdom—and of saints such as Bent El-Ḥmus, El-Khwatat, Lalla Luna Bat-Khalifa, Lalla Rḥima Ha-Cohanit, indicates a clear tendency for women to acquire sainthood by virtue of their own good deeds and special qualities.

In summary, one may assume that a combination of the high regard in which Jewry holds women, together with the background of Berber and Arab women's roles in the creation of saints in North Africa, contributed to the creation of this unique reality of Jewish female saints in Morocco. The emergence of learned women and female poets[3] in recent years has further reinforced this tendency.

83. Bent El-Ḥmus (Taourirt)

83.1 "There was a female saint in the town of Taourirt. Several rabbis, including the grandfather of my father, R. Makhluf and R. Yaʿaqob, as well as sages from Jerusalem, lodged in the home of a Jewish woman in Taourirt. Muslims came and falsely accused the rabbis of giving wine to Muslims and arrested them [the rabbis]. This Jewish woman, who was named Bent El-Ḥmus, said to them: *Gentlemen, if you will promise me Paradise, I shall tell them that I gave the* *wine.* They agreed. They took her to the Muslims and said that she had given the Muslims wine. The Muslims said this was a lie and that they were telling it to go free. They answered: *If you want us, we are in your hands.* The Jewish woman convinced them that she had sold the wine, and she was killed by the Muslims. After she was buried, a spring welled up near her grave."

84. El-Khwatat (Talate)

These are two saints, called "the two sisters," whose real names are unknown. According to tradition, they were well-known in their lifetime for their acts of charity. Any poor person who came to their house received from one sister a glass of oil and from the other a portion of fat. It seems they lived very long ago. They are buried in Talate, near Ait El-Cohen.[4] Their tombs are unusually large, and thus impressive from the perspective of their believers.[5] They are venerated by the Muslims also.

85. Imma Esther (Mogador)

The full name of "Mother Esther" was Esther Arobaz. She was buried in the local cemetary.

85.1 "I remember, when I was young, the house of my aunt was inundated by the sea. All called her Imma Esther. Every time workers went past the cemetery, one would say to the other: *Let us go and visit the grave of Imma Esther.*"

86. Lalla Brali (Ntifa)

This saint was known as a very righteous person who loved and cared for the poor.

87. Lalla Cohen (Fez)

She is buried in the local cemetery near her husband, R. Ḥayyim Cohen.[6] The *hillulah* in the honor of both is celebrated at the cemetery on *Lag b'Omer.*

88. Lalla Kherwiʿa (Beni Mellal)

Her name is derived from the name of a tree that grows near the grave of her husband, R. David Ben-Yamin.[7] According to tradition, she is buried near him.

89. Lalla Luna Bat-Khalifa (Rabat)

This saint became famous for her devotion to R. Yehudah Gadol Gilʿad during his lifetime and after his death.

89.1 "There was a female saint in Rabat named Lalla Luna Bat-Khalifa. She took care of the saint named R. Yehudah Gadol Gilʿad. When he died, she took care of his tombstone. She was 130 years old at the time of her death. Her grave was visited because she had taken care of the saint. She could heal people, especially [their] throats by grace of R. Yehudah Gadol Gilʿad. She treated them with saliva."

90. Lalla Mima (Tabia)

This saint is buried near her husband, R. Yisra'el Cohen, in the region of Tabia near Tilouine.

90.1 "My father came here [to Israel] and left me in my mother's womb. When the emissary of my grandfather, my mother's father, came to get the writ of divorce from him and told him that my mother had given birth to a baby girl, my father asked that the girl be named after R. Yisra'el's wife, therefore they called me Mima."

91. Lalla Miryam (Ntifa)

Known also as Lalla Miryam Ha-Tsaddiqah or Mamma Miryam, this saint had a *shammash* (caretaker), who was particularly close to her, and could not leave her without special permission. From the following story, it is apparent that a female saint had the same prerogatives and authority as a male saint.

91.1 "My mother became paralyzed in her hands and legs. I was still young. My mother was bedridden. They took her to the saint [to Lalla Miryam]. They stayed there seven days. One night, the saint came along with a woman doctor to take my mother to a spring. There she asked her to rub her hands and legs. Next day she got better and stood up on both legs. She dreamt of Lalla Miryam in the form of a nurse. They used to visit her grave. My brother was her caretaker. His name was Y. M. He wanted to come here [to Israel]. He sold everything. This was Passover Eve. Suddenly, a Jew appeared to him in a dream at night, in Casablanca, where he saw a woman shouting and crying. When people asked her [why], she told them: *Y. M. wants to leave me without my permission!*"

91.2 "Lalla Miryam Ha-Tsaddiqah, both Jews and Muslims visit her grave. She is from our village Ntifa. She is buried in Muslim surroundings. We used to visit that place, where Jews and Muslims are buried."[8]

92. Lalla Qafia (Anzour)

According to tradition, the saint is buried under a large stone near the grave of Sidi Bu-ʿAissa U-Sliman, who is believed to be her father.[9] The stone itself is called Lalla Qafia.

92.1 "We used to slaughter near a stone called Lalla Qafia. A black stone. You can slaughter even a hundred cows near it and not a drop of blood will leak from the stone; it drinks all the blood."

92.2 "There are two graves there. You slaughter there on that same stone a hundred sheep or a hundred bulls or even three hundred sheep, and you do not see even a drop of blood, even if you want the blood for medicine. If you slaughter a hundred thousand sheep there, no drop of blood will remain. All is absorbed and the place is clean. This stone is called Lalla Qafia."

93. Lalla Rḥima Ha-Cohanit (Iguidi)

More often called Imma Rḥima Ha-Cohanit, this saint was renowned for her great righteousness. According to tradition, seven of her sons are buried near her tomb. The Jews used to visit her grave, slaughter there, and prepare ritual meals. The *hillulah* in her honor is celebrated on the 7th of *Adar.*

94. Lalla Rivqah of Bene-Moshe (Marrakech)

Lalla Rivqah is a member of the Ait Bene-Moshe (Sons of Moses). According to a Moroccan Jewish tradition, the Bene-Moshe are contemporaries of Moses; they live in a closed society, and come to the aid of the Jews in times of trouble. Lalla Rivqah is also venerated by the

Muslims, who call her Sidi Bel-ʿAbbas (which is also the name of the Muslim patron saint of Marrakech).

94.1 "It happened in Marrakech and the saint is called Sidi Bel-ʿAbbas Shabbati. And the story goes like this: Once there was a Jewish apostate, who was the vizier of the king of Marrakech. One day, passing by Jewish villages, the vizier heard voices calling: *One of you will put to flight one thousand, and two [of you], ten thousand!* That is what this bastard, the apostate, told him [the king]. The king said: *What?* He [the vizier] answered: *The time will come when one of them will put to flight one thousand, and two [of them], ten thousand.* He [the king] said: *We want to know how they can do such a thing!* Then the vizier went to the Jews, and said: *I want to see one of you do such a thing!* At that time there was a rabbi who pronounced the Divine Name and went to the Bene-Moshe. . . . They say that there is a river, the Sambation, and by it they determine when it is *Sabbath* and when it is not. All the week it [the river] is fire, and on *Sabbath* stones come down. This is how they determine the *Sabbath.* It [the river] cannot be forded, and they say this is the place where the Bene-Moshe are to be found, and one of them can put to flight a thousand, and two [of them], ten thousand. So how to bring them? R. Yitsḥaq pronounced the Divine Name and went to them. He said: *Gentlemen, the Jews are in trouble. Do you want to send someone? If so, send someone. If not, the king will annihilate us!* So they had a lottery and the task fell to a woman, called Rivqah. He brought her and he said to them: *Gentlemen, one of these people is coming. Ready your soldiers!* They readied their soldiers. She rode a horse. She rode through one place and killed a thousand, she rode through another place and killed ten thousand. Since then we call the place *Zmaʿa Alfnah,* because so many people were killed there. The place was full of corpses. Suddenly her brother Yitsḥaq appeared and told her: *Rivqah, the Arabs saw your hands, and you must die!* They took her. She was called Sidi Bel-ʿAbbas Shabbati, meaning 'one of the persons of the *Sabbath.*' To this very day, Jews as well as Arabs visit the place."[10]

95. Lalla Saʿada (Casablanca)

According to one tradition, Lalla Saʿada was the wife of R. Eliyahu, buried in Casablanca; another tradition has it that she was a member of the Oḥana family.

95.1 "There was a female saint in Casablanca named Lalla Saᶜada. She was buried next to R. Eliyahu, side by side. We used to visit their tombs. When they moved the grave, they dug up the whole plot and buried them side by side in the new cemetery. Go see her wonderful deeds!"

95.2 "Lalla Saᶜada was the wife of R. Eliyahu. Of course she was a saint! They buried all bones in the new cemetery."

95.3 "Lalla Saᶜada Oḥana was buried near R. Eliyahu. She was a saint. Her grandson was a saint and her father was a saint as well. The Oḥana family. She was buried near R. Eliyahu. Then they took him [R. Eliyahu] and Lalla Saᶜada and the grandson and buried them in the new cemetery. Lalla Saᶜada was charitable and used to give alms, and she would never get involved in the affairs of others."

96. Lalla Saᶜada Alfassi (Aghbalou)

She is buried at the entrance of the synagogue in Aghbalou near Ourika, the site of the grave of R. Shelomoh Ben-Lḥans. There is a place to light candles near her tomb. The Hebrew inscription on her grave reads: "Tombstone of the righteous old woman Saᶜada Alfassi: she was a midwife, a member of the Burial Society and caretaker of the grave of R. Shelomoh Ben-Lḥans. She died on the 23rd of *Shebat* 5738. May her soul be bound in the bonds of eternal life."[11]

97. Lalla Saᶜada Bent-Ashqluḥ (Tasdremt)[12]

She is buried in the cemetery of Tasdremt, near Telouet. This very ancient cemetery is in the hills. There are no inscriptions on the graves. Tradition says that most of the graves belong to the Jewish Ashqluḥ family. The exact place of Lalla Saᶜada's grave is not known, and thus people make their pilgrimage to the cemetery as a whole.

Lalla Saᶜada was well-known for her acts of charity. According to tradition, she would make many pairs of shoes every week (thirty-six pairs in one version, one hundred pairs in another version) and sell them on Friday: all the money went to the poor. The epoch in which Lalla Saᶜada lived is not known. She was also venerated by the Muslims.

98. Lalla Safia (Agadir)

She is buried in a room in an old abandoned Jewish cemetery near Agadir.[13] The Muslims claim her as a Muslim saint, the daughter of Sidi Brahim U-ʿAli U-Tralimin, a famous saint of the Ida U-Tanan, and the sister of Lalla Yamin, buried in the kasba of Agadir. But they cannot explain why Lalla Safia is buried in a Jewish cemetery. Although the Jews claim that she is a Jewish saint, they do not interfere with the visits of Muslims to the site.

99. Lalla Safia (Souk El-Khemis)

This saint is buried in a high mountain not far from the grave of Mulay Yaʿqub,[14] who according to tradition is her father.

99.1 "I also went up to Lalla Safia. I climbed to her in the same way you climb a wall. And I was pregnant. There is a steep ascent, and if one falls there, nothing remains of him. I went up there with two men. I had no boys [only girls]. They told me to go there on pilgrimage to stop giving birth to baby girls. They take a string from the belt and bind it to her [around the grave]; they light candles there and go down. She is near Mulay Yaʿqub. We would bathe in Mulay Yaʿqub's springs and say 'Lalla Safia.' The Arabs don't go up there. Only the Jews go. They say that she is a Jew. They call her Lalla Safia Ha-Tsaddiqah like Lalla Solica Ha-Tsaddiqah. The sick and the people with no strength go there and are cured. Also a barren woman, she goes up to Lalla Safia and starts giving birth. She takes a string from her belt and leaves it on the grave. There is no tombstone there, only a large stone on which small stones like paving tiles are scattered. They light candles among the small stones. The place is not covered; it is in the open air, in the mountain. When you go up, you see mountains around on all sides. When you go down, you do not forget to say the name of any saint until you arrive successfully on the ground.[15] I made a bet with a man from Meknes who stayed with us in the rooms. He asked: *Which woman is strong enough to get up at four o'clock in the morning to go up to Lalla Safia?* [You go very early in the morning] because it is difficult to climb the mountain when it is very hot. I said: *I'll go up with you.* He said: *And if not?* I said: *If not, don't call me a woman!* I said to him: *I'll go up and I'll take my daughter on my back!* He said to me: *You are likely to kill your daughter and yourself as well.* I said to him: *If we die, then together.* I put her on my back and bound her with a sheet. We went up there. He went first and I followed him, until we arrived there. As soon as we arrived, I put her down. The people who remained down below cheered and applauded. When we came down, they received us with joy."

100. Lalla Setti Ben-Sasso (Rabat)

She is also called Imma Setti. She was known for her great righteousness.

100.1 "Every Thursday, she used to bake a loaf of bread as big as four loaves. The man who collected the alms for the poor every week received from her a loaf of bread that had the weight of four loaves. This *paqid* went with a porter from door to door. When he arrived at the door of Imma Setti, he would call: *Imma Setti, ask for mercy upon us!* She was ninety-four years old. Once David B. said to her: *Imma Setti, instead of baking such a loaf of bread, you should bake four loaves.* She replied: *You should not say such a thing to me. I want to give the poor person a loaf of bread that will satisfy him and his children.* She used to come to *bar-mitswah* and circumcision celebrations. *Has Elijah the Prophet already arrived?* she would ask. *Good, I'm coming, Elijah will arrive with me.* All respected her. When she died, people started to visit her grave."

101. Lalla Simḥa Ruben (Tazenakht)

This saint is buried in a mountain near Anrhaz, not far from Tazenakht.

101.1 "Lalla Simḥa Ruben was a saint. She was Jewish. The Muslims also called her Lalla Simḥa Ruben. I did not visit her grave. Who is able to climb that mountain?"

102. Lalla Sol Ha-Tsaddiqah (Fez)[16]

Sol Ḥatshuel, also known as Sol Ḥachuel, Ḥatchuel or Ḥatuel, the daughter of Ḥayyim and Simḥa, was born in Tangier in 1817. She is usually referred to as Sol Ha-Tsaddiqah (Sol the Saint) or Lalla Solica, and is the most famous female saint among Jews as well as Muslims in Morocco.

Versions of the story of her martyrdom are very widespread among the Jews of Morocco.[17] The historical facts are linked to the year 1834. Sol, a young girl of extraordinary beauty, was accused by her Muslim neighbor (a woman), of having embraced and then repudiated Islam. The governor of the city of Tangier had her arrested and sent her to the king in Fez for sentencing. She was condemned to death and executed. The Jews of Fez built her a special tomb.[18]

102.1 "Lalla Solica is [buried] in our cemetery, near R. Abner Ha-Tsarfati. We used to pray to her and light candles and say: *Lalla Solica, we beg you, have mercy upon us, heal us!* We used to beg all the saints! We celebrated her *hillulah* by lighting candles and singing to the skies. She was a God-fearing saint. She was something special, and she was learned in the *Torah.* They used to say that Lalla Solica is like 'Our Mother Rachel' [the Matriarch]. They would light candles on her tomb. R. Abner Ha-Tsarfati and R. El-Kebir Ben-ʿAttar were buried near her. We went every week, because it was near by. People would stay there late to read [Psalms]. They used to say that the *shekhinah* would descend upon those three graves."

102.2 "In Fez, [at the tomb of] Lalla Solica something happened to me. I had a son who is now twenty-four years old. When he was born, he weighed only one kilogram and 200 grams. There was a Dr. Ḥassin in Fez. The mother [my wife] took the child to him. The doctor told her that the child would not live, even if he would have the right treatment. The child was nothing but skin and bones. Injections didn't do him a bit of good. He stayed like that for seven months. The doctor marveled that he was still alive. I had a tailor shop, and we were a large family. Once I was sitting in the shop. It was in the month of *Ab* and it was hot. I went home to eat and I saw the boy there, in terrible shape. I thought: *He hasn't got a chance. I'll try the merit of the saints!* Because I placed my trust in them. I didn't eat lunch. I put the child in a basket. I covered him with a sheet and took him at noon, when it was very hot. I said: *Whatever will be will be! I am certain the saints will help, with God's help!* I took him to our tombs. There is a niche where they light candles. Lalla Solica had a large niche, and opposite her was R. Yehudah Ben-ʿAttar. Between them was a spring. So I took the child and put him inside the niche for the candles, and said: *Lalla Solica, if he is meant for this world, heal him, but if not, do as you wish!* I went to a corner and sat down there in the cemetery. Even during the day people are afraid to go there. But I was a member of the Burial Society, so I said to myself: *I have nothing to fear!* I sat there for three hours. My wife came home and started to look for the child. She even thought a cat had taken him, because he was so small. Three hours later I went there [to the niche], and I thought he was dead. But when I got [close], he smiled at me and waved his hands and feet. I took him to the spring and washed him and brought him back home in the basket. I got home and found everyone looking for the boy. They didn't know he was in the basket. I told them the whole story. That day I told my wife to make him some food, even though the doctor had forbidden it. From that time on, she gave him food and he ate with relish. I told my wife not to take him to the doctor anymore. He ate whatever we ate. Afterwards, when the doctor saw him, he was amazed and asked which doctor I had taken him to. I told him: *The doctor is the saints!* In less than a year he weighed four-and-a-half kilograms. And that was just fine. Now he is grown up and has never visited a doctor. During the war, his vehicle turned over three times, and each time he got up [unscathed] and never even went to a doctor."

102.3 "Lalla Solica once returned home, but instead of going into her father's house, she went into an Arab's house by mistake. The Muslim wanted her to be his daughter. She answered: *God forbid that the Devil should tempt me!* May she rest in peace! He kept trying to persuade her until he killed her. She herself gave him the knife so that he should kill her. She said to him: *You may kill me, but I shall not change my religion! I am a pure saint! I shall not marry a bastard, the son of a bastard!*"

102.4 "I named my daughter after her. My other daughters all died in infancy. They came and told me to take the girl and place her on [the tomb of] Lalla Solica. I went on a pilgrimage. I lit candles and said: *Lalla Solica! Grant life to what I have in my belly! If it is a girl, I'll put her in a dress; if it is a boy, I'll put him in a suit. And now have mercy on me!* And that's how it was. My daughter survived! Every time I went to Fez, I took my daughter and I lit many candles at the gravestone of Lalla Solica."

102.5 "I heard that she got into trouble with her mother. The Muslims spread the rumor that the Jewish girl had sworn by the name of Moḥammed. They caught her and they say that she was beautiful.

The sultan wanted to marry her and promised her many things, if she would marry him. She replied: *No!* On the Eve of the 9th of *Ab* [commemoration of the destruction of the Temple of Jerusalem], they mention her name in a dirge. And they say she chose to have her head cut off rather than marry the king."

103. Lalla Solica Wᶜaqnin (Tikhirat)

She was renowned for her extreme devotion to people.

103.1 "Lalla Solica Wᶜaqnin, the mother of the Ait Daḥu family. There was not a woman *tsaddiqah* like her. She fasted constantly. Once she fasted sixty times, each time for sixty days in a row. In that village Tikhirat. She was a fine person, a saint according to her deeds. Her sons were merchants. In her room she kept boxes named after about forty saints. Every time a caravan of Jews came to Tikhirat, she would lodge them, letting them wash their hands, eat and sleep. She would take care of them by herself. She knew well all the Jews in the village and every holiday eve she gave [alms] to the needy. She was a saintly person. Do you know people who do the same? She would look after a rabbi or a student who came to the village: she would wash his clothes, help him. She was old, she was eighty, and behaved the same way until her death. She also died on a Friday. They buried her and the sun stood still until they finished the burial ceremony. Before she died, she called her sons and told them that in the box of R. Shelomoh Ben-Yitsḥaq there is such and such an amount, in the box of R. Shelomoh Ben-Lḥans there is this amount, in the box of R. Ḥananiah Ha-Cohen there is this and this amount, in the box of R. Yosef Pinto there is so much, in the box of R. David Ben-Barukh there is this and this amount. And in her room the boxes in the name of the saints stood one alongside the other. She always went barefoot. When she died, the people started to visit her grave. . . . So it happened that when she died they found [in the boxes] the amounts of money that she had said. When somebody was in need of a loan, she would lend him the money from the box of R. Shelomoh Ben-Yitsḥaq. She would lend the money and ask the borrower to return the amount that he had received, and add more after some months. She had trust in them. She said to them that the money does not belong to her, but to the saints. That is what she said to those who came to ask for a loan."

104. Lalla Taqerquzt (Takerkouzt)[19]

There is a spring at the site that expands into a brook and then forms a pond bearing the name of the saint. The pond is full of turtles.[20] Lalla Taqerquzt is claimed by both Jews and Muslims, although many Jews recognize that she was a Muslim.

104.1 "There is a stream of water there. You see the water and suddenly it disappears and then appears. They say there was a girl, they don't know whether she was Jewish or Muslim. She is buried at the foot of the mountain. You see only heaps of stones. People do not cross the place, and if they do, they say: *Lalla Taqerquzt is over there.* That's all. I have not seen a place to light candles. There is no sign that people light candles there."

105. Lalla Tsaddiqah (Imi n'Timouga)

The saint's real name is not known.

105.1 "Our forefathers told that Lalla Tsaddiqah is buried there. We used to visit her grave. When I was young, my mother took me there. She said: *B-el-Lah u-b-elʿnaya* [*in the name of God and Providence*]. They called her Lalla Tsaddiqah. She is very ancient. Only our forefathers remembered her."

Notes

1. A brochure distributed in Jerusalem in 1992 (most of it in English, with some Hebrew) states: "A full Day's Travel and Prayer at the Tombs of our Foremothers in the Galilee . . . Women only . . . Mother Path in the Land . . . Devorah, the Prophetess, Yael, Yocheved Bat Levi, Zipporah, Wife of Moshe Rabenu, Elisheva, Wife of Aaron the Priest, Bilhah, Zilpah, Rachel, Wife of Rabbi Akiva, Dina, Daughter of Ya'akov Avinu." According to the chief organizer, men do not pay enough attention to the graves of female saints. In another bulletin entitled "Information regarding Customs & Laws while visiting Gravesites" (all in English), travelers are given general information pertaining to pilgrimages and visits to cemeteries. In the situation prevailing in Israel today, where traditions of different ethnic groups come together, the need occasionally arises to offer pilgrims guidance. Therefore, together with copious material in praise of saints and the miracles they

perform, pamphlets, guidebooks and other works are published about pilgrimages and relevant customs.

2. A. Chouraqui (1985, pp. 84–86); R. Attal (1973, p. xxiii).
3. J. Chétrit (1980, pp. 84–93). Concerning the contribution of Jewish women to poetry in Morocco, see J. Chétrit (1994).
4. L. Voinot (1948, p. 80) suggests that the two sainted sisters belonged to the family of Ait El-Cohen of Talate.
5. Near the tomb of R. David Naḥmias (Tazda) there are two 3-meter long graves in which two sainted Jewish brothers, also venerated by the Muslims, are said to be buried: L. Voinot (1948, p. 80).
6. R. Ḥayyim Cohen died in 1925. For information about him see: I. Ben-Ami (1984, pp. 359–60); Y. Benaim (1931, pp. 39–41); L. Brunot and E. Malka (1939, p. 277).
7. According to L. Voinot (1948, p. 57), the Muslims gave the name of the tree to R. David Ben-Yamin.
8. The fact that the saint is buried in Muslim surroundings indicates that the grave is very ancient and that in the interim the Jews left the place.
9. According to tradition, the saint Sidi Bu-ʿAissa U-Sliman and his two sainted brothers R. Yitsḥaq Ben-Sliman and Sidi Ftaḥ Ben-Sliman are the sons of King Salomon. They are venerated by both Jews and Muslims. See I. Ben-Ami (1984, pp. 497–98); L. Voinot (1948, pp. 38–39).
10. A similar version of this story is given by M. Mazal-Tarim (1939, p. 97), who writes that it happened at the time of R. Yitsḥaq Deluya. See also D. Noy (1964, p. 29); J. Lasri (1978, pp. 122–24).
11. The French inscription says: "Saada El Fassie decedée le 31.1.78 à l'age de 80." Lalla Saʿada's son and his wife were the caretakers of the grave when I visited it in 1981.
12. See L. Voinot (1948, pp. 69–70).
13. L. Voinot (1948, pp. 18–19) says that the old cemetery is found near the ravine that separates Founti from the Valley of Talbordj. According to our informant, the cemetery is situated between Taroudant and Agadir.
14. The saint Mulay Yaʿqub is venerated by both Jews and Muslims. He is buried in a Muslim area; the Jews could not visit his grave and bathe in the springs there without permission. See I. Ben-Ami (1984, pp. 451–52); L. Voinot (1948, p. 22).
15. The informant means that people called upon all the saints for help, because of the danger.
16. Much has been written about Lalla Sol Ha-Tsaddiqah. See Y. Benaim (1931, pp. 126–30); L. Voinot (1948, pp. 50–51); E. Doutté (1900,

p. 69); J. M. Toledano (1972, p. 254); E. Aubin (1904, p. 376); L. Brunot and E. Malka (1939, pp. 213–17); G. Vajda (1951, p. 100); E. Montet (1909, p. 55); N. Banon (1981, p. 373); I. Bendahan (s.d. *La heroína hebrea. Sol "la Saddika"* [drama histórico en prosa y verso en cinco actos]. Larache); A. Elmaleḥ (*Iyyar* 1946. "Sol Ha-Tsaddiqah." *Hed Hamizraḥ,* pp. 6–7); R. Boutet (31 July 1929 to 16 January 1930. "Sulika ou la vie de Sol Hatchuel." *Avenir Illustré*); A. Calle (1852. *El martírio de la joven Hachuel, o la heroína hebrea* [drama]. Seville); H. Iliowizi (1883. *Sol, an epic poem.* Minneapolis); Isidore Loeb (1880. "Une martyre juive au Maroc (1834)—Sol Hatchuel." *Archives Israélites,* vol. 41, pp. 181–97); E. Sumel (1858. *La heroína hebrea (Sol Hachuel).* Gibraltar); R. Tadjouri (30 April 1928. "Sol, la 'Sadiqa.' " *Avenir Illustré,* 3rd year, no. 15–16, pp. 4–6). Sol Ha-Tsaddiqah was also worshipped by the Muslims. The Catholic priest L. Godard (1859) claims the saint was a Catholic.

17. Several versions of Lalla Solica's martyrdom are known. Y. Benaim (1931, pp. 126–30) adopts the Muslim version that her mother, Fadina, beat her, and gives many details that appeared in an old manuscript. All versions agree on the fact that, even under pressure from her parents, the king, his son, and the rabbi, the saint refused to repudiate Judaism, preferring to die rather than give up her religion.
18. L. Voinot (1948, p. 50) gives a detailed description of the tomb. During my visit there in 1981, I copied the bilingual—Hebrew and French—inscription on the grave. The French inscription says: "Ici repose Mlle Solica Hatchouel. Nee a Tanger en 1817. Refusant de rentrer dans la religion islamisme les arabes l'ont assassinee a Fez en 1834 arrachee de sa famille tout le monde regrette cette enfant Sainte" (sic).
19. See E. Doutté (1914, p. 222); E. Dermenghem (1954, p. 146); L. Voinot (1948, p. 43); E. Westermarck (1926, vol. 1, p. 86).
20. Visitors used to slaughter at the spring and throw the meat to the turtles: see L. Voinot (1948, p. 44); E. Westermarck (1926, vol. 1, p. 86). L. Voinot tells of a tradition according to which at the end of the nineteenth century the turtles disappeared once for a period of three years because of a visit by a disguised Jew.

DATES OF THE *HILLULAH*

Tishri

8th *Tishri*	R. Abner Ha-Tsarfati
11th *Tishri*	R. Moshe Elbaz, R. Pinḥas El-Cohen, R. Shalom Zaʿafrani
23rd *Tishri*	R. Masʿud Bitton
26th *Tishri*	R. Eliyahu Abiḥatsira (Erfoud)
After *Sukkot*	Buri Khizo

Ḥeshwan

1st *Ḥeshwan*	R. David U-Moshe, R. Ḥayyim Cohen, Sepher Tislit
4th *Ḥeshwan*	R. Yosef Gabbay
15th *Ḥeshwan*	R. David Oḥnona
16th *Ḥeshwan*	R. Ḥayyim Pinto (Casablanca)
26th *Ḥeshwan*	R. Abba Abiḥatsira

Note: When the day of the saint's death is not known, the *hillulah* is usually celebrated on *Lag bʿOmer.* Sometimes, as in the case of R. ʿAmram Ben-Diwan, the central *hillulah* is celebrated on *Lag bʿOmer,* despite the fact that it is known that he died on the 15th of *Ab.* In addition, people went on pilgrimage to the holy graves in several fixed periods of the year, such as *Sukkot, Pesaḥ* and during the month of *Elul,* independently of the anniversary day of the saint's death.

Nowadays several *hillulot* are celebrated in Israel with a very large number of participants of North African origin:

R. Yisra'el Abiḥatsira—Baba Sale (Netivot)—4th *Shebat*
R. Yitsḥaq Abiḥatsira (Ramleh)—25th *Adar*
R. Meir Abiḥatsira—17th *Nisan*
Ḥoni Ha-meʿaggel (Galilean Hatsor)—5th *Iyyar* (Independence Day)
R. Ḥayyim Ḥuri (Beersheba)—25th *Iyyar*
Rabban Gamliel (Yavneh)—18th *Siwan*
R. Moshe Aharon Pinto (Kiriyat Malakhi)—5th *Elul*

Kislew

14th *Kislew*	R. David Abiḥatsira
15th *Kislew*	R. Raphael Aben-Tsur
25th *Kislew*	R. Eleʿazar Ha-Cohen (Iguenisaine)
28th *Kislew*	R. Yosef Knafo
29th *Kislew*	R. Shalom Zawi
Ḥanukkah	R. Aharon Assulin (Fercla), R. Yehudah Ben-Shabbat

Tebet

1st *Tebet*	Ait El-Cohen (Imini), R. Makhluf Ben-Yosef Abiḥatsira
2nd *Tebet*	R. Abraham Cohen Bu-Dwaya, R. Yosef Dayyan (Beni Hayoun)
3rd *Tebet*	R. Abraham Wazana, R. David Ben-Barukh (Azrou n'Bahamou)
10th *Tebet*	R. Eleʿazar Ha-Cohen (Aiounil)
14th *Tebet*	R. Abraham Turjman, R. Pinḥas Ha-Cohen
16th *Tebet*	R. Moshe Ḥaliwa
19th *Tebet*	R. David Perets (Telouet)
20th *Tebet*	R. Yaʿaqob Abiḥatsira

Shebat

14th *Shebat*	R. Yitsḥaq Abiḥatsira
15th *Shebat*	R. Aharon Assulin (Tinejdad), Bu-Sherif, R. Nwasser
23rd *Shebat*	Lalla Saʿada Alfassi
25th *Shebat*	R. Yannay Mul Lmekhfiya

Adar

1st *Adar*	R. Raḥamim Mizraḥi
2nd *Adar*	R. Barukh Assabagh
3rd *Adar*	R. Eliʿezer Davila
7th *Adar*	Lalla Rḥima Ha-Cohanit
9th *Adar*	R. Yitsḥaq Ben-Walid
14th *Adar (Purim)*	R. Eliʿezer Turei-Zahav, R. Yaḥya Laḥlu
24th *Adar*	Tsaddiq Azru

Nisan

8th *Nisan*	R. Moshe Ben-Yaᶜaqob Ḥayon
10th *Nisan*	R. David Elqayim
23rd *Nisan* *(Mimuna)*	R. Abraham Makhluf Ben-Yaḥya, R. Raphael Ha-Cohen (Achbarou), Tsaddiqe ᶜAyn Um-Krima

Iyyar

6th *Iyyar*	R. Yosef Ben-ᶜAttar
12th *Iyyar*	R. Masᶜud Abiḥatsira
18th *Iyyar* *(Lag b'Omer)*	R. Abraham Awriwer, R. Abraham Darᶜi, R. ᶜAmram Ben-Diwan, R. David Alshqar, R. David Ben-Safet (Marrakech), R. David Ben-Yamin, R. David Bussidan, Bu-Izzo Elbaz, R. Eliyahu Azulay, R. Eliyahu Demnati, R. Ḥayyim Amuyal, R. Ḥayyim Ben-Diwan, R. Hodi Elbaz, Lalla Cohen, R. Levi Ben-Levi, Mulay Igui, Mul El-Ḥazra El-Menzura, Mul El-Karma, Mul Timḥdart, R. Mussa Ben-Yishay, R. Nissim Ben-Nissim (Ait Bayoud), R. Raphael Anqawa, R. Raphael Berdugo, R. Shelomoh Asbaᶜ Boḥbot, R. Yaḥya Ben-Yaḥya (Boujad), R. Yaḥya El-Khdar, R. Yehudah Qadosh, R. Yitsḥaq Ha-Levi (Imi n'Tanoute)

Siwan

6th *Siwan* *(Shabuᶜot)*	R. David Ha-Levi Draᶜ
18th *Siwan*	R. Yisra'el Abiḥatsira
19th *Siwan*	R. Yehudah Ben-ᶜAttar
28th *Siwan*	R. Raphael Maman

Tammuz

17th *Tammuz*	R. Eliyahu Dahan
18th *Tammuz*	R. Masᶜud Ben-Moḥa
22nd *Tammuz*	R. Raphael Moshe Elbaz

Ab

4th *Ab*	R. Raphael Anqawa
15th *Ab*	R. ʿAmram Ben-Diwan, R. Yehudah Pinto
21st *Ab*	R. Meir Ben-Lolo

Elul

1st *Elul*	R. Abraham Azulay (Iguenisaine), R. Daniel Hashomer Ashkenazi
3rd *Elul*	R. Barukh Ha-Cohen (Taroudant), R. Khalifa Ben-Malka
6th *Elul*	R. Moshe Ha-Cohen (Fez)
15th *Elul*	R. Abba, R. Masʿud Naḥmias (Tazda), R. Moshe Ibn-Ḥammu
22th *Elul*	R. Aharon Abiḥatsira
26th *Elul*	R. Abba Elbaz, R. Ḥayyim Pinto (Mogador)
Elul (?)	Ait Naḥmias, R. David Naḥmias, R. Eliyahu (Casablanca)

Morocco: Map of Jewish Saints

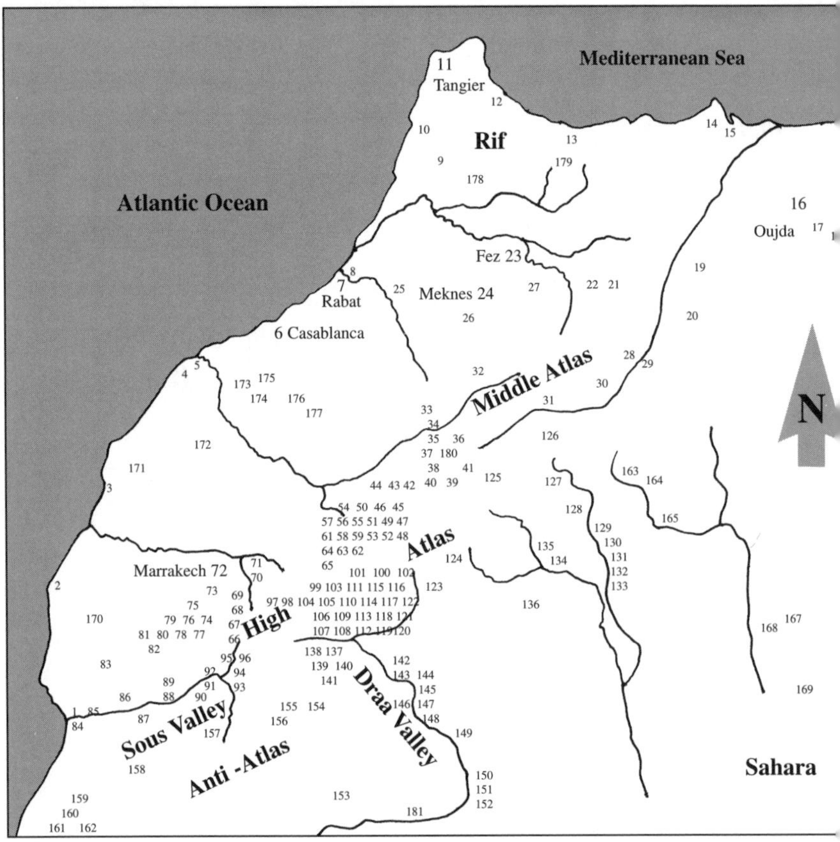

LIST OF SAINTS ACCORDING TO THEIR BURIAL PLACE

Achbarou (74): Raphael Ha-Cohen
Adig (102): Sidi Rghit
Agadir (1): Ḥayyim Ben-Shushan, Khalifa Ben-Malka, Lalla Safia, Nissim Afryat, Shelomoh Pinto, Yitsḥaq Afryat, Yosef Halaḥmi
Aghbalou (68): Lalla Saʿada Alfassi, Shelomoh Ben-Lḥans
Aghmat (61): Ait Bu-Aharon
Agourai (26): Makhluf Ben-Shetrit
Aguigal (153): Mul Aguiga
Aiounil (104): Eleʿazar Ha-Cohen
Ait Abbas (69*): Abraham Tangi, Shelomoh Tangi, Yosef Tangi
Ait Attab (41): Re'uben ʿAllu, Yosef Ben-ʿEli
Ait Bayoud (170): Abraham Abbetan, Eliyahu, Nissim Ben-Nissim, Yitsḥaq Ha-Levi
Ait Benhaddou (106): Shemuel Elḥadad
Ait Blal (50): Ḥayyim Waʿqnin
Ait Bou Dial (117): Abraham Wazana, David Wazana
Ait Bouguemes (48): Mul Taurirt, ʿObadiah Azulay
Ait Boujjou (38): Mulay Tamran
Ait Bou Hlau (107): ʿAremat Avanim
Ait Boulli (47): Ḥayyim Danino, ʿObadiah Ha-Levi, Yisra'el Danino
Ait Boulmane (31): Yaḥya Ben-Yosef
Ait Chaib (39): Mul El-Bit
Ait Hamza (42): Mulay Inguird
Ait Ourir (70): Ḥabib Ha-Mizraḥi
Ait Yaish (35): Abraham of Ait Yaʿish, Eliyahu Dahan, Shalom Dahan
Akka (146): Mordekhay Mul El-ʿAyn, Yehudah Ben-Ḥovav, Yissakhar Yisra'el

---

Note: The number in brackets indicates the localization of the burial place in the map of Morocco, opposite. The numbers marked with * indicate approximate localizations.

Amazrou (147): ʿAsarah Be-Kever
Amizmiz (77): Abraham Elmaleḥ, Makhluf, Raḥamim Eluq, Yehudah Elmaleḥ
Amzerkou (96): Ait El-Cohen
Amzouguin (137): Aharon Ha-Cohen, Moshe Ben-Shelomoh, Shelomoh Ben-Yitsḥaq
Anrhaz (66): Ḥayyim Ben-Diwan
Anzour (157): Lalla Qafia, Sidi Bu-ʿAissa U-Sliman
Aoulouz (92): Makhluf Ben-Yosef
Arba Touggana (63): Daniel Hashomer Ashkenazi, Shelomoh ʿAttar
Asni (67): Shalom Cohen
Assaka (154): Idbud Fassin
Assif El-Mal (78): Raphael Ben-Qas
Azemmour (5): Abraham Ben-Nathan, Abraham Mul Annes, Yossi Ha-Galili
Azjen (178): ʿAmram Ben-Diwan, David Cohen, Moshe El-Cohen
Azrou (32): Tsaddiq Azru
Azrou n'Bahamou (90): David Ben-Barukh
Bechar (167): Eliyahu Ha-Cohen, Ḥanina of Bechar, Shelomoh Bar-Beriro, Yisra'el Abiḥatsira, Yitsḥaq Bar-Beriro
Beni Hayoun (150): Yaʿaqob Dayyan, Yosef Dayyan
Beni Hmad (177): Cohanim, Yaḥya El-Khdar
Beni Mellal (37): David Ben-Yamin, Lalla Kherwiʿa, Shelomoh ʿAmar
Beni Sbih (151): Abraham Turjman, Ḥananiah Dayyan, Mordekhay Dayyan, Mordekhay Turjman, Mul Shejra
Boudenib (165): Abba Abiḥatsira, Yosef Dayyan
Bou Hallou (53): David Oḥnona, Moshe Ibn-Ḥammu, Mussa Ben-Yishay, Mwalin Bu-Ḥlu, Ulad Bu-Ḥlu, Yaʿaqob Sghir, Yannay Mul Lmekhfiya
Boujad (33): Bu-Izzo Elbaz, Eliyahu Demnati, Hodi Elbaz, Levi Ben-Levi, Shelomoh Asbaʿ Boḥbot, Shelomoh Ben-Levi, Shelomoh Ben-Lḥans, Yaḥya Ben-Sliman, Yaḥya Ben-Yaḥya, Yehudah Qadosh, Yisra'el Selluq, Yitsḥaq Ben-Levi, Yosef Gabbay
Bzou (43): Yitsḥaq Yisra'el Ha-Levi
Casablanca (6): Abraham Amselem, Abraham Yifraḥ, David Alshqar, David Dahan, David Danino, David Ḥadida, Eliyahu,

Ḥayyim Pinto, Ḥazzan Izzo, Lalla Saʿada, Masʿud Oḥana, Moshe Ḥay Elyaqim, Shelomoh ʿAllul, Sidi Belyut, Tsaddiqe ʿAyn Diab, Yitsḥaq Ben-Shetrit, Yitsḥaq Ḥadida, Yitsḥaq Qoriat

Cheriaa (14): Saʿadiah Dades

Dad (175): Abraham Awriwer, Nissim Ben-Nissim, Ulad Lyeshibah

Dades (124): David, Saʿadiah Ben-Yosef

Debdou (20): Ben-Zḥila, Daud Cohen, Moshe Mimun, Qayid El-Ghaba, Sayyid El-Merhirha, Shelomoh Ben-Zahir Cohen, Shelomoh Cohen Gadol, Shelomoh Mimun, Shemaʿyah Cohen, Sidi Moshe, Yitsḥaq El-Qansi, Yosef Ben-Bibi, Yosef Ben-Ghraba, Yosef Ben-Shemaʿyah, Yosef Ben-Wawa, Yosef Turjman

Demnate (51): Abraham Ḥamias, Aharon Ha-Cohen, David Dahan, David Danino, David Farḥi, Ḥayyim Boḥbot, Ḥazzan of Tirhermine, Mwalin El-Gomra, Shimʿon Elʿanqri, Sidi Mhasser, Sidi Mussa, Yaʿaqob Lḥor, Yeshuʿah Danino, Yitsḥaq Ben-Yamin, Yitsḥaq Ḥaziza, Yosef Cohen, Yosef Elmaleḥ, Yosef Ḥayyim Boḥbot, Yosef Melul

Djebel Bouiblan (21): Sidi Mussa U-Saleḥ

Douar Ait Ouaddi (36): Ḥayyim

Doukkala (172): Aharon Cohen

Draa (56): David Ha-Levi Draʿ, Yaʿaqob ʿAnido Ashkenazi, Yaʿish Bitton

Draa Valley (142): Baba Hena, Ulad Dayyan, Yitsḥaq Abettan

El Abid (40): Moshe Ben-Zohra

Erfoud (132): Eliyahu Abiḥatsira

Fercla (134): Aharon Assulin, Moshe Baya, Shelomoh Ben-Yaḥya, Shelomoh Ḥazzan

Fez (23): Abner Ha-Tsarfati, Aharon Monsonego, David Haqadmon, Ḥayyim Cohen, Iza Cohen, Lalla Cohen, Lalla Sol Ha-Tsaddiqah, Mattityahu Serero, Menashe Ibn-Danan, Moshe Ha-Cohen, Raphael Aben-Tsur, Sepher Zabaro, Shaul Serero, Shaul Serero, Shelomoh Ibn-Danan, Vidal Ha-Tsarfati, Yaʿaqob Qadosh, Yaʿaqob Qanizel, Yehonathan Serero, Yehudah Ben-ʿAttar

Figuig (166): Abraham Ben-Salem, Bene-Amuyal

Foum Djemaa (45): Yehudah Ben-Yisraʾel Ha-Levi

Foum el-Anser (180): Masʿud Ben-Ḥabib

Gourama (163): Hillel Ha-Galili, Makhluf Ha-Levi, Moshe Ben-Yaʿaqob Ḥayon
Ibaghaten (130*): Sidi Buzid
Ighi (101): Moshe, Mulay Ighi
Iguenisaine (64): Abraham Azulay, David Busqila, Eleʿazar Ben-ʿArakh, Eleʿazar Ha-Cohen, Meir Ben-Lolo, Raphael Ḥafota, Yamin Tsabbaḥ, Yehudah Cohen, Yehudah Ḥanokh, Yisra'el Sultan, Yosef Shem-Tov Ha-Yerushalmi
Iguidi (140*): Lalla Rḥima Ha-Cohanit, Yisra'el
Iguitimisa (111*): Yaʿaqob Ben-ʿAmram
Ikherkhouren (58): Shimʿon Cohen
Illigh (159): Abraham Amzalag
Imerhane (116): Ait El-Cohen, ʿAmram Moryossef, David El-Cohen, Sidi Buqassis
Imini (105): Ait El-Cohen
Imi n'Taga (83): Barukh Ha-Cohen
Imi n'Tanoute (82): Abraham Darʿi, Abraham Oḥayon, ʿEli Ben-Yitsḥaq, Masʿud Mani, Yehudah Saʿadon, Yitsḥaq Ha-Levi
Imi n'Timouga (81): Lalla Tsaddiqah
Inezgane (84): Haqadosh of Inezgane
Intektou (95*): Didokh
Jebha (13): Yaḥya Lordani
Kasba Tadla (34): Makhluf Ben-Yosef, Yaḥya Ben-Yaḥya
Kelaat (59): Shalom Azulay
Kelaat Mgouna (122): Tsaddiq Kelaʿat Al-Mguna
Kenadza (168): Moshe Ben-Shuqrun
Khemis of Sidi Bou Yahia (121): Sidi Bu-Zeggar
Khemisset (25): Yoab Ben-Tseruyah
Ksar Douar (128): Mulay Sedra
Ksar El-Kebir (9): Ḥazzan El-Ḥili, Meir Baʿal Ha-Nes, Yehudah Zabali
Ksar Es-Souk (129): Abraham Bu-Dwaya, Abraham Yafe, Lalla ʿAisha Alghzal, Moshe Lʿasri, Moshe Yitaḥ, Mul Sedra, Mul Terya, Raḥamim Ha-Yerushalmi, Shelomoh Illuz, Yaʿaqob Lʿasri, Yaḥya Laḥlu
Larache (10): Yosef Ha-Galili
Marrakech (72): Abraham Abikhzer, Abraham Abitbol, Abraham Azulay, ʿAzar Ha-Levi, Barukh ʿArama, Barukh Bemmafda, Cohanim, David Ben-Safet, David Tsabbaḥ, Eleʿazar Ha-Levi,

Eliyahu Yissan, Ḥananiah Ha-Cohen, Ḥayyim Messas, Ḥayyim Pinto, Kebur Shu, Lalla Rivqah of Bene-Moshe, Masʿud Bar-Mimuna, Masʿud Ben-Moḥa, Masʿud Bitton, Masʿud Naḥmias, Meir Bar-Sheshat, Mordekhay Ben-ʿAttar, Mordekhay Ben-Sal, Mordekhay Ben-Safet, Moshe Ben-Safet, Moshe Ḥaliwa, Mussa Taḥuni, Nissim Ben-Nissim, Pinḥas Ben-Yair, Pinḥas Ha-Cohen, Raphael Ben-ʿAttar, Re'uben Pinto, Shalom Kinizu, Shaul Naḥmias, Shelomoh Ben-ʿAttar, Shelomoh Ben-Tameshut, Shelomoh Cohen, Shelomoh Semana, Sidi Ḥmad El-Kamel, Yaʿaqob Abikhzer, Yaʿaqob Ḥazzan, Yaʿaqob Levi, Yehudah Ben-Yismʿael, Yehudah Tsarfati, Yisra'el Abikhzer, Yisra'el Ben-Moḥa, Yitsḥaq Ben-Safet, Yitsḥaq Deluya, Yosef Pinto

Mazagan (4): Yaḥya Ḥayyim Assulin

Meknes (24): David Bussidan, Gabriel, Makhluf Shetrit, Moshe Dahan, Mul El-Karma, Mul Sedra, Petaḥyah Mordekhay Berdugo, Raphael Berdugo, Raphael Elqubi, Shelomoh Ben-Eliʿezer, Shemuel ʿAmar

Mezguita (143): Ḥananiah Ḥaliwa

Mhamid (181): Shelomoh Ben-Lḥans, Shelomoh El-Maʿaravi, Yehudah Turjman

Midelt (126): Shelomoh Amselem, Yitsḥaq Abulʿafia, Yitsḥaq Ben-Ḥammu

Missour (30): Abraham Makhluf Ben-Yaḥya

Mogador (2): Abraham Ben-ʿAttar, Abraham Ben-Shushan, Abraham Knafo, Abraham Qoriat, Abraham Suissa, Abraham Tsabbaḥ, ʿAqqan Cohen, Baba Sidi, Cohanim, David ʿAttar, David Bel-Ḥazzan, David Ben-Barukh, David Ben-Zudi, David Elqayim, David Lusqi, David Yiflaḥ, Ḥayyim Pinto, Imma Esther, Kever Navi, Masʿud Ben-Tameshut, Masʿud Ḥarosh, Masʿud Knafo, Meir Ben-ʿAttar, Moshe Ha-Cohen, Nissim Sasson, Re'uben Ben-Re'uben, Shimʿon Beit-Halaḥmi, Yaʿaqob Ben-Yitaḥ, Yaʿaqob Bibas, Yehudah Pinto, Yonah Navon, Yosef Knafo, Yosef Malka

Mzab (173*): Aharon Dahan, Moshe Dahan

Nador (15): Mul Bab Jemaʿa

Ntifa (49): Ḥabib Yifraḥ, Lalla Brali, Lalla Miryam, Mul Bghi Bghi, Shalom Bar-Ḥani, Shelomoh, Yosef Bajayo

Ouarzazate (108): Daud, Yaʿaqob Bardiʿi, Yosef Ha-Cohen, Yosef Pinto

Oufran (160): Meʿarat Oufran, Shelomoh Ben-ʿAbbu, Yaʿaqob Ben-Shabbat, Yehudah Afryat

Oujda (16): Abraham Ben-Shuqrun, Eliyahu Azulay, Ḥayyim Amuyal, Shelomoh Sabban

Oulad Gfir (176): Shelomoh Laḥlu

Oulad Mansour (54): Cohanim, Moshe Waʿqnin

Oulad Said Ohayon (29*): Masʿud

Oulad Yahya (17): Asher, Nwasser, Sidi Ftaḥ Ben-Sliman, Yitsḥaq Ben-Sliman

Outat El-Hadj (28): Abraham ʿAbbu Ben-Yaḥya, Sidi ʿAbbud

Quermazdatine (94): Imin wa-Mumen

Rabat (7): Abraham Berdugo, Eliʿezer Davila, Eliyahu Merqado Malka, Ḥayyim Davila, Lalla Luna Bat-Khalifa, Lalla Setti Ben-Sasso, Masʿud Tsabbaḥ, Moshe Ben-Walid, Moshe Toledano, Raḥamim Mizraḥi, Raphael ʿAttiya, Shalom Zawi, Shelomoh Ben-Waʿish, Shemuel Abiḥatsira, Sidi Makhluf, Yaʿaqob Ben-Walid, Yehudah Gadol Gilʿad, Yequtiʾel Berdugo, Yosef Ben-ʿAttar

Rabat/Draa (144): Hillel Ha-Cohen, Sidi Sayyid

Rif (179*): Yaʿaqob Roshdi

Rissani (133): Abraham Abiḥatsira, David Abiḥatsira, Masʿud Abiḥatsira, Moshe Turjman, Shelomoh Oḥayon

Safi (3): Abraham Sultan, Aharon, Barukh Assabagh, Masʿud Bar-Mimuna, Masʿud Ben-Waʿish, Masʿud Perets, Raphael Ha-Cohen, Saʿadiah Reboḥ, Sidi Bu-Dheb, Ulad Zemmur, Yossi Ha-Galili

Salé (8): Abraham Revaḥ, ʿAmram Ben-Safet, David Ben-Safet, Ephraim Maymaran, Ḥayyim Ben-ʿAttar, Ḥayyim Toledano, Mordekhay Cohen, Moshe Amselem, Moshe Franco, Moshe Mamuna, Raphael Anqawa, Raphael Bibas, Shalom Zaguri, Shelomoh Ben-Lḥans, Shimʿon Zawi, Yaʿaqob Bibas, Yaḥya Ruimi, Yitsḥaq Qoriat, Yosef Bibas, Yosef Tsabbaḥ

Sefrou (27): Abba Elbaz, Abner Azini, Moshe Ben-Ḥammu, Mul Jebel El-Kebir, Nissim Cohen, Raphael Maman, Raphael Moshe Elbaz, Reʾuben Azini, Shelomoh Elbaz, Shimʿon ʿObadiah, Yehoshuaʿ Zekri, Yitsḥaq Ha-Cohen

Settat (174): Isso, Mimun Elghrabli, Shawil, Tsaddiq ʿAyn Nzar, Tsaddiqe ʿAyn Um-Krima, Yamin Yosef Dahan

Sidi Rahal (57): Abraham Ben-Ibgui, Abraham El-Cohen, Ait

Ḥaqon, Ḥabib Elqubi, Ḥaggai Perets, Shalom Cohen, Shelomoh Ḥamias, Ya'aqob Ashkenazi, Ya'aqob Ben-Qirat, Ya'aqob Ḥaqon, Yitsḥaq Davila
Sidi Yahia (18): Yaḥya Ben-Dossa
Skoura (118): Ait 'Arama, David 'Arama, Ele'azar Cohen, Isso Cohen, Lalla 'Aisha Asseraf, Makhluf 'Arama, Mas'ud 'Arama, Meir 'Arama, Moshe 'Arama, Moshe Ha-Cohen, Pinḥas Cohen, Shim'on Cohen, Sidi Moḥammed U-Belqassem, Sidi Mul El-Ḥazra, Yisra'el Cohen
Souk El-Khemis (171): Lalla Safia, Mulay Ya'qub
Sous (87): Makhluf Amata, Sidi Abraham, Sidi Mussa, Sidi Ya'qub
Tabia (80): David of Ait Ya'ish, Lalla Mima, Mimun Fḥima, Moshe, Mul Azadh, Mul Sandoq El-Khdar, Mul Tazghart, Mul Timḥdart, Yosef El-Bḥor
Tabia/Tilouine (91): Yisra'el Cohen
Tabia/Ziz (127): Mulay Tabia
Tabougimt (98): Aharon Abiḥatsira
Tadmout of Ait Otman (79): Cohanim and Leviim
Tadrhia (93): Mussa U-Re'uben, Yehudah U-Re'uben
Tagant (161): 'Akko 'Azran, Bu-Sherif, Ele'azar Ha-Cohen
Tagit (169): 'Eli Alghazi
Tagmout (162): Ele'azar Ha-Cohen, Shelomoh El-Ḥlu
Tagouidert (88): Sidi Bu-Lanwar
Tagounit (152): Shelomoh Afenjar, Ulad Siggar, Ya'aqob Ben-Semana, Yehudah Ben-Baba
Taguella (44): Sidi Irhrem n'Iduidhen
Tahanaout (73): Sliman Abayu, Sliman Adayyan
Takerkouzt (76): Lalla Taqerquzt
Talate (139): Ait El-Cohen, El-Khwatat
Talegjount (89): Irhir Izid
Tamaarouf (156): Eli'ezer Turei-Zahav
Tamaint El-Fouquia (85): Yitsḥaq Levi
Tamnougalt (145): Ait El-Cohen, Yosef Dahan
Tamzaourt (71*): Buri Khizo, Mul Tefillin, Shaul Zozot, Yosef Zozot
Tanant (46): Ḥayyim Ha-Mizraḥi
Tangier (11): Abraham Toledano, Ḥabib Toledano, Mordekhay Ben-Jo, Moshe Toledano, Vidal Bibas, Yehudah Azenqot
Taourirt (19): Bent El-Ḥmus, Mul Taurirt

Targa (120*): David Cohen, Menaḥem Cohen
Tarkellil (149): Ait El-Cohen, Eliyahu Abiḥatsira, Makhluf Ben-Yosef Abiḥatsira
Taroudant (86): Barukh Ha-Cohen, David Ben-Barukh, Moshe Elbaz, Pinḥas El-Cohen, Shalom Zaᶜafrani, Yamin Ha-Cohen
Tasdremt (97): Lalla Saᶜada Bent-Ashqluḥ
Tasemsela (112): Shem-Tov Ha-Mizraḥi
Tasbibt (75): Moshe Cohen
Taskast (141*): Yehudah Halaḥmi
Tasmesit (52): Meᶜarat Abuqassis, Meᶜarat Waᶜnono, Mimun Buqassis
Tassent (125): Eliᶜezer Ashkenazi
Tazda (138): Ait Naḥmias, David Naḥmias, Masᶜud Naḥmias, Yaᶜaqob Naḥmias, Yosef Naḥmias
Tazenakht (155): Aharon Ha-Cohen, Ait El-Cohen, Ephraim Ha-Cohen, Isso Ibgui, Lalla Simḥa Ruben, Moshe Wizeman, Sepher Tislit, Yaᶜaqob Ha-Cohen, Yosef Ha-Cohen
Tazzarine (103): Ḥayyim Lashqar, Sidi Brahim
Telouet (99): ᶜAmram Abiḥatsira, David Perets, Yaᶜaqob Pinto, Yaḥya Abiḥatsira, Yosef Abiḥatsira
Tetuan (12): Abraham Bibas, David Ben-ᶜAmram, El-Tsaddiq de la Piedra, Shemuel Nahon, Shemuel Yisra'el, Shem-Tov Nahon, Vidal Yisra'el, Yehudah Khalfon, Yitsḥaq Ben-Walid, Yitsḥaq Nahon
Tidghest (115): Shaul Ha-Cohen
Tidili (55): Abraham Cohen, Yaᶜaqob Bar-Ibgui
Tikhirat (110*): Ḥaggai Ha-Cohen, Lalla Solica Waᶜqnin, Shelomoh Suissa
Tikirt (119): Yonah Daudi, Yosef Bitton
Tillin (158): Mordekhay Ben-Shabbat, Mul El-Ḥazra El-Menzura, Shalom Ben-Shabbat, Shemuel, Tuqshusht, Yehudah Ben-Shabbat, Yissakhar Bihnan
Tillit (123): Abraham Cohen Bu-Dwaya
Timzerit (114): ᶜAzar Cohen, David Perets, David U-Moshe
Tinejdad (135): Aharon Assulin, Moshe Abikhzer
Tiskht (100): Abba
Todgha (134): Esqlila, Sepher Ait Yitsḥaq
Toulal (164): Makhluf Ha-Levi, Yitsḥaq Abiḥatsira
Touggana (62): Sidi Harun

Toundout (109): Abraham Abbetan, Aharon Moryossef, Ḥananiah Cohen, Moshe Ḥabib, Shalom Moryossef, Shaul Moryossef, Yisra'el Moryossef
Zagora (148): Makhluf Ben-Yosef
Zerekten (65): Meʿarat Hacohanim
Zrigat (131): Yitsḥaq Ben-Ḥarosh

GLOSSARY

Ab: The eleventh month of the Jewish calendar, corresponding to July-August.

Adar: The sixth month of the Jewish calendar, corresponding to February-March.

***Agurram**: Saint, marabout in Berber tribes.

***Ait**: Tribe (Berber).

*ʿ**Ar**: as used in Morocco: Petition made to a person with the pressure of an evil consequence if the petition is not granted.

Ashkenazim: Jews of Central and Eastern Europe or their descendants.

Baʿal Shem-Tov: Rabbi Israel Ben-Eliezer (1700–60), founder of the Hasidic movement in Eastern Europe; well-known among the Jews for the miracles he performed.

***Baraka**: Divine blessing; a power popularly believed in North Africa to be possessed by a saint, a sacred object or animal.

Bar-mitswah: Literally, son of commandment; ceremony to admit a thirteen-year-old boy as an adult member of the Jewish community.

Ben (*pl.* Bne): Son(s) of.

Cave of Makhpelah: Cave of the Patriarchs in Hebron.

Cohen (*pl.* Cohanim): Originally a member of the Jewish priestly class, descendant of Aaron, now having essentially honorific religious duties and prerogatives; still bound to strict rules of ritual purity according to Jewish law.

Dayyan: A judge in a rabbinical court.

***Djebel**: Mountain.

***El**: Prefix meaning "the."

***El-Khdar**: Literally, the green (a beneficent color).

Note: The Arabic and Berber words are preceded by an asterisk.

Elul: The last month of the Jewish calendar, corresponding to August-September.
Erets Yisra'el: The Holy Land, the Land of Israel.

Geulah: The redemption of the Jewish people by the Messiah.
Goy (*pl.* goyim): Gentile, non-Jew.

Ha: Prefix meaning "the."
Ḥakham: Sage, rabbi, a rabbi who teaches children; also the saint.
Ḥanukkah: Feast of Lights celebrated from the 25th of *Kislew* to the 2nd of *Tebet* to commemorate the rededication of the Second Temple by the Maccabees.
Ḥazzan: Cantor, the reader of the prayers in the synagogue; designation of the Jewish saint by the Muslims in North Africa.
Ḥebrah Qaddishah: Burial Society.
Ḥeshwan: The second month of the Jewish calendar, corresponding to October-November.
Hillulah (*pl.* hillulot): Festival to celebrate the anniversary of the death of a saint.

Iyyar: The ninth month of the Jewish calendar, corresponding to April-May.

Kislew: The third month of the Jewish calendar, corresponding to November-December.
Kosher: Food fit to be eaten, according to the Jewish dietary laws.

Lag bʿOmer: The 33rd day of the counting of the *Omer* (the period of 49 days from the 2nd day of Passover to *Shabuʿot*), a date which coincides with the 18th of *Iyyar;* the day of the *hillulah* of R. Shimʿon Bar-Yoḥay.
***Lalla**: Literally, madam (Berber). Designation given to female saints in North Africa by Jews and Muslims.

Maḥia: eau de vie, a coarse brandy prepared from dried fruits.
***Marabout**: A Muslim holy man believed to possess supernatural powers; the saint, his descendants, his shrine, and all sacred objects and animals.
Meʿarah: Cave, grotto.

Meʿarat Ha-Makhpelah: Cave of the Patriarchs in Hebron.
***Mellaḥ**: The Jewish quarter in North Africa corresponding to the ghetto in Eastern European countries.
Miqweh: A bath or a bathing place for immersion for purposes of ritual purification.
Mitswah (*pl.* mitswot): A commandment, precept, religious duty, good deed.
***Mul (*pl.* mwalin)**: Master; designation of Muslim saints in North Africa.
***Mulay**: Literally, my master; title of shereefs, sultans and the King of Morocco; also a designation for saints.
***Muqaddam**: Guardian of a holy place; caretaker of a saint's shrine.
***Mussem**: Feast in honor of a Muslim saint, celebrated once or twice a year; collective pilgrimage to a holy shrine on this occasion.
***Mwalin**: See "Mul."

Nisan: The seventh month of the Jewish calendar, corresponding to March-April.

Paqid (*pl.* pqidim): An officer of a confraternity, a religious organization, or a *hillulah.*
Paytan (*pl.* paytanim): Cantor(s).
Pesaḥ: Passover, celebrated from the 14th to the 22nd of *Nisan.*
Piyyut (*pl.* piyyutim): Liturgical poetry.
Purim: Festival celebrated on the 14th of *Adar.*

Qasida (*pl.* qasidot): Poem in Judeo-Arabic usually chanted by women.

Rabbi (R.): Title of respect for a Jewish scholar; a teacher of Jewish law, a spiritual leader of the Jewish community, a saint.
Rosh Hashanah: The Jewish New Year—a two-day holiday celebrated on the 1st and 2nd days of *Tishri.*

Sepher: Book, scroll.
Sepher Torah: *Torah* scroll.
Seʿudah: Festive meal.

Shabbat: *Sabbath.*

Shabuʿot: Literally, weeks; Feast of Weeks or Pentecost, celebrated on the 6th and 7th days of *Siwan.*

Shaliyaḥ (*pl.* sheliḥim): Rabbinical emissary who came from the Holy Land to collect alms.

Shammash: Caretaker of a saint's grave.

Shebat: The fifth month of the Jewish calendar, corresponding to January-February.

Sheḥitah: Ritual slaughtering.

Shekhinah: Divine Providence.

Shemaʿ: Liturgical prayer expressing Israel's ardent faith in and love of God, recited daily and when a person is dying.

Shofar: A ram's horn blown as a wind instrument in the synagogue on *Rosh Hashanah* and *Yom Kippur.*

Shoḥet: A person certified by Jewish law to slaughter animals for food in the manner prescribed by Jewish law.

***Sidi**: See "siyyid."

Siwan: The ninth month of the Jewish calendar, corresponding to May-June.

***Siyyid**: Master, saint, sanctuary.

Sukkot: Feast of Tabernacles or Feast of Booths, celebrated from the 15th to the 22nd of *Tishri.*

Talmud: The compilation of the discussions and interpretations of the Jewish Oral Law.

Tammuz: The tenth month of the Jewish calendar, corresponding to June-July.

Tebet: The fourth month of the Jewish calendar, corresponding to December-January.

Tefillin: Phylacteries.

Tishri: The first month of the Jewish calendar, corresponding to September-October.

Torah: The Pentateuch; the Old Testament itself; the entire body of Jewish law as contained chiefly in the Old Testament and the *Talmud.*

Tsaddiq (*pl.* tsaddiqim; *fem.* tsaddiqah): Saint; righteous man.

***Ulad**: Literally, son of; family, clan.

Yeshibah: Institution of Jewish learning in which young men study the *Torah* and the *Talmud.*
Yom Kippur: The Day of Atonement.

***Zgharit**: Joyful sound uttered by women on festive occasions.
***Ziyara**: Literally, visit; pilgrimage to the grave of a saint—to celebrate his birth or death, ask for his help, after making a vow to a saint, and so on.

BIBLIOGRAPHY

Aarne, Antti and Stith Thompson. 1961. *The Types of the Folktale.* FF Communications. Helsinki: Suomalainen Tiedeakatemia.

Achel-Hadas, I. 1961. "Deux sources miraculeuses du Rabbi de Tlemcen, Rabbi Ephraim Enkaoua." *Revue d'Histoire de la Médecine Hébraïque* 54: 183–87.

Al-Aflaki, Shams al-Din Ahmad. 1918–22. *Les Saints des derviches tourneurs* (trans. by Huart). 2 vols. Paris: E. Leroux.

Albert, Jean-Pierre. 1990. *Odeurs de Sainteté. La mythologie chrétienne des aromates.* Paris: Editions de l'EHESS.

Alqayim, David, and David Iflah. 1921. *Shir Yedidot.* Marrakech. Reprinted in 1979. Jerusalem: Joseph Lugassi (Hebrew).

Amar, Moshe. 1946. *Book of Miracles of Rabbi Daniel Hashomer.* Casablanca (Hebrew).

Attal, Robert. 1993. *Les Juifs d'Afrique du Nord: Bibliographie.* Jerusalem: Ben-Zvi Institute.

Attwater, Donald. 1973. *The Penguin Dictionary of Saints.* Harmondsworth: Penguin Books.

Aubin, Eugène. 1904. *Le Maroc d'aujourd'hui.* Paris: Librairie Armand Colin.

Avida, Yehuda. 1958. "The Miraculous Stories of Sason Hai Castiel." *Sefunot* 2: 103–27. Jerusalem: Ben-Zvi Institute (Hebrew).

Avishur, Yitzhak. 1982. "Judeo-Arabic Folksongs sung by Iraqi Jewry on Pilgrimages to Saints' Graves (Ziyyara)." *Studies on History and Culture of Iraqi Jewry* 2: 151–92. Or Yehuda: Institute for Research on Iraqi Jewry (Hebrew).

Banon, Nina. 1981. *Maroc, Guide et Histoire.* Casablanca: S.A.P.S.

Bar-Asher, Moshe. 1978. "ʿAl hayesodot ha-ʿibriyyim ba-ʿarabit ha-medubberet shel Yehudey Maroqo." *Leshonenu* 42, fasc. 3–4: 163–89 (Hebrew).

Barret, P., and J. N. Gurgand. 1978. *Priez pour nous à Compostelle.* Paris: Hachette.

Basset, Henri. 1920. *Le culte des grottes au Maroc.* Algiers: Carbonnel.

Basset, René. 1901. *Nedromah et les Traras.* Paris.

Bel, Alfred. 1938. *La religion musulmane en Berbérie.* Paris: Geuthner.

Benaim, Samuel Youssef. 1980. *Le pèlerinage juif des lieux saints au Maroc.* Casablanca.

Benaim, Yosef. 1931. *Malkhey Rabbanan.* Jerusalem: Hamaarav Press (Hebrew).

Ben-Ami, Issachar. 1971. "La Qsida chez les Juifs marocains." *Scripta Hierosolymitana* 22: 1–17. Jerusalem: Magnes Press.

———. 1972. "Magic rites among Moroccan Jews." In H. Z. Hirschberg, ed., *Zakhor le-Abraham, Mélanges Abraham Elmaleh.* Jerusalem: Comité de la Communauté Marocaine, pp. 195–205 (Hebrew).

———. 1973a. "Miracles. R. Daniel Hashomer Ashkenazi." In I. Ben-Ami, ed., *Folklore Research Center Studies* 3: 33–59. Jerusalem: Magnes Press (Hebrew).

———. 1973b. "The Presence of Ghosts in the Jewish Moroccan Home." *Proceedings of the Fifth World Congress of Jewish Studies* 5: 3–6. Jerusalem: World Union of Jewish Studies (Hebrew).

———. 1974a. "Folklore Research in Israel." *Ariel* 35: 32–47. Jerusalem: Ministry for Foreign Affairs, Cultural and Scientific Relations Division.

———. 1974b. "Le mariage traditionnel chez les Juifs marocains." In I. Ben-Ami and D. Noy, eds., *Studies in Marriage Customs. Folklore Research Center Studies* 4: 9–103. Reprint in I. Ben-Ami (1975a, pp. 9–104).

———. 1975a. *Moroccan Jewry: Ethno-Cultural Studies.* Jerusalem: Rubin Mass (Hebrew and French).

———. 1975b. "In Praise of Rabbi Hayyim Pinto." In I. Ben-Ami (1975a, pp. 209–20) (Hebrew).

———. 1975c. "Book of Miracles." *Yeda-ʿAm* 17: 1–9 (Hebrew).

———. 1977. "On the research of war folklore: the saint's motif." In S. Werses, N. Rotenstreich and H. Shmeruk, eds., *Sefer Dov Sedan.* Tel-Aviv: Hakibbutz Hameuchad Publishing House Ltd., pp. 87–105 (Hebrew).

———. 1980a. "The Saint Nissim Ben-Nissim." In M. Abitbol, ed., *Judaïsme d'Afrique du Nord aux XIXe–XXe siècles.* Jerusalem: Ben-Zvi Institute, pp. 150–63 (Hebrew).

———. 1980b. "Le culte des saints chez les Juifs et les Musulmans au

Maroc." *Les relations entre Juifs et Musulmans en Afrique du Nord, XIXe–XXe siècles.* Actes du Colloque International de l'Institut d'Histoire des Pays d'Outre-Mer. Paris: C.N.R.S., pp. 104–09.

———. 1980c. "Miraculous Legends of Wartime." In V. Newall, ed., *Folklore Studies in the Twentieth Century.* London, pp. 123–27.

———. 1981a. "Folk-Veneration of Saints among the Moroccan Jews. Tradition: Continuity and Change. The Case of the Holy Man, Rabbi David u-Moshe." In S. Morag, I. Ben-Ami and N. A. Stillman, eds., *Studies in Judaism and Islam.* Jerusalem: Magnes Press, pp. 283–344.

———. 1981b. "Saint worship among Jews and Muslims in Morocco." In M. Zohari et al., eds., *Hagut Ivrit Be'Artzot Ha'Islam.* Jerusalem: Brit Ivrit Olamit (World Hebrew Union), pp. 175–80 (Hebrew).

———. 1982a. "Community Organization at Saint Shrines in Morocco." In I. Ben-Ami, ed., *The Sepharadi and Oriental Jewish Heritage.* Jerusalem: Magnes Press, pp. 367–90 (Hebrew).

———. 1982b. "The Veneration of Saints among the Jews of the Draa Valley (South Morocco)." *Yeda-ʿAm* 21, nos. 49–50: 94–98 (Hebrew).

———. 1982c. "Songs of the *hillulah* and the *ziyara.*" In R. Mosheh Amar, ed., *Kav Lakav. Etudes sur le Judaïsme Maghrébin.* Jerusalem: Dovev Siftey Yeshanim Ner Hamaarav, pp. 124–42 (Hebrew).

———. 1983a. "Scrolls of the Law as Miracle Workers." In I. Ben-Ami and J. Dan, eds., *Studies in Aggadah and Jewish Folklore, Folklore Research Center Studies* 7: 299–321. Jerusalem: Magnes Press (Hebrew).

———. 1983b. "Relations between Jews and Muslims in the Veneration of Folk Saints in Morocco." *International Folklore Review* 3: 93–105.

———. 1986a. "The Cult of Saints among Moroccan Jews: The Beginnings of a Custom in Morocco and Israel." In J. Chétrit and Z. Yehuda, eds., *Miqqedem Umiyyam. Studies in the Jewry of Islamic Countries.* Haifa: University of Haifa, pp. 109–25 (Hebrew).

———. 1986b. "Folklore." In A. Serper, ed., *Encyclorama of Israel* 7: 229–329. Jerusalem: Edition et Diffusion Mondiale 1986.

———. 1989. "Le monde sacré et animal: contenu et message." In B. Levy and P. Wackers, eds., *Reinardus* 2: 32–41. Grave: Uitg. Alfa.

———. 1990. *Culte des saints et pèlerinages judeo-musulmans au Maroc.* Paris: Maisonneuve & Larose.

———. 1991. ed., *Studies on the Culture of the Jews of North Africa.* Jerusalem: Communauté Israélite Nord-Africaine (Hebrew, French and English).

———. 1993a. "The Veneration of Saints by Israeli Jews of Moroccan Origin." *International Folklore Review* 9: 21–23.

———. 1993b. "Customs of Pregnancy and Childbirth among Sephardic and Oriental Jews." In Y. K. Stillman and G. K. Zucker, eds., *New Horizons in Sephardic Studies.* Albany: State University of New York Press, pp. 253–267.

———. 1993c. "Saint Veneration among North African Jews." *Jewish Folklore and Ethnology Review* 15, no. 2: 78–83.

———. 1995. *Jewish Holy Men of Morocco and their Miracles.* Jerusalem: Joseph Lugassi Press.

Ben-Amos, Dan. 1976. *Folklore Genres.* Austin and London: University of Texas Press.

——— and Jerome R. Mintz. 1970. *In Praise of the Baal Shem Tov.* Bloomington and London: Indiana University Press.

Ben-Ari, E., and Y. Bilu. 1987. "Saints' Sanctuaries in Israeli Development Towns: On a Mechanism of Urban Transformation." *Urban Anthropology* 16, no. 2: 243–72.

Bénech, José. 1949. *Essai d'explication d'un mellah.* Baden-Baden.

Ben-Jacob, Abraham. 1973. *Holy Graves in Iraq.* Jerusalem: Mossad Harav Kook (Hebrew).

Bensimon, Raphael. 1994. *Le Judaïsme Marocain. Folklore: du berceau à la tombe.* Lod: Orot Yahdout Hamaghreb (Hebrew).

Bier, Aharon. 1988. *Jewish Holy Places In Eretz Israel.* Jerusalem: Rubin Mass (Hebrew).

Bilu, Yoram. 1978. *Traditional Psychiatry in Israel: Moroccan-born Moshav Members with Psychiatric Disorders and "Problems in Living" and their Traditional Healers.* Jerusalem: Hebrew University of Jerusalem (Ph. D. Thesis, Hebrew).

———. 1984. "Motivation personnelle et signification sociale du phenomène de la veneration des saints parmi les juifs marocains en Israel." In J. C. Lasri and C. Rapia, eds., *Juifs Nord-Africains D'Aujourd'hui.* Montreal: Presses de l'Université de Montreal.

———. 1987. "Dreams and Wishes of the Saint," in H. Goldberg, ed., *Judaism Viewed from Within and Without.* Albany: State University of New York Press, pp. 285–313.

———. 1993. *Without Bonds. The Life and Death of Rabbi Yaacov Wazana.* Jerusalem: Magnes Press (Hebrew).

Blackbourn, David. 1994. *Marpingen. Apparitions of the Virgin Mary in Nineteenth-Century Germany.* New York: Alfred A. Knopf.

Brauer, Erich. 1934. *Ethnologie der jemenitischen Juden.* Heidelberg.

———. 1948. *The Jews of Kurdistan: An Ethnological Study.* Ed. and trans. into Hebrew by Raphael Patai. Jerusalem: Palestine Institute of Folklore and Ethnology.

Brown, Peter. 1981. *The Cult of the Saints.* Chicago: University of Chicago Press.

Brunel, René. 1926. *Essai sur la confrérie religieuse des Aissaoua au Maroc.* Paris: Geuthner.

Brunot, Louis. 1931, 1952. *Textes arabes de Rabat.* 2 vols. Paris: Geuthner.

——— and Eli Malka. 1939. *Textes judéo-arabes de Fès.* Rabat: Ecole du Livre.

Canaan, Tewfik. 1927. *Mohammedan Saints and Sanctuaries in Palestine.* Jerusalem: Ariel Publishing House (facsimile of the 1927 original edition).

Castries, Henry de. 1924. "Les sept patrons de Marrakech." *Hespéris,* Tome 4, pp. 245–304. Paris: Larose.

Chebel, Malek. 1995. *Dictionnaire des symboles musulmans.* Paris: Albin Michel.

Chelhod, Joseph. 1964. *Les structures du sacré chez les Arabes.* Paris: G.-P. Maisonneuve et Larose.

Chénier, Louis de. 1787. *Recherches historiques sur les Maures et l'histoire de l'Empire de Maroc.* Paris.

Chétrit, Joseph. 1980. "Friha bat Yoseph—A Hebrew Poetess in the eighteenth century in Morocco." *Peʿamim* 4: 84–93 (Hebrew).

———. 1994. *Written Judeo-Arabic Poetry in Morocco. Poetic, Linguistic and Cultural Studies.* Jerusalem: Misgav Yerushalaym.

Chouraqui, André N. 1950. *La condition juridique de l'israélite marocain.* Paris: Presses du Livre Français. English trans. 1952. *The Social and Legal Status of the Jews in French Morocco.* New York: American Jewish Committee Publications.

———. 1968. *Between East and West. A History of the Jews of North Africa.* Philadelphia: Jewish Publication Society of America.

———. 1985. *Histoire des Juifs en Afrique du Nord.* Paris: Hachette.

Cohen, Shoshan. 1935. *The Miracles of the Saints.* Djerba: Imprimerie Jacob Haddad (Hebrew).

Colin, Georges S. 1926. "El Maqsad (Vie des Saints du Rif)." *Archives Marocaines,* vol. 26.

Corcos, David. 1976. *Studies in the History of the Jews of Morocco.* Jerusalem: Rubin Mass (Hebrew and French).

Coulson, John. 1958. *The Saints.* London: Burns and Oates.

Crapanzano, Vincent, 1973. *The Hamadsha. A Study in Moroccan Ethnopsychiatry.* Berkeley, Los Angeles and London: University of California Press.

———. 1975. "Saints, Jnuns and Dreams: An Essay in Moroccan Ethnopsychology." *Psychiatry* 38, no. 2: 145–59.

Delehaye, R.P.H. 1906. *Les légendes hagiographiques.* Brussels: Bollandistes.

Dermenghem, Emile. 1942. *Vies des saints musulmans.* Algiers: Baconnier. Reprinted 1981. Paris: Editions d'Aujourd'hui.

———. 1954. *Le culte des saints dans l'Islam maghrébin.* Paris: Gallimard.

Deshen, S. 1977. "Tunisian Hillulot." In M. Shokeid and S. Deshen, *The Generation of Transition: Continuity and Change among North African Immigrants in Israel.* Jerusalem: Ben-Zvi Institute, pp. 110–121 (Hebrew).

Desparmet, Joseph. 1935. "Ethnographie traditionnelle de la Mettidja." *Revue Africaine* 77: 178–88.

Dorson, Richard. 1972. *Folklore and Folklife.* Chicago: University of Chicago Press.

Doutté, Edmond. 1900. *Notes sur l'Islam Maghribin—Les Marabouts.* Paris: E. Leroux.

———. 1905. *Merrâkech.* Paris: Comité du Maroc.

———. 1909. *Magie et religion dans l'Afrique du Nord.* Algiers: Typographie Adolphe Jourdan. Reprinted 1984. Paris: Maisonneuve-Geuthner.

———. 1914. *En Tribu.* Paris: Geuthner.

Drague, Georges. 1951. *Esquisse d'histoire religieuse du Maroc.* Paris: J. Peyronnet.

Dreizin, F., A. Shenhar, H. Bar-Itzhak and G. Fridman. 1978. *Towards a computerized generation of sacred legends.* Haifa: University of Haifa.

———. 1979. *A Grammar of Expressiveness for Moroccan Jewish Sacred Legends.* Haifa: University of Haifa.
Dundes, Alan. 1965. *The Study of Folklore.* Englewood Cliffs: Prentice Hall.
———. 1968. *Every Man His Way. Readings in Cultural Anthropology.* Englewood Cliffs: Prentice Hall.
———. 1975. *Analytic Essays in Folklore.* The Hague and Paris: Mouton.
Durckheim, Emile. 1912. *Les formes élémentaires de la vie religieuse.* Paris: Alcan.
Eickelman, Dale F. 1972–1973. "Quelques aspects de l'organisation politique et économique d'une zawya marocaine au XIXe siècle." *Bulletin de la Société d'Histoire du Maroc* 4–5: 37–54.
———. 1976. *Moroccan Islam, Tradition and Society in a Pilgrimage Center.* Austin: University of Texas Press.
———. 1977. "Ideological Change and Regional Cults, Maraboutism and Ties of Closeness in Western Morocco." In R. Werbner (1977, pp. 3–28).
——— and Draioui Bouzekri. 1973. "Islamic Myths from Western Morocco." *Hespéris-Tamuda* 14: 195–225.
Elbaz, André. 1982. *Folktales of the Canadian Sephardim.* Toronto: Fitzhenry and Whiteside.
Eliade, Mircea. 1965. *Le sacré et le profane.* Paris: Gallimard.
———. 1969. *Le mythe de l'éternel retour.* Paris: Gallimard.
Encyclopaedia Judaica. 1977. Jerusalem: Keter Publishing House.
Epton, Nina. 1958. *Saints and Sorcerers, A Moroccan Journey.* London: Jarrolds.
Fahd, Toufic. 1987. *La divination arabe. Etudes religieuses sociologiques et folkloriques sur le milieu natif de l'Islam.* Paris: Sindbad.
Farid-ud-Din, ʿAttar. 1976. *Le mémorial des Saints.* Paris: Editions du Seuil.
Finnegan, Ruth. 1992. *Oral Poetry: Its Nature, Significance and Social Context,* Bloomington and Indianapolis: Indiana University Press.
Flamand, Pierre. 1952. *Un mellah en pays berbère: Demnate.* Paris: Librairie Générale de Droit & de Jurisprudence.
———. 1959. *Diaspora en Terre d'Islam: Les communautés israélites du sud marocain.* Casablanca: Imprimeries Reunies.
———. 1960. *Diaspora en Terre d'Islam: L'esprit populaire dans les Juiveries du sud marocain.* Casablanca: Imprimeries Reunies.

Foucauld, Charles de. 1888. *Reconnaissance au Maroc, 1883–1884.* Paris. Reprinted in Paris, Société d'Editions Géographiques, Maritimes et Coloniales.

Frazer, James G. 1960–61. *The Golden Bough.* London: St. Martin's Library; Macmillan & Co. Ltd. Abridged edition by the author in 2 vols. (first printed in 1922).

Geertz, Clifford. 1968. *Islam Observed. Religious Development in Morocco and Indonesia.* New Haven and London: Yale University Press.

Gellner, Ernest. 1969. *Saints of the Atlas.* Chicago: University of Chicago Press.

Gennep, Arnold van. 1909. *Les rites de passage.* Paris: Emile Nourry. English trans. The Rites of Passage. 1960. London: Routledge and Kegan Paul.

———. 1914. *En Algérie.* Paris.

———. 1943–1956. *Manuel de folklore français contemporain.* 4 tomes. Reprinted 1982. Paris: A. & J. Picard.

———. 1973. *Le culte populaire des saints en Savoie.* Paris: Maisonneuve & Larose.

Gerber, Jane. 1972. *Jewish Society in Fes. Studies in Communal and Economic Life.* Columbia University: Ph. D. Thesis.

Godard, Léon. 1859. *Le Maroc—Notes d'un voyageur (1858–1859).* Algiers.

Goldenberg, A. 1954. "Pèlerinages israélites au Maroc." *Cahiers de l'Alliance Israélite Universelle* 83: 33–34.

Goldziher, Ignaz. 1880. "Le culte des saints chez les Musulmans." *Revue de l'Histoire des Religions* 2: 256–351.

———. 1884. "Le culte des ancêtres et le culte des morts chez les Arabes." *Revue de l'Histoire des Religions* 10: 332–59.

Goulven, J. 1927. *Les Mellahs de Rabat-Salé.* Paris: Geuthner.

Gruel-Alpert, Lise. 1995. *La Tradition orale russe.* Paris: Presses Universitaires de France.

Gsell, S. 1913. *Histoire ancienne de l'Afrique du Nord.* Vol. 1. Paris: Hachette.

Hakohen, Mordekhay. 1971. *Holy Places in Eretz Israel.* Jerusalem: Ministry for Religion Affairs (Hebrew).

Hassin, David. 1807. *Tehilla le-Dawid* (Poetic Anthology: *piyyutim* and *qinot*). Amsterdam. Reprinted in 1931. Casablanca: Imprimerie Razon.

Hayyat, Shimon. 1973. "Pilgrimage Songs to Holy Places in Iraq." *Shebet wa-ʿam.* Jerusalem: Council of the Sephardi Community, pp. 461–75 (Hebrew).

Hazan, Ephraim. 1979. "Poetry and Piyyut in North-Africa—Continuity and Innovation. The Rise of a new Genre." *Peʿamim* 2: 39–47 (Hebrew).

Herber, J. 1923. "Les Hamadcha et les Dghoughiyyin." *Hespéris* 3: 217–36.

Hertz, Robert. 1970. "Saint Besse, Etude d'un culte alpestre." *Sociologie religieuse et Folklore.* Paris: Presses Universitaires de France, pp. 110–60.

Hirschberg, Haim Zeev. 1957. *From the Maghreb.* Jerusalem: Jewish Agency (Hebrew).

———. 1965. *A History of the Jews in North Africa.* 2 vols. Jerusalem: Bialik Institute (Hebrew). English trans. 1974–82. Leiden: E. J. Brill.

Houri, Shushan. 1985. *The Life and Works of Rabbi Hayyim Houri.* Beersheba: Hemed Press (Hebrew).

Huizinga, J. 1979. *The Waning of the Middle Ages.* Harmondsworth: Penguin Books.

Hurwitz, Abraham M.H. 1969. "Pilgrimage to holy graves and holy places." *Noʿam* 12: 169–238 (Hebrew).

Jamous, Raymond. 1981. *Honneur et Baraka. Les structures sociales traditionnelles dans le Rif.* Paris and Cambridge: Cambridge University Press.

Jansen, Hugh Wm. 1965. "The Esoteric-Exoteric Factor in Folklore." In A. Dundes (1965, pp. 43–51).

Jourdan, François. 1983. *La tradition des sept dormants.* Paris: Maisonneuve et Larose.

Kriss, Rudolph. 1955. *Peregrinatio neohellenika. Wahlfartswanderungen in heutigen Griechenland und in Unteritalien.* Vienna: Verlag des Osterreichischen Museums für Volskunde.

——— and Hubert Kriss. 1975. *Volkskundliche Anteile in Kult und Legend Athiopischer Heiligen.* Wiesbaden: O. Harrassowitz.

———. 1960–62. *Volksglaube im Bereich des Islams.* 2 vols. Wiesbaden: O. Harrassowitz.

Langlois, Christine. 1955. ed., *La fabrication des Saints, Terrain* 24. Paris: Ministère de la Culture et de la Francophonie.

Laredo, Abraham I. 1954. *Berberes y Hebreos de Marruecos.* Madrid: Instituto de Estudios Africanos del C. S. I. C.

———. 1978. *Les noms des Juifs du Maroc.* Madrid: Instituto "B. Arias Montano."

Lasri, Jacob. 1978. *Close to sages and rabbis.* Beersheba: Hazi Mor (Hebrew).

Lease, E. 1919. "The Number Three. Mysterious, Mystic, Magic." *Classical Philology* 14: 56–73.

Legey, Françoise. 1926. *Essai de folklore marocain.* Paris: Paul Geuthner.

Leibovici, Sarah. 1984. *Chronique des Juifs de Tétouan (1860–1896).* Paris: Maisonneuve & Larose.

Les Pèlerinages. 1960. Sources Orientales, vol. 3. Paris: Editions du Seuil.

Lewinsky, Yom-Tov (ed.). 1961. "Elijah the Prophet in Folklore, Traditions and Folk-Life." *Yeda-ʿAm* 7, no. 1 (25) (Hebrew).

Mach, Rudolph. 1957. *Der Zaddik in Talmud und Midrash.* Leiden: E. J. Brill.

Malka, Elie. 1946. *Essai d'ethnographie traditionnelle des mellahs ou croyances, rites de passage et vieilles pratiques de Israélites marocains.* Rabat.

Manor, Dan. 1982. *Kabbale et Ethique au Maroc. La voie de Rabbi Jacob Abihatsira.* Jerusalem: Ben-Zvi Institute (Hebrew).

Marcus, Eliezer. 1983. "The Oicotype of the 'The Desecrator's Punishment' (AT* 771)." In I. Ben-Ami and J. Dan, eds., *Studies in Aggadah and Jewish Folklore, Folklore Research Center Studies* 7: 337–66. Jerusalem: Magnes Press (Hebrew).

Marks, Emmanuel. 1977. "Communal and Individual Pilgrimage. The Region of Saints' Tombs in South Sinai." In R. Werbner (1977, pp. 29–51).

Massignon, Louis. 1908. "Les Saints musulmans enterrés à Bagdad." *Revue de l'Histoire des Religions,* pp. 329–38.

———. 1950. "Les Sept Dormants. Apocalypse de l'Islam." In *Analecta Bollandiana, 68: Mélanges Paul Peeters,* vol. 2. Brussels: Société des Bollandistes.

Mathieu, J. and R. Maneville. 1952. *Les accoucheuses musulmanes traditionnelles de Casablanca.* Paris: Publications de l'Institut des Hautes Etudes Marocaines.

Mauchamp, Emile. n.d. *La sorcellerie au Maroc.* Paris: Dorbon Aine.
Mazal-Tarim, Makhlouf. 1939. *Book in Praise of Rabbi Hayyim Pinto.* Casablanca (Judeo-Arabic).
Meunié, J. 1951. "Sur le culte des Saints et les fêtes rituelles dans le Moyen-Dra et la région de Tazarine." *Hespéris* 38: 365–80. Paris: Larose.
Michaux-Bellaire, E. 1921. "Essai sur l'Histoire des Confréries Marocaines." *Hespéris* 1: 141–59. Paris: Larose.
Mograbi, Abraham. 1968. *Ma'aseh Nissim: Book of Miracles of Rabbi Yaaqob Abihatsira.* Jerusalem (Hebrew).
Montagne, Robert. 1924. "Coutumes et légendes de la côte berbère." *Hespéris* 4: 101–16. Paris: Larose.
Montet, Edouard. 1909. *Le culte des saints musulmans dans l'Afrique du Nord et plus spécialement au Maroc.* Geneva: Georg.
———. 1911. *De l'état présent et de l'avenir de l'Islam.* Paris: Geuthner.
Morsy, Magaly. 1972. "*Les Ahansala. Examen du rôle historique d'une famille maraboutique de l'Atlas marocain au XVIII*[e] *siècle.* Paris: Mouton.
Moulieras, Auguste. 1895–99. *Le Maroc inconnu.* 2 vols. Paris: Challamel.
Nigal, Gedalya. 1982. "In Praise of R. Hayyim Ben-Attar." In R. Mosheh Amar, ed., *Kav Lakav. Etudes sur le Judaïsme Maghrébin.* Jerusalem: Dovev Siftey Yeshanim Ner Hamaarav, pp. 73–93 (Hebrew).
Noy, Dov. 1964. *Jewish Folktales from Morocco.* Jerusalem: Bitfuzot Hagolah (Hebrew).
Olrik, Axel. 1965. "Epic Laws of Folk Narrative." In A. Dundes (1965, pp. 129–41).
Oursel, Raymond. 1978. *Pèlerins du Moyen Age.* Paris: Fayard.
Ovadia, David. 1974–77. *The Community of Sefrou.* 3 vols. Jerusalem: Institute for Research of the History of Jewish Communities in Morocco (Hebrew).
———. 1979. *Fes and its sages.* Jerusalem: Beit Oved (Hebrew).
Pâcques, Viviane. 1971. "Les fêtes du Mwulud dans la région de Marrakech." *Journal de la Société des Africanistes* 41: 133–43.

Patai, Raphael. 1942–43. *Man and Earth.* 2 vols. Jerusalem: Magnes Press (Hebrew).

Pinto, Haim and David Pinto. n.d. *And the Man Moshe* (R. Moshe Abraham Pinto) n.p. (Hebrew).

Raphael, Freddy et al. 1973. *Les pèlerinages de l'antiquité biblique et classique à l'occident médiéval.* Paris: Geuthner.

Röhrich, L. 1973. *Probleme der Sagenforschung.* Freiburg.

Rouche, Isaac. 1936. "Un grand rabbin à Tlemcen au XVe siècle." *Bulletin de la Société de Géographie et d'Archéologie de la Province d'Oran* 57: 280–86; 1943. 64: 43–73.

Roussel, Romain. 1972. *Les Pèlerinages.* Paris: Presses Universitaires de France.

Rubinstein, Avraham. 1991. *In Praise of the Baʿal Shem Tov.* Jerusalem: Rubin Mass (Hebrew).

Sabban, A. 1978–79. *Book in Praise of the Saints.* Jerusalem (Hebrew and Judeo-Arabic).

Schnitzler, Otto. 1970. "The Particularity of the Number Seven and the Origin of the Seven Day's Week." In D. Noy and I. Ben-Ami, eds., *Folklore Research Center Studies* 1: 73–80. Jerusalem: Magnes Press.

Scholem, Gershom. 1980. *Elements of the Kabbalah and its Symbolism.* Jerusalem: Bialik Institute (Hebrew).

Schwarzbaum, Haim. 1975. *The folkloristic aspects of Judaism and Islam.* Tel Aviv: Don Publishing House (Hebrew).

———. 1982. *Biblical and Extra-Biblical Legends in Islamic Folk-Literature.* Walldorf-Hessen: Verlag für Orientkunde Dr. H. Vorndran.

Semach, Y. D. 1937–38. "Les Saints de l'Atlas." *Paix et Droit* 17, no. 10: 10–11; 18, no. 1: 7–8; 18, no. 2: 10–11.

Shiloah, Amnon. 1992. *Jewish Musical Traditions.* Detroit: Wayne State University Press.

Shils, Edward. 1975. *Center and Periphery. Essays in Macrosociology.* Chicago: University of Chicago Press.

Shinar, Pinhas. 1980. "La recherche relative aux rapports judéo-musulmans dans le Maghreb contemporain." *Les relations entre Juifs et Musulmans en Afrique du Nord—XIXe–XXe siècles.* Paris: C. N. R. S., pp. 1–31.

Shokeid, Moshe, and Shlomo Deshen. 1977. *The Generation of Transition: Continuity and Change among North African Immigrants in Israel.* Jerusalem: Ben-Zvi Institute (Hebrew).

Slouschz, Nahum. 1927. *Travels in North Africa.* Philadelphia: Jewish Publication Society of America.

———. 1944. *The Jews of North Africa.* Philadelphia: Jewish Publication Society of America.

Slyomovics, Susan. 1993. "The Pilgrimage of Rabbi Ephraim Al-Naqawa, Tlemcen, Algeria." *Jewish Folklore and Ethnology Review* 15, no. 2: 84–88.

Smith, C. A. 1976. *Regional Analysis: Social Systems.* Vol. 2. New York: Academic Press.

Smith, William R. 1894. *The Religion of the Semites. The Fundamental Institutions.* London. Reprinted in 1957. New York: Meridian Books.

Stillman, Norman A. 1973. "The Sefrou remnant." *Jewish Social Studies* 35: 255–63.

———. 1982. "Saddiq and Marabout in Morocco." In I. Ben-Ami, ed., *The Sepharadi and Oriental Jewish Heritage.* Jerusalem: Magnes Press, pp. 489–500.

———. 1988. *The Language and Culture of the Jews of Sefrou, Morocco: an Ethnolinguistic Study.* Manchester: University of Manchester.

Stillman, Yedida K. 1982. *From Southern Morocco to Northern Israel: A Study in the Material Culture of Shelomi.* Haifa: University of Haifa (Hebrew).

Tavenner, E. 1916. "Three as a Magic Number in Latin Literature." *Transactions of the American Philological Association* 47: 117–43.

Thompson, Stith. 1955–58. *Motif-Index of Folk-Literature.* 6 vols. Bloomington: Indiana University Press.

———. 1967. *The Folktale.* New York: Holt, Rinehart and Winston.

Tishbi, Isaiah. 1957. *The Doctrine of the Zohar.* 2 vols. Jerusalem: Bialik Institute (Hebrew).

Toledano, Jacob M. 1911. *Ner ha-Ma'arab* (History of the Jews of Morocco). 1972. Reprinted in Jerusalem: Hamaarav Press (Hebrew).

Touati, H. 1994. *Entre Dieu et les Hommes. Lettrés, saints et sorciers au Maghreb (XVIIe siècle).* Paris: Editions de l'EHESS.

Trachtenberg, Joshua. 1970. *Jewish Magic and Superstition.* New York: Atheneum.

Turner, Victor. 1974. *Dramas, Fields and Metaphors. Symbolic Action in Human Society.* Ithaca: Cornell University Press.

———. 1979. *Process, Performance and Pilgrimage: A Study in Comparative Symbology.* New Delhi.

Urbach, Ephraim E. 1969. *The Sages, Their Concepts and Beliefs.* Jerusalem: Magnes Press (Hebrew).

Vajda, Georges. 1951. *Un recueil de textes historiques judéo-marocains.* Paris: Larose.

Valadji, Jacob. 1902. "L'arrivée des Issawis à Mequinez." *Revue des Ecoles de l'Alliance Israélite Universelle* 6: 406–11.

Vansina, Jan. 1973. *Oral Tradition. A Study in Historical Methodology.* London: Penguin Books.

Vehel, J. 1930. "Pèlerinages nord-africains." *Univers Israélite* 85: 170–02, 208–09.

Vilnay, Zeev. 1985–86. *Holy Graves in Eretz Israel.* 2 vols. Jerusalem: Ahiever Press (Hebrew).

Voinot, Louis. 1948. *Pèlerinages judéo-musulmans du Maroc.* Paris: Larose.

Weingrod, Alex. 1990. *The Saint of Beersheba.* Albany: State University of New York Press.

Weiss, Shraga. 1976. *Sephardic Sages in the Holy Land.* Jerusalem: Rubin Mass (Hebrew).

Werblowsky, Z. 1977. "Saints." *Encyclopaedia Hebraica.* Vol. 29, pp. 146–65 (Hebrew).

Werbner, Richard P., ed. 1977. *Regional Cults.* London: Academic Press.

Westermarck, Edward. 1926. *Ritual and Belief in Morocco.* 2 vols. London: Macmillan.

Yaʿari, Abraham. 1962. "History of the *Hillulah* in Meron." *Tarbiz* 31: 91 (Hebrew).

———. 1977. *Emissaries from the Holy Land.* Jerusalem: Mosad Harav Kook (Hebrew).

Zafrani, Haïm. 1972. *Les Juifs du Maroc. Vie sociale, économique et religieuse. Etudes de Taqqanot et Responsa.* Paris: Geuthner.

———. 1977. *Poésie juive en Occident musulman.* Paris: Geuthner.

Zenner, Walter P. 1965. "Saints and Piecemeal Supernaturalism among the Jerusalem Sephardim." *Anthropological Quarterly* 38: 201–17.

INDEX OF SAINTS AND THEIR TOMBS

B

C

D

E

G

H

GENERAL INDEX

Ab. See Year cycle
Ablution, ritual, 29, 65, 79, 80, 94, 215, 230, 237, 242, 250, 251, 253, 255, 256, 267, 269, 271, 284, 291, 295. *See also* Purification
Adar. See Year cycle
Agurram, 151, 152, 167nn.19, 24, 182
Almsgiving, 26, 33n.3, 89, 98, 127, 191, 192, 222, 230, 232, 233, 241, 243, 244, 246, 278, 281, 309, 313, 315, 318. *See also* Charity
Amulet, 81, 97, 140, 146n.7, 155, 211, 212, 225, 234, 249, 264, 268, 306
Animals, 24, 32, 43, 50, 52, 54, 55, 66, 67, 68, 72n.22, 77, 89, 95, 98, 99, 101, 118, 132, 133, 136, 137, 138, 145n.15, 146n.17, 153, 155, 156, 160, 161, 163, 164, 168nn.29, 31, 169nn.40, 47, 189, 191, 201, 205, 208, 209, 211, 213, 216, 223, 225, 226, 231, 232, 233, 235, 236, 240, 242, 243, 245, 246, 254, 255, 256, 259, 261, 262, 263, 269, 272, 273, 276, 277, 278, 279, 282, 283, 285, 286, 288, 289, 290, 292, 294, 295, 296, 311, 312, 319, 321n.20; sanctified, 156, 160, 168n.31. *See also* Camel; Connection of saints with animals; Dove; Lion; Snake
Appearance of saint after his death, 61, 69, 70, 85, 86, 87, 89, 90, 92n.7, 93, 156, 258, 285; in dreams (*see* Dreams)
Arabs. *See* Muslims
Auction: of candles, 100, 170n.64, 179n.3, 190, 192, 241, 260; of glasses in honor of the saint, 100, 106, 111–12, 120–22, 179n.3, 190, 192, 240–41; of internal organs of sacrificed animal, 99–100; of privilege of burying the saint, 265, 268; of right to open the shrine, 241, 260; of saint's room, 241; of saint's shroud, 264, 267–68

Ba'al Shem-Tov, 43, 178, 273
Baba Ḥaki, 22n.6, 37, 174
Baba Sale, 22n.6, 37, 71n.8, 174, 178, 180nn.10, 11, 292
Baraka, 33n.5, 83n.9, 148, 149, 151, 156, 161, 166nn.4, 11, 168n.31
Barrenness, 54, 62, 71n.5, 79, 81, 87, 90, 96, 97, 133, 138, 145, 155, 168n.27, 175, 189, 202, 203, 204, 205, 209, 212, 221, 224, 232, 238, 255, 256, 264, 277, 285, 306, 314
Bath, ritual. *See* Ablution, ritual
Believer. *See* Worshipper
Biblical figures. See *Erets Yisra'el*
Birkat Ha-levanah (Blessing of the New Moon), 243, 292
Blessing by the saint, 51, 52, 55, 58n.4, 70, 85, 88, 94, 97, 151, 177, 243, 244, 265, 266, 271

Slaughter, ritual (*continued*) 163, 164, 172, 179n.3, 190, 191, 209, 210, 222, 226, 228, 232, 246, 247, 256, 282, 283, 286, 292, 311, 321n.20; by Muslims, 59n.12, 209, 212, 217, 228, 232, 272, 292, 295, 296

Sleeping at the shrine, 63, 64, 72n.23, 85, 86, 90, 101, 145n.9, 154, 168n.26, 172, 207, 225, 232, 239, 250, 278, 292, 296, 298n.12

Snake, 58n.5, 68, 72nn.22–23, 90, 91, 101, 135, 137, 155, 168nn.28–29, 203, 210, 214, 232, 234, 245, 247, 263, 275–77, 297n.12

Society in the saint's name, 129n.5, 208, 209

Source, 32, 65, 67, 75, 79, 81n.1, 83n.9, 86, 91, 96, 97, 144n.6, 150, 160, 161, 169n.44, 183, 202, 224, 225, 230, 231, 253, 256, 275, 294, 309, 310, 314, 316, 317, 320n.14, 321n.20

Spring. *See* Source

Stone, 28, 32, 50, 59n.14, 63, 64, 75–78, 80, 81n.1, 96, 97, 102, 132, 133, 134, 138, 146n.17, 157, 159, 160, 164, 202, 203, 205, 206, 213, 215, 216, 230, 231, 232, 234, 244, 250, 251, 252, 256, 263, 267, 269, 275, 278, 282, 283, 289, 296, 311, 314

Stream. *See* River

Students, 26, 39, 208, 218, 226, 228, 232, 238, 278; buried near a saint, 39, 76, 202, 208, 237

Study of *Torah* and Talmud, 24–25, 68, 69, 94, 119, 137, 157, 208, 220, 262, 264, 268, 270, 276, 286, 287, 288, 307, 316; by saints after their death, 25, 69, 132, 136, 208; by saints with Elijah the Prophet, 24, 25

Sukkot. See Year cycle

Sun stands still, 28, 66, 72n.16, 156, 204, 253, 269, 318

Synagogue, 26, 52, 53, 55, 56, 59, 69, 70, 73, 90, 94, 99, 105, 111, 114, 118, 119, 127, 133, 139, 162, 163, 172, 173, 174, 175, 176, 178, 179n.5, 180n.12, 192, 211, 213, 218, 227, 228, 235, 236, 237, 238, 239, 250, 254, 258, 263, 271, 272, 273, 274, 277, 282, 288, 293, 297n.4, 298n.15, 302n.59, 306, 307, 313

Talisman. *See* Amulet

Tammuz. See Year cycle

Tebet. See Year cycle

Tebilah. See Ablution, ritual

Tefillin. See Phylacteries

Tetragrammaton, 68, 145n.8, 235, 272, 283, 312

Tishri. See Year cycle

Tombs. *See* Graves; Shrines

Tombstones, 54, 59n.14, 70, 73n.27, 76, 89, 133, 202, 216, 234, 265, 283

Torah, 68, 119, 288; Scroll, 30, 41, 46n.4, 117, 118, 259, 262, 271–73. *See also* Study of *Torah* and Talmud

Tqaf, 64

Tree, 20, 28, 31, 32, 50, 62, 66, 68, 75, 80, 81, 81n.1, 97, 138, 146n.17, 154, 157, 159, 160, 161, 163, 169n.45, 203, 210, 211, 213, 224, 225, 234, 240,

Books in the Raphael Patai Series
in Jewish Folklore and Anthropology

The Myth of the Jewish Race, revised edition,
by Raphael Patai and Jennifer Patai, 1989

The Hebrew Goddess, third enlarged edition,
by Raphael Patai, 1990

Robert Graves and the Hebrew Myths: A Collaboration,
by Raphael Patai, 1991

Jewish Musical Traditions, by Amnon Shiloah, 1992

The Jews of Kurdistan, by Erich Brauer,
completed and edited by Raphael Patai, 1993

Jewish Moroccan Folk Narratives from Israel,
by Haya Bar-Itzhak and Aliza Shenhar, 1993

For Our Soul: The Ethiopian Jews in Israel,
by Teshome G. Wagaw, 1993

Book of Fables: The Yiddish Fable Collection of Reb Moshe Wallich Frankfurt am Main, 1697, translated and edited by Eli Katz, 1994

From Sofia to Jaffa: The Jews of Bulgaria and Israel,
by Guy H. Haskell, 1994

Jadīd al-Islām: The Jewish "New Muslims" of Meshed,
by Raphael Patai, 1997

Saint Veneration among the Jews in Morocco,
by Issachar Ben-Ami, 1997